Critical Policy Studies........................

Critical Policy Studies

Edited by Michael Orsini and
Miriam Smith

UBCPress · Vancouver · Toronto

15 14 13 12 11 10 09 08 07   5 4 3 2 1

Printed in Canada on ancient-forest-free paper (100% post-consumer recycled) that is
processed chlorine- and acid-free, with vegetable-based inks.

Library and Archives Canada Cataloguing in Publication

Critical policy studies / edited by Michael Orsini and Miriam Smith.

Includes bibliographical references and index.
ISBN-13: 978-0-7748-1317-4 (bound); 978-0-7748-1318-1 (pbk.)

1. Political planning – Canada. I. Orsini, Michael, 1967- II. Smith, Miriam
Catherine

JL86.P64C75 2006   320.60971   C2006-905139-9

Canadä

UBC Press gratefully acknowledges the financial support for our publishing program
of the Government of Canada through the Book Publishing Industry Development
Program (BPIDP), and of the Canada Council for the Arts, and the British Columbia
Arts Council.

This book has been published with the help of a grant from the Canadian Federation
for the Humanities and Social Sciences, through the Aid to Scholarly Publications
Programme, using funds provided by the Social Sciences and Humanities Research
Council of Canada.

The editors and publisher acknowledge the financial assistance of the Research and
Publications Committee of the Faculty of Social Sciences, University of Ottawa.

UBC Press
The University of British Columbia
2029 West Mall
Vancouver, BC V6T 1Z2
604-822-5959 / Fax: 604-822-6083
www.ubcpress.ca

Contents

Figures and Tables

Acknowledgments

This book explores new approaches to policy studies in Canada, focusing especially (but not exclusively) on work by junior scholars who have tackled new topics and theoretical approaches, sometimes borrowed from other disciplines such as geography, law, and sociology. The book seeks to widen the field of what is defined as public policy and to introduce new concepts into Canadian policy analysis. Given this, our most important debt is to an outstanding group of contributors, who wrote wonderful pieces, many of which, we believe, will become widely cited in the public policy literature. We would like to thank the contributors for responding quickly to our many requests for revision. We would also like to acknowledge the work of the anonymous referees for UBC Press who pressed us and our contributors to improve the book. Emily Andrew was a supportive editor throughout and we would like to thank her for her invaluable assistance in shepherding this project to completion. Karine Levasseur assisted in preparing the manuscript for publication and her work is gratefully acknowledged.

Michael would like to thank his wife Victoria and "ankle biters" Emma and Lucca for putting it all in perspective, as well as his parents for continued support.

Critical Policy Studies

1
Critical Policy Studies

Michael Orsini and Miriam Smith

The public policy world is in a state of flux. Globalization, the transition to a knowledge-based economy, and the rise of new technologies are transforming the policy world as we know it. These changes are catapulting new, substantive issues onto the policy agenda, or, at the very least, transforming the policy problems that have been with us for decades. Mad cow disease, border screening, and global warming are just some of the new policy problems that dominate the daily headlines. The "real world" of policy making, Leslie A. Pal (2005) explains in a recent edition of his popular public policy text *Beyond Policy Analysis*, is increasingly marked by crisis. Policy makers and students of public policy alike need to re-examine their tool kits and reflect on just what policy analysis is supposed to achieve. This volume uses the term "critical policy studies" as a container for an ensemble of approaches and perspectives that we believe are best suited to the changing policy context in which we find ourselves. Critical policy studies is not an ideological straitjacket; rather, it is an orientation to policy analysis inspired by the Lasswellian tradition and by a desire to speak truth to power.

As Maarten Hajer (2003, 175) has recently emphasized, policy making and politics increasingly take place in an "institutional void" where "there are no clear rules and norms according to which politics is to be conducted and policy measures are to be agreed upon." As he makes clear, this does not mean that traditional political institutions cease to matter: rather, there are policy problems that have necessitated political action of a different order. In some cases, state authority or legitimacy may be at issue; in other instances, the action may take place alongside the traditional state apparatus. What are some of the implications of this new world of policy making? Hajer (2003, 179-80) lays out five: the dispersal of decision making, the "new spatiality of policy making and politics," a rethinking of standard views of participation and governance, the undermining of scientific expertise, and an expansion of the context of policy making. Although states nonetheless remain important units of analyses, politics and policy occur at a number of scales, across different spatial horizons. Moreover, a recognition of the importance of the spatial question and the dispersal of decision making requires a re-examination of widely held views of democratic participation and governance. The time-honoured tradition of citizen consultations and hearings, often convened by governments eager to control the agenda or at the very least guide the direction of the discussion, may be insufficient in an age in which citizens demand a greater say in the decisions that affect them. The role of citizens in policy making invariably raises the question of how evidence, whether scientific or experiential, can and should be incorporated in decision making. This dilemma has been made all the more thorny by the profound mistrust and distrust of "science" to provide authoritative answers to complex policy problems, as the recent controversy over vCJD (the human form of mad cow disease), among others, powerfully demonstrates. If traditional policy problems were not complex enough, a host of new themes raises profound questions about nature itself, including the social and ethical challenges associated with genetics and biotechnology, for instance.

In this way, traditional arenas of policy making, such as economic and trade policy, have been cross-cut by the complex pressures of globalization and by the emergence of new political actors who take advantage of transnational access points and the uncertainty of the locus of power to try to circumvent the state. New forms of political agency, such as transnationalism, and the enhanced legitimacy of civil society organizations in policy fields such as the environment and human rights, have undermined the position of traditional state-based power-holders in the policy process.

Government-sponsored policy templates such as social cohesion, social exclusion, civic engagement, and the voluntary sector have been advanced as legitimate responses to the numerous social ills that plague societies. Poverty, in the new formulation made popular by Third Way governments such as Tony Blair's New Labour government in the UK, is recast as a social phenomenon, not solely a material deprivation. Under such a scenario, governments become charged with the task of "facilitating" the fight against social exclusion, sometimes without doing anything to address the underlying socioeconomic problems that drive citizens into poverty in the first place. These new templates and the policies attached to them construct a range of ways of connecting citizens to the state and of purportedly bringing citizens into the policy-making process, but they bring with them their own unique set of challenges. Communities that were once marginal to or frozen out of public policy – such as Aboriginal people, children, the poor, lesbians and gay men, ethnocultural communities, and women – are increasingly viewed as "stakeholders" in public policy debates, not to mention important sources of legitimacy for governments facing an increasingly disaffected electorate. Public policy areas that were once the monopoly of the federal government have been undercut by the rise of cities, regions, provinces, and transnational networks as politics is decentred – and recentred – from the federal state. This phenomenon is more than simply the downloading or offloading of responsibilities from federal governments to provincial or local governments. New governance arrangements that involve a mix of public, private, and voluntary sectors are altering the policy landscape in ways that cannot be captured by a singular focus on downloading.

Like public policy itself, the study of public policy has undergone significant change, and is gaining increased legitimacy in the field of political science. Journals such as *Governance, Policy Sciences, Policy and Politics,* and the *Journal of Public Policy* publish some of the most interesting scholarship in the field. And as is amply demonstrated by this edited collection, the subdiscipline of policy studies has begun to embrace radically different theoretical and methodological approaches borrowed from other subfields of political science such as historical institutionalism, feminist analysis (Hawkesworth 1994; Burt 1995; Phillips 1996), social movement analysis, and Foucauldian analysis, which have injected new life and vigour into the public policy field. Public policy scholars are also borrowing liberally from other disciplines, including sociology and geography. Indeed, much of the renewed interest in public policy might be traced to the openness of some scholars to think beyond the disciplinary paradigm of rational choice, which has maintained a stranglehold on American political science in recent years.

One of the exemplars of this new approach to public policy is Frank Fischer's recent book *Reframing Public Policy* (2003), which makes a compelling case for a post-empiricist alternative to the technocratic form of policy analysis which has occupied the mainstream for several years. Postempiricists such as Fischer, Douglas Torgerson (1996), Maarten Hajer (2005), and John Dryzek (1990) do not necessarily cling to a core set of unshakeable beliefs. Rather, they share a concern with moving beyond objectivist conceptions of reality, especially the fact/value dichotomy. In recent work, this newfound interest in expanding theoretical boundaries has been accompanied by a renewed commitment by public policy scholars to undertake comparative and global analyses. Further, this juxtaposition of traditional fields of policy analysis is helping to supercede and transcend the old boundaries of policy analysis. In these ways, the volume contributes to critical policy studies and provides an alternative to mainstream approaches and topics.

In the past, classic texts in Canadian and comparative public policy have focused on explaining what the state does and why states vary in the types of policies they undertake (Dobuzinskis, Howlett, and Laycock 1996). Usually, discussions centred on the traditional domains of policy as reflected in the organization of the state and the policy-making apparatus, such as, for example, economic policy, social policy, foreign policy, and agricultural policy. The main theories of policy making were organized around the society/state binary: pluralism and neo-Marxism saw social forces as driving public policy, and state-based analyses explored the impact of factors such as the organization of the state and the role of policy communities in shaping public policy outcomes.

Contemporary theories of public policy challenge this traditional picture in a number of ways. As noted earlier, extensive interdisciplinary cross-fertilization has resulted in the adoption of theoretical approaches from other disciplines such as geography, sociology, communication, and cultural studies. This edited collection charts some of these changes in the context of policy making discussed earlier by Hajer (2003) and in the approaches undertaken to grasp what is unfolding in a public policy world set against the ambiguous and contradictory backdrop of globalization and neo-liberalism. Although the volume covers a lot of ground, it is based on the assumption that there are horizontal synergies across new policy areas which render some of the traditional divisions outdated. Our contributors include a number of respected analysts as well as some of the new, exciting voices in the discipline. Some, if hard pressed, might not self-identify as public policy scholars, but their scholarship has wider implications for how we understand public policy generally and policy analysis specifically. This edited collection is distinctive in providing a discussion of a range of policy fields, some of which have emerged only recently on the policy agenda and will no doubt occupy policy makers for years to come. In addition, we hope this collection will help to ignite a much-needed discussion of the appropriate boundaries of the discipline of policy studies within a Canadian and comparative context. Policy issues associated with risk, compensation, sexuality, and Aboriginal people, for instance, have not generally been accorded their rightful place in the study of public policy. We hope, therefore, that this book will contribute to correcting this problem.

Main Themes of the Volume

The themes of the volume reflect the concern with new voices in policy debates as well as recent theoretical developments in critical policy studies. The book is divided into four main sections, "Political Economy," "Citizens and Diversity," "Discourse and Knowledge," and "Risky Subjects."

POLITICAL ECONOMY

The first section draws on Canada's rich political economy tradition. In Chapter 2, Peter Graefe demonstrates quite convincingly that, though it is a longstanding approach, political economy is flexible enough to accommodate a range of intellectual and practical concerns. Graefe offers a particularly clear discussion of the distinction between political economy as a form of policy analysis and the pluralist and neo-pluralist assumptions of much mainstream policy analysis. For Graefe, political economy is centrally concerned with the exploration of public policy as an exercise of economic and political power. He dismisses the claim that political economy is reductionist and presents a rich distillation of recent literatures on political economy and intersectionality, focusing specifically on feminist political economy. Graefe's chapter presages Karen Murray's Chapter 8 discussion of governmentality by focusing on the advantages and disadvantages of a governmentality approach from the perspective of feminist political economy.

Chapter 3, by Rianne Mahon, Caroline Andrew, and Robert Johnson, presents an overview of recent thinking about the rescaling of political economy. They question concepts that have been central to traditional public policy analysis and political economy. Drawing on new developments in geography, Mahon, Andrew, and Johnson argue that policy studies must develop a more nuanced approach to the theorization of space. Traditional policy analysis has recognized the diminished importance of the nation-state in the global era, the downloading of responsibilities to subnational levels of government, the importance of cities, and the role of new policy actors (such as the voluntary sector) in governance. Nonetheless, the policy literature overwhelmingly assumes that the national scale is the privileged level for public policy action and analysis. Yet, the authors argue that the process of rescaling that is under way in the global era requires us to rethink the dominant place of the nation-state in public policy. Understanding scale means paying attention to the many spaces in which policies are constructed and in which contestation over policy occurs. Globalization entails not simply the decline of the nation-state but the emergence of new forms of contestation over space and scale. In this light, it is essential to view scale as a set of dynamic relationships, rather than as fixed spaces. The authors provide a useful summary of the ways in which central concepts of policy analysis such as the "policy community" or "knowledge transfer" are rooted in specific assumptions about the importance of the national scale and how these limit the consideration of the multi-scalar nature of shifting policy responsibilities.

CITIZENS AND DIVERSITY

The second section is concerned with the public policy challenges associated with the politicization of diversity in Canadian society. Chapter 4, by Rachel Laforest and Susan Phillips, asks whether the policy process needs to be "rewired" in order to bring citizens' voices into policy making in a significant and meaningful way. Such forms of engagement would circumvent the traditional forms of representation of interests through the party system or through interest associations or social movement organizations. Instead, citizen engagement aims to empower ordinary citizens to participate in policy processes, especially in holding governments accountable for policies and performance. However, Laforest and Phillips caution that "the emerging performance-based model of engagement is not an expansion, but in fact a potential contraction of the influence of citizens in political representation and policy development" (p. 68). In this sense, claims to tap the knowledge of ordinary citizens in the policy process may legitimate less participatory forms of policy making.

Although citizen engagement is based on the assumption of the undifferentiated individual, one who is divorced from his or her civil society involvement and who always speaks as a citizen, Chapters 5 and 6, by Miriam Smith and Olena Hankivsky, respectively, discuss how the situated knowledge of groups can be brought into the policy-making process. In each case, new knowledges challenge the existing structure of policy making, the definition of policy issues, and the nature of the policy process itself – each of which is a perennial concern of policy scholars. All three chapters – Laforest and Phillips, Smith, and Hankivsky – refer to the ways in which the specific experiences of groups that have historically been excluded can be integrated into policy making.

Smith argues that public policy also needs to be "queered," as a way of taking seriously the interests and identities of lesbian and gay citizens; Hankivsky focuses on gendering the analysis of public policy. Challenging "heteronormativity" in the policy process, as suggested by Smith, requires the kind of restructuring that is discussed and developed in Hankivsky's chapter on gender mainstreaming. Hankivsky provides a survey of current Canadian efforts at gender mainstreaming, that is, evaluating policy from the perspective of its impact on gender equality and ensuring gender equity in the policy process itself. Like Laforest and Phillips, in their discussion of citizen engagement, Hankivsky finds that the discourse of gender mainstreaming and gender-based analysis has not matched reality. Both the Smith and Hankivsky chapters discuss the dangers of an essentialized definition of gender-based identities. A liberal approach to difference assumes that "women" or "lesbian and gay" citizens can fit into neat analytical boxes and be added into the policy-making process; however, feminist analysis, queer theory, and postcolonialism all point to the intersections among different identities, as well as to the role of broader social and political structures as patterned power relationships that set important limits on the policy-making process. Similarly, these chapters highlight the importance of the patterns of political mobilization in civil society and their relevance for the policy process. As Hankivsky notes, the declining political power of the women's movement at the federal level has seriously undermined efforts to deepen gender analysis.

In Chapter 7, Yasmeen Abu-Laban argues that the central concept of the nation-state in Canadian policy analysis has been based on specific assumptions about colonialism and race, assumptions that must be re-examined in the global era. Abu-Laban asserts that the consideration of race and ethnicity in Canadian policy studies and political science must move beyond multiculturalism as a policy arena to consider the ways in which what the Canadian state does (or does not do) is linked to the legacy of European colonialism and to specific assumptions about the nature of Canadian society. Abu-Laban shows how areas of policy such as the census, immigration, borders, and the war on terror must be linked to and integrated with an approach that pays attention to the intersections of race and ethnicity.

These chapters present very diverse views on how citizens influence policy making, ranging from the individual citizen of Laforest and Phillips' chapter through the group politics and structural reworking of public policy that is suggested by gender-based analysis, challenging heteronormativity, or engaging with the colonial legacy of Canadian public policy analysis.

DISCOURSE AND KNOWLEDGE

The chapters in this section ask, in different but complementary ways, how one might incorporate new knowledges into the policy process or whether these new ways of knowing require us to redraw the contours of the public policy field. Just as feminists were correct to point out that gender is not simply an add-on to policy analysis ("add gender and stir"), the chapters in this section outline a similar challenge when trying to bring new, often "situated knowledges," to borrow a phrase from Donna J. Haraway (1991), to the table. Policy makers are facing formidable challenges in opening up the policy process to non-state actors. For one, there is greater pressure to consult with and engage actors who may not be traditionally consulted on policy issues. It is fairly straightforward for governments wishing to hear the range of civil society opinion on, for instance, specific environmental policies. This normally involves canvassing the groups which are often vocal on the issue. It is quite another thing for governments, at all levels, to confront an issue with disparate interests, unorganized interests, or newly mobilized citizens who may not follow the institutional rules of engagement.

Karen Bridget Murray's Chapter 8 discussion of governmentality and policy studies reflects the growing influence of Foucauldian thought in the social sciences in fields as diverse as medical sociology, criminology, and security studies. Murray's chapter demonstrates the ways in which this analytic approach can be used to interrogate comparative welfare state scholarship. Governmentality poses a fundamental challenge to the mainstream social science methodologies on which comparative welfare state scholarship is based, methodologies that assume that competing explanatory claims can be adjudicated with reference to empirical evidence, both quantitative and qualitative. Murray's chapter shows how comparative welfare state research is based on the assumption of the reality of a liberal zone of freedom in which power is absent; in contrast, the governmentality approach explores the ways in which the individual is constituted to participate as a "free" subject through the use and deployment of various fields of knowledge. As Murray argues, "expert knowledge was drawn upon in various ways and at various times to justify a whole range of endeavours: educators relied on knowledge about pedagogy; counsellors trusted theories of human nature; parents turned to parenting journals in determining how to raise their children; administrators drew upon organizational theory, and so on" (p. 164). This illustrates how governmentality is concerned with the micro level at which public policies play themselves out; however, it also illustrates the two other themes of this volume: the emergence of new areas of public policy such as health promotion (described in Chapter 16) or assimilationist political strategies in queer politics (described in Chapter 5) as well as the importance of knowledge and ideas in the policy process. Governmentality points to the construction of fields of expert knowledge which provide contested parameters for policy. This is true not only in the sense of the well-worn literature in comparative welfare state studies on the impact of ideas, as Murray argues. The governmentality approach also suggests a much more profound critique of knowledge deployment as means of governing people and, perhaps even more importantly, as means by which people actively govern themselves.

In Chapter 9, Stuart N. Soroka uses the example of Canadian environmental policy making to present an introduction to the role of agenda-setting and issue framing in public policy. Soroka's chapter offers a counterpoint to the other chapters in this section by drawing on a long-standing public policy literature in political communication and public opinion studies. In a careful review of the wealth of literature on the subjects of agenda-setting and issue definition, Soroka notes that both perspectives have something to offer to policy studies, even though they may appear to be "unlikely bedfellows." As he explains, "Agenda-setting is premised in large part on empirical rational-choice-inspired theories of policy making. Issue definition, however, finds its roots in constructionist or interpretivist – even anti-empirical – research strategies in political communications, emphasizing the importance of language and the subjective, manipulable descriptions that structure everyday politics" (p. 188).

Francesca Scala's Chapter 10 examination of the boundaries between state and non-state actors in producing knowledge in the policy process applies the concept of "boundary work" to the rapidly expanding subfield of "social studies of science," posing important questions about the blurring of the boundaries between state and non-state actors, which have important implications for how we conceptualize knowledge. As Scala explains, boundary work theories are useful in explaining how "different disciplines, professions, and social organizations negotiate and maintain the boundaries that delineate their activities and spheres of influence and authority" (p. 213). More importantly, the concept of boundary work highlights the constructed nature of scientific knowledge and authority, in contrast to claims that scientific knowledge is pure, untainted, and can speak for itself. It is clear, then, that introducing the idea that scientific knowledge could also be viewed as "situated knowledge" has important implications for how we view the knowledge presented by non-experts who are trying to mould policy discourses that are heavily influenced by science and/or medicine.

In Chapter 11, Frances Abele tackles a particularly challenging area, namely, the use of traditional Indigenous knowledge in policy making. Abele argues that, because of the strength of Aboriginal political organizations in Canada, debates over the use of Indigenous knowledge have centred on the ways in which it can be brought into the policy process, rather than on how it can be exploited for profit or "bio-prospecting." Abele's analysis shows the ways in which claims about who is expert and who is defined to have knowledge form a central element in social movement challenges to traditional policy analysis. In advancing claims about knowledge, Aboriginal peoples are also making claims about participation in policy creation and respect for traditional forms of Aboriginal governance that themselves privilege certain types of knowledge (such as that of elders).

In Chapter 12, the final study in this section, Luc Juillet draws on Fischer's (2003) post-empiricist approach to explore the discursive framing of policy debates over migratory birds. Juillet shows how scientists and Aboriginal peoples put forth conflicting policy frames regarding conservation and environmental policies in this area and how this "inter-frame conflict" prevents policy change. Juillet demonstrates that the discursive frameworks of policy debates are linked to and embedded in other frames in Canadian politics, such as constitutional politics. Shifts in constitutional politics legitimated First Nations' demands for national recognition, which, in turn, reinforced the Aboriginal framing of conservation policy regarding migratory birds.

Together, these chapters suggest diverse methodological and theoretical approaches to understanding the role of discourse and knowledge in policy making: they range from the Foucauldian approach of Murray to the media-focused framing and agenda-setting of Soroka; Scala's chapter scrutinizes the role of experts in setting policy boundaries, and Abele's chapter examines challenges to experts and the reassertion of grassroots policy knowledge epitomized by debates between elders and "experts"; finally, Juillet's chapter takes a post-empiricist approach to discursive framing.

RISKY SUBJECTS

The final section groups chapters by Denis Saint-Martin, Mark B. Salter, Matt James, and Michael Orsini. Each chapter deals with conceptions of risk, vividly demonstrating that risk talk has permeated not only popular but policy discourses as well. We speak of "at risk" populations (Saint-Martin), "risky" physical environments (Salter, James), and "risky" lifestyles (Orsini). What is new, one might argue, is how the social is being reshaped through the prism of risk. For instance, in 2004, Social Development Canada, a recently reconstituted federal government department, and the McGill Institute for the Study of Canada co-sponsored a large conference entitled "New Century, New Risks," which dealt with the emergence of new "social" risks; in 2002, the Policy Research Initiative devoted its annual conference to the theme of risk in all its various guises, from security to unemployment to infectious diseases to risk management in the public service. What is often lost in many discussions of risk and public policy is how risk discourses are altering citizens' subjectivities. Governments, and by extension, policies, have internalized the language of risk in their conception of vulnerable populations (Murray 2004). Policies directed at subpopulations such as Aboriginals, people with AIDS, and single mothers construct these citizens in ways that ultimately remove their agency, all the while using the language of community empowerment and capacity building. Such language assumes that individuals as consumers will behave rationally (in a risk averse manner) to evade risky situations, whether that means making healthy food choices so as to avoid obesity, or remaining in a dead-end job to avoid unemployment or, worse, social assistance. Meanwhile, governments are saddled with the arduous task of trying to protect individuals from their own bad habits or unwise choices, and from situations, often beyond their control, which may place them at risk, whether in the short, medium, or long term. For instance, the precautionary principle, which has defined the environmental movement, is concerned primarily with hardwiring the decision-making process in such a way as to act decisively in the face of scientific uncertainty regarding potential dangers or hazards. At the same time, there is a paradoxical movement toward evidence-based policy making, itself a by-product of the shift toward evidence-based medicine, which has its firm roots in the randomized clinical trial, the so-called Gold Standard.

It is not surprising that there are immense public policy challenges associated with making decisions in an environment increasingly marked by risk. As Martin J. Smith (2004) explains, there are three dimensions of risk which are often confused in policy discourse: risk as science, risk as perception, and the risk society approach. The first approach holds that risks are identifiable, knowable, and thus measurable; the second focuses on the cultural aspects of risk, and tries to take issue with the claim that measuring risk is possible. The risk society approach is best associated with the work of Ulrich Beck

(1992), who links the proliferation of risk to a crisis of modernity. Risk, Smith says, is being used in all three ways – in the objective sense, in terms of risk perception, and in terms of responding to greater anxieties in society (risk society thesis). The problem of risk in government policy, he says, is fairly complex. First, he notes, the general approach to risk is objective and positivist; it is also based on a number of questionable assumptions: risks are measurable, policy making is rational (governments can use risk assessment to make the right decisions), and the process of risk assessment is independent of human agency. In addition, although some lip service is paid to the subjective nature of risk, there is an assumption that the public's overreaction to risk can be limited if only the "facts" are communicated to it in a proper manner. When examining the British case of BSE (mad cow disease), Smith argues that most analysts underplay the contingent nature of risk and the way it has been used as a form of power/knowledge to legitimize certain behaviour. He also argues that the management of risk has failed because the notions of risk are contested, risk is intersubjective (interventions create new risks), and perceptions of risk vary according to political, economic, and social positions. Since the definition of risk is inherently political, it is critical for policy scholars to examine how risks are conceptualized, identified, and acted upon, and why some risks gain prominence in public discourse while others remain largely hidden from public view; they must also study the respective roles of science, government, the public, and the media in these processes.

In Chapter 13, Denis Saint-Martin discusses the recent evolution of social policy in Canada, as elsewhere, in terms of the shift from the Keynesian welfare state to the social investment state. Following Anthony Giddens (1998) and others, Saint-Martin argues that one of the key shifts in contemporary social policy breaks with the assumption of a separation of politics and economics, viewing social policy as a tool of "social investment" for economic development. Linking back to issues raised by Graefe and Murray in Chapters 2 and 8, Saint-Martin asserts that this paradigm involves investing to create responsible citizens who can manage risk: in the social investment state, the purpose of social policy is to prepare citizens to participate in the market economy, rather than to insulate them from its vagaries. For Saint-Martin, the social investment state might be appropriately renamed the "risk management state," following the work of thinkers such as Peter Baldwin (1990) and Pierre Rosanvallon (2000). As David Garland (2004, 63) explains, what is disconcerting about the shift to a risk-management state is

the "attention away from conflicts over the means of production and towards conflicts over the means of security." Saint-Martin ultimately suggests
that decommodification is no longer a sufficient criterion on which to judge
the generosity of welfare states.

Mark B. Salter's Chapter 14 examination of security typifies the reconceptualization of traditional arenas of public policy, which were based on a
separation between foreign and domestic spheres of policy. Salter's chapter
represents part of a growing trend to reconceptualize "border policy" as an
important new arena of Canadian public policy, one that brings together a
broad range of concerns about immigration, security, crime, and health. Salter
explores the ways in which the border is defined as a problem in public
policy discourse, showing that how the problem is perceived or constructed
often shapes the policy solutions that are proposed; the trend toward
securitization of the border has important implications for other policy areas
such as those concerning health, criminal law, and immigration/refugees, a
phenomenon he characterizes as "spillover securitization."

In Chapter 15, Matt James' discussion of the new politics of redress shows
how the growth and failures of redress movements have led to the creation of
a new category – the "innocent victims" of natural disasters. The politics of
compensation for such victims is a moral commitment for a neo-liberal era,
drawing on the age-old distinction between the deserving and undeserving
recipients of material commitments from the community. Drawing these
themes together, James links the politics of compensation, redress, and reparations to the modern politics of social policy in the neo-liberal period.

Finally, in Chapter 16, Michael Orsini examines health politics and policy,
and offers an alternative to the usual discussion of health care spending and
intergovernmentalism by tracing the main paradigms that have influenced
Canadian health policy from the sixties to the present. Orsini provides the
lens through which we can read a broad range of health debates as moving
from a focus on health promotion and population health to one on the
responsibilization of health. Against the backdrop of the omnipresent "risk
society," Orsini's discussion offers a critique of these shifting paradigms based
on a narrative analysis of health policy.

Conclusion

The chapters offered here depart, in different ways, from the traditional definition of Canadian public policy. They develop and explore the application
of new theoretical approaches to public policy such as governmentality and

rescaling while building on older theoretical traditions such as political economy, agenda-setting, and issue framing. Many of the contributions discuss the ways in which knowledge is used in the policy process, where policy knowledge(s) come from, and in which interests they are developed and deployed. Although the chapters range in their assessment of the truths of policy-relevant knowledge, many reflect a post-positivist sensibility in which the social and political construction of policy problems and the expert or situated knowledges used to "solve" them are viewed as dynamic interactions that are shaped by power relations. Many of the chapters draw on insights from disciplines beyond political science. Unlike so much of American political science, which borrows from economics and public choice theory, these chapters build on scholarship from the English-speaking world beyond the US as well as from neglected American voices and European traditions of social theory. In both geographical and disciplinary terms, the chapters open up new terrain for Canadian policy analysis by showing how theories, methods, and research questions from other disciplines and traditions can inform research questions and approaches to Canadian material. Although much of Canadian public policy analysis has had a strong public administration bent and has been directly or indirectly tied to the state's political projects, this book offers a critical perspective on public policy and on the policy process, suggesting that the knowledge(s) that are claimed by state actors in making policy must be subjected to questioning, contestation, and critique.

The chapters also suggest a new delineation of policy fields: rather than employing the traditional focus on economic policy, social policy, and so forth, the chapters suggest the emergence of new areas of public policy or, to put it another way, the redefinition and reconceptualization of substantive areas of public policy. The politics of risk and compensation are new areas of public policy; the redefinition of security in terms of borders or of social policy in terms of social investment all offer new ways of thinking about old policy areas.

Finally, much more than most volumes on public policy, the book takes seriously the perspectives of marginalized groups in Canadian society, whose interests and identities have often been absent from discussions and debates on public policy. By integrating the views and interests of Aboriginal people, ethnic and racial minorities, women, and lesbian and gay citizens, the volume offers a critical perspective on Canadian public policy. The authors may quibble about how best to integrate the interests of previously marginalized groups into the policy-making process, but many of them agree on the importance of doing so. The analysis of Canadian public policy must be open to a critical rethinking of fundamental assumptions about political power and about the social and political structures that underpin the policy process.

REFERENCES

Baldwin, Peter. 1990. *The Politics of Social Solidarity: Class Bases of the European Welfare State, 1875-1975.* Cambridge: Cambridge University Press.

Beck, Ulrich. 1992. *Risk Society: Towards a New Modernity.* New York: Sage Publications.

Burt, Sandra. 1995. "The Several Worlds of Policy Analysis: Traditional Approaches and Feminist Critiques." In *Changing Methods: Feminists Transforming Practice,* ed. Sandra Burt and Lorraine Code, 357-78. Peterborough: Broadview Press.

Dobuzinskis, Laurent, Michael Howlett, and David Laycock, eds. 1996. *Policy Studies in Canada: The State of the Art.* Toronto: University of Toronto Press.

Dryzek, John. 1990. *Discursive Democracy: Politics, Policy and Political Science.* New York: Cambridge University Press.

Fischer, Frank. 2003. *Reframing Public Policy: Discursive Politics and Deliberative Practices.* Oxford and New York: Oxford University Press.

Garland, David. 2004. "The Rise of Risk." In *Risk and Morality,* ed. Richard Ericson and Aaron Doyle, 48-87. Toronto: University of Toronto Press.

Giddens, Anthony. 1998. *The Third Way: The Renewal of Social Democracy.* Cambridge: Polity Press.

Hajer, Maarten. 2003. "Policy without Polity: Policy Analysis and the Institutional Void." *Policy Sciences* 36: 175-95.

—. 2005. "Setting the Stage: A Dramaturgy of Policy Deliberation." *Administration and Society* 35(6): 624-47.

Haraway, Donna J. 1991. "Situated Knowledges: The Science Question in Feminism and the Privilege of Partial Perspective." In *Simians, Cyborgs, and Women: The Reinvention of Nature,* ed. Donna J. Haraway, 183-201. New York: Routledge.

Hawkesworth, Mary. 1994. "Policy Studies within a Feminist Frame." *Policy Sciences* 27: 97-118.

Murray, Karen. 2004. "Do Not Disturb: 'Vulnerable Populations' in Federal Government Policy Discourses and Practices." *Canadian Journal of Urban Research* 13(1): 50-69.

Pal, Leslie A. 2005. *Beyond Policy Analysis: Public Issue Management in Turbulent Times.* 3rd ed. Scarborough: Nelson Thomson Learning.

Phillips, Susan. 1996. "Discourse, Identity, and Voice: Feminist Contributions to Policy Studies." In *Policy Studies in Canada: The State of the Art,* ed. Laurent Dobuzinskis, Michael Howlett, and David Laycock, 242-65. Toronto: University of Toronto Press.

Rosanvallon, Pierre. 2000. *The New Social Question: Rethinking the Welfare State*. Princeton, NJ: Princeton University Press.

Smith, Martin J. 2004. "Mad Cows and Mad Money: Problems of Risk in the Making and Understanding of Policy." *British Journal of Politics and International Relations* 6(3): 312-32.

Torgerson, Douglas. 1996. "Power and Insight in Policy Discourse: Post-positivism and Problem Definition." In *Policy Studies in Canada: The State of the Art*, ed. Laurent Dobuzinskis, Michael Howlett, and David Laycock, 266-98. Toronto: University of Toronto Press.

PART ONE

Political Economy

2
Political Economy
and Canadian Public Policy

Peter Graefe

Canadian political economists have long analyzed public policies, whether in the context of studying the labour market or the welfare state, but have largely not defined themselves as public policy scholars. They have sought to intervene in debates in political sociology, comparative politics, or political economy, rather than engaging in the field of public policy studies as conventionally defined. Yet, as Stephen McBride (1996, 49-50) perceptively underlines, the fields of political economy and public policy converge on important questions. If public policy focuses on what the state chooses to do or not do, political economy has an interest in studying the state as a key locus of power. More particularly, political economy's concern with the interaction of economic, social, cultural, and economic-political factors, its interest in the distribution of social power between actors, and its close attention to the question of "who benefits," provides useful tools for understanding and explaining variations in policy across space and time. In a period where globalization, imperialism, increased social diversity, and declining public confidence in representative democratic institutions have questioned the capacity of the state to make policies, or at least to make policies contrary to the decisions of powerful private economic actors, political economy's most important contribution may be to illustrate and explain the linkages between such large-scale structural changes and the more immediate realm of policy and policy making.

Any attempt at enumerating political economy approaches to public policy is bound to be unsatisfactory, given the variety of mainstream and critical approaches. In this chapter, I will pay attention to a portion of the field, providing a lean presentation of basic concepts and ideas underlying some promising recent work. The point in focusing on only a section of the field is not to deny the variety and diversity of political economy approaches, including critical ones, nor is it to suggest that I am laying out a "one best way." I hope instead to bring together and give some coherence to a variety of recent works in political economy and public policy, and to suggest that these works provide a promising set of tools for policy analysis. Those wishing for a synthetic overview of the field and of its historic development can consult the comprehensive reviews provided by McBride (1996) and Wallace Clement (2001). Clement and Leah F. Vosko's (2003) collection, *Changing Canada: Political Economy as Transformation*, also provides well-crafted chapters applying political economy approaches to various policy fields.

This chapter begins by briefly considering how the political and the economic are linked in political economy through the study of social relations, and then by presenting a conceptualization of the state that sets the political economy approaches considered here apart from most mainstream approaches. In so doing, I question many of the *ad hominem* critiques made of political economy approaches in terms of their economism, class reductionism, and determinism. This first section situates the contribution of political economy in embedding public policy processes and outcomes within broader structures of power in society. The second section illustrates how the concepts elaborated in the first section can be employed to study policy, and includes some strengths and weaknesses of the approach.

Political/Economy

Political economists have generated numerous approaches through which to connect the political and the economic. For example, Professor Stephen Clarkson introduces the subject to his students by saying that they will be studying S&M – that is, states and markets. Although presented with humour, Clarkson's connection between the political (states) and the economic (markets) is a useful one. It recognizes that markets are socially embedded institutions: contrary to some widely held myths, they are not self-regulating, but in fact demand the exercise of political power in order to enforce contracts and protect private property. This approach allows analysts to assess how public policies shape markets, affecting forms of competition, forms of interaction between industrial and finance capital, and the protection of workers in the labour market. It also allows analysts to consider how markets and different forms of economic organization constrain the range of viable choices open to governments. Indeed, it highlights the limits of public policy analysis that does not pay attention to how the organization of the economy affects the shape of policy making and policy outcomes, and suggests that variation in policies across space and time may result from differences between econo-mies and the organization of economic actors (see, for example, Ebbinghaus and Manow 2001; Hall and Soskice 2001).

This view shares some features of a neo-pluralist understanding of the state and public policy (for example, Lindblom 1977, chap. 14). Neo-pluralism recognizes that business has a privileged position in policy making, arising from the importance of business decisions (for example, concerning em-ployment or investment) for the welfare of society (levels of employment, environmental outcomes of economic activity). As a result, policy makers need to remain highly attuned to the needs of business in order to ensure that business continues to contribute to that welfare. Their interest is not evidence of a conspiracy: it simply reflects the dependence of capitalist de-mocracies on decisions taken privately by business in a context where busi-nesses must compete to survive. Charles Lindblom famously spoke of "the market as prison" to emphasize how dependence on free market mecha-nisms to make important decisions for society meant that policies which interfered with the functioning of markets would lead to a punishing recoil. Investment and employment would drop off through the regular working of the market, not because business people put any overt pressure on the gov-ernment (Lindblom 1982). This view was labelled "neo-pluralist" because it broke partially with pluralism, wherein business was perceived as simply one interest among others. True, pluralists felt that business held more re-sources than other groups and had more access to decision-making institu-tions and forums, but they believed that other interests could check business if they organized properly. Neo-pluralism goes further by recognizing that a market economy tips the playing field before any interest groups make them-selves heard. It would not surprise a neo-pluralist to learn that even NDP provincial governments have adopted formal administrative practices such as scanning new policies through a "business lens" to ensure their accept-ability to the business community (Carroll and Ratner 2005).

There are important problems with the neo-pluralist approach that may explain why it has been largely ignored: business groups in fact do expend resources to lobby government and participate in policy networks; govern-ments do introduce legislation that is contrary to the expressed wishes of business; different countries have very different levels of state intervention in the economy and yet maintain similar levels of economic activity; and poli-cies can sometimes improve the functioning of markets (see Smith 1990). It is nevertheless remarkable that much mainstream work in policy studies fails to systematically recognize the fact that, because policies are adopted in the context of a capitalist economy, the range of policy options considered feasible will be affected. Instead, the work sticks to the pluralist view that despite inequalities of power and access, power is sufficiently diffuse, multifaceted (not just wealth, but also skills, expertise, time, information), and variable between issue areas to allow the less powerful to organize and gain influence and to ensure that no group can dominate in multiple fields of decision making.

The "states and markets" and neo-pluralist approaches are fine, as far as they go. But two problems with these views are worth noting here. First, they erect a false distinction between the political and the economic. Second, if our interest lies in understanding what the state does and why, the "state" of states-and-markets political economy needs to be unpacked and theorized rather than taken as an unproblematic unitary actor representing some form of "general interest." The next two subsections take up the first issue by sketching out a field of political economy based on the analysis of social relations; the third subsection expands on the second issue by proposing an alternative vision of the state.

Production and Social Relations

A states-and-markets approach to political economy runs the risk of exaggerating the distinction between the political and the economic. The formal division of the economic and the political is a peculiar feature of capitalist social formations, and it risks masking the extent to which relations of power and inequality hold across the division (Wood 1995, chap. 1). It masks, for instance, how the state supports and reproduces the power of employers in the economy through the protection of property rights. It also conceals how relations in the "private" realm of the workplace or household affect the capacities of individuals and groups to perform in the "public realm" of politics and the state. It is likewise mistaken to assume that unequal social relations, such as those related to class, gender, race/ethnicity, and sexuality, exist only in some realm outside the state and the economy. These relations are played out across all realms of social life.

How, then, should we conceptualize the political and the economic in a more integrated sense? One means is to consider the world as continually produced and reproduced. This day-by-day process of producing the material basis of human existence, not to mention the ideas and ideologies that make sense of this existence, involves humans in relationships with others. The positions occupied by people in these processes often vary, and in ways that significantly influence their life chances and experiences. Individuals are hard pressed to challenge any particular set of unequal relationships since these relations are central to the production and reproduction of social life. These relations can be thought of as "structured," since, as Jim Glassman (2003, 681) points out, "people must participate, whether they wish to (or are aware of doing so) or not." In sum, then, certain groups and individuals are relatively enabled and empowered by their location within a web of social relations.

In a capitalist system, attention must be paid to the role of class relations in production and reproduction, and particularly to the power that different classes possess based on their different positions in the process. Critics of political economy have seized on this to claim that it is class and/or economic reductionist – that it seeks to explain everything through class struggle and the economic structures shaping it (Skocpol 1985, 5; 1980, 200; Thelen and Steinmo 1992, 10; Almond 1996, 85). Yet, the broad view of production laid out here requires that attention be paid to an array of structural relations beyond those of class. After all, this process of production and reproduction also implicates other relations such as gender, race/ethnicity, and sexuality, and the structuring of these relations into systems of patriarchy, racism, and heterosexism. We can therefore speak of an "intersectional" approach that considers the meshed and overlapping impacts of these different structural relations on social processes, and which focuses on determining their relative causal efficacy in concrete historical situations (rather than positing the trans-historical dominance of certain structural relations over others) (Glassman 2003, 684; Vosko 2002b).

The intersectional approach is not immune from criticism, but its development points to the inadequacy of dismissing political economy for being solely interested in class relations and economic domination. Indeed, I would argue that the most dynamic tendency in Canadian political economy is precisely that of feminist political economy, which looks both at the gendered impacts of neo-liberal state restructuring (Vosko 2002a) and at the organization of the women's movement and its allies in seeking to advance women's equality and citizenship through policy advocacy and participation (Brodie 1995; Masson 1999, 2001; McKeen 2004; Porter 2003). Less work has been done at the intersection of class and race, although Yasmeen Abu-Laban and Christina Gabriel (2002) have carefully documented how policies of multiculturalism and immigration have been redefined and recentred as part of the more general neo-liberalization of the Canadian state. Similarly, questions of sexuality need to be better integrated (see Smith 2005). Still, the difficulty integrating these perspectives seems less theoretical (as in a reluctance of political economy to analyze unequal social relations other than class) than methodological (such that omissions arise from habitual research and writing emphases) (Purcell 2003, 317-18). Collaborative research processes promise to reduce these problems.

The intersectional approach responds to the challenge of postmodernists and post-structuralists, who criticized the narrowness of earlier political economy work focused largely on class and the workplace. A leading feminist welfare state scholar recently called on researchers to "exorcise" Marxism from social policy studies and to take a Foucauldian turn that emphasizes the analysis of "the whole set of regulatory, capillary, disciplinary and discursive analytic themes" (Orloff 2003, 26). This approach is attractive in its ability to deal directly with the power bound up in symbols, discourses, and forms of knowledge, and to thus interrogate how state policies "regard and reward, position and place" different identities and behaviour (Brush 2003, 52, emphasis in original). It looks explicitly at how needs or client categories come to be formed through the mobilization of expertise by professionals and bureaucrats. The underlying ontology and epistemology of these approaches nevertheless eschews the burdens of explanation and causation, focusing instead on how authorities have posed themselves questions about such things as their power, the ends to which it is exercised, and what they need to know in order to govern (Rose and Miller 1992, 177; Murray, this volume). This is ultimately too steep a price to pay since most political economists are interested in unpacking determination (by posing causal, historical, and explanatory questions) in order to intervene in the world (MacDonald 1998). This may explain why many feminist political economists have only partially followed this call. They have continued to work at the margins of political economy and governmentality approaches, trying to reach an understanding of how discourses and knowledge are tied up in ongoing conflicts over the production and reproduction of unequal social relations (Brush 2003; Larner 2000; Masson 1999; Michaud 2000). Moreover, though governmentality decentres the state and argues that oppression can be overcome by reconstituting basic presuppositions shaping norms about how government is to be exercised, to what ends, by what means, for and by whom, political economists continue to see the state as an important site of political struggle and representation, and to seek change through policy participation, mobilization, and organization (Masson 2005, 18), as well as through struggles over language and cognitive frames.

AGENCY

Political economy analyses have often been criticized for being reductionist. Some crudely assert that such analyses simply conclude that the capitalists always get their way, or that "politics always works optimally for capitalism and capitalists, leaving only the 'how' to be systematically explained" (Skocpol 1980, 200; see Smith 1990, 319; Taylor 2003, 87). If we indeed left analysis at the level of establishing structured systems of inequality such as capitalism or patriarchy, and of elaborating how any policy outcome served the purposes of capitalism or male dominance, then the charge might stick. However, this deductive mode of analysis has more in common with elite theory than with major strands of political economy since it ignores the latter's interest in social relations. Elite theory was based on the idea of an economic and governmental elite ruling in its own interests (see Dye and Zeigler 1975, 3-6); political economy stresses how rule is constantly negotiated. Relationships may be unequal, but they nevertheless involve mutual dependencies. They can be renegotiated when one party changes its power relative to the other. To take a simplified example, capitalists exercise structural power through their ability to make investment decisions, and they can extract policies from governments and concessions from workers by threatening to invest elsewhere. Workers can nevertheless also act to limit this power by collectively withdrawing their labour or by offering forms of cooperation and partnership leading to positive-sum compromises (on the latter, see Wright 2000).

Analysis must thus go beyond an appreciation of systems of structured inequality to also pay attention to the means in which actors attempt to transform the social relations in which they are implicated. It must be added that the existence of an unequal social relation is by no means sufficient to spur challenges, since actors must first be able to recognize and name the inequality. This situation was traditionally rendered in terms of the distinction between "class structure" and "class formation." The idea here was that though structural relations created class inequalities, one could not speak of class struggle until actors defined their situation in such terms and proposed solutions, organized on that basis, created institutions (such as mutual associations, parties, and unions), and developed a shared culture giving meaning to their situation and goals (Esping-Andersen 1985, 27, 31). This insight has subsequently been extended to other social relations, as in Barbara Hobson's (1999) work on the development of women's citizenship rights. Political economy analysis must thus also consider the interactive processes of identity and interest formation, as actors define new identities (and the interests felt to follow from those identities) to make sense of their place in social relations, and to attempt to mobilize the similarly situated to transform those relations.

It is here that political economy and public policy have a first interface. Public policies act as resources and constraints, both in identity and interest construction and in the contestation of social relations. Policies can be seen as institutionalized compromises between social forces. To take a simplified Canadian example, the move from treating unions as criminal conspiracies in the nineteenth century through various forms of partial legal recognition through the first half of the twentieth century reflected the growing strength of the working class. Partial recognition, in turn, provided resources and bases for the working class to strengthen its position, by, for instance, facilitating the organization of a greater share of the workforce into unions. However, the forms taken by legal recognition also affected the development of working-class identities and interests. By favouring the organization of male-dominated manufacturing industries, and the settlement of disputes through legalistic grievance procedures, the unions came to define working-class interests narrowly around the confines of the legal framework, and to embrace a particular identity of the male breadwinner that proved problematic for reaching women, workers in non-standard employment, and ethnic and sexual minorities.

This description of the interface of public policy and social relations nevertheless makes clear that the relationship is an interactive one that cannot be easily boiled down into independent and dependent variables. Public policies affect the relative power of actors in reproducing social relations, but they also institutionalize social relations. In order to understand how policies serve as institutionalized compromises, we need to return to a consideration of the state. In the next section, I will attempt to show that "states versus markets" approaches are untenable in this context because they provide no political sociology of the state. By sociology of the state, I mean an attempt at explaining what goes on inside the state to produce certain results. There is some overlap with governmentality approaches, which, as Murray (this volume) suggests, also seek to make the state an object of empirical study. Governmentality research focuses on what I might call a "psychology of the state," seeking to uncover the rationalities employed by political authorities. Political economy, by contrast, seeks to understand the power-laden processes of conflict and compromise through which these rationalities are put into practice, and to analyze how this is reflected in both the organization of the state's institutions and the receptiveness of the state to the demands of different social actors.

THE STATE

In his book on neo-Marxist state theory, Bob Jessop (1990, 341) suggests that "the core of the state apparatus comprises a distinct ensemble of institutions and organizations whose socially accepted function is to define and enforce collectively binding decisions on the members of a society in the name of their common interest or general will." He then emphasizes that terms such as "socially accepted," "common interest," and "general will" are inevitably disputed and notes that their definition will render the state more permeable to some interests rather than others. For instance, if the common interest is defined to include economic growth, this has ramifications for the relative legitimacy of business, labour, and environmental interests within the state. The state, including conceptions of the institutions and organizations that are considered as being within the state, representations of proper relations of hierarchy between these institutions, and renderings of "common interests" must therefore be placed within an analysis of social relations.

One way of doing this is to consider the state as a space, and not, as is often the case, as an actor or as a series of institutions. It is a space in which different social actors struggle to represent themselves and their projects through the creation and transformation of institutions and public policies. The state does not act: rather, social forces act through the state. This can involve attempting to create new institutions within that space, such as departments or advisory committees, to represent a social actor's project and discourse within the state. It may involve contesting existing patterns of representation within·existing institutions, such as the exclusion of particular actors from a policy network, or their confinement to an "attentive public" (rather than "subgovernment") role. It can also mean attempting to rearrange the relative hierarchy of different institutions within the space of the state, as, for instance, in changing the relative precedence given to particular policy committees (such as international trade versus agriculture), or in altering the extent of control the Department of Finance is granted over line departments. In analyzing the action of social forces, we can pay particular attention to their *state projects* (such as to what ends power will be exercised through the state, or what policy outputs are sought) and *state strategies* (such as how the different institutions and interests within the state are to be assembled or mobilized to fulfill state projects).

This discussion of actors struggling within the state must not become disconnected from an understanding of structured social relations. The state may be a space, but it is not a blank space. The institutions within the state represent earlier compromises between actors of uneven power, and can be transformed only within the present context of uneven power relations existing within and outside the state. Attention needs to be given to the ongoing negotiation of compromises between relatively dominant and relatively dominated actors concerning the "common interest" or "general will," particularly over fundamental questions of economic planning and development, the distribution of wealth, and the contours of citizenship and belonging. Negotiations and conflict about these questions take place both inside the state, in conflict over appropriate policies, and outside the state, as, for instance, through strikes or claims to public space (such as take-back-the-night marches or free-speech fights) (Mitchell 2003). Dominant social forces nevertheless will attempt to rally subordinate social forces to their program through a series of partial concessions. They can be said to have imposed a hegemonic project when they succeed in largely stabilizing contradictory social relations and aligning them behind shared visions of the "common interest" (Jenson 1989; Jessop 1990, 207-9). Some of these compromises occur within the state, including the representation of subordinate actors and of their projects. These compromises nevertheless have the state projects and state strategies of dominant social forces as their reference point. Although they provide points of leverage for subordinate actors to exercise power through the state, the overall matrix of institutions and projects within the state nevertheless favour the exercise of power by the relatively dominant. In less abstract terms, the representation of relatively dominated actors is likely to be doubly peripheralized: at the periphery of policy networks and in bodies at the periphery of the state. It is in this context that the state can be said to have a "strategic selectivity" since its institutional arrangements and the "common interest" it is set up to serve privilege the projects of certain social actors over others (Jessop 1990, 209).

Chapter 13, Denis Saint-Martin's discussion of the "social investment state," may serve as a partial illustration here. His chapter is not a political

economy analysis, as the causes of the change from the welfare state to the
social investment state are largely unexplored, with some vague references to
the role of ideas. The lack of attention to power relations within the state is
evident in the questionable proposition that assuring equality and social
justice to all citizens was the primary business of the postwar welfare state.
However, we could read his reference to a new paradigm in social policy as a
sign that the neo-liberal state project is being renegotiated in order to shore
up some of its shortcomings in terms of social exclusion. In the process, new
identities are recognized and prioritized, and new knowledge bases mobilized. This renegotiation is taking place against the backdrop of an English
Canadian left that is still struggling to overcome the setbacks of the 1980s
and 1990s, be they in terms of reduced union power, the virtual disappearance of the National Action Committee on the Status of Women, or the crisis
of social democratic parties such as the NDP. In this context, it is not surprising that Saint-Martin finds that workers and women experience difficulty in
having their identities and claims recognized within emergent state policies.
Class and gender inequalities have not disappeared, nor have movements
vying for equality. However, the relative weakness of these movements has
reduced their capacity to check changes that roll back or subordinate the
places in the state where their projects were rooted in the postwar period.

Looking at the state as a condensation of social struggles has some advantages for making sense of contemporary debates over globalization and
the state. Much of the research in this vein sees globalization as an external
constraint on national states, limiting the range of possible policy options
and forcing the abandonment of existing non-market-conforming policies.
Some writing on policy transfer, for instance, considers that countries are
coerced, in varying extents, to accept the policy ideas of international institutions (Dolowitz and Marsh 1996). The external constraint outlook is represented in a recent edited collection that asks to what extent Canada "is free to
choose" distinct public policies in light of continental integration (Hoberg
2001). A key problem with such work is that it assumes that the state acts
where it can to ensure some sort of transcendent public interest, and does
not consider how observed changes in the state may suit the interests of
powerful social actors, even if they impose costs or losses on the majority. It
would otherwise be a strange coincidence that the dictates of "external constraints" mapped so clearly onto the policy program laid out by employers'
associations and their think tanks (Langille 1987; Carroll and Shaw 2001).
Rather than considering globalization as an "out there" pressure limiting the

state, we should look at how particular social actors have used globalization to legitimize particular strategies of state reform reflecting their interests. Instead of "less state," we have observed the creation of a different kind of state, with institutions with close links to capital and its project, such as Treasuries and Ministries of Finance, coming to the fore and ensuring that other state institutions either remake themselves along neo-liberal lines or remain in marginal positions within the state hierarchy (Panitch 1999). This view enables analysts to consider how globalization involves restructuring the state and public policies in order to serve the global economy, in response to powerful domestic social forces seeking precisely that end (Findlay 2004, 44-48; McBride 2005).

Another strength of this approach to the state is that it gives a handle for analyzing the spatiality of the state, and particularly conflicts over the scales at which particular processes are regulated. In other words, rather than assuming that the growing importance of supranational or subnational governments in policy making reflects its functionality and "fit" with the scale of given policy problems, the view of the state as a space allows analysts to investigate these changes of scales as conflicts between different social actors over appropriate scales of social regulation (see Brenner 2003; Brenner et al. 2003; Mahon, Andrew, and Johnson, this volume). In the Canadian context, this perspective has been employed to explain the particular course taken by child care policy (Mahon 2003) and the regional policy strategies of women's movements (Masson 2001). The growing permeability of nation-state borders and the shift in certain scales of state regulation have posed significant challenges to mainstream policy studies, given the emphasis on the nation-state as the primary unit of analysis (DeLeon and Resnick-Terry 1999; Richardson 2000). This is less challenging for political economy approaches since the analysis of conflicting social relations within the state can easily add a scalar dimension. By seeing the state as a space of struggle between social actors rather than as a black box, political economy provides tools for analyzing and making sense of these developments, much as neo-Gramscian theory provides useful tools for dealing with these questions of permeability and scale in international relations (Gill 2003).

In this context, the dismissal of political economy approaches on the grounds of having an instrumentalist or functionalist view of the state, whereby the state is simply an instrument of the bourgeoisie or acted to ensure the reproduction of capital, is even less convincing than it used to be. As Leo Panitch (1999, 31) argues, "to understand how certain institutions or policies evolve through the push and pull of policy debate and class struggle ... in such a way as to sustain or conform with capitalist social relations is not at all about ascribing perfect strategic foresight to subjects. Nor does it entail the notion that everything that happens is unidimensionally reproductive of the system."

Application: Some Strengths and Weaknesses

The political economy approach laid out here appears more or less consistent with many recent policy studies, particularly those tracing the rise, adoption, and differentiated effects of neo-liberal policy prescriptions generally (for example, Bradford 1999; McBride 2005, 2003), as well as those in specific policy areas such as employment insurance (Porter 2003; Pulkingham 1998), income security (McKeen 2004), immigration and multiculturalism (Abu-Laban and Gabriel 2002), health care (Armstrong and Armstrong 2003), industrial relations (Panitch and Swartz 2003), labour-market policy (Cameron 1996; Vosko 2000), and child policy (Jenson 2000).

The approach suggested here has its strengths and weaknesses. Some Marxian perspectives would rightfully underline its "politicist" tendencies. The emphasis on politics, particularly in terms of struggles and compromises within the state over the status of different institutions and the projects to be pursued through them, confronts old charges of economism, determinism, and class reductionism. However, this comes at the expense of paying sustained attention to economic structures and material conditions that affect the power of different actors, and the range of possible outcomes. For instance, research on economic and social development strategies has revealed how the shared tendency toward forms of "competitive austerity" (Albo 1997; Coates 2000; Zuege 1999) or "varieties of neoliberalism" (Albo and Fast 2003) results from the limits that competitive imperatives and pressures of contemporary capitalism place on social democratic strategies. Recent neo-institutionalist analyses of the welfare state underline how structural economic changes force stark trade-offs in post-industrial welfare states, eliminating the ability to set public policies that achieve full employment, diminish earnings inequality, and establish sound public finances at the same time (Esping-Andersen 1999; Wren 2001). Neo-Marxist interventions in this latter debate (for example, Leys 2001; Mahon 2001) have criticized the rigid determinism of the neo-institutionalists' trade-offs – an indication that the charge of determinism is perhaps more correctly levelled at institutionalists than at Marxists – but they do accept that social struggles over policy are forged against and around the particular constraints of post-industrial political economies. In sum, care must be taken in handling the "politicist" bias apparent in many recent political economy analyses, or one will end up assuming rather than assessing the real possibilities open to the diverse actors in their varying places in the broader political economy, and thus tend to a voluntarism by overstating the agency open to actors, particularly subordinate ones.

In some cases, this voluntarism might raise the question of what, besides jargon and some ontological and epistemological gymnastics, differentiates the approach described here from sophisticated versions of reformed pluralism or neo-pluralism (see Smith 1990). In other words, does this approach simply import the pluralist's understanding of policy as profoundly shaped by interest-group competition (albeit heavily mediated by institutions in the reformed pluralism of agenda-setting, policy transfer, and policy network studies) into what claims to be a radical analysis? Two axes of difference with pluralism are worth noting for clarity's sake. First, the understandings of society differ, with political economy approaches insisting on structural relations of inequality running throughout state and society, as compared to the pluralist view of a neutral state, and of varying relations of power between groups, depending on the issue area. The political economist thus challenges the popular association of state action with the public interest, recognizing that the state participates in relations of exploitation and inequality. "More state" is therefore not necessarily synonymous with democratization or progressive politics. As recent work on democratic administration has argued, attaining more egalitarian outcomes requires the democratization of the state to render it more permeable to progressive actors and movements (McElligott 2001; Shields and Evans 1998). In addition, as noted in the section on production, political economy problematizes the formation of identities and collective actors, whereas pluralism seems to assume that the "interests" of interest groups are more or less pre-given (Smith 1999).

Second, the emphasis on relations of power running throughout state and society leads political economy analyses, in contrast to pluralism and most institutional approaches, always to place the study of a given public policy in a broader context. One cannot properly assess the development or evolution of a policy without situating it with respect to dominant state projects and ideologies and the social base of the state. As policy network and advocacy coalition scholars admit, they are hard pressed to explain change within a particular field (for instance, agriculture) solely with reference to endogenous factors (Marsh and Smith 2000; Richardson 2000; Sabatier and Jenkins-Smith 1993). Placing these networks within the field of the state provides one means of systematically accounting for exogenous pressures, by noting how struggles within the state lead to changes in the hierarchy of the networks with respect to each other, and in the membership and bodies of expertise constituting individual networks. For instance, the push by Canadian capital for neo-liberal restructuring displaced the locus of social policy making from departments such as Health and Welfare to the Department of Finance, and thereby helped transform the terms of consultation, debates, and acceptable policy options, for the social policy network (McKeen 2004, 70-71). This question of context also involves levels of analysis. Policy is considered not simply at the micro level of particular actor interactions, nor at the meso level of political institutions shaping the direction of policy development. Instead, it is viewed as the struggle of social forces acting within contexts set by institutions and structural relations of power.

Of course, Paul Pierson and Theda Skocpol (2002, 706) have recently argued that one of historical institutionalism's main strengths is to look at context, and thus to "probe uneasy balances of power and resources, and see institutions as the developing products of struggle among unequal actors." Although historical institutionalism may look at institutions as products of struggle, it generally cannot theorize that struggle since it does not come down on a particular theory of society, be it a pluralist one or one structured by social relations such as gender or class. It seeks to ground explanation and determination in a limited range of political (and occasionally collective bargaining) institutions, and thus consciously sidelines consideration of the contribution of deeper economic and social structures (to say nothing of agency) to policy variation in time and space (Pontusson 1995, 126, 128, 131). Although we cannot deny the considerable ingenuity and analytical refinement of historical institutionalism, its failure to engage with structure limits its ability to embed policy within context, a drawback which becomes especially noticeable when institutionalism is compared to political economy approaches.

As one makes this case, a particular limit to the approach becomes clear. In emphasizing social relations cutting across society, and the linkage of the macro, meso, and micro levels, analysis can lose explanatory leverage as it approaches concrete processes on the micro level. It is hard pressed to theorize the role of individual actors or the creative elements of politics leading to outcomes other than those predicted from a reading of the forces present.

Conversely, the further analysis extends into particular policy-making institutions and forums, the more tenuous the link to broad questions of social relations. Moreover, given the space constraints of the journal article form, not to mention limits of expertise, attempts to situate the micro in the macro context are plagued with difficulties. This issue of the difficult macro-micro linkage nevertheless has been confronted in imaginative ways. Wendy McKeen (2004), for instance, extended Janine Brodie's (1995) general analysis of the women's movement and policy restructuring by analyzing the organization and discourses in the federal income security policy network. Brodie made a general argument about how neo-liberal restructuring eroded many of the political identities and institutional spaces that Canadian feminists had used in the 1960s and 1970s to advance their claims and policy demands. She emphasized how new dominant policy discourses "re-privatized" social policy provision by increasing familial responsibilities, even as, on the grounds that men and women should be treated equally, it ignored the fact that women provide the bulk of unpaid care work. McKeen enriched and nuanced this account by moving beyond Brodie's emphasis on dominant discourses to look more closely at the impact of more marginalized actors and of the social policy network. This allowed for a more textured analysis of policy change, uncovering the previously unremarked yet crucial role of the progressive social policy community. By mobilizing under the banner of "child poverty," this community closed spaces for engagement which the more radical projects of the women's and labour movements had held in the social policy debates of the 1990s, thereby contributing to the erosion Brodie identified. McKeen's work added this texture without losing sight of the broader economic, political, and ideological changes framing actors' strategies.

Indeed, these examples suggest the value of collective research projects that move from a relatively macro analysis of the social base of the state and state projects through to studies of particular policies and policy networks. Such an approach would verify the macro analysis and identify exceptions, tensions, and sources of agency missed by the macro analysis. These micro studies should in turn be spun out to the macro level to help identify potential sources and directions of policy change.

Conclusion

Political economy provides an exciting window onto the study of public policy, highlighting how social inequalities are played out in struggles over what the state chooses to do or not do. At a time when citizens are interrogating the social sciences to answer big questions about sovereignty, imperialism, and the attenuation of representative democracy, political economy provides a number of useful tools for understanding the linkages between large-scale structural forces and the adoption of particular public policies. It grounds its understanding of policy in structured relations of power and in the efforts of actors to reproduce or transform these relations. These struggles are played out across society, including the state as a central site for the exercise of power. Without denying the role of institutions, of knowledge, or of learning, it insists that policy making be seen as an act of power, and not simply as a technical exercise of sorting and evaluating policy options. Policies reflect the structural relations of power in the society from which they emerge, yet serve also as points of leverage and resources for groups attempting to transform these structural relations. Students of political economy approaches thus start from an understanding of contemporary capitalist society as fundamentally divided along such lines as class, gender, race/ethnicity, and sexuality. They are led to study policy in terms of how actors have mobilized and organized to make sense of, transform, or reproduce these divisions through the state.

As noted in this chapter, painting political economy approaches as determinist or class reductionist is lazy and inadequate. Yet, despite its emphasis on context and on linkages between the macro, meso, and micro levels of analysis, there are aspects of policy making related to bargaining dynamics, chance, and creativity that elude political economy's analytical grasp. Nevertheless, as mainstream policy studies continue to work from a largely pluralist understanding of power as diffused, political economy provides a useful set of tools for those with more radical understandings of society and power.

ACKNOWLEDGMENTS
My thinking in the section on the state is greatly indebted to Rianne Mahon (1977) and Pascale Dufour (2004, 162-73). I thank my PS783 students for helping me work through the arguments of this essay as a whole.

REFERENCES
Abu-Laban, Yasmeen, and Christina Gabriel. 2002. *Selling Diversity: Immigration, Multiculturalism, Employment Equity, and Globalization.* Peterborough: Broadview Press.

Albo, Gregory. 1997. "A World Market of Opportunities? Capitalist Obstacles and Left Economic Policy." In *The Socialist Register 1997*, ed. Leo Panitch, 5-47. Halifax: Fernwood.

Albo, Gregory, and Travis Fast. 2003. "Varieties of Neoliberalism: Trajectories of Workfare in the Advanced Capitalist Countries." Paper presented to the annual meeting of the Canadian Political Science Association, Halifax, 1 June.

Almond, Gabriel. 1996. "Political Science: The History of the Discipline." In *A New Handbook of Political Science*, ed. Robert Goodin and Hans-Dieter Klingemann, 50-96. Oxford: Oxford University Press.

Armstrong, Hugh, and Pat Armstrong. 2003. *Wasting Away: The Undermining of Canadian Health Care.* 2nd ed. Toronto: Oxford University Press.

Bradford, Neil. 1999. "The Policy Influence of Economic Ideas: Interests, Institutions and Innovation in Canada." *Studies in Political Economy* 59: 17-60.

Brenner, Neil. 2003. "'Glocalization' as a State Spatial Strategy: Urban Entrepreneur-ship and the New Politics of Uneven Development in Western Europe." In *Remaking the Global Economy: Economic-Geographical Perspectives,* ed. Jamie Peck and Henry Wai-chung Yeung, 197-215. London: Sage Publications.

Brenner, Neil, Bob Jessop, Martin Jones, and Gordon MacLeod. 2003. "Introduction: State Space in Question." In *State/Space: A Reader,* ed. Neil Brenner, Bob Jessop, Martin Jones, and Gordon MacLeod, 1-26. Malden: Blackwell.

Brodie, Janine. 1995. *Politics on the Margins: Restructuring and the Canadian Women's Movement.* Halifax: Fernwood.

Brush, Lisa. 2003. *Gender and Governance.* Walnut Creek: Altamira.

Cameron, Barbara. 1996. "From Equal Opportunity to Symbolic Equity: Three Decades of Federal Training Policy for Women." In *Rethinking Restructuring: Gender and Change in Canada,* ed. Isabella Bakker, 55-81. Toronto: University of Toronto Press.

Carroll, William K., and Bob Ratner. 2005. "The NDP Regime in British Columbia, 1991-2001: A Post-mortem." *Canadian Review of Sociology and Anthropology* 42(2): 1-30.

Carroll, William K., and Murray Shaw. 2001. "Consolidating a Neoliberal Policy Bloc in Canada, 1976 to 1996." *Canadian Public Policy* 27(2): 195-217.

Clement, Wallace. 2001. "Canadian Political Economy's Legacy for Sociology." *Canadian Journal of Sociology* 26(3): 405-20.

Clement, Wallace, and Leah F. Vosko, eds. 2003. *Changing Canada: Political Economy as Transformation.* Montreal and Kingston: McGill-Queen's University Press.

Coates, David. 2000. *Models of Capitalism: Growth and Stagnation in the Modern Era.* Cambridge: Policy Press.

DeLeon, Peter, and Phyllis Resnick-Terry. 1999. "Comparative Policy Analysis: Déjà Vu All Over Again?" *Journal of Comparative Policy Analysis: Research and Practice* 1(1): 9-22.

Dolowitz, David, and David Marsh. 1996. "Who Learns What from Whom? A Review of the Policy Transfer Literature." *Political Studies* 44: 343-57.

Dufour, Pascale. 2004. "L'adoption du projet de loi 112 au Québec: Le produit d'une mobilisation ou une simple question de conjoncture politique?" *Politique et sociétés* 23(2-3): 159-82.

Dye, Thomas R., and L. Harmon Zeigler. 1975. *The Irony of Democracy: An Uncommon Introduction to American Politics.* 3rd ed. Belmont: Duxbury Press.

Ebbinghaus, Bernhard, and Philip Manow. 2001. "Studying Varieties of Welfare Capitalism." In *Comparing Welfare Capitalism: Social Policy and Political Economy in Europe, Japan and the USA,* ed. Bernhard Ebbinghaus and Philip Manow, 1-24. London: Routledge.

Esping-Andersen, Gøsta. 1985. *Politics against Markets: The Social Democratic Road to Power.* Princeton: Princeton University Press.

—. 1999. *Social Foundations of Postindustrial Economies.* Oxford: Oxford University Press.

Findlay, Tammy. 2004. "Getting Our Act Together: Gender, Globalization, and the State." *Socialism and Democracy* 18(1): 43-83.

Gill, Stephen. 2003. *Power and Resistance in the New World Order.* New York: Palgrave.

Glassman, Jim. 2003. "Rethinking Overdetermination, Structural Power and Social Change: A Critique of Gibson-Graham, Resnick, and Wolff." *Antipode* 35(4): 678-98.

Hall, Peter A., and David Soskice. 2001. "An Introduction to Varieties of Capitalism." In *Varieties of Capitalism: The Institutional Foundations of Comparative Advantage,* ed. Peter A. Hall and David Soskice, 1-68. Oxford: Oxford University Press.

Hoberg, George, ed. 2001. *Capacity for Choice: Canada in the New North America.* Toronto: University of Toronto Press.

Hobson, Barbara. 1999. "Women's Collective Agency, Power Resources, and the Framing of Citizenship Rights." In *Extending Citizenship, Reconfiguring States,* ed. Michael Hanagan and Charles Tilly, 149-78. London: Rowman and Littlefield.

Jenson, Jane. 1989. "'Different' but Not 'Exceptional': Canada's Permeable Fordism." *Canadian Review of Sociology and Anthropology* 26(1): 69-94.

—. 2000. "Le nouveau régime de citoyenneté du Canada: Investir dans l'enfance." *Lien social et politiques* 44: 11-23.

Jessop, Bob. 1990. *State Theory: Putting the Capitalist State in Its Place.* Cambridge: Polity Press.

Langille, David. 1987. "The Business Council on National Issues and the Canadian State." *Studies in Political Economy* 24: 41-85.

Larner, Wendy. 2000. "Neo-liberalism: Policy, Ideology, Governmentality." *Studies in Political Economy* 63: 5-25.

Leys, Colin. 2001. *Market-Driven Politics: Neoliberal Democracy and the Public Interest.* London: Verso.

Lindblom, Charles. 1977. *Politics and Markets: The World's Political-Economic Systems.* New York: Basic Books.

—. 1982. "The Market as Prison." *Journal of Politics* 44(2): 324-36.

MacDonald, Eleanor. 1998. "Vectors of Identity: Determination, Association, and Intervention." *Studies in Political Economy* 57: 7-35.

Mahon, Rianne. 1977. "Canadian Public Policy: The Unequal Structure of Representation." In *The Canadian State: Political Economy and Political Power,* ed. Leo Panitch, 165-98. Toronto: University of Toronto Press.

—. 2001. "Theorizing Welfare Regimes: Towards a Dialogue?" *Social Politics* 8(1): 24-35.

—. 2003. "Yet Another R? The Redesign *and* Rescaling of Welfare Regimes." Paper presented at the Workshop of the ISA Research Committee 19, University of Toronto, 21-24 August.

Marsh, David, and Martin Smith. 2000. "Understanding Policy Networks: Towards a Dialectical Approach." *Political Studies* 48(1): 4-21.

Masson, Dominique. 1999. "Constituting 'Post-welfare State' Welfare Arrangements: The Role of Women's Movement Service Groups in Québec." *Resources for Feminist Research* 27(3-4): 49-69.

—. 2001. "Gouvernance partagée, associations et démocratie: Les femmes dans le développement régional." *Politique et Sociétés* 20(2-3): 89-116.

—. 2005. "Introduction." In *Femmes et politiques: L'État en mutation,* ed. Dominique Masson, 1-22. Ottawa: Presses de l'Université d'Ottawa.

McBride, Stephen. 1996. "The Political Economy Tradition and Canadian Policy Studies." In *Policy Studies in Canada: The State of the Art,* ed. Laurent Dobuzinskis, Michael Howlett, and David Laycock, 49-66. Toronto: University of Toronto Press.

—. 2003. "Quiet Constitutionalism: The International Political Economy of Domestic Institutional Change." *Canadian Journal of Political Science* 36(2): 251-73.

—. 2005. *Paradigm Shift: Globalization and the Canadian State.* 2nd ed. Halifax: Fernwood.

McElligott, Greg. 2001. *Beyond Service: State Workers, Public Policy, and the Prospects for Democratic Administration.* Toronto: University of Toronto Press.

McKeen, Wendy. 2004. *Money in Their Own Name: The Feminist Voice in Poverty Debate in Canada, 1970-1995.* Toronto: University of Toronto Press.

Michaud, Jacinthe. 2000. "The Restructuring of the Health Care System in Québec: Its Impact on the Women's Health Movement." *Studies in Political Economy* 61: 31-48.

Mitchell, Don. 2003. *The Right to the City: Social Justice and the Fight for Public Space.* New York: Guilford Press.

Orloff, Ann Shola. 2003. "Systems of Social Provision and Regulation." Paper presented at the annual meeting of the Canadian Political Science Association, Halifax, 31 May.

Panitch, Leo. 1999. "The Impoverishment of State Theory." *Socialism and Democracy* 13(2): 19-35.

Panitch, Leo, and Donald Swartz. 2003. *From Consent to Coercion: The Assault on Trade Union Freedoms.* Toronto: Garamond.

Pierson, Paul, and Theda Skocpol. 2002. "Historical Institutionalism in Contemporary Political Science." In *Political Science: The State of the Discipline,* ed. Ira Katznelson and Helen V. Milner, 693-721. New York: W.W. Norton.

Pontusson, Jonas. 1995. "From Comparative Public Policy to Political Economy: Putting Political Institutions in Their Place and Taking Interests Seriously." *Comparative Political Studies* 28(1): 117-47.

Porter, Ann. 2003. *Gendered States: Women, Unemployment Insurance, and the Political Economy of the Welfare State in Canada, 1945-1997.* Montreal and Kingston: McGill-Queen's University Press.

Pulkingham, Jane. 1998. "Remaking the Social Divisions of Welfare: Gender, 'Dependency,' and UI Reform." *Studies in Political Economy* 56: 7-48.

Purcell, Mark. 2003. "Islands of Practice and the Marston/Brenner Debate: Toward a More Synthetic Critical Human Geography." *Progress in Human Geography* 27(3): 317-32.

Richardson, Jeremy. 2000. "Government, Interest Groups and Policy Change." *Political Studies* 48(5): 1006-25.

Rose, Nikolas, and Peter Miller. 1992. "Political Power beyond the State: Problematics of Government." *British Journal of Sociology* 43(2): 173-205.

Sabatier, Paul, and Hank C. Jenkins-Smith, eds. 1993. *Policy Change and Learning: An Advocacy Coalition Approach.* Boulder: Westview Press.

Shields, John, and B. Mitchell Evans. 1998. *Shrinking the State: Globalization and Public Administration "Reform."* Halifax: Fernwood.

Skocpol, Theda. 1980. "Political Response to Capitalist Crisis: Neo-Marxist Theories of the State and the Case of the New Deal." *Politics and Society* 10(2): 155-201.

—. 1985. "Bringing the State Back In: Strategies of Analysis in Current Research." In *Bringing the State Back In,* ed. Peter B. Evans, Dietrich Rueschemeyer, and Theda Skocpol, 3-37. Cambridge: Cambridge University Press.

Smith, Martin J. 1990. "Pluralism, Reformed Pluralism and Neopluralism: The Role of Pressure Groups in Policy-Making." *Political Studies* 38(2): 302-22.

Smith, Miriam. 1999. *Lesbian and Gay Rights in Canada: Social Movements and Equality-Seeking: 1971-1995.* Toronto: University of Toronto Press.

—. 2005. "Resisting and Reinforcing Neoliberalism: Lesbian and Gay Organizing at the Federal and Local Levels in Canada." *Policy and Politics* 33(1): 75-94.

Taylor, Marilyn. 2003. *Public Policy in the Community.* New York: Palgrave.

Thelen, Kathleen, and Sven Steinmo. 1992. "Historical Institutionalism in Comparative Politics." In *Structuring Politics: Historical Institutionalism in Comparative Analysis,* ed. Sven Steinmo, Kathleen Thelen, and Frank Longstreth, 1-32. Cambridge: Cambridge University Press.

Vosko, Leah F. 2000. *Temporary Work: The Gendered Rise of a Precarious Employment Relationship*. Toronto: University of Toronto Press.

—. 2002a. "Mandatory 'Marriage' or Obligatory Waged Work: Social Assistance and Single Mothers in Wisconsin and Ontario." In *Women's Work Is Never Done: Comparative Studies in Care-Giving, Employment, and Social Policy Reform*, ed. Sylvia Bashevkin, 165-200. New York: Routledge.

—. 2002b. "The Pasts (and Futures) of Feminist Political Economy in Canada: Reviving the Debate." *Studies in Political Economy* 68: 55-83.

Wood, Ellen Meiksins. 1995. *Democracy against Capitalism: Renewing Historical Materialism*. Cambridge: Cambridge University Press.

Wren, Anne. 2001. "The Challenge of De-industrialization: Divergent Ideological Responses to Welfare State Reform." In *Comparing Welfare Capitalism: Social Policy and Political Economy in Europe, Japan and the USA*, ed. Bernhard Ebbinghaus and Philip Manow, 239-69. London: Routledge.

Wright, Erik Olin. 2000. "Working-Class Power, Capitalist-Class Interests, and Class Compromise." *American Journal of Sociology* 105(4): 957-1002.

Zuege, Alan. 1999. "The Chimera of the Third Way." In *The Socialist Register 2000: Necessary and Unnecessary Utopias*, ed. Leo Panitch and Colin Leys, 87-114. London: Merlin.

3
Policy Analysis in an Era of "Globalization": Capturing Spatial Dimensions and Scalar Strategies

Rianne Mahon, Caroline Andrew, and Robert Johnson

This chapter reflects on how best to capture the spatial dimension of policy analysis in an era of globalization. The view that space cannot simply be seen as a passive container for the flows of time has been gaining ground, in the first place, with the development of theoretical insights coming out of the discipline of geography (Castells 1996; Harvey 2001; Massey and Allen 1984; Soja 1989), and second, because of the need to grapple with the spatial implications of "globalization" for policy analysis and policy responses (Skogstad 2000). The approach taken here is centred on the concept of scale, rooted in the kind of political economy discussed by Peter Graefe in Chapter 2 of this volume; the relation to other concepts such as place and region is explored only briefly in this chapter (for a discussion, see Paasi 2004).

Policy analysis, like much of the social science theory on which it draws, has assumed the centrality of the nation-state. Thus, the main focus has been on national policies, though the reality of federalism often forced students of Canadian policy to include federal-provincial bargaining and sometimes analyses of policy development at the provincial scale. Even here, however, this has been seen as Canadian exceptionalism from the norm of national decision making. Canadian exceptionalism could in fact be linked to Charles Tilly's (1990) argument that the nation-state emerged as the dominant form from among other alternatives such as empire and city-states; in this regard, Canada might be considered an example where traces of empire and city-states remained in existence somewhat longer than elsewhere. National-state centrism (or "methodological nationalism") made good sense for much of the twentieth century but as the century drew to a close, the adequacy of such a uni-scalar analysis came increasingly under question.

This chapter begins with a brief critique of methodological nationalism in light of what has been defined as globalization and then turns to examine the specifically Canadian tradition of incorporating scalar dimensions into the study of public policy. The next section considers some of the analytical tools policy analysts have used to reflect on how these new conditions affect policy making. This is followed by a discussion of the outlines of a multi-scalar approach. The final section uses these analytical tools to look at current issues (child care and urban policy) in Canada, showing how local policy making needs to be included in analyzing the effects of scalar arrangements on public policy in Canada.

Canadian Public Policy Analysis: Provinces and Regions as Spatial Actors

Policy studies draw on a modern social science that betrays its roots in the nineteenth and twentieth centuries, an era when the national state form, pioneered in Europe, gradually spread across the globe. By the end of the Second World War, the national state had become the normal way of organizing social, economic, and political life. It occupied a pivotal position in the Keynesian welfare states of advanced capitalist countries, the "development" states of Africa, Asia, and Latin America, and the Soviet and Chinese communist regimes alike. In these circumstances, policies were most often national policies. As Bob Jessop (1999, 382) argues, "International as well as urban and regional policies had supporting roles to play ... but they were mapped onto and organized around these 'imagined' national economies and their national states."

It is not surprising, therefore, that the centrality of the national scale has operated as an epistemological assumption deeply embedded in policy studies and the modern social sciences on which they draw. In fact, students of policy have typically seen national economies, national cultures, and national social relations as the natural objects of public policies, formed and implemented through national political and administrative institutions. They thus share the "methodological nationalism" – the assumption "that all social relations are organized at a national scale or are undergoing processes of nationalization" (Brenner 2004, 28) – which characterizes much of modern social science.

Trends of political activity at geographical scales smaller than the nation-state were seen as being "below" the national level or as "lower" levels; the "below" or "lower" clearly implied a relationship of inferiority to the "higher" levels. In particular, municipal government in Canada was contrasted to the "senior" levels of government, again a description of hierarchy. There was a recognition that politics occurred in different arenas but these arenas were seen as existing in a fixed order below the national level. Within nation-states, a greater geographic scope was equated with greater importance.

This was not true beyond the nation-state in pre-globalization thinking where greater geographic spread did not equate with greater power. Nation-states were seen as the key actors of international relations. In this sense, the mid-twentieth century represents the heyday of a multi-scalar hierarchy in which the national state acted as the linchpin.

Today, however, new technologies of transport and communication have combined with neo-liberal discourses and policies to render "national econo-mies" increasingly permeable to flows of goods, services, and, to a lesser ex-tent, people. New and revamped supra- and international arrangements have given rise to forms of "supra-national constitutionalism," establishing norms that "control government behaviour even though they are not part of the do-mestic constitution" (Clarkson 2002, 4). At the same time, devolution and decentralization, celebrated in the canons of the new public management, have shifted attention from the national to subnational governments. Such downscaling is reinforced by the growing interest in city-regions as the scale best able to capitalize on newly important economies of agglomeration.

What this has meant is that the clear hierarchical assumption from the nation-state period is no longer operative. There is no clear agreement as to what arena of politics is the most significant or the most structuring. For instance, Warren Magnusson (2005, 119) makes an argument for the impor-tance of urban government that situates this both locally and globally: "We need to open ourselves up to the extensiveness and messiness of urban life and to take the politics and government of it more seriously ... It can be a model of multiple centres of initiative. In such a model, local authorities can play an especially important part, not only in organizing whatever is most immediate but also in laying the ground for a cosmopolitan order." Other authors would argue for regions or the global or the body. A hierarchical vision of scales focused on the nation-state can no longer command alle-giance – as every imaginable scale in a multi-scalar model has its examples and its proponents.

In some respects, such a multi-scalar approach is not new to students of Canadian public policy, as Canadian conditions have imposed a greater con-cern for thinking about other spatial dimensions. This of course relates to the federal structure of Canadian government as well as to the imperial links to Great Britain and later to the United States. In particular, there is a Canad-ian tradition of the analysis of the impact of federalism and regionalism on policy making and it is important to understand the contribution those studies made to the analysis of the spatial dimension of policy.

The Canadian institutional approach, as reflected in Richard Simeon's (1972) analysis of federal-provincial diplomacy in policy making, brought to the fore the impact of federal-provincial negotiations on policy formation. Simeon (1972, 285) argued that executive federalism had led to a greater policy role for the provinces but without eliminating the federal power: "More generally, the negotiation process both reflects and contributes to a greater provincial role ... These shifts in relative status have not, however, made Ottawa powerless." Although Simeon recognized the increasing policy strength of the provincial governments, he gave too little space to non-state actors and therefore ignored the interplay of state and civil society (Schultz 1977). In addition, his analysis reflected a form of methodological nationalism, as he himself admitted. His primary interest remained national policy making: "Provincial governments are major participants in national policy formation" (Simeon 1972, 285). He thus did not deal with provincial policy and its influence on national policy or pan-Canadian policy outcomes. Others, however, have built on Simeon's work. Richard Schultz (1977) analyzed the impact of federalism on state-civil society relations. Looking at interest-group participation, he admonished that "it would seem unwise to underestimate the activities, influence and costs of interest group participation in the intergovernmental bargaining process" (1977, 394). The study of manpower policy in Ontario by Stephan Dupré et al. (1973) added a depth of analysis by pointing out that the clash between the Ontario and the federal governments reflected a disagreement between (provincial) educators and (federal) economists. Thus, ideological and professional interests were being played out in spatial terms.

The older political economy tradition in Canada, particularly that of Harold Innis, had a clear interest in the spatialization of politics. The idea of the relationship between the metropolis and the hinterland connected both to the spaces of empire and the spaces of city-states (thus reflecting our earlier comment on the influence of alternatives to the nation-state in Canada), and so did the analysis of the relations between Canada, Britain, and the United States. This older political economy tradition also looked at the impact of regions and regional arenas of politics or policy making in Canada. James R. Mallory's (1954) analysis of the conflict between the policies of the Alberta and federal governments is one such example. Mallory's argument was that behind the intergovernmental conflicts were class interests that manifested themselves in spatial terms. His study gives importance both to the state actors, with their political parties and their policies, and to the economic interests acting through different political structures. The spatial dimension remains critical as Western Canada has a different economic position and interests in the world than do Ontario and Quebec. Or, to quote Mallory (1954, 176-77), "these circumstances have tended to make of the disallowance power an imperial device for holding other provinces under the sway of the predominant economic interest of the central provinces. The outlying provinces are still Canada's empire."

Mallory's analysis has been described in part to illustrate the rich Canadian tradition of spatial analysis in policy making – federal policy is understood within an international and a local context. Janine Brodie (1990, 77) built on this tradition, examining "how the state, through its national development strategies, established, legitimized, and enforced particular spatial contours in the national economy and how this activity gave rise to spatially based political conflict." She makes the important point that regions are politically constructed through the impact of policies that reflect class forces in an international context. Certainly both non-state and state actors are central, but the focus is on the national state and its development policies. Yet for the most part, the studies of Canadian public policy have not followed the Mallory tradition. Perhaps more typical is the conclusion to J.E. Hodgetts' (1971) classic piece on regional interests and policy in a federal structure. For Hodgetts (1971, 346), "the growing recognition of regions is basically an artifice of administrators who, working within the political system, play a creative role in constructing regions appropriate to the functions entrusted to them ... If this development persists we must abandon any hopes we have of gearing our institutions and policies to the conception of a single Canadian political system." This certainly raises the issue of methodological nationalism and also of an overemphasis on state actors. Alan Cairns (1986), in his classic article on institutional versus sociological forces in shaping regional policies in Canada, offers a somewhat similar conclusion.

Federal-provincial relations, and the changing interscalar rule regime governing these, have received greater emphasis in areas of divided jurisdiction, such as labour-market and social policy. In the case of labour-market policy, the ambiguous nature of constitutional responsibility led to what Jamie Peck (1998, 101) has called "jurisdictional entanglement," as witnessed in the federal-provincial conflicts in the area of training during the immediate postwar period. Due to federal-provincial cost-sharing arrangements, federal

funding for such training was skewed toward the largest provinces and Ontario in particular; wishing to assert unilateral control over the situation,
Ottawa tried to invoke constitutional grounds, claiming that labour-market
policy was a national – not a provincial – economic priority (Dupré et al.
1973). Federalism is therefore said to have played a significant role in this
area, ultimately leading to federal recognition of provincial jurisdiction in
the aftermath of the 1995 Quebec referendum (McIntosh 2000). Others
working within the varieties of capitalism approach (Bradford 2003; Noël
2004) argue, however, that the broader institutional structures underpinning
a (liberal) market economy are of greater importance.

With regard to social policy, Keith Banting (1982) argued that, in the
postwar period, income security came to constitute one of the few exemplars
of a centralist conception of Canadian federalism, through the liberal use of
its spending powers. Leslie A. Pal's (1988) study of unemployment insurance, which devoted a whole chapter to federalism, also concluded that intergovernmental coordination was less of an issue here – though Quebec
contested federal dominance even in the heyday of the postwar rule regime,
preferring instead to establish a coherent system of its own. In his study of
social assistance, Gerard Boychuk (1998) suggested that, in fact, the Canada
Assistance Plan (CAP) had little impact on the existence of ten distinct provincial social assistance regimes. This "patchwork of purpose" was even more
marked in the fields of education and health, where the provinces remained
dominant despite the role played by federal transfers. With the passage of the
Canada Health and Social Transfer (CHST) in 1996, moreover, the federal
government appeared to concede the primacy of the provinces throughout
the social policy field.

What these studies do indicate is the growing recognition that the provincial arena is important and can influence the way in which federal policy
making operates. The Ontario capacity to use federal cost-sharing formulas
to its advantage both influenced the spatial impact of federal policies and
triggered the challenges of the western provinces, and certainly fuelled Quebec determination to achieve greater policy autonomy. The studies dealt with
federal policy making but their results gave greater space and greater weight
to the impact of provincial policies and policy making.

Political economists, from Innis through to the 1970s generation of
political economists such as Wallace Clement (1977) and Jim Laxer (1970,
1981), have long emphasized the importance of the continental scale. The
conclusion of the Canada-US Free Trade and the North American Free Trade

Agreements (CUFTA and NAFTA) has drawn others to reflect on the "internationalization" of policy (Doern, Tomlin, and Pal 1996). Here the main preoccupation has been to determine whether these agreements have led to policy convergence with the United States (Banting, Hoberg, and Simeon 1997; Hoberg 2001). Thomas Courchene (2001) would take this further, suggesting that increasingly dense north-south economic ties are generating pressure for policy convergence at the regional and municipal level. Stephen Clarkson (2002), operating within the Canadian political economy tradition, explores the complex ways in which these international agreements have triggered shifts in federal-provincial relations as well as having an impact on the municipal level.

Thus, a Canadian tradition in including spatial dimensions and space-based actors has existed in policy studies, and this awareness of the international (or imperial) context and of regional and provincial interests and actors has pushed many to move beyond a singular focus on national policy. Nevertheless, methodological nationalism has crept in through the back door in tones of regret that the Canadian state deviates from the qualities of a "real" nation-state. For example, Hugh Thorburn (1984) bemoaned the degeneration of federal-provincial cooperation in the 1970s and 1980s for inhibiting the development of indicative planning as an alternative to neo-liberal restructuring. Michael Atkinson and William Coleman (1989) argued that Canada failed to develop a strong industrial policy, not only because of the limitations imposed by the Westminster tradition and the strength of the business community, but also due to federalism. And many on the left in English-speaking Canada have regretted what they see as the weakening of national standards through the space given to the provinces.

There are a variety of very different imperatives that lie behind these analyses of Canadian exceptionalism. There are, for some, methodological imperatives, as seen in the development of comparative analyses and particularly in the cross-national studies that focus on the nation-state. However, it is interesting to note that there have been very few cross-provincial or cross-municipal comparative studies in Canada, whereas the cross-national focus has been more attractive.

How Has the Impact of Globalization on Policy Making Been Examined?

Contemporary policy studies increasingly call for a conceptual shift from government to governance. The literature on policy communities/policy networks represents an early expression of this shift: "Policy networks are mechanisms for political resource mobilization where the capacity for decision making, program formulation, and implementation is widely distrib-uted or dispersed among public and private actors" (Kenis and Schneider 1991, 41). Policy networks are thus seen as a means to move beyond the dichotomy of (macro-level) state versus society-centred analyses (Bradford 1998). This approach has the virtue of mapping out the particular institutionalized relations between governmental and civil society actors in a particular policy field or sector. It does not, however, come without its own limitations. Of particular import, it tends to miss the "horizontal" and "vertical" dimension of governance (Saint-Martin 2004; Zeitlin 2003). It fails to capture the dynamic way in which policy responsibilities are shifted among different, and indeed newly created, institutional scales such as the European Union (EU). Instead, it reproduces the "centralization" versus "decentralization" dichotomy found in some studies of the impact of federalism on policy making, contrasting the centralization found in the state to the associational system pertinent to a particular sector or policy field (Pal 2001, 244-46). It also fails to shed light on the way in which the ideas underpinning public policies move across national boundaries.

The literature on policy transfer takes up the way that policy ideas travel between nation-states. The classic study of policy transfer is Hugh Heclo's 1974 *Modern Social Policy in Britain and Sweden*, which explored the role of cross-national policy learning in the formation of modern (national) welfare states. Although these studies tend to treat the national regimes as largely closed to transnational influences, these attempts to theorize national policy regimes, including the "varieties of capitalism," which postulates a strong connection or complementarity of policies and practices across a number of areas (Hall and Soskice 2001), are not without insight. Problems arise, however, when policy regimes assume a life of their own and are treated as homogeneous, self-reproducing entities. This is particularly evident in the thesis common to all versions of "policy regime" analysis, namely, that each regime will respond to contemporary challenges in path-dependent ways.

The contemporary literature on policy transfer does draw attention to the ways in which seemingly closed national policy routines can be disrupted by the transnational flow of ideas, from the policy prescriptions of inter- and supranational organizations to the expertise provided by transnational consultants (Saint-Martin 2000). For David P. Dolowitz and David Marsh (2000, 5), policy transfer involves "a process in which knowledge about policies, administrative arrangements, institutions and ideas in one political setting (past or present) is used in the development of policies, administrative arrangements, institutions, and ideas in another political setting." The most interesting work on policy transfer links it to recent developments in policy regime theory, which ease the "iron law" of path-dependent responses to contemporary challenges. Jonathan Zeitlin and David M. Trubeck (2003, 11) challenge the tendency of national policy regime approaches to ignore "prospects for mutual learning and policy transfer across welfare and production regimes." In this they join Maurizio Ferrera, Anton Hemerijck, and Martin Rhodes (2000), who argue that often the most successful responses to new policy issues have involved the formation of "hybrids." These emerge when policy makers draw on traditions that were previously submerged by the dominant national regime, or when they look outside for the source of new policy ideas.

In their openness to the possibility of path-breaking policy learning, Zeitlin and Trubeck (2003) connect with the cutting-edge work being done by historical institutionalists such as Colin Crouch (2001) and Wolfgang Streeck and Kathleen Thelen (2005). Their work represents an important development in comparative political economy because it recognizes the severity of the contemporary challenges to the *ancien* (policy) *régimes*. In particular, Crouch's work highlights the complex "hybrid" character of actually existing societies and the way in which these "untidy bits" provide resources for actors seeking to shape new paths. Streeck and Thelen focus on the ways in which apparently incremental responses to neo-liberalism are eroding the non-liberal models of capitalism previously established in countries such as Japan and Germany. They describe four kinds of path-reshaping strategies: displacement, layering, drift, and conversion. Common to their work is a richer, more dynamic conception of policy, one in which power and contestation receive their due.

Nevertheless, these new developments in historical institutionalism, like those in the policy transfer literature, continue to take the national as the primary scale of analysis. Both implicitly adopt a mechanical "Russian dolls" conception of nested locales, which understands each doll/scale as largely capable of being considered on its own, even while located in its (fixed) position in a preordained hierarchy (Herod and Wright 2002, 8). Such a conception was inadequate even in the heyday of the nation-state-centred hierarchy and it is even more so today, as interscalar arrangements are being reconfigured. To some extent this is recognized by Dolowitz and Marsh (2000,

12), who acknowledge that policy learning can take place across, as well as between, levels of government. Yet, for the latter, each level is still thought of as a container – no longer airtight perhaps, but still a clearly bounded space. This is in marked contrast not only to the political economy of scale but also to the literature on multi-level governance.

Although the concept of multi-level governance (MLG) was initially developed to make sense of the structure of governance emerging within the EU, it has been extended to illuminate the dynamics of devolution in the UK and has had some resonance with students of Canadian intergovernmental relations. Like the political economy of scale, MLG recognizes the challenge that such developments pose to the Westphalian model and the Russian dolls conception of political space. Liesbeth Hooghe and Gary Marks' work (2001) has been particularly important. Critical of the view that policy making in the EU is determined "primarily by state executives constrained by political interests, nested within autonomous state arenas that connect subnational groups to European affairs," they argue that decision-making competencies are shared by actors at different levels (Marks and Hooghe 1996, 345). Policy is thus the result of the interplay between the member states, directly and through organs such as the Council of Ministers; EU organs such as the Commission, the Court, and increasingly the Parliament; and subnational forces (subnational governments, the social partners, and other social movements), who have established a direct presence in the EU policy arena. Together these shape the EU policy agenda and take and implement policy decisions.

MLG is based on the methodological individualism characteristic of the public or rational choice variant of political economy where self-interest-maximizing individuals face different incentive structures (and time horizons) given by the institutional setting in which they are operating. From this perspective, multi-level governance is the outcome of the games played within and across a particular combination of institutional incentive structures, even if macro-level issues are not completely ignored (see Hooghe and Marks 2001, chap. 6). Thus, for instance, the willingness of national states to cede (some) sovereignty to the EU is understood in terms of the key role played by elected government officials, who have short time horizons and aim to maximize the probability of being re-elected: "To the extent that political leaders have a short time horizon (and thus a high discount rate), and the substantial policy stream of European integration is more salient for powerful domestic constituencies than its decisional implications, so state sovereignty may be sacrificed for efficient policy provision" (Marks and Hooghe 1996, 349).

This trilogy of analytical tools – policy networks, policy transfer, and multi-level governance – suggests how some students of public policy are grappling with the global context and the multiplicity of actors. Although these studies have made a contribution to the field, the primacy they accord to nation-state actors limits their ability to theorize the highly contested and complex reconfiguration of relations among and across scales of action. A multi-scalar approach to policy analysis rooted in macro political economy can transcend these limitations.

A Multi-Scalar Perspective on the Spatial Dimension of Public Policy

Not surprisingly, the concept of "scale" used here derives from geography, where space and spatial relations constitute the centre of inquiry. Yet it is not the cartographic definition – scale as relation between distance on a map and distance on the ground – that is deployed. John Agnew (1997, 100) defines scale as "the level of geographic resolution at which a given phenomenon is thought of, acted upon or studied" or "the focal setting at which spatial boundaries are defined for a specific social claim, activity or behavior." These definitions draw attention to the scale/spatial reach of a policy and to the scale at which actors mobilize to secure or to challenge it. They fail, however, to bring out the critical relational – or multi-scalar – dimension: each scale has to be understood in terms of its position relative to other scales. As Edward Soja (1989) put it, the world is a *mutable* hierarchy of locales or scales. Mutability here refers both to the scales themselves – as, for example, the construction of new scales of action such as the European Union – and to the complex hierarchies in which they operate.

To identify more concretely how this multi-scalar perspective leads to a fuller understanding of public policy, we will use three basic concepts: scalar discourses, interscalar rule regimes, and jumping scale.

. Contemporary developments, and the scalar discourses associated with them, are drawing new attention to other scales of thought and action. Thus, neo-liberal scalar discourses represent the global as the scale of immutable market forces and the local as the scale for creating competitive advantage (global cities as "engines of growth" in the post-industrial economy), while seeking to reduce the national to the scale of deregulation, devolution, and privatization (Peck 2002, 334). The shift is not just discursive, even if competing scalar discourses play an important part in the struggle over the definition and allocation of functions across scales. It is embedded in new institutions, such as the World Trade Organization (WTO), which support the global reach of transnational capital while simultaneously constraining the options of national states. At the same time, policy responsibilities are being devolved, giving local scales of action a new prominence. Associated with this is the growth of trans-local linkages not mediated by national states (Jessop 1999, 389).

Two examples of scalar discourses that have a clear impact on policy making at the urban level derive from the work of Manuel Castells (1996) and Richard Florida (2002). Castells' arguments about the network of "world cities" as the economic force of the twenty-first century have underpinned urban economic development strategies, particularly around the support to information technology development. Cities have rushed to help support the development of high-tech clusters, or technopoles. Florida's work also highlights urban economic development strategies, calling for spending on cultural policies and on a variety of quality-of-life measures destined to try to attract the "creative class." Such scalar discourses create justifications for local actions designed to attract broad-based support from the local population.

Although certain theorists abandon the national to focus on these "urban nodes" and the global flows that bind them, the greater discursive space for local action does not mean that the nation-state has been hollowed out. As Neil Brenner (2004, 30) suggests, "the effort to transcend state-centric modes of analysis does not entail a denial of the national state's continued relevance, as a major locus of political-economic regulation. What such a project requires ... is a reconceptualization of how the geographies of state space are being transformed at various geographic scales under contemporary geo-economic conditions." In fact, rescaling is not a zero sum process in which new policy roles at the supra- and subnational scale mean the eclipse of the national state. Rather, what is at stake is a reconfiguration of a complex set of hierarchical arrangements – a contested process, but one that is not without a certain order. What is involved is constitution of new multi-scalar arrangements – or, as Jamie Peck (2002, 256) puts it, interscalar rule regimes – which are superimposed upon the old. In the process, the national scale, far from withering away, often retains a critical role as "scale manager" in a range of policy processes.

Finally, rescaling is a not a process through which one hierarchy/multi-scalar rule regime is replaced by another. In fact, Ash Amin (2002, 387) notes, "sites such as cities and nations continue to exist as territorial units, now with different external orientations ... and different scalar involvement (for example, national welfare policies, continental trade agreements, global environmental regulations, local tax regimes)." In other words, even less than in the past is there one singular interscalar rule regime. Rather, there is a multiplicity of differently structured interscalar rule regimes, operative in and across diverse policy fields. The national state often plays an important role in organizing their intersection.

There is, of course, a debate among scale theorists about the relative weight given to structure versus agency. Brenner (2004), Jessop (1999), and Chris Collinge (1999) tend to focus on the way in which scale is articulated with processes of capital accumulation and associated structural relations. Others, such as Agnew (1997), Andrew Herod and Melissa Wright (2002), and Conway (2004) focus on social movements and/or political parties, as these incorporate scale into their strategic calculations. Nevertheless, both stress the power-laden and contested nature of interscalar arrangements. In this respect, the political economy of scale intersects with the literature on contentious politics in situating political conflict as part of scalar strategies. As William H. Sewell Jr. (2001, 67) indicates, "Questions of scale figure prominently in social movements and revolutions."

Thus, scale theorists are interested in how interscalar rule regimes operate to reinforce (or counteract) class and gender inequality (Conway 2004). Precisely because such interscalar arrangements have an impact on social relations of power, they themselves become the target of struggles designed to change those relations. Scalar discourses can play a role here, contributing to collective actors' ability to "jump scale" (Smith 1992). Jumping scale can be done for a variety of reasons, both by state and non-state actors. Actors can decide to move to a scale of political action where they can define themselves, or be defined, as central rather than peripheral. For instance, the James Bay Cree and local environmental groups jumped scale from local to national (Quebec and Canada) and then to an international context in which their struggle became an example of the worldwide struggle for the recognition of the rights of Indigenous peoples (Rousseau 2000).

The notion of interscalar rule regimes may seem familiar to students of Canadian federalism, as might the concept of scalar discourses to students of Canadian regionalism and its impact on policy. Jumping scale speaks especially to students of the policy impact of interest group (Schultz 1977) and social movement mobilization. More attention needs to be paid to

Canada's cities and their place – past and present – in a multi-scalar policy process.

Canada's Cities in a Multi-Scalar Policy Process

The growing proportion of Canadians who are metropolitan residents is one of the drivers of the increased visibility of urban policy issues. So too are the interscalar discourses that portray global cities as the "nodes of the network society" and as the "engines of growth" of the knowledge economy. Yet the interscalar rule regime formally governing Canada's cities has put provincial governments in the central policy-making position. Article 92.8 of the BNA Act gave the provincial governments exclusive jurisdiction over "Municipal Institutions in the Province," and postwar institutional developments reinforced this.

Despite the BNA Act, municipalities have in fact had an important influence on policy at both the provincial and the federal levels. Rejecting the common view about municipal incapacity during the Depression, Michèle Dagenais (1992) argues in her study of Montreal that cities may have served as models for the emerging welfare state in Canada.

Daycare is another area in which municipal governments have been policy innovators. Non-parental child care was initially isolated to the local scale as a charitable service for children whose mothers were forced to work because of the lack of a male breadwinner. To the extent that it entered the political arena, therefore, it did so at the municipal scale. This situation briefly changed during the Second World War, when the federal government stepped in to help fund daycare (mainly in Toronto and Montreal) in order to enable married women to fill key war-effort jobs left vacant by the men who had gone overseas. At the end of the war, the federal government withdrew. As Susan Prentice (1993) documents, protests by a local coalition of parents, child care providers, and municipal councillors in Toronto were insufficient to persuade the federal government to change its mind – but they were able to jump scale to seek provincial support. As a result, Ontario became the first province to recognize child care at that scale, adopting the Day Nursery Act several decades in advance of other provinces. Under the act, initiative remained with the municipality but access to provincial funds meant conformity to provincially set standards.

The next step came as part of the development of the postwar interscalar rule regime governing social policy. The 1966 passage of the Canada Assistance Plan (CAP), which was designed, inter alia, to support and encourage the shift of responsibility for community services from the local to the provincial scale, opened the way to renewed federal involvement, this time via federal-provincial cost-sharing arrangements. Although this occurred prior to the formation of a new generation of child care advocacy groups, the director of the federal Women's Bureau encouraged the Family and Child Welfare Division of the Canadian Welfare Council to use its network of social planning councils in major cities across Canada to document the growing need for child care (Finkel 1995; Mahon 2000). In this way, activities at the municipal scale lent force to arguments made at the national scale, as the director of the Canadian Women's Bureau used her position within the bureaucracy quietly to lobby for a renewed federal commitment. Neither she nor the Royal Commission on the Status of Women, which reported in 1970, were able to secure independent child care legislation, however. As a consequence, the interscalar rule regime governing access to federal funds continued to treat child care as part of an anti-poverty program rather than a citizen right available to all who wanted and needed it.

Although CAP's welfare orientation cast its shadow over child care programs across the country, it did not entirely preclude local initiatives which sought to move in a different direction. Thus, even though Alberta's funding mechanism – the Preventive Social Services Act – reflected the federal government's welfare bias, it, like the Day Nursery Act, made provision for government funding: the Alberta government was prepared to absorb (with federal assistance) up to 80 percent of the costs, while leaving it to the municipalities to decide how much and what kind of child care would be provided. In Edmonton and several other large municipalities (Langford 1997), local advocates used these provisions to lay the foundations of a quality public child care system, one that looked to the continental scale (the Child Welfare League of America) to establish its (high) standards (Campbell 2001, 90).

In the late 1970s, however, the provincial government moved to simultaneously centralize control over child care and to promote the expansion of commercial child care (Hayden 1997). In response, local child care advocates developed the capacity to act more effectively at the provincial scale, forming the Alberta Association for Young Children (Campbell 2001, 91), even while they also mobilized support at the municipal scale. In some cities, they proved strong enough to retain control over existing centres (Campbell 2001; Langford 1997). More broadly, municipalities remained in charge of after-school care and were allowed to "pass through" the province to get federal funding under CAP (Jenson and Mahon 2002). This established an important exception to the rule that requests for federal CAP funds had to come from provinces.

The child care example has been given at length because it illustrates the way in which cities have been involved in policy areas historically governed by federal-provincial relations. In fact, the twentieth century in Canada saw many areas of social policy being rescaled from municipal to provincial and federal governments. The reform period of the 1880s to the 1920s resulted in provincial and federal reforms that took over many local policy areas, with the support of local politicians. This rescaling, which touched the fields of health, education, and social welfare, was in part driven by an increasing concern for geographical, and social, equality in access to services (Andrew 1995, 2003). It had the effect, however, of centralizing policy and program control at the provincial scale.

Today, however, there are new calls for federal urban policy, from international and national sources. A recent OECD study criticized Canada's fragmented approach to urban policy and the lack of national engagement (Bradford 2004, 40). The large cities themselves are beginning to argue for greater autonomy and a greater policy capacity. Roger Keil (2005, 14) talks of a "progressive urban wave" at the level of mayoral politics and, in the case of Toronto, "to a clearly urban (as opposed to the previously suburban) policy agenda." Thus, the City of Toronto (2002, 2) supports the idea of a city charter that would, among other elements, "give Toronto powers and responsibilities that match the City's needs" and "enable the City to communicate directly with the federal government on matters of mutual interest such as urban infrastructure, housing construction incentives, immigrant settlement and the development of a national agenda on urban issues." Toronto is clearly trying to contest the current interscalar role regime.

The last time in which urban affairs issues were visibly and explicitly on the federal policy agenda was when the Ministry of State for Urban Affairs (MSUA) was created in 1971 (Andrew 1994; Wolfe 2003). This period saw important developments in urban growth patterns, with rapid urbanization or, more accurately, rapid suburbanization and redevelopment pressures on the urban core. These changes gave rise to the urban reform movements of the 1960s, and parts of their local agendas reached the national scale, especially in the aftermath of the 1968 election, when the Trudeau Liberals swept all but one of the seats of the three largest urban areas. The MSUA was abolished in 1979, however, and urban *policy* as such eliminated from the federal government policy agenda.

The politics of scale re-emerged around the issue of infrastructure decay and the attendant need for substantial new investment. This issue was rescaled from the municipal to the federal level through the efforts of the Federation of Canadian Municipalities (FCM), the formal network linking Canadian municipal governments and giving them a voice at the national scale. Throughout the 1980s, the FCM worked hard to build the case for federal and provincial support for municipal infrastructure, arguing that Canada's cities had reached the breaking point (Andrew and Morrison 2002). Their efforts were successful: the newly elected Liberal Party put in place a new infrastructure program, which was followed by a succession of infrastructure programs through the 1990s. The political success of these programs led to the federal government establishment of Infrastructure Canada, dedicated to negotiating tri-level agreements for specific infrastructure projects. These programs can be seen as an example of jumping scale, in that municipal (and sometimes provincial) priorities dominated the federal expenditures in this field.

If infrastructure was being rescaled from municipal to federal, in the 1990s housing policy moved in the opposite direction. The federal government's budget cutting included passing responsibility for social housing to the provinces, most of whom, in turn, rescaled social housing policy to the municipalities. The resulting rise in the numbers of homeless in Canada, however, generated pressure on the federal government to re-enter the social housing field. To date, the federal government has created the Homelessness Secretariat and increased spending on transition housing while trying to resist the political pressure to fully move back into social housing. This involves much "jumping" of scale – federal to provincial to municipal but then back, via policies focused on the homeless, from local to provincial and federal.

The federal government also set up a Prime Minister's Caucus Task Force on Urban Issues, which argued for federal activity in three areas – housing, transportation, and infrastructure (Task Force 2002) – where Ottawa would face less active hostility from the provincial governments. With Paul Martin as prime minister, an Urban Secretariat was set up in the Privy Council Office, with Mike Harcourt, former mayor of Vancouver and former BC premier, acting as senior policy advisor. After the 2004 election, a new Ministry of Infrastructure and Communities was established.

The big-city mayors' focus on gaining federal money for major public transportation projects and other large infrastructure initiatives, at the expense of certain important areas, especially those relating to poverty reduction (Wolfe 2003, 16). Yet the latter are being brought to the surface in federal politics (through the Metropolis Project and the Policy Research Initiative) around questions of ethnocultural diversity, urban Aboriginal policy, and the links between neighbourhoods, poverty, and issues of social exclusion (for further details on the Metropolis Project, see the 2004 issue of *Our Diverse Cities*; Andrew, Graham, and Phillips 2002).

The politics of scale is not, however, about the federal policy agenda only: it is also about urban mobilization to resist what Keil (2002) has described as the regulation of everyday life by the neo-liberal state. In other words, it is not about state actors only but also those from civil society. An area that illustrates these "contradictory processes of social struggles and conflict" which attempt to resist "the controlled, marketized, consumerist capitalization of everydayness" (Keil 2002, 586) is women's urban safety (Whitzman 1992; Andrew, Graham, and Phillips 2002). This illustrates many aspects of scalar politics, from jumping scale to policy transfers both local and international.

Policy transfers have been local – Toronto to Montreal, Toronto to Ottawa, Montreal to Ottawa, and so on. They have also been international – from Montreal to European networks (Wekerle and Whitzman 1995) and from Europe back to Canadian cities – with models of programs, policies, and activities around time, cities, and women. These have often taken place through actors jumping scale; here, municipal government actors play roles in international forums and national networks. Thus, Toronto's women's safety initiatives influenced Montreal's, and Montreal's activity formed the basis for the FCM document *Une ville à la mesure des femmes* (Michaud 2004) and has also been a model for European approaches. Policy transfers have been local to local, on a global and a national level. These can be seen as part of the resistance to the form of everyday urban life in Canadian city-regions. Mobilization of civil society implies policy that is both in partnership with cities and in opposition to their policies.

Policy making for Canadian cities thus needs to be understood in a multiscalar perspective. The contemporary debate around urban policy and scale illustrates Agnew's (1997) definition, quoted earlier, that describes scale as the geographic level at which issues are thought of or acted upon. At present, both the level of thinking about urban issues and acting upon them are multiple and contested, harmonious and conflictual. What is needed is "a robust national framework for local problem-solving," a multi-scalar policy for Canada's cities (Bradford 2004, 44).

Conclusion

In this chapter, we have put forward an alternative approach to conventional policy analysis that argues for close attention to the *spatial* factors in any account of policy development and implementation. To capture these dynamics of public policy changes associated with contemporary developments, a practitioner adopting a multi-scalar perspective would start with the following guidelines/assumptions:

- Public policy, in the first instance, has a spatial reach, with boundaries that cannot be taken as pre-given. Instead, these are socially constructed and contested.
- This is reflected in the use of scalar discourses (in policy documents and in the language of political, state, and social actors), and in the political contestation and negotiation between actors over the (re-)allocation of policy responsibilities to another or new scale – a process we have termed as rescaling and involving a politics of scale.
- The outputs and outcomes of policy formation and implementation cannot be seen in isolation, but need to be considered in a relational fashion as part of the creation of interscalar policy regimes.

Thus, the political economy of scale brings a new perspective to public policy analysis, in showing how the formation and development of public policy is intimately tied to the way that social actors construct, contest, and negotiate larger societal arrangements at particular scales.

REFERENCES

Agnew, John. 1997. "The Dramaturgy of Horizons: Geographical Scale in the 'Reconstruction of Italy' by the New Italian Political Parties, 1992-1995." *Political Geography* 16: 99-121.

Amin, Ash. 2002. "Spatialities of Globalisation." *Environment and Planning A* 34(3): 385-99.

Andrew, Caroline. 1994. "Federal Urban Activity: Intergovernmental Relations in an Age of Restraint." In *The Changing Canadian Metropolis: A Public Policy Perspective*, ed. Frances Frisken, 427-55. Toronto: Canadian Urban Institute.

—. 1995. "Provincial-Municipal Relations: Or Hyper-fractionalized Quasi-subordination Revisited." In *Canadian Metropolitics*, ed. James Lightbody, 137-60. Toronto: Copp Clark.

—. 2003. "Municipal Restructuring, Urban Services and the Potential for the Creation of Transformative Political Spaces." In *Changing Canada: Political Economy as Transformation*, ed. Wallace Clement and Leah Vosko, 311-34. Montreal and Kingston: McGill-Queen's University Press.

Andrew, Caroline, Katherine Graham, and Susan Phillips, eds. 2002. *Urban Affairs: Back on the Policy Agenda*. Montreal and Kingston: McGill-Queen's University Press.

Andrew, Caroline, and Jeff Morrison. 2002. "Infrastructure." In *Urban Policy Issues: Canadian Perspectives*, ed. E.P. Fowler and David Siegel, 237-52. Don Mills: Oxford University Press.

Atkinson, Michael, and William Coleman. 1989. *The State, Business and Industrial Change in Canada*. Toronto: University of Toronto Press.

Banting, Keith. 1982. *The Welfare State and Canadian Federalism*. Montreal and Kingston: McGill-Queen's University Press.

Banting, Keith, George Hoberg, and Richard Simeon. 1997. *Degrees of Freedom: Canada and the US in a Changing World*. Montreal and Kingston: McGill-Queen's University Press.

Boychuk, Gerard. 1998. *Patchworks of Purpose: The Development of Provincial Social Assistance Regimes in Canada*. Montreal and Kingston: McGill-Queen's University Press.

Bradford, Neil. 1998. *Commissioning Ideas: Canadian National Policy Innovation in Comparative Perspective*. Toronto: Oxford University Press.

—. 2003. "Public-Private Partnership? Shifting Paradigms of Economic Governance in Ontario." *Canadian Journal of Political Science* 36: 1005-33.

—. 2004. "Place Matters and Multi-level Governance: Perspectives on a New Urban Policy Paradigm." *Policy Options* 25, 2: 39-44.

Brenner, Neil. 2004. *New State Spaces: Urban Governance and the Rescaling of Statehood*. New York: Oxford University Press.

Brodie, Janine. 1990. *The Political Economy of Canadian Regionalism*. Toronto: Harcourt Brace Jovanovich.

Cairns, Alan. 1986. "The Embedded State: State-Society Relations in Canada." In *State and Society: Canada in Comparative Perspective*, ed. Keith Banting, 53-86. Toronto: University of Toronto Press.

Campbell, Sheila. 2001. "Acting Locally: Community Activism in Edmonton, 1940-1970." In *Changing Child Care: Five Decades of Child Care Advocacy and Policy in Canada*, ed. Susan Prentice, 81-95. Halifax: Fernwood.

Castells, Manuel. 1996. *The Rise of the Network Society*. Vol. 1 of *The Information Age: Economy, Society and Culture*. Oxford: Blackwell.

City of Toronto. 2002. *Establishing a New Relationship with the Federal and Provincial Governments: Progress Report on Toronto's Initiatives*. Policy and Finance Committee Report No. 12, City of Toronto.

Clarkson, Stephen. 2002. *Uncle Sam and Us: Globalization, Neo-conservatism and the Canadian State*. Toronto: University of Toronto Press.

Clement, Wallace. 1977. *Continental Corporate Power: Economic Elite Linkages between Canada and the United States.* Toronto: McClelland and Stewart.

Collinge, Chris. 1999. "Self-Organisation of Society by Scale: A Spatial Reworking of Regulation Theory." *Environment and Planning D: Society and Space* 17: 557-74.

Conway, Janet. 2004. *Identity, Place, Knowledge: Social Movements Contesting Globalization.* Halifax: Fernwood.

Courchene, Thomas. 2001. "Ontario as a North American Region-State: Toronto as Global City-Region: Responses to the NAFTA Challenge." In *Global City-Regions,* ed. Allen J. Scott, 158-92. Toronto: Oxford University Press.

Crouch, Colin. 2001. "Welfare State Regimes and Industrial Relations Systems: The Questionable Role of Path Dependency Theory." In *Comparing Welfare Capitalisms: Social Policy and Political Economy in Europe, Japan and the US,* ed. Bernard Ebbinghaus and Philip Manow, 105-24. London: Routledge.

Dagenais, Michèle. 1992. "Une bureaucratie en voie de formation: L'administration municipale de Montréal dans la première moitié du XX siècle." *Revue d'histoire de l'Amérique française* 46: 177-205.

Doern, Bruce, Brian Tomlin, and Leslie A. Pal. 1996. *Border Crossings: The Internationalization of Canadian Public Policy.* Toronto: Oxford University Press.

Dolowitz, David P., and David Marsh. 2000. "Learning from Abroad: The Role of Policy Transfer in Contemporary Policy-Making." *Governance* 13: 5-24.

Dupré, Stephan, David Cameron, Graeme McKechnie, and Theodore Rotenberg. 1973. *Federalism and Policy Development.* Toronto: University of Toronto Press.

Ferrera, Maurizio, Anton Hemerijck, and Martin Rhodes. 2000. "The Future of Social Europe: Recasting Work and Welfare in the New Economy." Report for the Portuguese Presidency of the European Union.

Finkel, Alvin. 1995. "Even the Little Children Cooperated: Family Strategies, Childcare Discourses and Social Welfare Debates, 1945-1975." *Labour/le travail* 36: 91-118.

Florida, Richard. 2002. *The Rise of the Creative Class and How It Has Transformed Work, Leisure, Culture and Everyday Life.* New York: Basic Books.

Hall, Peter, and David Soskice, eds. 2001. *Varieties of Capitalism: The Institutional Foundations of Comparative Advantage.* New York: Oxford University Press.

Harvey, David. 2001. *Spaces of Capital: Towards a Critical Geography.* New York: Routledge.

Hayden, Jacqueline. 1997. *Neo-conservatism and Childcare Services in Alberta: A Case Study.* Occasional Paper No. 9. Centre for Urban and Community Studies. Toronto: University of Toronto Press.

Heclo, Hugh. 1974. *Modern Social Policy in Britain and Sweden.* New Haven: Yale University Press.

Herod, Andrew, and Melissa Wright. 2002. "Placing Scale: An Introduction." In *Geographies of Power: Placing Scale,* ed. Andrew Herod and Melissa Wright, 1-14. Oxford: Blackwell.

Hoberg, George, ed. 2001. *Capacity for Choice: Canada in the New North America.* Toronto: University of Toronto Press.

Hodgetts, J.E. 1971. "Regional Interests and Policy in a Federal Structure." In *Canadian Federalism: Myth or Reality?* 2nd ed., ed. Peter J. Meekison, 339-49. Toronto: Methuen.

Hooghe, Liesbeth, and Gary Marks. 2001. *Multi-level Governance and European Integration.* Boulder: Rowman and Littlefield.

Innis, Harold. 1956. *The Fur Trade in Canada.* Toronto: University of Toronto Press.

Jenson, Jane, and Rianne Mahon. 2002. *Bringing Cities to the Table: Child Care and Intergovernmental Affairs.* CPRN Discussion Paper F/26. Ottawa: Canadian Policy Research Networks.

Jessop, Bob. 1999. "Narrating the Future of the National Economy and the National State." In *State/Culture: State-Formation after the Cultural Turn,* ed. George Steinmetz, 378-405. Ithaca: Cornell University Press.

Keil, Roger. 2002. "'Common-Sense' Neoliberalism: Progressive Conservative Urbanism in Toronto, Canada." *Antipode* 34: 578-601.

—. 2005. "New State Spaces in Canada: Metropolitanization in Montreal and Toronto." Paper presented at the annual meeting of the Canadian Political Science Association, London, Ontario.

Kenis, Patrick, and Volker Schneider. 1991. "Policy Networks and Policy Analysis: Scrutinizing a New Analytical Toolbox." In *Policy Networks: Empirical Evidence and Theoretical Considerations,* ed. Bernd Marin and Renate Mayntz, 25-59. Boulder: Westview Press.

Langford, Tom. 1997. "Municipal-Provincial Conflict over Child Care in Alberta 1966-1996." Paper presented at the annual meeting of the Canadian Political Science Association, St. John's, Newfoundland.

Laxer, Jim. 1970. *The Energy Poker Game: The Politics of Continental Resource Deals.* Toronto: New Press.

—. 1981. *Canada's Economic Strategy.* Toronto: McClelland and Stewart.

Magnusson, Warren. 2005. "Urbanism, Cities and Local Self-Government." *Canadian Public Administration* 48: 96-123.

Mahon, Rianne. 2000. "The Never-Ending Story: The Struggle for Universal Child Care Policy in the 1970s." *Canadian Historical Review* 81: 582-674.

Mallory, James R. 1954. *Social Credit and the Federal Power in Canada.* Toronto: University of Toronto Press.

Marks, Gary, and Liesbeth Hooghe. 1996. "European Integration from the 1980s: State-Centric or Multi-level Governance?" *Journal of Common Market Studies* 34: 343-78.

Massey, Doreen, and John Allen, eds. 1984. *Geography Matters! A Reader.* New York: Cambridge University Press.

McIntosh, Thomas, ed. 2000. *Federalism, Democracy and Labour Market Policy in Canada.* Montreal and Kingston: McGill-Queen's University Press.

Michaud, Anne. 2004. *Une ville à la mesure des femmes.* Ottawa: Fédération canadienne des municipalités; Montreal: Femmes et Ville.

Noël, Alain. 2004. "Introduction: Varieties of Capitalism, Varieties of Federalism." In *Federalism and Labour Market Policy,* ed. Alain Noël, 1-23. Montreal and Kingston: McGill-Queen's University Press.

Paasi, Anssi. 2004. "Place and Region: Looking through the Prism of Scale." *Progress in Human Geography* 28: 536-46.

Pal, Leslie A. 1988. *State, Class and Bureaucracy: Canadian Unemployment Insurance and Public Policy.* Montreal and Kingston: McGill-Queen's University Press.

—. 2001. *Beyond Public Policy Analysis.* 2nd ed. Scarborough: Nelson.

Peck, Jamie. 1998. "From Federal Welfare to Local Workfare? Remaking Canada's Work-Welfare Regime." In *An Unruly World? Globalization, Governance and Geography,* ed. Andrew Herod, Gearóid Ó Tuathail, and Susan Roberts, 95-115. London and New York: Routledge.

—. 2002. "Political Economies of Scale: Fast Policy, Interscalar Relations and Neoliberal Workfare." *Economic Geography* 78: 331-60.

Prentice, Susan. 1993. "Militant Mothers in Domestic Times: Toronto's Postwar Childcare Struggle." PhD diss., Sociology, York University.

Rousseau, Jean. 2000. "The New Political Scales of Citizenship in a Global Era: The Politics of Hydro-Electric Development in the James Bay Region." PhD diss., Political Science, Carleton University.

Saint-Martin, Denis. 2000. *Building the New Managerialist State: Consultants and the Politics of Public Sector Reform in Comparative Perspective.* Toronto: Oxford University Press.

—. 2004. *Coordinating Interdependence: Governance and Social Policy Redesign in Britain, the European Union and Canada.* CPRN Social Architecture Papers Research Report F/41. Ottawa: Canadian Policy Research Networks.

Schultz, Richard. 1977. "Interest Groups and Intergovernmental Negotiations: Caught in the Vise of Federalism." In *Canadian Federalism: Myth or Reality?* 3rd ed., ed. Peter J. Meekison, 59-75. Toronto: Methuen.

Sewell, William H., Jr. 2001. "Space in Contentious Politics." In *Silence and Voice in the Study of Contentious Politics,* ed. Ronald R. Aminzade, Jack Goldstone, Doug McAdam, Elizabeth Perry, William H. Sewell Jr., Sidney Tarrow, Douglas McAdam, and Charles Tilly, 51-88. New York: Cambridge University Press.

Simeon, Richard. 1972. *Federal-Provincial Diplomacy: The Making of Recent Policy in Canada.* Toronto: University of Toronto Press.

Skogstad, Grace. 2000. "Globalization and Public Policy: Situating Canadian Analyses." *Canadian Journal of Political Science* 33: 805-28.

Smith, Neil. 1992. "Homeless/Global: Scaling Places." In *Mapping the Future: Local Cultures, Global Change,* ed. Jon Bird, Barry Curtis, Tim Putnam, George Robertson, and Lisa Tickner, 87-119. London: Routledge.

Soja, Edward. 1989. *Postmodern Geographies: The Reassertion of Space in Critical Social Theory.* London: Verso.

Streeck, Wolfgang, and Kathleen Thelen. 2005. "Introduction: Institutional Change in Advanced Political Economies." In *Beyond Continuity: Institutional Change in Advanced Political Economies,* ed. Wolfgang Streeck and Kathleen Thelen, 1-39. Oxford: Oxford University Press.

Task Force (Prime Minister's Caucus Task Force on Urban Issues). 2002. *Canada's Urban Strategy: A Blueprint for Action.* Final Report.

Thorburn, Hugh. 1984. *Planning and the Economy: Building Federal-Provincial Consensus.* Ottawa: Canadian Institute for Economic Policy.

Tilly, Charles. 1990. *Coercion, Capital and European States.* Cambridge: Blackwell.

Wekerle, Gerda, and Carolyn Whitzman. 1995. *Safe Cities: Guidelines for Planning, Design, and Management.* New York: Van Nostrand Reinhold.

Whitzman, Carolyn. 1992. "Taking Back Planning: Promoting Women's Safety in Public Places – The Toronto Experience." *Journal of Architectural and Planning Research* 9: 169-79.

Wolfe, Jeanne. 2003. "A National Urban Policy for Canada: Prospects and Challenges." *Canadian Journal of Urban Research* 12: 1-21.

Zeitlin, Jonathan. 2003. "Introduction: Governing Work and Welfare in a New Economy: European and American Experiments." In *Governing Work and Welfare in a New Economy: European and American Experiments,* ed. Jonathan Zeitlin and David M. Trubeck, 1-30. New York: Oxford University Press.

Zeitlin, Jonathan, and David M. Trubeck, eds. 2003. *Governing Work and Welfare in a New Economy: European and American Experiments.* New York: Oxford University Press.

PART TWO

Citizens and Diversity

. . . . . .

4
Citizen Engagement: Rewiring the Policy Process

Rachel Laforest and Susan Phillips

The role of the Canadian public in policy making has undergone a profound transformation over the past three decades. The channels for public input into policy have evolved and expanded from the historical reliance on political parties as the primary mechanisms for interest mobilization, articulation, and aggregation and on elite accommodation in which strong, organized interests and powerful insiders dominated access to the policy process. "Citizen engagement" based on the principles of deliberative dialogue is seen to be a sound alternative for clarifying values, discussing issues, and assessing policy options. With citizen engagement, the aim is to extend participation in decision making beyond the traditional actors, interest groups, social movements, and voluntary associations in order to involve the "ordinary citizen" – the citizen acting as a representative of himself or herself, not of an organized group. Such engagement is argued to produce not only better policy, but more active, "better" citizens. Rather than assuming that elected officials will serve as trustees for their constituents from one election to the next, citizens are expected to have access to the policy process at various points and on a regular basis. Although there is, of course, still a role for legislators in interacting with and speaking on behalf of their constituents, many of the new forms of citizen engagement are being led by the public service, independent commissions, think tanks, or citizens themselves.

The goal of citizen engagement is to supplement, not replace, representative democracy. By facilitating the direct and active involvement of the citizenry outside of the mechanisms of representative democracy, however, governments are contorting old assumptions and are, in effect, redesigning the institutional links between the citizens and the state, thus remaking the policy process in some fundamental ways. This chapter takes a critical look at the state of the art of the involvement of citizens in policy making in Canada. First, it briefly outlines representative and deliberative democracy as "ideal" or stylized models that anchor two ends of a continuum for describing the ways in which citizens have input into the policy process and for structuring broader relationships between the state and civil society (see Figure 4.1). Along this continuum have come a broad range of experiments in citizen involvement over the past thirty years, of which a few highlights are worth noting.

In spite of considerable effort by governments and a desire and expectation on the part of citizens to have a greater voice in policy development, recent polls show that citizens remain "underwhelmed" with the current means by which they are consulted and engaged in policy (Ekos Research 2004). Why do the results fall so short of the theory, rhetoric, and amount of activity around citizen engagement? The second part of the chapter explores some of the inherent shortcomings and incompatibilities of wedding a model of deliberative citizen engagement onto existing practices of representative democracy. The current interest in democratic renewal at the federal level and in several provinces is primarily a means of bolstering representative democracy, but doing so in ways that open more spaces for direct involvement of citizens. The most dramatic change in the role of citizens in policy making is not likely to come through current efforts at democratic renewal, however.

The real shift that is occurring is not from representative to deliberative models of democracy, but from representative to results-based models. This entails a fundamental change in *when* citizens have input into policy: from input into the development and design of public policy at the front end to watching over outcomes and holding governments to account on the basis of reported performance at the back end. The idea of citizens diligently poring over reports on wait times for hip replacements and knee surgeries or over the performance of high-school students on standardized tests so that, on the basis of hard evidence, they can hold governments to account and pressure them to change their policies or budget allocations may seem to give them new tools for involvement. Although attractive in theory, we suggest that the emerging performance-based model of engagement is not an expansion, but in fact a potential contraction of the influence of citizens in political representation and policy development.

From Representative to Deliberative Democracy:
A Continuum of Engagement

Political representation is at the heart of our democratic system. It ensures that a diversity of views and interests are heard and fed into the policy process.

Central to this process are the functions of interest aggregation and articulation. These concepts were initially developed as the core elements of rather mechanistic input-output models of democracy, which have since been largely dismissed as being too simplistic. Although we do not base our analysis on either the Schumpeterian or the pluralistic assumptions that drove these input and output models, the fundamental concepts are nevertheless useful as a framework for analyzing the evolution of citizen engagement.[1] How are interests (and identities) articulated and claims made, and by whom? Who has responsibility for aggregating these interests into coherent policy positions, recommendations, and decisions, and how does this happen? The answers to these basic questions have produced quite different approaches to involving citizens and their organizations in policy making that can be described in a general way as a contrast between the traditional model of representative democracy and the more recent approach of deliberative democracy. As we will see, the reality of the Canadian experience with citizen involvement lies somewhere between these two idealized types, and the emerging direction of a performance-based model could be seen as tangential to both.

THE TRADITION: REPRESENTATIVE DEMOCRACY

Under a traditional system of representative democracy, the process of representing the views of citizens is facilitated directly through voting and indirectly by political parties and interest groups. In the electoral process, candidates and their parties offer platforms and broker ideas so as to appeal to the largest number of voters, and it is at this point that citizens express their preferences. Assuming this competitive process for votes is open and fair, the electoral outcome supposedly reflects the aggregation of the most widely held preferences, and hence this model is often called an "aggregative" model of democracy (Young 2000, 19; see also Cohen 1997, 411, and Mansbridge 1980, 17). In Canada, the traditional post-election practice has been to regard the elected official as a "trustee" for voters, acting according to what he or she judges to be in the best interests of constituents until being held accountable at the next election (Aucoin and Turnbull 2003).

Voting is not the only route to representation, however. Political parties and interest groups also play an important role in the policy process because they both articulate and aggregate interests and they hold elected officials accountable. They bring together people who share some common interests; they simplify policy issues, generate symbols of identification, and mobilize

citizens around these issues. In so doing, they play a vital role in fostering citizen involvement by drawing attention to policy issues, by encouraging the involvement of citizens in political affairs, by providing venues for debating and compromising on policy positions, and by serving as conduits between citizens and government. This connection not only expresses the views of citizens to the state, but transmits and disseminates policy information from the state to the citizenry. Political parties are fundamental to interest aggregation in a classic representative model, but the role of interest groups is contested. In populist versions of democracy, such as that advocated by the Reform/Alliance predecessor of the current Conservative Party, interest groups and other voluntary organizations are seen to interfere with or bypass the most important relationship – that between citizen and legislator – and to overload governments with conflicting demands. In this view, the citizen-legislator relationship does not need to be mediated by third parties, but reinforced through the use of townhalls, referenda, recall, and other means through which citizens can express their views directly to elected officials and can hold them to account if they are not appropriate delegates and voices on behalf of their constituents.

Criticisms of the effectiveness of political representation under this model of representative democracy have been a staple of political science for many years and do not need to be repeated at length here. In brief, the criticisms highlight a number of serious inadequacies including the following: the method of aggregation of preferences through first-past-the-post voting systems diminishes representation of minorities; political parties tend to be thin mechanisms, often functional as vehicles for active participation only every four years or so during election campaigns, and even then do not facilitate effective dialogue on issues (Dobrowolsky and Jenson 1994; Lortie Commission 1992); brokerage parties aggregate interests in such an opportunistic manner that it is difficult to determine what the party really stands for; many citizens do not have easy access to their elected officials, and even if they do, the practice of party discipline in a parliamentary system means that legislators vote according to party lines rather than according to constituent preferences. In addition, the public policy process is simply too complex and dynamic for periodic participation at election times or contact with elected officials alone to enable the diversity of citizens to effectively make their claims known or to contribute their experience and knowledge in useful ways. Given the deficiencies in traditional means of political representation, citizens have for some time appealed for greater access to the political sphere, and evolving theories of democracy have issued some serious conceptual challenges to representative democracy.[2] Since the early 1970s, governments at all levels have experimented, with varying degrees of effort and success, with an array of new ways to involve citizens in the policy process.[3] Citizen engagement has not replaced representative democracy in Canada, but has attempted to create new spaces for participation and representation within it.

The Newcomer: Deliberative Democracy

The model of deliberative democracy that emerged in the 1990s starts from the premise that political *representation* is not enough: active *participation* by citizens is as important as having their interests represented by third parties. In this way, deliberative democracy could be seen as a variant – imbued with very prescriptive requirements for process – of the notions of participatory democracy that have been around since the 1970s. By focusing on citizens who participate as individuals rather than as group representatives and by embracing the value of genuine two-way dialogue, rather than merely a one-way transmission of information from citizens to governments, notions of deliberative democracy prompted a self-conscious and purposeful attempt in the late 1990s to recast and rename public participation or public consultation as *citizen engagement* (Phillips with Orsini 2002, 3).

Conceptual approaches to deliberative democracy lay out several essential requirements for process (see Bohman 1996; Cohen 1997; Gutman and Thompson 1996; Macedo 1999). First, it must involve *reciprocity*, that is, free and open deliberation and dialogue, not merely the declaration of preferences or claims. In this sense, it must be dialogical, not merely discursive (Bohman 1996). A second requirement is that there be public *reasoning* in which citizens and officials justify their claims to one another and are accountable to each other; people must be treated as equals in the process. The underlying assumption is that people have a responsibility to come to the process willing to be moved by reason. Third, the process rests on *publicity* by which the reasons that citizens and officials give to justify their actions be made public and the process itself transparent (Gutman and Thompson 1996, 95). A final aspect of a deliberative process is that all citizens have an equal opportunity to participate and that those affected by the resulting decisions are included in the discussion – a criteria that is compelling in theory, but hard to pull off in practice (Young 2000, 23). Although deliberative theorists have been consumed with process and, in particular, with outlining the nature of public reasoning, deliberation is by no means intended to be divorced

from decision making. Indeed, as Joshua Cohen (1997, 99) argues, deliberative democracy is tied to the principle of accountability: "Not simply a form
of politics, democracy, in the deliberative view, is a framework of social and
institutional conditions that facilitates free discussion among equal citizens
– by providing favorable conditions for participation, association, and expression – and ties the authorization to exercise public power (and the exercise itself) to such discussion."

In practice, the interest in deliberation has given rise to a variety of experimentation with and commercialization of small-group methods for engaging citizens in dialogue that include citizen assemblies, the "citizen jury,"[4]
and deliberative polling (Fishkin 1991). All of these techniques bring small
groups of randomly selected citizens together to address a policy problem,
give them background information and access to experts who may be called
upon as needed, and provide space and time to discuss and debate various
solutions. At the end of the process, it is normally expected that a consensus
position be reached. The analogy to jury duty is not accidental as the intent
is that citizens come to realize that, as citizens, they have a civic responsibility to serve from time to time as called upon to do so. One implication of
being embedded in a theoretical framework that emphasizes process is that
deliberative democracy serves as a buttress against arguments for more extensive use of the methods of direct democracy (such as referenda, plebiscites,
and recall). Deliberative democrats have never been fans of referenda because they do not solve the aggregation problem since most use simple majorities to determine outcomes, and because they are not necessarily
accompanied by a process of genuine dialogue (Gutman and Thompson
1996; Schauer 1999). In fact, for most deliberative theorists, referenda offer

FIGURE 4.1

A continuum of citizen involvement

Representative		**Deliberative**	
Articulation:	Political parties, interest groups, legislators	Articulation:	Citizens
Aggregation:	Parties, interest groups, legislators	Aggregation:	Public service, legislators, consultants
Accountability:	Opposition parties, interest groups	Accountability:	Citizens, public service, legislators

little added value over voting, and when the issues at hand are complex or have polarized positions and parties, they may actually afford less real debate than the traditional representative model.[5]

Opening Up Political Representation

Citizen involvement in policy making has evolved in both concept and practice in Canada from an elitist basis where representation was mainly by invitation to more open and inclusive processes. This evolution should not be read as a clear and steady movement toward a deliberative model, however.

Many of the early Canadian efforts at involving citizens came through royal commissions mandated to examine critical policy issues, receive feedback, and draw policy recommendations. The testing of ideas meant that the politically nominated commissioners usually led public hearings or consultations, and they were ultimately accountable for the recommendations because the final report bore their names. Because such inquiries were designed to provide in-depth examination of particular issues or problems, experts and researchers were normally the targeted participants, both as witnesses and as part of the extensive research that was often commissioned.[6] The findings of a commission or inquiry would be tabled with Parliament, Cabinet, or the prime minister for appropriate action. Because of the nature of the appointments to the commission and their links to the political system, the head of the commission often championed the recommendations within the state.

The Berger Inquiry into the Mackenzie Valley pipeline in the mid-1970s set a new standard – that in many respects is still seen to be the gold standard – for enabling citizens, particularly those potentially affected by development, to have their say alongside industry experts and representatives of organized groups in a manner that had a direct and transparent impact on policy outcomes (see Patten 2000; Torgerson 1996).[7] Over the course of seventeen months, the inquiry conducted formal hearings in which representation was made by legal counsel, and it held less formal sessions on the socio-economic impact of the proposed pipeline, going to nearly all the communities in the North that would have been affected by the development.[8] The Berger Inquiry is noted for more than its numbers and breadth of participation, although both were key achievements. What also stands out is the fact that the process was made accessible to citizens who had little political experience: "at the community hearings northerners were encouraged to tell the judge what they wished, in their own time, language and fashion, in their own communities among familiar faces, and without the formality of counsel and cross-examination" (Beakhust 1978, 315).[9] Second, funding was provided so that environmental and other citizen groups could conduct research, travel to make interventions, and produce regular summaries that would keep their memberships informed.[10] Third, the impact was not just process, but process that influenced policy in a transparent manner. The policy makers – in this case, Justice Berger and his staff – were present throughout the hearings so that they heard the information first-hand, listened carefully to it, and explained the rationale for the decision using the various inputs to the commission's report. Finally, the process enhanced the legitimacy of the policy decision. As Beakhust (1978, 320) argues, the lesson of the Berger Inquiry was "not so much that it persuaded people to participate, but that the process of doing so helped to make a wide public take its conclusions seriously."

During the 1980s, public involvement became a component of most major policy decisions and was quite routinely undertaken by legislative committees and the public service rather than being reserved to special events such as royal commissions. Governments sought assurances that a broad representation of the Canadian public had been consulted, as both a means of obtaining input into policy and of legitimizing policy decisions: how many participated became a prime indicator of success, and national consultations routinely travelled across the country as well as provided toll-free numbers for telephone access. Focus on the breadth of participation (the numbers) rather than on the depth (the quality of input) was reinforced by neo-liberalism and by populism. As neo-liberalism took hold in the late 1980s, a deep mistrust of civil society organizations set in at the political level, a tendency that was reinforced by the brand of populism asserted by the then Reform Party. The result was to question whom groups represented and dismiss them as merely getting in the way of the relationship between citizen and elected official (Jenson and Phillips 1996). The first major experiment with an individual-only consultation, and still one of the most expensive consultations in Canadian history, was the 1990 Citizen's Forum on Canada's Future. Its chief commissioner, Keith Spicer, declared that he wanted to hear from one million Canadians in three months; only individuals, not representatives of organized interests, were allowed to participate.[11] Given the situation – a highly political environment and a process in which citizens were asked extremely vague, complex questions – it is not surprising that the forum resulted in an outpouring of raw, unfocused emotion that had no direct impact on shaping public policy.

The involvement of individuals was taken further by the Social Security Review of 1994, which followed a two-pronged process: a parliamentary committee that, in the face of opposition to welfare state restructuring from a wide range of social policy groups, decided to restrict the range of views heard or counted as meaningful;[12] and a parallel departmental process that provided a counterweight by using a variety of consultative tools, such as townhalls, focus groups, public opinion surveys, and policy workbooks, to obtain input from individuals.[13] Given the impression that representation was actively constrained and that the input from individuals was never really used in decision making, the review was a low point in relationships between the department and social policy groups, relationships that remained highly fractured for a long time (Institute on Governance 1996, 7).

The trend of the 1990s toward a preference for the involvement of individuals signalled a shift in the purpose of public input: to add experiential knowledge, often through the sharing of personal stories, rather than to provide technical expertise. Although in some cases, such experience added significantly to the knowledge base supporting policy development, in other instances it was seen as adding little that was new or as a means of shutting out organized groups.[14] Research-based knowledge was, of course, still desirable as part of policy development, but the ante was upped for voluntary associations. If they wanted to be part of policy development, they would have to produce research that could stand alongside that of academics, think tanks, and in-house government researchers. In contrast, their experiential knowledge that came from service provision or from close contact with the users of these services was devalued or excluded since the users were being asked to speak for themselves. Although the downloading that came with neo-liberalism meant that voluntary organizations were delivering a greater range of services on behalf of governments, and thus often had much more direct knowledge than governments as to how effectively those programs were actually working, they were often not heard from in this capacity.

The emphasis on individuals also meant that citizen engagement was better equipped to produce interest articulation than interest aggregation. The state provided the venues for claims making by individuals, and often the mobilization of interests in the first place by determining who was invited to participate. In the absence of a serious role for intermediary organizations, the identification of common positions and aggregation of interests of the hundreds or thousands of citizens who participated in these consultations fell to the public servants, or more likely to the third-party consultants who prepared the consultation reports.

As consultations multiplied, the real goals were sometimes questionable, often seen by the public to be aimed at legitimating policy or raising awareness about it, rather than actually being intended to help design policy. For instance, the massive consultation on the Green Plan in 1990 began with high expectations from environmental groups and citizens for the development of innovative approaches to environmental sustainability, but ended as a failed exercise in legitimation. In spite of the many policy ideas that emerged from the meetings in some forty centres across the country, ministers were preparing to announce a more limited Green Plan and were not prepared to share drafts of it with participants so that alternatives could be discussed (Patten 2000, 232-33). As Steve Patten (2000, 233) suggests, the lesson of the Green Plan consultation is that "processes not meaningfully linked to the *real* policy process will amount to little more than an exchange of information. Non-state actors gain a platform for policy advocacy, but no real opportunity for policy participation."

The introduction in the mid-1990s of ideas that sprang from theories of *deliberative* democracy, stressing the need for genuine dialogue and transparency, were thus well timed given a considerable public mistrust of the motivations and effectiveness of existing consultation practices. Borrowing from the lead of the United States, the UK, and Europe, all levels of government in Canada tried a variety of experiments with citizen juries,[15] assemblies, and other mechanisms for deliberation. These included, for example, deliberative mechanisms for constitutional reform,[16] developing municipal and provincial budgets,[17] electoral reform,[18] and nuclear waste management.[19] Interest in deliberation also promoted more bottom-up exercises in which citizens come together for dialogue not at the behest of government, but on their own accord or as animated by an independent organization or think tank. The discussions called "The Society We Want" and the "Citizens' Dialogue on the Future of Health Care in Canada," both organized by the Canadian Policy Research Networks (CPRN),[20] are perhaps the best-known examples of these (Abelson and Gauvin 2004; MacKinnon 2004).

As the involvement of citizens became routinized in policy development, the sheer volume of activity had several effects. First, it produced a large and sophisticated communications and consultation industry available for hire as specialists in process. Second, the public service eclipsed legislators and legislative committees as the primary locus of organized consultation.[21] Third, the need for information and coordination by federal departments of the multitude of consultations occurring at the same time became evident, and technology afforded the opportunity not only to share information about events but to facilitate input and discussions online. In February 2003, the federal government launched a pilot project of an online consultation portal (http://www.consultingcanadians.gc.ca); currently, seventeen participating departments list their public consultations, complete with background documents and, in many cases, the opportunity to provide input online. Accompanying the communication of their activities by federal departments was a need for some consistency or standards of practice so that citizens knew what to realistically expect and demand. The Privy Council Office had drafted a set of principles in the early 1990s to guide public consultation within the Government of Canada, but it was never officially adopted as government-wide policy (although several departments developed their own guidelines).[22] Many of these principles were incorporated into the Code of Good Practice on Policy Dialogue that was developed under the accord signed between the government and the voluntary sector in December 2001.[23] If actually implemented and incorporated into departmental practices, the code could go a long way toward reasserting the role of organizations in policy development by requiring government to respect and seek out their input in the analysis and design of policy initiatives, and by committing groups to enhance their policy capacity and ability to represent the view of their constituencies. Whether the code is widely adopted and used by both federal government departments and voluntary organizations is still an open question, as is its impact on the practice of engagement with citizens rather than organizations.

It cannot be said that experiments with citizen engagement have fully transformed our democratic model from a representative to a truly deliberative one, but significant changes in the relationship between state, citizen, and civil society have certainly occurred. And these changes raise a number of key challenges for democratic practice and for policy making.

The Challenges: When Deliberation Meets Representation in the Policy Process

The creation of more opportunities for citizens to participate in policy should, at least in theory, result in more informed policy and a more knowledgeable, efficacious, and activist citizenry. Although the opportunities for citizen involvement in policy making have clearly expanded over the past decade, it is

questionable whether this has actually increased citizen influence on the policy
process or its outcomes. In many respects, the practices of citizen engagement may be attenuating linkages to the decision-making process, both because such engagement often occurs outside the realm of traditional political
institutions and because there are new intermediaries. The new intermediaries are not voluntary organizations which directly represent their members,
constituents, or users, but are consultation specialists and contractors hired
to perform a service. Responsibility for leading consultations is increasingly
being contracted out to professional for-profit facilitators or consultants who
have no direct responsibility to the public. Sometimes voluntary organizations are paid to take on this role. Whether these third parties are engaged to
conduct meetings and focus groups with citizens at large, as in the case of the
professional, or with relevant constituents, in the case of the voluntary organization,[24] it is these contracted agents who now play a lead role in providing
policy recommendations based on the consultations. In this scenario, voluntary organizations do have a renewed role, but a different one: they are not
acting as political, accountable representatives of their own memberships
and constituencies, but as contractors to government. This may put them in
an awkward position: their members may see them as agents of government;
government will view them as contractors responsible for ensuring that other
voices are heard without contributing their own.

What really stands out is the lack of participation and "engagement" on
the part of the policy makers, who are once removed from the contracted
consultation process. Without any formal ties to the policy process, they cannot be expected to support and champion the recommendations that have
emerged out of citizen public engagement. Moreover, if decision makers decide to disregard the recommendations, it may not carry a high political price.
As a result, consultations increasingly fail to provide an organizational home
for the discussion of issues, the development of agendas, and the formulation of policies. Deliberative theory reminds us that in order to be effective,
policy makers also need to be involved in the process of deliberation, and
seek to understand the views of the citizens. For the deliberative model to
actually develop ongoing relationships between citizens and policy makers,
participation must link back to decision making (Fischer 2003; Fischer and
Forester 1993; Healey 1997).

The second problem with the current popularity of deliberative initiatives is the old aggregation issue. In order to facilitate active participation
and deliberation, such forums by nature involve small numbers of people

who are representing themselves. Thus, the challenge is to truly make the process inclusive (often by repeating it a number of times, as the Romanow Commission did) and to test the extent to which these citizens are reflecting views of broader communities. A consequence, whether intended or not, of such initiatives that call upon different sets of independently selected individuals who collectively represent a broad cross-section of society is that they may undermine existing forms of representation – notably civil society organizations – through which citizens have already affiliated because they have a collective identity and an ongoing interest in the issues. When organizations and their networks are not involved, the responsibility of aggregation rests with the contractors or the public service, and in fact seldom occurs. The aggregation of interests is thus weak, and can arrive at highly generalized positions only.

 A third challenge lies in showing participants and the population at large how the information gathered through the engagement process was used in policy. In effect, many of the consultations require the paid consultants to aggregate a high volume of public input in the form of written, verbal, and electronic communications. Although aggregation involves weighting and combining these various information streams, the process required to manage, analyze, and use the information gathered is often unclear or time-pressured. Consequently, consultation reports often provide only selective but pithy quotes from citizens, rather than a solid analysis of the strength and extent of support for these opinions. Thus, they represent neither good social science nor good politics. Moreover, because no means exist to assure how input is being weighted and measured, questions remain as to the real impact that public input is having on policy. Participants in many deliberative or other consultative exercises seem to have no idea whether their involvement made any difference at all – nor could they, in the absence of feedback. Although the process of deliberation may produce reasoned positions and help people develop the citizenship skills of debating and compromising, process alone is not enough. Unless the product of their deliberation is seen to be connected to policy making, citizens are unlikely to feel more efficacious or empowered, or to be more trusting of governments over the longer term.

Due to these difficulties, Canadian experience may have produced plenty of deliberation, but has fallen short of a truly deliberative model of democracy. Moreover, as we move away from the representative model of democracy, citizens are losing some important routes for political representation – those provided by intermediary voluntary organizations. Increasingly, the onus is on citizens themselves to articulate their own preferences. The function of organizations that traditionally played this role under the representative model is being recast in the policy process. Their purpose is no longer to bring together citizens with similar ideas and interests, nor is it to convey the experiential knowledge acquired as service providers. Rather, they are increasingly asked to furnish outcome-based evidence and "scientific" research in order to substantiate their position when engaging in policy debates. Therefore, they no longer serve as a conduit to transmit and translate preferences into the policy process, but are an additional source of data generation, a *partner* of the state in the search for evidence, which by the same token is no longer grounded in experiential knowledge. The double whammy is that not only has the value of their role as representatives of members and constituents been diminished, but most Canadian voluntary associations lack the policy capacity to take on this new role of evidence-based research in any serious way. Indeed, more than half of the medium-to-large voluntary organizations in Canada reported in a recent national survey that they have difficulty participating in the development of public policy, which could be read as being due both to issues of internal capacity and limited political opportunities.[25] The diminution in both the representative role and the policy role of voluntary organizations has profound implications for the overall capacity of citizens to influence policy. Under the deliberative model, direct participation in the policy process is seen as both empowering and enabling. Without *voice*, however, individuals may find it hard to truly exercise influence or have any real sense that participation makes a difference.

From Input to Output Models

Although citizen engagement has opened some new spaces for policy dialogue, it has not reversed the decline in public trust and confidence in political institutions. The need to address the democratic deficit – the difference between what citizens expect of political institutions and what is perceived to be reality – has been a common refrain at both the federal and provincial levels of government in recent years. At the federal level, the Martin government started out with a commitment to reducing the democratic deficit, including a commitment to promote "the participation, the engagement, the active debate of all Canadians."[26] A number of provinces are also actively committed to reform agendas that will make government more citizen-centred, and to involving citizens in determining the nature of such reforms.[27]

So far, most of the reforms, slowed significantly at the federal level by the cautiousness of a minority government situation, have been aimed at reforming parliamentary and electoral institutions, including increasing citizen engagement through parliamentary processes. Parliamentary reform that seriously enhances citizen engagement, Peter Aucoin and Lori Turnbull (2003, 433-44) suggest, would see ministers allowing MPs to conduct dialogue with constituents before legislation is set in stone, making greater use of committees to examine draft bills, and ensuring that the major consultative exercises conducted by the public service do not bypass parliamentarians, a practice that increases the perceived irrelevance of MPs. Although much-needed parliamentary reform may re-tip the balance between Parliament and the public service, it may do little to address the challenges outlined above.

Parliamentary reform, even if substantial, is not the most significant way in which citizen involvement in policy making is being reshaped. Rather, the real change in the expected roles of citizens is taking place through the implementation of performance-based accountability. This takes citizen engagement in a direction quite different from that of inching along the continuum from representative to deliberative democracy. It shifts the involvement of citizens in the policy process from the input to the output end of policy development.

One legacy of the philosophy of New Public Management that dominated most governments in Canada as elsewhere in the 1990s was an "explosion" in the interest in accountability (Good 2003; Osborne, McLaughlin, and Ferlie 2002; Power 1997; Savoie 2003). What is new in accountability is that government departments are being compelled to provide outcome measures that, in theory, enable policy results to be compared across jurisdictions or over time to determine if "investments" are paying off (Saint-Martin 2004), or to hold provincial governments accountable for federal transfers. Such evidence-based reporting was a key part of the logic of the Social Union Framework Agreement (SUFA), in which both the federal and provincial/ territorial governments committed to measuring outcomes of their social programs, reporting regularly to their constituents on the performance of these programs, and using "third parties" as appropriate to assess progress (Phillips 2003, 107). Although SUFA was never invoked as a means of guiding intergovernmental relationships before its sunset clause ran out, the SUFA policy frame remains in play. As the federal government increases transfers for health, urban infrastructure, and other programs, it is seeking accountability, but cannot directly impose national standards in areas of provincial jurisdiction. By requiring or encouraging governments to produce evidence of results and by promoting the vigilance of citizens in analyzing such information, it can achieve accountability through the back door that it cannot through the front door. Interest in accountability is not driven by the federal government alone, however, as provincial governments, notably Alberta, are also requiring departments to produce annual reports indicating performance targets and outcomes.[28] Private and public foundations, too, increasingly demand that the organizations they fund produce outcome measures of performance assessment (see Hall et al. 2003).

This shift in accountability regimes has transformed the playing field for policy making. It not only involves, on the part of citizens and their organizations, that they observe and monitor the policy process as well as review, analyze, and compare policy outcomes, but that they share this information with the broader public and in some cases, mobilize the public in order to hold governments to account. In effect, it turns citizens into social scientists and casts them in the role of perpetual watchdogs. Although the ideas of evidence-based accountability and citizen watchdogs may be appealing in theory, they are improbable in reality. At best, outcome measurement is a complex task; public debate concerning it requires access to relevant data and technical information, the ability to assess the quality of measurement, and the establishment of institutional venues for debate on the adequacy and policy implications of the data (Phillips 2003, 107). Most citizens have neither the time nor the research skills to be effective in this role, nor do many of the voluntary organizations which might do this on their behalf. Moreover, the formation of informed opinions, the aggregation of voices, and their articulation into concrete political claims are all vital for accountability. And as we argued above, it is these spaces – that exist in intermediary voluntary associations – that are being squeezed out in the redesign of citizen engagement and policy development.

Conclusion

From a policy-making perspective, the developments around citizen engagement have the potential to break down some of the basic pillars of democratic decision-making processes: how interests are articulated and aggregated, and how governments are held accountable. At the front end of policy making, interest articulation and aggregation are essential functions for developing legitimate, publicly binding decisions. Interest mediation plays a large role in helping determine the content of policies. The accountability function ensures the evaluation and monitoring of outcomes.

From the 1970s, when Canadian governments began to actively experiment with citizen involvement in policy making, there has undoubtedly been the creation of new and multiple spaces for political representation and participation in representative democracy. There have also been important changes in who and what gets represented, and how this occurs. Citizen engagement has come to give primacy to the participation of citizens instead of, or at least in parallel with, organized groups. Active participation (personally attending a meeting or being involved in a chat group) trumps representation by third parties. Experiential knowledge is more likely than expert knowledge to be produced from such involvement, except for the organizations that must trade more exclusively in highly specialized policy research. New forms of deliberative dialogue are taking place that involve citizens over extended periods of time, rather than for the few hours required to attend a public consultation or a parliamentary committee. The overall effect has been to expand the ability of citizens to articulate their values, concerns, and preferences, and to make these claims known. With a diminished role for organizations, however, aggregation of interests falls to either the public servants or the contractors who manage and conduct exercises in citizen engagement, or it is not done at all. Although performance-based accountability may provide more and better information, and is carving out a new role for citizens as watchdogs at the evaluation end of policy making, the notion that citizens and their organizations can effectively take up these opportunities or that this will enhance citizens' ability to exert influence on policy is over-optimistic at best and illusory at worst.

With many more opportunities to have input, citizens may be more wired (both electronically and through more traditional face-to-face interactions) into the policy process, but this does not necessarily mean that they actually have a greater influence on policy decisions. The wiring may exist, but the power is not always on. The point of this chapter is not to argue against continued efforts at achieving more truly deliberative forms of dialogue as a means to enhancing a meaningful role for citizens in policy development. Rather, it suggests the need to ensure that the new deliberative wiring is effectively plugged into decision making. It also suggests that such additional means for increasing citizen engagement need not and should not be done at the expense of all forms of representative democracy. This includes not only parliamentary processes, but the wide array of voluntary associations that serve as important mechanisms for interest aggregation, that can themselves be sites for the exercise of the skills of citizenship through deliberation and debate, and that play a vital role in accountability. Ultimately, if the democratic deficit is to be addressed in any serious manner, three developments must occur: first, parliamentary reform needs to proceed; second, the recognition that interest groups and voluntary associations can play a constructive role in mediating between citizens and the state needs to be reinserted into contemporary thinking about citizen engagement; and third, the capacity for the realization of their role needs to be strengthened.

NOTES

1   For a recent critique of input-output models from a deliberative perspective, see Robert E. Goodin (2003, 161-68).

2   See research from the Institute for Research on Public Policy survey, "Strengthening Canadian Democracy: The Views for Canadians," by Paul Howe and David Northrup (2000); the Centre for Research and Information on Canada 2003 survey, "Citizen Participation and Canadian Democracy: An Overview."

3   For example, the first national conference on public participation in Canada was held in 1977, by which time such a sufficient range of experience had occurred that it could be documented in a series of case studies as well as comparative analysis. See Barry Sadler (1978).

4   The term "citizen jury" is a trademark of the Jefferson Center in the USA but the convening of such juries began simultaneously in the UK. The commercialization of the methods of deliberative democracy has become a major consulting industry, particularly in the United States. See http://www.jefferson-center.org.

5   Canada's major experiments with direct democracy, the Quebec referenda on sovereignty (which were squeakers that produced a "no" vote by very slim majorities) and the national 1992 referendum on the Charlottetown Accord (which was defeated), have been traumatic events for the country, leaving considerable criticism of the process as part of their legacy (see Pal and Seidle 1993). Afterward, the main interest in direct democracy existed in the populist challenge of the Reform/Alliance Party, which would have reshaped the role of MP from that of trustee to delegate, using referenda and recall to ensure that the citizen could keep the elected official on a short leash (Aucoin and Turnbull 2003, 441). Such ideas found no resonance – indeed, were dismissed without comment – in Prime Minister Martin's approach to reducing the democratic deficit.

6   For example, the 1985 Royal Commission on the Economic Union and Development Prospects for Canada, also known as the Macdonald Commission,

generated over seventy background research studies that were then published in 1986 as a series. For a discussion of the roles of commissioners, research staff, and the consultation component of commissions, see Jane Jenson (1994).

7   The commission was established by the federal government in response to pressure from a coalition of environmental groups (see Beakhust 1978). From the beginning, Justice Berger made it clear that he was not going to be rushed to judgment. Instead, he conducted preliminary hearings to get a sense of the depth and nature of the concerns, and on that basis designed a consultation process that enabled a broad spectrum of interests to be heard.

8   In total, over three hundred expert witnesses and a thousand northerners participated, generating more than thirty-two thousand pages of testimony (Berger 1977).

9   To keep people informed during the process, daily summaries in local Aboriginal languages were prepared for broadcast over the northern CBC network and many of the community hearings were themselves televised.

10 The commission encouraged environmental groups to work together in a coalition, rather than funding each group separately; similarly, many of the Aboriginal organizations agreed to joint representation. This enabled the coalitions to have counsel available at every important session to examine and cross-examine witnesses (Beakhust 1978, 315). Many of the environmental groups which received intervenor funding from the federal government via the commission also had, like many citizen organizations, a platform of core operational funding to support their representation and other activities. Thus, though participating in such an intense manner for a lengthy period may have been taxing, they had some funding that was not project-based and could be directed toward providing policy capacity.

11 Even one provincial premier who had asked to address the forum was told that he could call the 1-800 number just like anybody else. Citizens were given exceedingly complex questions, such as how to balance individual and group rights, which they were expected to discuss and comment upon in a short period of time; they received no background information or indication from the commission of how this could inform policy (Phillips 1991, 193).

12 Part way through the process, the minister declared that he no longer wanted to hear from groups which advocated policy change that was not in line with the government's intended direction. Éric Montpetit (2003, 107) has argued that a similar restriction of political actors took place with Health Canada's review of assisted reproductive technologies. Although adhering to commitments made in the 1997 election campaign to obtain further input concerning Health Canada policies on reproductive technologies by holding a workshop, Health Canada officials knew where they wanted to take the issue and thus were not interested in hearing ideas that would challenge their own. Numerous other "multi-stakeholder"

sessions are seen to have the similar effect of containing debate and thus limiting input into policy.

13   This was the first widespread use of workbooks, of which approximately one million were distributed and forty thousand returned. However, before it could fully analyze these workbooks and use them in the development of policy, the process ran out of time. House of Commons, 17 March 1995, *Hansard* transcripts.

14   Perhaps the most overt example of this was the 1992 Panel on Violence against Women, which chose to hear only from individuals who could relate their personal experiences as victims of violence. The panel ignored the multitude of agencies which, through experience, understood that some of the issues and the possible remedies for violence against women differed from community to community.

15   Citizen juries are being used extensively in Scotland, for example. See http://www.communitiesscotland.gov.uk/Web/Site/Engagement/techniques/citizens_juries.asp. For other examples from Europe, see the website's References section.

16   See Matthew Mendelsohn (2000) and Leslie A. Pal and F. Leslie Seidle (1993).

17   In January 2004 the city of Hamilton launched a public consultation process entitled "Working Together towards Fiscal Stability" in order to foster greater public involvement in developing the 2004 city budget. See http://www.myhamilton.ca, under Mayors News Releases, 21 January 2004. For more information on public involvement in municipal budgeting, see Fenn 1999. The premier of Ontario, Dalton McGuinty, also launched a series of citizen juries in January 2004 in order to receive public input in the budgetary process and to develop a more "transparent and accountable budget." For more information, see http://www.fin.gov.on.ca/english/budget/bud04/papere.html.

18   For details on electoral reform in British Columbia, see the Citizens' Assembly on Electoral Reform website, http://www.citizensassembly.bc.ca/.

19   See Watling et al. (2004).

20   CPRN conducted more than twenty roundtables across the country on behalf of the Commission on the Future of Health Care in Canada (Romanow Commission). These citizen deliberation mechanisms were viewed as important counterweights to the input that the commission received from experts and interest groups. As for The Society We Want, CPRN held day-long dialogues with more than three hundred Ontarians, selected at random. Citizen juries were formed with approximately eighteen individuals.

21   A number of parliamentarians have taken the active involvement of their constituents very seriously, and regularly sponsor townhall meetings in their ridings, host online discussions, or have developed other means for ongoing dialogue about policy. One of the leaders in such practices has been Dr. Carolyn Bennett, MP for St. Paul and former minister of state (public health) (see http://www.carolynbennett.com). These are still probably more exception than norm, however.

22 See, for example, Health Canada's *Policy Toolkit for Public Involvement in Decision Making*, at http://www.hc-sc.gc.ca/hppb/voluntarysector/building_partners. html; Environment Canada's *Commitment to Effective Consultations*, at http:// www.ec.gc.ca/consult/policy_e.html; and the Department of Justice's policy at http://canada.justice.gc.ca/en/cons/pc_policy.html.

23 See also Voluntary Sector Initiative, *Participating in Federal Public Policy: A Guide for the Voluntary Sector*, at http://www.vsi-isbc.ca/eng/index.cfm.

24 For example, the Canadian Public Health Association conducted consultations across Canada on the issue of xenotransplantation; the National Children's Alliance was contracted to conduct consultations with the early child development and child care communities across Canada as part of the National Children's Agenda. A private consulting firm, eLab by Design, conducted "Canada's Foreign Policy Dialogue" in 2003 on behalf of the Department of Foreign Affairs and International Trade (DFAIT) to consult Canadian citizens on the future of foreign policy.

25 Fifty percent of the voluntary and charitable organizations with annual revenues of over $100,000 reported that they had difficulties participating in public policy development; the problem was most significant for organizations with annual revenues of between $1 and $9 million. Percentages reported by such bodies were even higher for those areas in which citizen involvement has expanded in recent years: health (62 percent); law, advocacy, and politics (57 percent); environment (56 percent); and social services (54 percent). The charitable organizations of universities and colleges reported the highest level of difficulty: 64 percent indicated that they had problems being effective participants in policy development. See Statistics Canada et al. (2004).

26 See Prime Minister's Reply to the Speech from the Throne, 3 February 2004, at http://pm.gc.ca.

27 The governments of both Ontario and Quebec have established ministers and secretariats for democratic renewal. The Ontario minister promised that his government would deliver positive change so that "Ontarians become engaged in our democracy as never before, improving the way our government does its job" ("McGuinty government to strengthen our democracy and improve the way government serves people," press release, 8 December 2003, 2), and has committed to creating a citizens' jury as a means to determine electoral reform. In British Columbia, a citizens' assembly was established in 2004 to make recommendations on changes to the electoral system. In New Brunswick, a commission has been created to identify options for an enhanced "citizen-centred democracy" (http://www.gnb.ca/0100/index-e.asp).

28 Alberta was one of the first provinces to progress toward a performance-based model of accountability as it moved to adopting clearer "business" lines in the

1990s. Under its 1998 Government Accountability Act, departments report annually on how they have met their targets.

REFERENCES

Abelson, Julia, and François-Pierre Gauvin. 2004. *Engaging Citizens: One Route to Health Care Accountability*. Ottawa: Canadian Policy Research Networks.

Aucoin, Peter, and Lori Turnbull. 2003. "The Democratic Deficit: Paul Martin and Parliamentary Reform." *Canadian Public Administration* 46(4): 427-49.

Beakhust, Grahame. 1978. "The Berger Inquiry." In *Involvement and Environment: Proceedings of the Canadian Conference on Public Participation*. Vol. 2, ed. Barry Sadler. Edmonton: Environment Council of Alberta.

Berger, Justice Thomas R. 1977. *Northern Frontier, Northern Homeland: Report of the Mackenzie Valley Pipeline Inquiry*. Vol. 1. Toronto: James Lorimer.

Bohman, James. 1996. *Public Deliberation: Pluralism, Complexity, and Democracy*. Cambridge, MA: MIT Press.

Cohen, Joshua. 1997. "Procedure and Substance in Deliberative Democracy." In *Deliberative Democracy: Essays on Reason and Politics*, ed. James Bohman and William Rehg, 407-37. Cambridge, MA: MIT Press.

Council for Research and Information on Canada. 2003. "Citizen Participation and Canadian Democracy: An Overview." http://www.cric.ca/en_re/etudes/index.html.

Dobrowolsky, Alexandra, and Jane Jenson. 1994. "Reforming the Parties." In *How Ottawa Spends 1993-1994: A More Democratic Canada ... ?* ed. Susan D. Phillips, 43-81. Montreal and Kingston: McGill-Queen's University Press.

Ekos Research. 2004. *Rethinking Citizen Engagement 2004*. Ottawa: Ekos Research.

Fenn, W. Michael. 1999. "Expanding the Frontiers of Public Participation: Public Involvement in Municipal Budgeting and Finance." In *Citizen Engagement: Lessons in Participation in Local Government*, ed. Katherine A. Graham and Susan D. Phillips, 113-36. Toronto: IPAC.

Fischer, Frank. 2003. *Reframing Public Policy. Discursive Politics and Deliberative Practices*. New York: Oxford University Press.

Fischer, Frank, and John Forester. 1993. *The Argumentative Turn in Policy Analysis and Planning*. Durham, NC: Duke University Press.

Fishkin, James. 1991. *Democracy and Deliberation: New Directions for Democratic Reform*. New Haven: Yale University Press.

Good, David A. 2003. *The Politics of Public Management*. Toronto: IPAC.

Goodin, Robert E. 2003. *Reflective Democracy*. Oxford: Oxford University Press.

Gutman, Amy, and Dennis Thompson. 1996. *Democracy and Disagreement*. Cambridge, MA: Belknap Press.

Hall, Michael, Susan D. Phillips, Claudia Meillat, and Donna Pickering. 2003. *Assessing Performance: Evaluation Practices and Perspectives in Canada's Voluntary Sector*. Toronto: Canadian Centre for Philanthropy.

Healey, Patsy. 1997. *Collaborative Planning: Shaping Places in Fragmented Societies.* London: Macmillan.

Howe, Paul, and David Northrup. 2000. "Strengthening Canadian Democracy: The Views of Canadians." *Policy Matters* 1(5), July. Institute for Research on Public Policy.

Institute on Governance. 1996. *The Citizen Engagement Round Table: The Social Security Review and the Aboriginal Claims Process in B.C.* http://www.iog.ca/publications/cert7.pdf.

Jenson, Jane. 1994. "Commissioning Ideas: Representation and Royal Commissions." In *How Ottawa Spends 1994-95: Making Change,* ed. Susan D. Phillips, 39-70. Ottawa: Carleton University Press.

Jenson, Jane, and Susan D. Phillips. 1996. "Regime Shift: New Citizenship Practices in Canada." *International Journal of Canadian Studies* 14(Fall): 111-36.

Lortie Commission (Royal Commission on Electoral Reform and Party Financing). 1992. *Reforming Electoral Democracy: Final Report.* Vol. 2. Ottawa: Minister of Supply and Services.

Macedo, Stephen. 1999. *Deliberative Politics: Essays on Democracy and Disagreement.* New York: Oxford University Press.

MacKinnon, Mary Pat. 2004. "Institutionalizing Citizen Participation: What We Hoped For and Where We Are Today." Paper presented to the fourteenth John K. Friesen Conference, Simon Fraser University, Vancouver, 20 May.

Mansbridge, Jane. 1980. *Beyond Adversary Democracy.* New York: Basic Books.

Mendelsohn, Matthew. 2000. "Public Brokerage: Constitutional Reform and the Accommodation of Mass Publics." *Canadian Journal of Political Science* 33(2): 245-72.

Montpetit, Éric. 2003. "Public Consultations in Policy Network Environments: The Case of Assisted Reproductive Technology Policy in Canada." *Canadian Public Policy* 29(1): 95-110.

Osborne, Stephen, Kate McLaughlin, and Ewan Ferlie. 2002. *The New Public Management: Current Trends and Future Prospects.* London: Routledge.

Pal, Leslie A., and F. Leslie Seidle. 1993. "Constitutional Politics 1990-92: The Paradox of Participation." In *How Ottawa Spends 1993-1994: A More Democratic Canada ... ?* ed. Susan D. Phillips, 143-202. Ottawa: Carleton University Press.

Patten, Steve. 2000. "Democratizing the Institutions of Policy-Making: Democratic Consultation and Participatory Administration." *Journal of Canadian Studies* 35(4): 221-39.

Phillips, Susan D. 1991. "How Ottawa Blends: Shifting Government Relationships with Interest Groups." In *How Ottawa Spends 1991-1992: The Politics of Fragmentation,* ed. Frances Abele, 183-228. Ottawa: Carleton University Press.

—. 2003. "SUFA and Citizen Engagement: Fake or Genuine Masterpiece?" In *Forging the Canadian Social Union: SUFA and Beyond,* ed. Sarah Fortin, Alain Noël, and France St-Hilaire, 1-36. Montreal: IRPP.

Phillips, Susan D., with Michael Orsini. 2002. *Mapping the Links: Citizen Involvement in Policy Processes.* Ottawa: Canadian Policy Research Networks.

Power, Michael. 1997. *The Audit Society: Rituals of Verification.* Oxford: Oxford University Press.

Sadler, Barry, ed. 1978. *Involvement and Environment: Proceedings of the Canadian Conference on Public Participation.* Vol. 2. Edmonton: Environment Council of Alberta.

Saint-Martin, Denis. 2004. *Coordinating Interdependence: Governance and Social Policy Redesign in Britain, the European Union and Canada.* CPRN Social Architecture Papers Research Report F/41. Ottawa: Canadian Policy Research Networks.

Savoie, Donald J. 2003. *Breaking the Bargain: Public Servants, Ministers, and Parliament.* Toronto: University of Toronto Press.

Schauer, Frederick. 1999. "Talking as Decision Procedure." In *Deliberative Politics: Essays on Democracy and Deliberation,* ed. Stephen Macedo, 17-28. Oxford: Oxford University Press.

Statistics Canada et al. 2004. *Cornerstones of Community: Highlights from the National Survey of Nonprofit and Voluntary Organizations.* Ottawa: Ministry of Industry.

Torgerson, Douglas. 1996. "Power and Insight in Policy Discourse: Post-positivism and Problem Definition." In *Policy Studies in Canada: The State of the Art,* ed. Laurent Dobuzinskis, Michael Howlett, and David Laycock, 266-98. Toronto: University of Toronto Press.

Watling, Judy, Judith Maxwell, Nandini Saxena, and Suzanne Taschereau. 2004. *Responsible Action: Citizens' Dialogue on the Long-Term Management of Used Nuclear Fuel.* Ottawa: Canadian Policy Research Networks.

→ Young, Iris Marion. 2000. *Inclusion and Democracy.* Oxford: Oxford University Press.

5
Queering Public Policy: A Canadian Perspective

Miriam Smith

Canada is in the forefront of lesbian and gay rights in the world. It is one of the few countries that systematically bans discrimination against lesbians and gay men in areas such as housing and employment while, at the same time, extending recognition to same-sex couples. Same-sex marriage is on the Canadian policy agenda and is fast becoming a legal fact across jurisdictions. Lesbian, gay, bisexual, and transgender (LGBT) struggles over the last twenty years have centred on litigation. Drawing on the powerful template of rights discourse, one that is deeply rooted in Canadian society, the LGBT movement has claimed the rights of citizenship on equal terms with heterosexuals. This chapter argues that the quest for legal rights is only one stage of LGBT struggles and that, as legal recognition and protection is increasingly extended to lesbian and gay citizens and as the drive for legal equality reaches its apex with the legal recognition of same-sex marriage, the policy agenda of the lesbian and gay movement will increasingly focus on advancing queer identities and interests within social institutions such as the education system, the health care system, and broader fields of social policy. As the lesbian and gay movement progresses beyond the drive for legal citizenship, many of these struggles will focus on overcoming both the social stigma that still attaches to LGBT identities and the myriad social practices that reinforce this stigma. These efforts will highlight the heteronormative organization of social life and, by extension, the heteronormative organization of public policy and of the policy process itself. The term "heteronormative" refers to the ways in which heterosexuality is treated as an often unstated social norm. For example, social policies are often based on a heteronormative concept of the family (opposite-sex partners and their children). At the same time as the contemporary LGBT movement sets out to challenge heteronormative forms of policy and practice, the prospective policy agenda in the lesbian and gay sector promises to reinforce a liberal and state-focused citizenship.

This chapter sets out to define this policy terrain and to suggest the ways in which LGBT people are currently organized into (and out of) the policy process. The first section explores the LGBT public policy issues that have been put forward by LGBT activists and advocates, including anti-discrimination measures, relationship recognition, parenting rights, hate crimes/hate speech, sexual regulation, and social policy (health, education, and housing). The balance of the discussion situates these concrete policy debates within the broader concept of sexual citizenship. In doing so, it highlights the extent to which public policy is organized around profoundly heteronormative assumptions about the nature of Canadian economic, social, and political life. LGBT citizens have been organized into the policy process in ways that reflect and reinforce a liberal model of sexual citizenship. This model of liberal sexual citizenship has yielded tremendous "advances" in LGBT legal rights and recognition in Canada; yet, this model of citizenship restricts LGBT interests and issues in ways that forestall a more profound excavation of the project of a queer public policy. By drawing on burgeoning studies of sexual citizenship, this analysis follows many other analysts of queer politics in pointing to the complex ambiguity of the project of inclusion and recognition (see, for example, Epstein 2003; Gotell 2002; Herman 1989; Rubin 1984).

Lesbian, Gay, Bisexual, and Transgender Public Policy Issues: An Overview

In November 2003, the e-mail list of the main Canadian LGBT public advocacy group, Egale, had a debate over the future of LGBT public policy issues. In the wake of court decisions in favour of same-sex marriage, one contributor to the list suggested that there were few lesbian and gay (as opposed to transgender) issues left to be dealt with on the political agenda, except the question of the higher age of consent for anal sex (eighteen, versus fourteen for vaginal intercourse). Joining the e-mail debate on 3 November, Egale board member and Calgary activist Stephen Lock pointed out that sexual regulation of queer people was still very much a live issue in the wake of bar and bath raids in Montreal and Calgary in 2003. These raids, undertaken under the federal Criminal Code bawdy house laws, resulted in the arrest of eight people and, according to Lock, constituted an "attack on gay space." Lock went on to say, "The most basic issue of our equality is not whether we can marry or not marry. Our sexuality is the most basic issue upon which we continue to be vilified and attacked." This debate demonstrates the different views of LGBT public policy issues that are held even among the politically active segment of the LGBT community. To begin, then, we will survey the most common types of public policy issues that have been raised by the Canadian LGBT movement.

FREEDOM FROM DISCRIMINATION

As for other marginalized groups in Canadian society, a basic area of LGBT public policy concerns freedom from discrimination based on sexual preference in areas such as employment and housing. Freedom from such discrimination was a central goal of the gay liberation movement from its inception in the early 1970s, and was the subject of many of the struggles of the early movement. In the 1970s, activists pushed forward challenges to the exclusion of sexual orientation as a prohibited ground of discrimination in human rights legislation at the federal and provincial levels. These efforts were largely unsuccessful in securing basic human rights protections, except in Quebec where the provincial human rights code was amended to include sexual orientation in 1977.

The entrenchment of the Charter of Rights in 1982 was an important turning point with respect to the inclusion of sexual orientation in federal and provincial human rights legislation. In many provinces, the spectre of Charter litigation moved the policy debate toward the inclusion of sexual orientation in human rights legislation over the course of the eighties and nineties, beginning in Ontario in 1986 (Rayside 1988). Early litigation, such as that by Graham Haig over discrimination against gay and lesbian members of the Canadian Forces *(Haig v. Canada)*, established that sexual orientation had to be included in the federal Human Rights Act, even though the act itself was not formally amended until 1996. Jim Egan and Jack Nesbit's 1995 case *(Egan & Nesbit v. Canada)* established that sexual orientation was included in the ambit of the Charter's equality rights clause. Delwyn Vriend's 1996 Charter challenge established the primacy of the Charter's equality rights provisions over provincial human rights legislation, forcing Alberta to include sexual orientation in its human rights legislation as a prohibited ground of discrimination *(Vriend v. Alberta)*. By 2003, when Nunavut passed its human rights legislation, sexual orientation discrimination was prohibited in every province and territory, as well as in federal jurisdiction. The most important outstanding issue in this area is that of transgender (trans) discrimination – discrimination based on gender identity. Some court and tribunal decisions have indicated that trans people are protected under the rubric of sex discrimination in federal, provincial, and territorial human rights legislation. Yet, as advocates for trans people have argued, where explicit and visible protections are concerned, de facto protection is not as useful for marginalized groups as a prohibition against discrimination based on gender identity. Therefore, many trans people would prefer explicit human rights protections.

RELATIONSHIP RECOGNITION

The second major area of LGBT public policy focuses on claims for relationship recognition such as the right to receive same-sex benefits in the public and private sectors, the right to adopt, the right to receive support upon breakdown of a relationship, and the right to marry. Relationship recognition can be characterized as freedom from discrimination in the sense that lesbians and gay litigants and advocacy organizations are demanding that lesbian and gay relationships be treated in the same way as straight relationships under law and public policy. However, spousal and parenting rights potentially involve a much deeper level of recognition of LGBT people as citizens. Relationship recognition is controversial in the lesbian and gay male communities in ways that the first type of equality seeking is not. Within the communities, there are some who oppose relationship recognition as a co-optation of the original goals of the gay liberation movement – sexual freedom – and as marking the conservatization of the movement (Hannon 1999). Others have called attention to the feminist critique of family as a patriarchal institution and wondered if relationship recognition will radicalize and transform the heterosexual family (Cossman 1994; Herman 1989). Increasingly, relationship recognition and same-sex marriage are viewed as mechanisms for the inclusion of LGBT citizens on terms that reinforce neo-liberal citizenship (Gotell 2002; Boyd and Young 2003; Smith 2005b).

If judged by their actions and political effort, the main organizations of the lesbian and gay rights movement at the federal level currently view relationship recognition as the main goal of their political activism. Although such organizations recognize that there are lively debates on the legitimacy of relationship recognition within the gay male and lesbian communities, in general, rights-based organizations are caught up in a political dynamic which demands the articulation of a clear-cut, almost "ethnic" identity in order to make their rights claims legible to the Canadian public, the media, the courts, the governing caucus, and policy makers. In a similar vein, LGBT organizations usually present an equality rights argument that is based on the moral and political equation of lesbian and gay male couples with straight couples.

An increasingly important subset of relationship recognition concerns parental rights, especially on custody and adoption (Rayside 2002). Some of the earliest legal cases that were covered by the gay press in Canada during the seventies were custody hearings, most commonly those in which lesbians lost custody of their children upon the breakup of their marriage. This was an important issue around which lesbians organized during the late seventies and early eighties. As the baby-boomer generation of "out" lesbians and gay men settled into mid-life in the eighties and nineties, some members of this group were either partnered with women or men who had children from a previous heterosexual relationship or decided to have children of their own, through adoption or through the use of new reproductive technologies or other private arrangements. Because of the lack of accurate census data about the LGBT population and families, there is no firm estimate of how many such families exist in Canada. However, they are certainly an important political constituency within the LGBT community in Canada and have shaped the recent politics of the movement. In some measure because of the growing importance of LGBT couples with children, a change which opened up a new political space between lesbians and gay men around human rights issues, lesbians and gays have done more organizing together over the last twenty years.

These new forms of family gave rise to new sets of political issues including the rights to legal adoption, both for same-sex couples wishing to adopt children and for those wishing to adopt each other's biological children. Families headed by same-sex couples have also challenged the two-parent assumption of Canadian law by arguing that children should have the right to three parents, a legal issue that arose in an Ontario case in which two lesbians were raising a child together with the biological father of the child, who did not live in the house. All three wished to be the legal parents of the child but were denied by an Ontario court (Cossman 2003). Another issue in the parenting area concerns access to new reproductive technologies for lesbians (Lüttichau 2004). Lesbians played an active role in the Royal Commission on New Reproductive Technologies in pushing for the right to access these technologies; some tensions arose between lesbians and other feminists who were skeptical of the new technologies and their implications for women (Fortier, Montpetit, and Scala 2003).

Recasting Canadian public policies and law so as to recognize same-sex couples in other areas is complicated because the heterosexual family has traditionally been the cornerstone of civil society, and because, as in other

Western countries, the dominance of this family form underpins Canadian law, public policy, and social practice. Everything from registering a motor vehicle to going to the dentist potentially involves recognition of hetero-sexual spousal relationships in law, practice, and policy, and thus the recog-nition of same-sex relationships entails a wholesale restructuring of these policies in both the public and private sector. However, over the last twenty-five years, there has been a strong push from common law straight couples for recognition of their relationships on par with relationships between le-gally married heterosexual Canadians. In law and social practice, the firm distinction between legally married and common law or *union de fait* rela-tionships has been weakened, with Quebec leading the way in the decline of legal marriage and the rise of long-term non-married partnerships between heterosexuals, including heterosexuals raising children. Opposite-sex couples who lived together "common law" in the provinces governed by English com-mon law, or *union de fait* in Quebec, governed by the civil code, indirectly contributed to the social, political, and legal weakening of the special status of legal marriage, creating political opportunities for same-sex couples to claim recognition.

Advocacy organizations and trade unions have played a key role in push-ing for relationship recognition. Since the advent of the Charter, many LGBT organizations, most notably Egale at the federal level as well as trade unions such as the Canadian Union of Public Employees, have undertaken political work around the project of Charter litigation and have intervened in court and tribunal cases concerning relationship recognition. These efforts have resulted in consistent court decisions in favour of same-sex relationship rec-ognition, by far the most important of which is *M. v. H.*, an Ontario case in which a lesbian sued her former partner for spousal support upon the breakup of their long-time relationship. As in common law heterosexual partnerships, M. had contributed to building H.'s business and claimed that H.'s income in part depended on her labour in both household and business. She claimed that this relationship had been based on financial interdependence, an inter-dependence that had to be recognized at the end of the relationship, just as it would have been for a straight couple, whether common law or married. The Supreme Court of Canada agreed. The federal government and many of the provinces responded to this decision by overhauling their legal regimes with respect to relationship recognition. Of these initiatives, three affected the greatest number of Canadians: the first was the federal government's 2000 Modernization of Benefits and Obligations bill, which amended sixty-nine federal laws and regulations so that any provisions affecting spousal benefits and obligations were extended to same-sex couples; the second was Quebec's 1999 legislation which redefined the term "spouse" in thirty-nine provincial laws and regulations; the third was Ontario's Act to Amend Certain Statutes, Because of the Supreme Court of Canada Decision in M. v. H. (Bill 5), which amended sixty-seven Ontario laws ranging from the Estates Act to the Land Transfer Tax Act (including the Family Law Act, the specific statute at issue in M. v. H.).

These changes formed the background to the issue of same-sex marriage, which was a natural next step after the changes signalled by M. v. H. If common law couples and those living in union de fait had rights in federal, provincial, and territorial law that resembled those of married couples, and if, in the wake of M. v. H., same-sex couples were accorded rights similar to those of such couples, then it was only logical that same-sex couples should have the right to access legal marriage as the final measure of legal, political, social, economic, and symbolic equality. In important respects, non-marital heterosexual relationships are no longer stigmatized. Given that heterosexual marriage is no longer as important as it was, one might ask why militant heterosexual activists in the evangelical Protestant organizations, the Catholic Church, and the Reform/Alliance wing of the Conservative Party are so keen to continue to restrict access to legal marriage and why gay and lesbian couples are so eager to get it.

For many same-sex couples, the solution lies in the idea of full equality. Even though the differences in practice between marriage and common law partnership are relatively trivial, especially outside of Quebec, there is still an important symbolic dimension to the public and legal recognition of a sanctified relationship. By the same token, this is why a political counter-movement of heterosexual militancy has emerged regarding the marriage issue. Further, legal marriage still confers some specific benefits that are not available to common law same-sex couples. These vary by provincial and territorial jurisdiction but some of the most important are the fact that same-sex couples face formidable complexities in sponsoring their partners for immigration to Canada, barriers that are not faced by married heterosexuals. A series of court decisions in 2002-03 in BC, Ontario, and Quebec led the federal government to propose legislation that would recognize same-sex marriage and to refer the question of its constitutionality to the Supreme Court of Canada. In Reference re Same-Sex Marriage (2004), the court ruled that the legislation was constitutionally valid and the legislation was passed by the Martin government on 29 June 2005. Same-sex marriage is now the law in Canada. Although the Harper government has promised to reopen the issue, the force of the court's decision means that the government would have to circumvent the Charter rights of same-sex couples by using the not-withstanding clause in order to roll back same-sex marriage.

HATE CRIMES/HATE SPEECH

Another important area of public policy for LGBT citizens has been that of combating violence and hatred (Janoff 2005). Despite legal recognition and anti-discrimination measures, LGBT people are often the victims of violence and hate speech, ranging from the bullying and teasing of school-aged children through to gay-bashing and murder, motivated by hatred of LGBT people. In some cases, young men who are thought to be gay have been attacked by their peers. A series of murders of gay men in Montreal in the early nineties led to a human rights inquiry by the Quebec human rights commission, and the 2001 murder of Aaron Webster, a gay Vancouverite, led to a new campaign to stop anti-gay violence (Matas 2001). Transsexuals have also been targeted, as in the cases of three young transsexual sex trade workers who were murdered in Toronto in 1996, and the more recent murder case of a transsexual sex trade worker. Viviane K. Namaste (1996) has argued that those who break with normative gender/sex identities are most likely to be targets of violence, as the perpetrators use violence to police their own self-presentation. Namaste's analysis suggests that because of the central importance of gender identities in this type of violence, it must be understood as much more than simply "gay-bashing," and that men, women, and transsexual citizens have different experiences of violence. Grassroots organizing in the LGBT community on anti-violence increasingly recognizes these differences.

In public policy terms, anti-gay violence has translated into a number of initiatives in federal politics. The most important of these are the 1995 Criminal Code amendment which included sexual orientation as a ground in sentencing for hate crimes, and the Bill C-250 amendment on hate speech, which strengthened the code's hate-sentencing provisions. The bill, proposed in 2003 by NDP MP Svend Robinson, was intended to amend the code's section 18 on hate propaganda to add sexual orientation to its list of prohibited grounds. Both the 1995 amendment and Robinson's bill provoked substantial public debate, including the mobilization of the Christian right against them. Although the Bill C-250 amendment was opposed by the Canadian Alliance Party, it was supported by MPs from other parties and passed into law just prior to the 2004 federal election (Dunfield 2003). Due to this expansion of the Criminal Code definition of hate propaganda, inciting hatred against an identifiable group on the basis of its sexual orientation is now a criminal offence.

SEXUAL FREEDOM AND MORAL REGULATION

Sexual freedom was the central characteristic of the gay liberation movement which, in itself, was inspired by the youth revolt and sexual revolution of the sixties. Sexual freedom continues to be a live issue in lesbian and gay politics. For some, sexual freedom is the main goal of the movement and a key dimension of lesbian and, especially, gay political identity. The freedom to engage in "various forms of sexual practice in personal relationships" is a central feature of sexual citizenship (Richardson 2000, 108). In concrete policy terms, in the Canadian context, this area has included issues such as censorship of lesbian and gay bookstores, pornography, criminalization of anal sex, police attempts to regulate public sex, and age of consent laws. These policy issues sparked the first waves of gay liberation organizing in the 1970s. Many gay and lesbian communities were on the receiving end of police repression and violence, and the counter-movement against policing practices was an important component of queer politics, especially in urban centres. The Toronto bath raids of 1981, the policing of a string of gay murders in Montreal in the early nineties, and the murder of Aaron Webster in Vancouver in 2001 (a victim of gay-bashing) are cases in which policing has been politicized in the lesbian and gay communities. Censorship of lesbian and gay reading materials by Canada Customs has been the subject of a string of court challenges, led by Little Sister's bookstore in Vancouver (Fuller and Blackley 1995).

In the earlier period of its history, Egale was less interested in such issues, both because the relationship between the police and the gay community has usually been treated as a local concern and because it feared that such issues would tarnish its public image and drive away potential supporters (Griffin 2000). As a public policy issue, sexual freedom tends to emphasize differences between lesbians/gays, on the one hand, and straights, on the other hand; the first two issues – freedom from basic forms of discrimination and relationship recognition – tend to emphasize the similarities between queers and straights. Sexual freedom issues have the potential to challenge openly the line between "good sex" and "bad sex," and between sexual order and sexual chaos, in Gayle Rubin's (1984) terms. Fighting for relationship recognition, parenting rights, and same-sex marriage suggests that lesbian and gay couples fit into an acceptable "family" model (precisely the point of the feminist and gay liberationist critiques of "family" in the lesbian and gay communities); the political issues around sexual regulation and sexual freedom threaten this cozy picture of middle-class and mono-gamously coupled respectability by pushing at the line between "good" and "bad." Advocacy organizations are often caught up in the dynamic of pre-senting the "good" face of the community to those outside of it. This dy-namic has been well documented in other communities. For example, Cathy Cohen's (1999) work on AIDS and African American political organizations shows how marginalized peoples often produce advocacy organizations that seek accommodation and assimilation with dominant economic, political, and social models.

SOCIAL POLICY

A fourth area of public policy for LGBT citizens concerns the provision of social services to queer communities and the ways in which the interests of LGBT people are represented in social services and social service delivery. This issue is most often raised by urban LGBT non-profit organizations who work on the front lines with marginalized subpopulations within the LGBT community, such as youth. This policy area is the least understood and the most neglected, yet has the greatest potential to lead to the project of "queer-ing" public policy – questioning and contesting the heteronormative organi-zation of public policies. This heteronormative organization of public policy is particularly visible in the area of social services, in which policies are predi-cated on the heterosexual nuclear family model. Struggles around relation-ship recognition, LGBT parenting, and same-sex marriage were long thought to have the potential to contest the traditional definition of the family. Yet, much of the discursive construction of queer rights in these areas has been based on the idea that same-sex couples or LGBT people are the same as heterosexuals and wish to access the same rights and obligations as those enjoyed by straights on a level playing field. In contrast, what is being recog-nized in public policy is what is different about queer people. This same dynamic applies in the broader area of social service provision; as with sexual regulation by the state, the policy issues here highlight what is different about LGBT people and hence rest on claims for the recognition of specific identi-ties. Moreover, the complexities and diversities of the LGBT population mean that a broad range of issues arise. The health needs of bisexual citizens are not the same as those of transsexual citizens. Hence, these policy areas pose a deeper challenge to conventional policy processes and policy analysis than the simple inclusion of LGBT citizens as an undigested group defined by "sexual orientation"; rather, they question the heteronormative organization and assumptions of the policy process and assert distinctive LGBT identities, needs, and interests.

Over the last ten years, the recognition of LGBT parents and their children in the school system has emerged as a political issue in diverse communities across Canada. These issues centre on the recognition of the needs of LGBT youth in the school system as well as on the recognition of families with same-sex parents (Rayside 2003). In British Columbia, the strength of the evangelical movement has produced challenges to the use of gay/lesbian-positive reading materials in the elementary school classroom (the Surrey book-banning case) as well as debates over the evangelical campus codes that condemn homosexuality and their relationship to teacher training for public schools (the Trinity Western University case) (Smith 2004). In Ontario, high-school student Marc Hall sparked an ongoing legal battle when he sought to take his boyfriend to the prom at his Catholic high school. These high-profile cases have been accompanied by organizing in school boards across Canada on the issue of combating homophobia in the school system, providing support and resources for LGBT students and families, and designing and implementing equity policies for public schools.

As in education, LGBT activism in health policy is long-standing. The AIDS crisis of the eighties sparked critically important challenges to the expertise of doctors, scientists, governments, and corporations. The LGBT communities, which were in the forefront of AIDS organizing, pioneered new forms of social movement organizing through the theatre and direct action of groups such as ACT UP! The LGBT movement across the medical professions worked hard to remove the equation of queer sexuality with mental, sexual, or medical deviance. In this, the LGBT community was one of the key actors – along with the women's movement – in challenging medical and scientific expertise in policy making in the health care field. The questioning by AIDS activists of the dominant expertise of the medical community is echoed by the contemporary health movement among LGBT activists. The newly established Canadian Rainbow Health Coalition, which has brought together health practitioners and stakeholders, pushes for more recognition of LGBT health needs in the health care system.

Health policy is particularly important for transgender people, especially for transsexuals who may wish to undergo surgical reassignment. Increasingly, sexual reassignment surgery (SRS) is defined as the most important human rights issue in the trans communities. Recent struggles over trans inclusion within Egale and other organizations have highlighted the double marginalization of the transgender communities, whose interests and identities have often been submerged and marginalized within the broader spectrum of gay and lesbian politics (see Broad 2002). The emergence of trans health as a human rights issue builds on a long tradition in LGBT politics in which health has been politicized.

Another emerging social policy area is that of housing and social assistance policies. Although these are usually not defined as LGBT issues, they are particularly important for LGBT youth. The ongoing stigmatization of LGBT youth in their families, schools, and communities is at the core of this set of issues as LGBT youth are more likely than other young people to be rejected by their families and to face bullying and harassment in school and community settings. Because of these factors, such youth are more likely to suffer from mental health problems leading to suicide and more likely to migrate from smaller communities into large cities such as Toronto, Vancouver, and Montreal where they may encounter homelessness, street life, and the sex trade. Social assistance and affordable housing are critically important for queer youth, yet their specific needs are not taken into account in the design of housing and social assistance policies, which are predicated on the heterosexual model of family and intimate relationships (Grundy 2003).

Queering Public Policy: Sexual Citizenship

The LGBT policy area entails much more than simply recognizing or granting rights to LGBT citizens. As this survey of policy issues has demonstrated, LGBT political issues are not restricted to formal legal citizenship rights such as relationship recognition or anti-discrimination measures. Drawing on the interdisciplinary literature on sexual citizenship and gender, this section presents an analysis of the distinctive means by which public policy can be "queered."

Feminist analyses of public policy and citizenship offer important guidance for understanding LGBT political dynamics. Feminists fought for formal legal equality measures and equal treatment for women on issues such as the right to vote, the right to hold property, and the right to education. However, feminists also fought for differential treatment that would produce equality of results for women, such as the right to maternity leave. Some feminist claims focused on the equal treatment of women and men, but others emphasized the recognition of difference. Similarly, in analyzing LGBT claims, we can differentiate between those that focus on the similar treatment of LGBT people and straights (for example, in non-discrimination measures, relationship recognition, and same-sex marriage) and those that focus on treating LGBT people differently in the name of equality of results (for example, in parenting rights and access to new reproductive technologies). The perils and pitfalls for LGBT people of engagement with the state are paralleled in the experience of women's organizations. The dilemmas of feminist engagement have been well documented in Canada (Bashevkin 1996; Dobrowolsky 2000; Findlay 1987; Young 2000).

However, feminist experience also suggests that political claims may go beyond the similar/different debate to a recognition of the existence of patriarchy as an organized set of political, economic, and social structures that oppresses women. In this area, feminists have mounted a wholesale challenge to the existing structures of citizenship and public policy in liberal democracies, arguing that liberal citizenship is fundamentally gendered and that public policies, taken as a whole, rest on the assumptions of a patriarchal society. In policy studies, these forms of feminist analysis have led to important critiques of the traditional welfare state model for failing to understand social policy as a gendered project. The work of Sylvia Bashevkin (1996) and Jane Jenson (1989) demonstrates how the comparative welfare state literature has failed to account for gender and has given rise to a new comparative analysis and classification of welfare states in terms of gender equality. Similarly, the moves toward the gendering of policy analysis and the policy process reflect analyses that are based on an understanding of systemic gender inequality. In these approaches, women are not simply a homogeneous and unitary category, dealt with as one of many stakeholders in public policy making. Rather, gender is treated as a set of power relations that is central to policy analysis.

The project of queering public policy is analogous to these projects of gender analysis. Heteronormative social organization is an analogue to patriarchy, although its structural power has not been theorized fully in terms of its implications for social policy and political economy. Lesbian feminists in particular have emphasized that heteronormativity is intimately tied to the reproduction of patriarchy because of the importance of controlling sexuality and reproduction in setting the terms of gender relations. In the ferment of the late sixties and early seventies, many of the early gay liberation and lesbian feminist activists emphasized the importance of the links between feminism and gay liberation, arguing that patriarchy was inherently hetero-normative and highlighting the common interest of feminists, bisexuals, gay men, and transgender people in fighting state regulation of sexuality as well as the dominant social norms of sexual orientation and gender identity. This argument has been restated in the analysis of the recent evolution of US policies on lesbian and gay rights recognition, policies which have developed very differently from those of Canada. Anna Marie Smith (2001) posits that the campaign in defence of heterosexual marriage in the US is linked to the attempted sexual regulation of single mothers by welfare reformers. Smith (2001, 315) asserts that US welfare reform has focused on the "poor single mother" who is "explicitly expected to marry her way out of poverty, both for her own sake and for that of her children." As Smith argues, "patriarchal heterosexual marriage is more than a moral category; it is an institution that is supposed to replace the state's obligations toward the poor. The promotion of patriarchal heterosexual marriage ... is therefore integral to the post-welfare state regime." This is an important example of potential links between feminist and queer analyses of social policies.

Just as some feminist policy analysis has suggested that gendering public policy must mean more than simply "add women and stir," so too the project of queering public policy entails bringing a queer perspective to bear in all areas of policy analysis. At a simple level, this means that queer advocacy groups must be included as policy stakeholders across all sectors of public policy, from tax policy to housing and health. On issues of policy process such as citizen consultation, citizen engagement, and state policies toward the voluntary sector and advocacy organizations, LGBT groups would be included, rather than excluded (Smith 2005a). In other words, queer people and their issues would no longer be ghettoized in the bailiwick of Charter-based equality rights but would become policy "citizens" (Grundy and Smith 2005).

This project of formal inclusion is similar to that demanded by feminist organizations in the 1970s; its importance is underlined by recognizing the extent of the current exclusion of LGBT organizations from the policy process from the local to the federal levels of government. LGBT citizens are far behind other groups in terms of their formal inclusion. For example, LGBT organizations are not routinely consulted in exercises on citizenship engagement or the voluntary sector, and LGBT interests are not systematically taken into account in health, education, and housing. The first steps toward inclusion, then, are based on claims of sameness – LGBT groups should be included as are organizations representing other groups in Canadian society. However, when LGBT organizations and perspectives are included, claims based on differences immediately ensue. For example, LGBT perspectives on health policy emphasize the distinctive needs of LGBT citizens, distinctive needs that arise out of the specific effects of social marginalization for some segments of the LGBT community or that reflect specific interests of the community. The specific experiences of LGBT people with depression, suicidal thoughts, or breast cancer are not the same as those of straights, and specific policies are needed to deal with these differences. Steven Epstein (2003), in discussing LGBT health activism in the US, refers to this as the "inclusion-difference" dynamic, meaning that, once LGBT people are "included" in the policy process, their "difference" from heterosexuals becomes the primary focus.

In this sense, the project of queering public policy eventually must move beyond the analogue of feminist analysis of public policy by recognizing the distinctive subcultures of LGBT life and ensuring that the state steps out of certain areas of regulation of sexuality and sexual practices. Because they focus on LGBT targets, the ongoing Canada Customs censorship of lesbian and gay erotic and reading material, the police raids on bathhouses and the Toronto lesbian club the Pussy Palace in 2000, and police attempts to regulate public sex in parks and washrooms entail a tacit recognition of the distinctive cultural practices of LGBT communities. This aspect of the project of queering public policy is somewhat analogous to debates about racialization of public policy. Citizenship regimes that are based on the historically dominant English or French Canadian concepts of culture must take account of ethnocultural groups whose cultural and religious practices may differ from the dominant norm and whose histories of marginalization may give rise to distinctive interests and identities. Obviously, the recognition of cultural difference in citizenship practices is one of the most important public policy issues of our time in Canada, as elsewhere (as we see in the French debate over the wearing of the hijab in school or the US debates over bilingual education). The analogy here to heteronormative social organization is that, for LGBT communities, the history of marginalization and the nature of queer difference give rise to distinctive subcultural communities. The recognition of these communities may entail inclusion in public policy formation and public policy itself, but it may also entail policies that are tailored to respecting difference by rolling back the repressive role of the state in regulating queer sexualities.

A long and important thread of literature in queer theory and LGBT politics calls attention to the dangers of inclusion. Inclusion based on assertions of sameness creates "good queers" and "bad queers," a distinction alluded to in Gayle Rubin's good sex, bad sex dichotomy. Those who settle down with partners and children are integrated into Canadian society with the rights and obligations of citizenship, but the "bad queers" who live out sexual freedom through the sexual subcultures of urban life are criminalized. Inclusion in public policy may mean that lesbian and gay organizations are turned into agents of the state's project of investing in responsibilized citizenry for the knowledge economy. LGBT engagement in health policy debates may erase queer sexuality and identity, as Epstein (2003) has argued. Epstein traces the tensions in health policy for gay men between a sex-positive approach that celebrates gay sexuality and a medicalized approach that turns gay men into objects of biomedical expertise and that erases gay male identity from health policy (see also Kinsman 1996).

These debates demonstrate the dangers of the policy process for LGBT communities. Being included – even with a difference – may eventually extinguish queer identity.

Conclusion

To date, most of the literature on sexuality, citizenship, and public policy has focused on the myriad ways in which LGBT people have been excluded from the regime of liberal citizenship; most of the rights struggles of the last twenty years have centred on classic issues of formal legal equality. In the areas of anti-discrimination and human rights legislation and litigation, and the ongoing debates over relationship recognition, adoption, parenting rights, and same-sex marriage, LGBT claims rest on the assertion that LGBT relationships and families are the same as those of straights and that, therefore, LGBT relationships and families should be included in the regime of benefits and obligations that surround straight relationships and families. This chapter has argued that the formal legal equality phase of LGBT political struggles is nearing its end and that the next phase will entail broader demands for the inclusion of LGBT interests and identities across the spectrum of public policy, especially in areas such as education, health care, and social services. This expansion of focus will pose a serious challenge for LGBT organizations, which, reflecting the subcultural nature of the communities, are strongest and best organized at the local (especially urban) level. For this reason, organizational restructuring is to be expected in the LGBT area. Egale has already expanded its advocacy focus beyond discrimination and relationship recognition, has undertaken new policy initiatives on social policy, and has proactively sought to develop and reflect the diversities of LGBT communities through the establishment of caucuses within the organization that represent trans people, First Nations two-spirit people, and people of colour. From a policy-making perspective, it must be recognized that LGBT political interests extend beyond the area of Charter-based human rights. LGBT activism in health care, social policy, housing, and urban issues must be incorporated and recognized in the policy-making process.

Inclusion in the public policy mainstream poses challenges and risks for queer citizens. Just as feminists have negotiated debates over co-optation, so too, queer organizations, activists, and citizens will encounter the challenge of retaining their distinctive identities and interests in the face of new opportunities for participation in policy processes.

REFERENCES

Cases

Egan & Nesbit v. Canada, [1995] 124 D.L.R. (4th) 609 SCC.

Haig v. Canada (1992), 94 D.L.R. (4th) 1.

M. v. H., [1999] S.C.J. No. 23.

Reference re Same-Sex Marriage (2004), SCC 79.

Vriend v. Alberta, [1998] 1 S.C.R. 493.

Secondary Sources

Bashevkin, Sylvia. 1996. "Rethinking Retrenchment: North American Social Policy during the Early Clinton and Chrétien Years." *Canadian Journal of Political Science* 33(1): 7-36.

Boyd, Susan B., and Claire F.L. Young. 2003. "From Same-Sex to No Sex? Trends towards Recognition of (Same-Sex) Relationships in Canada." *Seattle Journal for Social Justice* 1(3): 757-93.

Broad, Kendal L. 2002. "'GLB + T? Gender/Sexuality Movements and Transgender Collective Identity (De)constructions.'" *International Journal of Sexuality and Gender Studies* 7(4): 241-63.

Cohen, Cathy. 1999. *The Boundaries of Blackness: AIDS and the Breakdown of Black Politics.* Chicago: University of Chicago Press.

Cossman, Brenda. 1994. "Family Inside/Out." *University of Toronto Law Journal* 44: 1-39.

—. 2003. "Telling Straight People How to Live." *Xtra*, 1 May. http://www.xtra.ca/site/toronto2/arch/body1381.shtm.

Dobrowolsky, Alexandra. 2000. *The Politics of Pragmatism.* Toronto: Oxford University Press.

Dunfield, Allison. 2003. "MP's Vote to Extend Hate Crime Protection." *Globe and Mail,* 17 September, A3.

Epstein, Steven. 2003. "Sexualizing Governance and Medicalizing Identities: The Emergence of 'State-Centered' LGBT Health Politics in the United States." *Sexualities* 6(2): 131-71.

Findlay, Sue. 1987. "Facing the State: The Politics of the Women's Movement Reconsidered." In *Feminism and Political Economy,* ed. Heather Jon Maroney and Meg Luxton, 31-50. Toronto: Methuen.

Fortier, Isabelle, Éric Montpetit, and Francesca Scala. 2003. "Democratic Practices vs. Expertise: The National Action Committee on the Status of Women and Canada's Policy on Reproductive Technology." Paper presented at the annual meeting of the Canadian Political Science Association, Halifax, 1-3 June.

Fuller, Janine, and Stuart Blackley. 1995. *Restricted Entry: Censorship on Trial.* Vancouver: Press Gang.

Gotell, Lise. 2002. "Queering Law by Same Sex Marriage?" Paper presented at the annual meeting of the Canadian Political Science Association, Toronto, 31 May-1 June.

Griffin, Andrew. 2000. "EGALE Abandons Queer Teens." *Capital Xtra,* 18 February, 7.

Grundy, John. 2003. "The Political Economy of Toronto's LGBT Voluntary and Non Profit Sector." Paper presented at the annual meeting of the Canadian Lesbian and Gay Studies Association, Halifax, 31 May-2 June.

Grundy, John, and Miriam Smith. 2005. "The Politics of Multiscalar Citizenship: The Case of Lesbian and Gay Organizing in Canada." *Citizenship Studies* 9(4): 389-404.

Hannon, Philip. 1999. "Sexual Outlaws or Respectable In-Laws?" *Capital Xtra,* 3 June, 3.

Herman, Didi. 1989. "Are We Family? Lesbian Rights and Women's Liberation." *Osgoode Hall Law Journal* 28(4): 789-815.

Janoff, Douglas Victor. 2005. *Pink Blood: Homophobic Violence in Canada.* Toronto: University of Toronto Press.

Jenson, Jane. 1989. "Paradigms and Political Discourse: Protective Legislation in France and the United States before 1914." *Canadian Journal of Political Science* 22(2): 235-58.

Kinsman, Gary. 1996. "Responsibility as a Strategy of Governance: Regulating People Living with AIDS and Lesbians and Gay Men in Ontario." *Economy and Society* 213(3): 393-409.

Lüttichau, Ingrid. 2004. "'We Are Family': The Regulation of 'Female-Only' Reproduction." *Social and Legal Studies* 13(1): 81-101.

Matas, Robert. 2001. "Vancouver Gays Outraged by Killing." *Globe and Mail,* 19 November, A11.

Namaste, Viviane K. 1996. "Genderbashing: Sexuality, Gender, and the Regulation of Public Space." *Environment and Planning D: Society and Space* 14: 221-40.

Rayside, David. 1988. "Gay Rights and Family Values: The Passage of Bill 7 in Ontario." *Studies in Political Economy* 26 (Summer): 109-47.

—. 2002. "The Politics of Lesbian and Gay Parenting in Canada and the United States." Paper presented at the annual meeting of the Canadian Political Science Association, Toronto, 31 May-1 June.

—. 2003. "Sexual Diversity in Public Schooling in Canada and the United States." Paper presented at the annual meeting of the American Political Science Association, Philadelphia, 28-31 August.

Richardson, Diane. 2000. "Constructing Sexual Citizenship: Theorizing Sexual Rights." *Critical Social Policy* 20(1): 105-35.

Rubin, Gayle. 1984. "Thinking Sex: Notes for a Radical Theory of the Politics of Sexuality." In *Pleasure and Danger: Exploring Female Sexuality,* ed. Carole S. Vance, 267-319. Boston: Routledge and Kegan Paul.

Smith, Anna Marie. 2001. "The Politicization of Marriage in Contemporary American Public Policy: The Defense of Marriage Act and the Personal Responsibility Act." *Citizenship Studies* 5(3): 303-20.

Smith, Miriam. 2004. "Questioning Heteronormativity: Lesbian and Gay Challenges to Educational Practice in British Columbia, Canada." *Social Movement Studies* 3(2): 131-45.

—. 2005a. "Diversity and Identity in the Nonprofit Sector: Lessons from LGBT Organizing in Toronto, Canada." *Social Policy and Administration* 39(5): 463-80.

—. 2005b. "Resisting and Reinforcing Neoliberalism: Lesbian and Gay Organizing at the Federal and Local Levels in Canada." *Policy and Politics* 33(1): 75-93.

Young, Lisa. 2000. *Feminists and Party Politics.* Vancouver: UBC Press.

6
Gender Mainstreaming in the Canadian Context: "One Step Forward and Two Steps Back"

Olena Hankivsky

Recent attention to a "new" strategy of gender mainstreaming (GM) has taken hold both internationally and nationally. This strategy illuminates the significance of gender as a central element of thinking and acting (Vlassov and Moreno 2002) and recognizes its role in power relations and institutions (Woodward 2003). GM assumes that women and men are differentially affected by policies; its overall aim is to integrate such knowledge and concomitant analyses into all dimensions of policy decision making. Specifically, GM requires that from inception all policies should be analyzed for their gendered impact so that they can benefit men and women equally. In focusing on the respective situations, priorities, and needs of both genders, GM is thought to hold much promise for the realization of social justice. Not surprisingly, GM has been described as representing a paradigm shift in policy and practice (Rees 1998).

Although Canada has been recognized as a leader in the advancement of gender equality, serious criticisms can be levelled at this country's approach to GM. To date, few critical examinations of GM in the Canadian context have been undertaken. There is little available analysis to explain why policies and programs continue to show limited and compartmentalized concerns with gender equality. The purpose of this chapter is twofold: to contribute to the understanding of why GM has not realized its potential and in the process, to demonstrate the need for an alternative strategy of diversity mainstreaming. I begin by briefly tracing the development of GM in Canada and examining existing understandings of this strategy. Drawing on Thorgerdur Einarsdóttir's (2003) framework for effective gender mainstreaming, which consists of three interconnected key pillars – institutionalized gender equality machinery, the women's movement, and gender research within academe – I investigate the current shortcomings of GM in the Canadian context. Although the discussion covers issues associated with each pillar, tracing important developments within government machinery and women's movements in Canada, I especially concentrate on the conceptual foundation of GM – feminist theory. I discuss the implications of the dissociation between GM and contemporary feminist theory, that is, the narrow approach to gender equality and a lack of attention to intersecting factors of discrimination and oppression currently informing GM strategies, methodologies, and tools.

In response to these shortcomings, I propose a new direction for mainstreaming which I refer to as diversity mainstreaming. Embedding my approach within an intersectional analysis that seeks to understand and explain multiple, interlocking, and interactive social categories of experience (such as "race"/ethnicity, class, sexuality, ability, and geographic location) in the political context, I argue that diversity mainstreaming is better able to capture, articulate, and make visible the relationships between simultaneously interlocking forms of oppression that include but are not limited to gender. Its potential lies in its capacity to more effectively uncover and respond to complex systems of domination and subordination, privilege and disadvantage. Thus, diversity mainstreaming challenges the unidimensional approach to justice currently grounded within the strategy of GM and provides an improved and effective "policy strategy for change" (Woodward 2003, 65).

The Context for Gender Mainstreaming

In Canada, a number of key historic events and policy developments have created what can be considered an ideal or "enabling" environment for GM. According to Mieke Verloo (2001), Canada is considered one of the first countries internationally to stress the importance of trying to effect change by fully integrating women and their concerns throughout the policy process. The concept of GM took hold and became an international strategy for gender equality at the 1995 World Conference on Women in Beijing, but a brief historic overview demonstrates that GM is in fact not a new strategy, but rather one that has a substantial history.

For example, in 1967, the Royal Commission on the Status of Women was appointed to "inquire into and report upon the status of women in Canada, and to recommend what steps might be taken by the Federal Government to ensure for women equal opportunities with men" (Canada 1967). In 1970, the commission made 167 recommendations aimed at improving the lives of women. A committee that eventually became known as Status of Women Canada (SWC) oversaw implementation of these recommendations. The 1970s also saw the establishment of the Women's Program (1973) to assist women's and other organizations working for gender equality, as well as the Canadian Advisory Council on the Status of Women (1973), which produced research and advised Parliament on issues related to women's equality (SWC 2002). SWC had the responsibility of monitoring Canada's first official strategy of integrating an assessment of federal initiatives and decisions on women in 1976 (ibid.). In 1982, the Canadian Charter of Rights and Freedoms constitutionally entrenched equality rights under Sections 15 and 28. Canada's commitment to gender equality has also been solidified through its ratification of a number of key international human rights agreements, including the 1979 Convention on the Elimination of All Forms of Discrimination against Women (CEDAW) and the 1948 Universal Declaration of Human Rights.

In 1995, in preparation for the Fourth World Conference on Women in Beijing, the Government of Canada, along with twenty-four federal departments and agencies, developed its *Setting the Stage for the Next Century: The Federal Plan for Gender Equality (1995-2000)*, which outlined Canada's commitment to implementing gender-based analysis (GBA) in policies, programs, and legislation. The plan's objectives were to implement GBA throughout federal departments and agencies, improve women's economic autonomy and well-being as well as women's physical and psychological well-being, reduce violence in society, particularly violence against women and children, promote gender equality in all aspects of Canada's cultural life, incorporate women's perspectives in governance, promote and support global gender equality, and advance gender equality for employees of federal departments and agencies. *Setting the Stage* also established procedures to develop and apply tools and methodologies for carrying out and evaluating this work. This includes promoting public understandings of the benefits of equality and engaging citizens in its achievements (SWC 2004a). In 2000, the federal government renewed its commitment to gender equality with the Agenda for Gender Equality (2000-05).

The 1995 Beijing Platform for Action, which was adopted by 189 countries, and the more recent Beijing +5 and +10 reviews, formalized a global plan for promoting gender equality and, in particular, for addressing gender-blind and gender-biased policies. Since Beijing, there has been growing political support for this strategy, more effort has been made to understand this approach, and numerous methodologies and tools have been developed for gender mainstreaming (Verloo 2001). In Canada, federal and provincial governments have adopted policies requiring gender-based analyses, and in most cases have developed accompanying training manuals. The guide most frequently referred to is *Gender-Based Analysis: A Guide for Policy-Making*, produced by the SWC. The guide (SWC 1998, 1) was developed to "increase awareness at all levels of government of the importance of gender as an organizing principle (a way of conceptualizing information; a way of looking at the world)"; it was also designed to "facilitate the development and assessment of policies and legislation from a gender perspective so that they will have intended and equitable results for women and men, girls and boys."

Defining Gender Mainstreaming

Although GM is widely supported in principle, some confusion exists as to what exactly it means. There is no clear consensus concerning its definition or how it should be operationalized. According to the Beijing Platform for Action resolution (*Report of the Fourth World Conference on Women* 1995, c. H, para. 202), for example, "in addressing the issues and mechanisms for promoting the advancement of women, governments and other actors should promote an active and visible policy of mainstreaming a gender perspective in all policies and programmes so that, *before decisions are made*, an analysis is made of the effects on women and men, respectively." The Council of Europe (1998, 15) emphasizes the importance of gender equality in its definition: "Gender mainstreaming is the (re)organization, improvement, development and evaluation of policy processes, so that a gender equality perspective is incorporated in all policies and at all stages, by the actors normally involved in policy making."

In Canada, the terminology of gender-based analysis (GBA), rather than that of GM, has been adopted. According to *Setting the Stage* (SWC 1995), "mainstreaming a gender perspective in all policies and programs so that, before any decisions are taken, an analysis is made of the effects on women and men respectively." SWC's *Gender-Based Analysis* guide (SWC 1998, 4) puts forward the following definition: "Gender-based analysis is a process that assesses the differential impact of proposed and/or existing policies, programs and legislation on women and men. It makes it possible for policy to be undertaken with an appreciation of gender differences, of the nature of relationships between women and men and of their different social realities, life expectations and economic circumstances. It is a tool for understanding social processes and for responding with informed and equitable options."

GM recognizes gender as an essential variable in policy analysis. This requires a solid knowledge of gender trends in society and the collection of information that furthers the understanding of the ways that gender interacts with policy, how policy may reinforce existing power structures based on gender, or how policy may produce gender inequalities. GM is considered a comprehensive approach to equality, one that responds directly to the short-comings of formal equality – the assumption that men and women can be treated equally to ensure equality of results for both genders (Rankin and Vickers 2001, 29). Instead, GM prioritizes substantive equality, which requires the accommodation of differences and the consideration of how gender burdens and benefits are shaped by policy. Accordingly, it does recognize that to overcome past and persistent inequities, women-specific policies and programs may be required. In so doing, it rejects the traditional "one size fits all" approach to equality.

GM also seeks to reorient the nature of the mainstream by reorganizing all stages of policy. Untested assumptions about gender are challenged because each step of the policy process, including development, implementation, monitoring, and evaluation, is subject to an explicit gender analysis. Questions that inform such an analysis vary but may include the following: Are the differences in the contexts of the lives of men and women, boys and girls addressed? What attempts have already been made to remedy the issue or problem? What were some of the outcomes of these attempts? Who controls the decision-making processes and resources related to this policy/ program? Are intended and unintended outcomes (both short and long term) identified? How will the outcome of this policy or program be evaluated? What changes should be made in the policy or program to make it more responsive to the needs of diverse groups of men and women (Health Canada et al. 2003; SWC 2004b)? An essential component of this work, and indeed of any good GBA, is having appropriate information and research data derived from gender auditing or proofing of policies, gender-disaggregated statistics, gender budgets, gender indicators, gender training, and gender-impact assessments. In sum, GBA is intended to ensure not only gender equity but also accountable, effective, and efficient policies.

Success to Date

Internationally, the introduction of GM has been embraced by a wide range of countries with varying policy machineries. As a formal government strategy, it has without doubt produced new knowledge about gender and gender relations and how these intersect with public policy. For example, in Canada, an impressive body of knowledge is being created by Statistics Canada, the

Policy Research Fund at SWC, the Bureau of Women's Health and Gender Analysis at Health Canada, Indian and Northern Affairs, Citizenship and Immigration, and the Canadian International Development Agency. It has also been recognized that GBA constitutes an effective use of public monies because it enables policy to more accurately reflect the lives of women and men (Greaves et al. 1999; Williams 2000).

However, GM is also an extremely demanding strategy (Bretherton 2001); this is indicated by the fact that its overall impact has been uneven in Canada as well as in other jurisdictions. The differing socio-economic circumstances of women and men are not consistently considered in government policy-making processes, and an assumption is still often held that as long as both genders are treated equally, a policy has achieved its desired outcome (Dwyer-Renaud 2000). In fact, despite the historic attention to gender, gender neutrality – treating women and men as interchangeable – has characterized much of Canadian public policy (Burt 1995). For example, in the mid-1990s, referring to the publication record of the journal *Canadian Public Policy*, Sandra Burt (1995, 361-62) demonstrated the absence of gender-based analysis in the field of policy. Between 1975 and 1993, the journal published 509 articles: of these, only 6 were concerned with narrowly defined women's issues; in other articles, issues which had gendered dimensions were not subject to any kind of gender analysis.

In addition, since the introduction of GBA, Canada has in fact witnessed a shift away from women's equality to a concern for the needs of children in many areas of social policy (Burt and Hardman 2001). And even when GBA is integrated in some areas of policy, it is rarely applied in a systematic fashion to include, for example, economic and technology policies (Rankin and Vickers 2001), trade policies (Hankivsky et al. 2004), or foreign policy (Standing Committee on the Status of Women 2005f). As Verloo (2001, 5-6) correctly observes about Canada, "the integration of gender mainstreaming in general policies has been hindered by a lack of political will and bureaucratic indifference if not hostility." Recently, Liza Frulla (Standing Committee on the Status of Women 2004f, 2), the former minister responsible for SWC, similarly acknowledged that "there remains the urgent need to continue to mainstream gender in all areas of the government through programs, services, and legislation."

Kathleen Lahey (2002, 10) is therefore right to caution that "those who are concerned with the status of women ... should be aware ... that a simple commitment to gender mainstreaming will not, by itself, generate change."

Indeed, government departments at all levels are criticized for not reflecting women's realities and experiences (SWC 2002, 29). So, despite Canada's international reputation for its work on gender equality and specifically GBA, what occurs at the level of domestic policy making has not been transformative (Standing Committee on the Status of Women 2005e). Not surprisingly, in 2005, the Standing Committee on the Status of Women (2005f, 31) concluded that despite ten years of effort, "GBA is still not being systematically incorporated into policy-making in all government departments."

One way to understand why there has been so little progress in engendering policy is to investigate the three key interrelated pillars of GM: the institutionalized gender equality policy machinery, the women's movement, and gender research. According to Einarsdóttir (2003, 2), it is essential to "investigate the configuration of the three pillars and their interaction," as these are key to the project of gender equality and, by extension, GM. These pillars constitute an important analytic framework from which to reveal the problems with GBA in Canada and to signal the need for an expanded strategy of diversity mainstreaming.

National Gender Equality Machinery

It has been noted (SWC 2002, 2) that an "enabling environment" for GBA includes "a national machinery with a clearly defined role, mechanisms to support gender equality with other government departments, intergovernmental collaborative mechanisms, and mechanisms for information exchange and collaboration among federal, provincial and territorial governments." Without this first pillar, governments would lack the necessary infrastructure to follow through on their commitments of gender mainstreaming throughout the policy process.

Status of Women Canada, through its Gender-Based Analysis Directorate established in 1999, is the department that oversees the implementation and evaluation of GBA in Canada. Along with a number of key departments which participate in an Interdepartmental Committee on Gender-Based Analysis headed by the directorate,[1] SWC represents the key gender equality policy machinery in Canada. The cornerstone of SWC's approach to GBA is a six-point strategy consisting of training; tool development; policy case studies; research, information, and education promotion; evaluation and accountability; and coordination. In addition, it is worth noting that a number of provinces and territories have also committed to the implementation of GBA, and in some instances, dedicate government personnel to this initiative.

Although femocrats claim that they can effectively use GBA inside government (Williams 2000), the reality is that GM remains in the hands of specialized divisions rather than being present and central in all divisions of government – an essential requirement of effective GM (Dwyer-Renaud 2000, 23). The inadequacy of giving a single department so much responsibility for GM is evidenced by the experiences of SWC. According to the Standing Committee on the Status of Women (2005f), SWC has an international reputation for its "ground-breaking, leading-edge work," especially in terms of training and tool development. However, these international perceptions are not borne out by effective implementation of GBA in Canada.

To begin, SWC has never been particularly effective within government. It has been under-resourced, understaffed, and marginalized because of its peripheral location. As Sandra Burt and Sonya L. Hardman (2001, 213) explain, "from its inception, Status of Women has had internal, organizational problems, as well as the problems of visibility and effectiveness characteristic of all horizontal departments." In addition, SWC itself has acknowledged the difficulties of trying to implement GM across so many varied government departments: "because of the number or complexity of policy issues associated with gender equality, SWC must react to the full spectrum of new and changing issues on the government's economic, legal and social agenda. The fact that responsibility for policies that affect women is shared by a large number of federal departments, therefore, presents special challenges" (SWC 2002, 28). Moreover, as SWC is not centrally located vis-à-vis government planning and coordination, it clearly does not have the power to effect policy in any meaningful way. According to SWC (ibid.) itself, though the department "can and does influence other departments, it seldom possesses the direct authority to lead policy development." A good example of its lack of influence appeared most recently in trade policy-making processes. In this policy context, SWC "is not seen as an important voice within trade negotiations" (Hassanali 2000, 10). In general, other departments do not always recognize or take the responsibility to see the gender aspects of their policy areas.

Especially challenging is that, over the last decade, SWC has had to pursue the GBA strategy within a policy environment characterized by significant political, economic, and social restructuring and downsizing resulting from the proliferation of neo-liberalism and economic globalization. In the current environment, shifts from state responsibility for social justice to market-based individualistic solutions have forced women's machineries to focus on ensuring "least worst outcomes" (IDRC 2003) rather than on progressing forward in terms of gender equality. In this kind of market-oriented policy context, "the low priority accorded to gender issues ... demonstrates that obligations to mainstream gender equality will not be permitted to obstruct the real mainstream" (Bretherton 2001, 75).

Consequently, recommendations for improving mainstreaming efforts are being put forward. These include ensuring adequate resources, both human and financial, for gender equality initiatives (Standing Committee on the Status of Women 2005c), strengthening institutional infrastructures, and developing increased capacity for undertaking such policy work. It has also been argued that the responsibility for and ownership of GM need to be more widely shared, especially across central government agencies, and that the horizontal coordination of government actions requires improvement (Standing Committee on the Status of Women 2005a). If this does not occur, it is easy for policy analysts to simply say, "We don't have to worry about that. That's someone else's job" (Standing Committee on the Status of Women 2005b, 26). Moreover, legislative mechanisms, such as the Immigration and Refugee Protection Act, which obligates the Department of Citizenship and Immigration to report its application of GBA to Parliament, are considered effective accountability mechanisms that should be more widely adopted. Sanctions for non-compliance have also been suggested (Rankin and Vickers 2001). Also worth highlighting is the Justice Canada (Standing Committee on the Status of Women 2005d, 10) position that though formal evaluations of GBA are essential, it is equally important "to determine what constitutes a success in terms of doing a diversity analysis in gender analysis."

Finally, as the president of the Newfoundland and Labrador Provincial Advisory Council on the Status of Women noted a short time ago (Standing Committee on the Status of Women 2004e, 8), "we need a sustained presence of equality-seeking women's organizations in communities and regions if we are to move forward on equality. We need respect for the experiences and analysis of grassroots women and organizations, and we need resourcing for the work we do." Indeed, it is essential to consider how government currently interacts and consults with organizations in the Canadian women's movement, especially because many women's NGOs "don't even know what GBA is" (Standing Committee on the Status of Women 2005e, 19).

Canadian Women's Movement

The second wave of the women's movement is thought to have been the key mobilizing force behind the establishment of equality policy machinery and gender research within academia (Einarsdóttir 2003). Indeed, because "women's movements have, through many decades, repeatedly put high pressure on state agents and international agencies, such as the UN, to bring gender equality issues forward" (ibid., 3), they are considered an essential pillar in GM. In the Canadian context, the women's movements have played an important role in shaping the machinery that is in place to promote women's interests and gender equality (Andrew 1984; Rankin and Vickers 2004). Consultations on policy issues with women's organizations are seen as key to shaping GBA policies and strategies (SWC 2002).

Currently, Canada has over fifteen hundred formal women's organizations. Status of Women Canada (2002, 21) maintains that this network "plays a significant role in progress toward gender equality." Specifically, it asserts that these organizations "contribute to setting local, regional and national agendas for gender equality" and that "SWC's network of regional representatives maintains regular contact with equality seeking organizations across the country" (ibid.). Despite these claims, consultative processes between women's movements and the state are fraught (Rankin and Vickers 2004). Historically and currently, women's groups and equality-seeking organizations have, and should continue to have, an important role to play in terms of driving forward a gender equality and gender research agenda. Because these groups are outside the political establishment, they are able to maintain clarity of analysis when it comes to promoting transformational goals vis-à-vis women's lives. However, as Pauline L. Rankin and Jill Vickers (2004, 45) note, "although women's movements in Canada were generally willing to engage with state institutions for the two decades after 1970, the negative experiences many report in recent years are leading some to refocus their attention away from official politics." Concerns are growing regarding the co-optation of femocrats into government agendas and the consequent loss of their ability to speak with a feminist voice (Burt and Hardman 2001).

In general, certain organizations within the women's movement in Canada have lost their momentum. Contributing factors include the backlash against feminism, divisive internal politics, and significantly, radical state funding cuts to front-line and advocacy NGOs. For instance, the National Action Committee on the Status of Women (NAC), founded in 1972 and representing over five hundred organizations nationally, has almost dissolved during the last decade. This "premier, mass-based feminist organization" (Carlyle 2002, 14), which has played a key role in women's rights and equality in Canada, has been troubled by its own internal struggles. As Rankin and

Vickers (2004, 48) explain, "important efforts to deal with critical, complex issues such as racism, ableism and homophobia within feminist institutions such as NAC, unfortunately, resulted in diminished solidarity."

Moreover, government funding cuts during the last decade have literally devastated NAC. Its confrontational stances regarding Meech Lake, the Charlottetown Accord, free trade, and other policies (Bashevkin 1989; Rebick 1999) have cost the organization political support and funding. As Elizabeth Carlyle (2002, 14) reports, Liberals on Parliament Hill have "openly mocked NAC, denied most funding requests, sent backbenchers to NAC lobby sessions and aggressively defamed the organization in public." The overall lack of funding has resulted in a shoestring operation with a barely operational website, no paid staff, no office, and little political credibility. Consequently, the absence of a general national feminist umbrella organization has left a vacuum in terms of a well-structured driving force for gender equality in Canada.

Quebec is something of an exception to this trend of decline: there, the women's movement has always been distinct and women's organizations, most notably the Fédération des femmes du Québec (FFQ), have gone through a regeneration process, though even these bodies are demanding more provincial funding for ethnocultural and racial women's groups. Throughout English Canada, however, federal government cuts, not limited solely to NAC, have especially undermined the ability of women's non-governmental organizations to participate effectively in the democratic process. In particular, funding criteria for SWC's Women's Program were changed in 1998; the impact on women's organizations, and movements more generally, have been profound. Instead of providing core funding for operations, SWC now funds only project-based initiatives. As a result, many equality-seeking women's groups have ceased to exist. This has led some activists, such as the interim president of NAC, to argue that "What is a fact for many women's groups is that Status of Women Canada has increased the state of women's inequality" (Standing Committee on the Status of Women 2004h, 14).

Aboriginal women's organizations, including the Métis National Council of Women, Pauktuutit Inuit Women's Association, Quebec Native Women, and the Native Women's Association of Canada, criticize SWC for being discriminatory and excluding them from "capacity-building processes and policy development and implementation on an equal basis" (Standing Committee on the Status of Women 2004g, 10). During her testimony to the Standing Committee on the Status of Women, Jennifer Dickson, executive director,

Pauktuutit Inuit Women's Association remarked "if you think of Status of Women Canada as some place for women in Canada to take their status issues to, it ain't the place to go" (Standing Committee on the Status of Women 2004d, 29). It is also worth noting that, with the exception of Quebec Native Women, women's organizations from Quebec were absent from consultations undertaken by the Standing Committee.

In sum, the significance of the changes to Canadian women's movements cannot be underestimated. According to Einarsdóttir (2003), ambitious projects to change all policies, as is the case of GM, require participation and pressure from an *all-inclusive women's movement*. Although it is problematic to assume a unitary, all-inclusive women's movement, it is true that participation by a range of representative civil society groups and actors is needed in the policy process. And though present circumstances may force women's groups across the country to become more educated about public policy (Standing Committee on the Status of Women 2005e), the fact that they are losing their strength and influence, and are becoming less willing and able to consult effectively with governments to share emerging issues and concerns of Canadian women is problematic. A strong mobilizing network, one which can articulate the diversity of women's voices nationally, is required to further the project of social justice and gender equality. This type of work cannot be done in government silos without connecting with women at the grassroots (Standing Committee on the Status of Women 2004h, 25). As Lahey (2002) argues, gender-based analysis cannot improve the overall conditions of women without the direct involvement of women in the analysis.

However, it is not enough simply to think through strategies to improve the funding and political participation of women's movements: the adequacy and effectiveness of current Canadian GBA approaches need to be seriously contemplated. Burt and Hardman (2001, 209) have made similar observations by arguing that "policy-makers need to articulate their vision of equality. Equality is a highly contested concept that could be so extensive as to include reforms in child care provisions and family law, or limited to improving opportunities for women to compete for jobs in the public sphere." In fact, the problems go beyond disagreements regarding definitions and extend to the very theoretical foundation upon which GM is based.

Feminist Research and Feminist Theory
The third and arguably least-investigated pillar of GM is that of feminist research. GM was developed within feminism, in particular, within feminist

theory. As Gemma Carney (2004, 15) argues, "at a broad political level, [feminist theory] provides normative theoretical arguments on which the *raison d'être* of gender mainstreaming rests." To be effective and reach its transformational potential, GM should be "anchored in a sophisticated theoretical understanding of gender relations" (Woodward 2001, 19). Similarly, Lahey (2002, 10) has asserted that "the administrative incorporation of gender-based analysis into ongoing policy-making will have to be grounded in the best of women's studies and legal theory, research and training techniques."

Feminist scholars have made important contributions in terms of raising the issue of gender in public policy analysis (see, for example, Bacchi 1999; Mazur 2002; Vickers 1997). In the Canadian context, the gendered effects of policies, and more recently restructuring and dismantling of the welfare state, have been interrogated (Bakker 1996; Bashevkin 1989, 2002; Brodie 1996; Burt 1995; Morrow, Hankivsky, and Varcoe 2004). Susan Phillips (in Rankin and Vickers 2001, 28-29) has effectively outlined the three key contributions that feminists make to policy studies: first, they expose the ways in which gender relations have been institutionalized and made normative within traditional approaches to policy making; second, they problematize issues of identity by deconstructing the category of "women"; and third, they challenge objective knowledge claims of policy makers and encourage alternative epistemological approaches. In *Women, Policy and Politics* (1999), Carol Bacchi recommends that, when analyzing policies, we ask the question "What's the problem?" so as to interrogate how and why certain issues are accepted, or alternatively, overlooked as policy problems. It is in this spirit of reflecting on the assumptions and perspectives informing policy that GBA has developed within Canada.

The problem, however, is that the concepts of gender and gender analysis currently in use are grounded in liberal feminist thinking and are not at all congruent with contemporary feminist theorizing about differences. They are especially unable to address what is required for inclusivity and sensitivity to the diversity and plurality of lived experiences. Most GBA approaches focus on integrating "women" into policies, draw on simplistic divisions between men and women, and perpetuate the assumption that gender is the primary axis through which inequality and discrimination are experienced. In a word, GM as currently conceptualized, both in Canada and abroad, reflects an overly simplistic approach to gender, one that is largely essentialist and which wrongly suggests that gender issues are relatively tractable rather than intractable (Shaw 2001). At present, GM is woefully undertheorized.

Consequently, its operationalization in the realm of policy can lead to mixed or poor results only.

For instance, the GBA guide produced by SWC (1998, 14) offers weak directives: its analytical tools for understanding women's diversity consist of considering how the experiences of women and men will differ geographically and are influenced by poverty, colour, Aboriginal ancestry, and disability/ability. Health Canada's *Gender-Based Analysis Policy* (2003) states that the GBA framework should be "overlaid" with a diversity analysis. Although *CIDA's Policy on Gender Equality* (CIDA 1999, 17) does contend that the use of gender analysis provides information on "the difference among women and men and the diversity of their circumstances, social relationships, and consequent states" (for example, their class, race, caste, ethnicity, age, culture, and abilities), it does not adequately incorporate these considerations into its implementation strategies. And though the *Gender Equality Analysis Policy* of Indian and Northern Affairs Canada (1999, 6) emphasizes the importance of considering diversity, it lists diversity as a factor "in addition to gender."

These policies and guides do acknowledge difference and diversity, but their standard approach treats differences as a kind of "add-on characteristics of some women" (Agnew 2003, 17). This type of method is ineffective because it essentially prioritizes gender while relegating other factors such as race, class, ability, and sexuality to a secondary status. As Katherine Teghtsoonian (1999, 5) argues, "despite drawing attention to the specific circumstances of multiply marginalized women, the focus in these documents tends to remain on gender-in-general." Moreover, even when differences are recognized, they are essentialized. Thus, according to Rankin and Vickers (2001, v), "women who do not belong to the dominant culture, or who are different because of their race, sexual orientation or disability, continue to confront marginalization in the policy-making process and require different strategies to integrate their agendas into the public policy process."

Moreover, the current approach to GBA in Canada is not consistent with present-day feminist theorizing which has demonstrated the complexities of intersecting forms of discrimination and privilege, and shown how these affect the ways in which gender and equality should be understood. To better understand the disassociation between contemporary theorizing and current practices of GM, it is useful to consider the way in which feminist theorizing in regard to gender and equality has evolved. The category of gender was introduced in reaction to the category of sex and traditional theoretical tendencies to define women's nature through biological sex (Young 1990).

Feminists have rejected such framing on the basis that there is nothing about being female that naturally binds women (Haraway 1991). More recently, the assumptions of the foundational category of gender have been interrogated. In particular, postmodern feminism has done much to challenge foundationalist and essentialist assumptions in theory (Butler 1990; Fraser and Nicholson 1990). Feminist theorists have critiqued the reductionist nature of gender and the lack of recognition for differences of race, class, culture, religion, nationality, ableness, and sexuality (Spelman 1988). Without doubt, most constructs and conceptualizations of gender privilege a universal model of women who are portrayed as middle-class, heterosexual, and able-bodied.

Other important critiques of the primacy, universalism, and colonialism of Western feminist theory have been articulated by post-colonial theorists, particularly around the implications such approaches have had for understanding diversity and for discursive constructs of "Third World women" (Mohanty 1997; Yuval-Davis 1997).

Examinations of the consequences of the intersection of two or more forms of discrimination or systems of discrimination have been undertaken, with the work of Audre Lorde (1994), Patricia Hill Collins (1990), and Kimberle Crenshaw (1991, 2000) at the forefront of these efforts. This focus has been invaluable for revealing how systems of discrimination or subordination overlap and create complex intersections (Hannan 2001), and for clarifying, as Stuart Hall explains, how they "articulate" with one another (quoted in Slack 1996). And of course, the focus on difference (Young 1990) and issues of redistribution/recognition (Fraser 1997) has further complicated the discourse around gender equality. In fact, it has been argued that difference has supplanted equality as the central concern of feminists (Fox-Genovese in Arneil 1999).

What all these recent developments have in common is that they seriously question the usefulness and adequacy of focusing on gender as the primary axis for understanding inequalities and oppression. That is, contemporary feminist theorizing has moved beyond the conceptual understanding of gender and gender equality that informs GM frameworks. Of course, this raises the key issue of whether GM should be replaced by a framework that would effectively capture differences and diversity stemming from race, class, sexuality, and ability, *as well as* gender. As Vijay Agnew (2003, 2) observes, "diversity in feminist conceptualizations (and theories) of gender, identity, location, epistemology, and discourse has opened up the debate in interpretation and application." Without doubt, it is important to acknowledge that putting gender theory to practical application is not easy. However, most feminist theorizing has been motivated by the quest for social change and social justice (Haslanger and Tuana 2003). Given this, the most comprehensive, inclusive, and up-to-date theorizing should be used in practical applications of GM.

Diversity Mainstreaming

Both women's organizations and academics have questioned whether existing GBA and its tools adequately meet the needs of Canada's diverse populations of visible minorities, women with disabilities, and Aboriginal and Métis women (Kartini International 2001), or indeed those populations with complex identities that cross such categorical constructs. During consultation with the Standing Committee on the Status of Women, the National Organization of Immigrant and Visible Minority Women called for both a gender lens and a racial-ethnic lens (Standing Committee on the Status of Women 2004a, 40); a number of different Aboriginal women's organizations called for "culturally based gender analysis" (Standing Committee on the Status of Women 2004c, 36). In response, one of the committee members stated, "what we are asking departments to do is not culturally based. It's just male and female" (Standing Committee on the Status of Women 2004b, 36). This underscores the disconnect between the intersectional approach that is prioritized by women of colour and Aboriginal women and the unidimensional understanding of gender and equality reflected in government policy and GBA in particular.

Moreover, as I have argued elsewhere (Hankivsky 2005, 978), "if we take seriously the need to apply the insights of recent feminist theorizing, it becomes clear that there are in fact no real possibilities to adequately improve or expand the gender mainstreaming framework." What is in fact required is a diversity mainstreaming framework that prioritizes intersectionalities, that is, the various forms of oppression that include but are not limited to gender (ibid.). In other words, current GM frameworks, with their constrictive nature, need to be replaced by an alternative which challenges hegemonic conceptualizations of gender and ensures a better link between intellectual and practical work.

Diversity mainstreaming does not reject the category of gender, but rather displaces it as *the* primary axis for understanding discrimination, inequality, and oppression. This creates a more sophisticated and comprehensive approach to understanding the lived experience of all women and men, especially those who have been and continue to be marginalized by current perspectives and practices of GM. Because it is informed by the concept of "intersectionality," diversity mainstreaming begins with the premise that "the combination of various oppressions ... produce something unique and distinct from any one form of discrimination standing alone" (Eaton 1994, 229). It seeks to go beyond singular categories to capture multiple grounds of discrimination so that power and privilege, and intersecting domains of inclusion, exclusion, and inequality, are better understood. For instance, this form of analysis has the capacity to "address the manner in which racism, patriarchy, class oppression and other discriminatory systems create inequalities that structure the relative positions of women, races, ethnicities, classes" (CWGL 2004).

Accordingly, diversity mainstreaming challenges the monocultural approaches of liberal neutrality, as reflected in the works of John Rawls (1971), Brian Barry (2001), and Chandran Kukathas (1998), which fail to capture adequately the distribution of goods and services on the grounds of identity-based differences. It also goes deeper than standard accounts of liberal pluralism, such as William A. Galston (2002); Joseph H. Carens (2000); Will Kymlicka (1989, 1995, 1997, 2001); Charles Taylor (1994, 1998, 1999); Joseph Raz (1994); and Jeff Spinner (1994). Although diversity mainstreaming is similar to liberal pluralism in its focus on accommodating diverse groups and individuals, it differs in a number of significant ways. First, it rejects notions of unitary subjects, choosing instead to see identities as socially constructed and consisting of multiple intersecting categories of experience, which are changeable and fluid. Second, it holds that attention to diversity does not equate with simply inserting various axes of "race," ethnicity, ability, sexuality, class, geographic location, and so on into considerations of gender. Put simply, diversity mainstreaming does not take an additive approach to various categories of experience, but rather sees them as "interlocking, interactive, and relational" (Mullings 2002). It requires an analytic framework that promotes a relational understanding of such multiple and mutually constitutive forces. That is, diversity mainstreaming allows for the linkages between group experiences to be highlighted and systems of power in creating structural inequalities to be revealed and interrogated. In employing this distinct approach, we can better understand that, despite liberal pluralist demands that different groups should have "different influence in public life according to the degree that they are impacted upon by a particular issue," "not all interests in society are in an equal position to assert themselves" (Vincent 2003, 6). Diversity mainstreaming's explicit attention to power therefore has the potential to provide direction regarding what approaches and tools are needed for the "mainstream" to be transformed, not simply influenced by those who seek social justice in the realm of public policy.

Not everyone is convinced that GBA in the Canadian context should be displaced by diversity mainstreaming. For example, Rankin (Standing Committee on the Status of Women 2005e, 29) asserts, "some people would argue that the move to gender analysis has homogenized things – you know, women versus men, so women are just a single category. My concern is that if we ... pile on all those other kinds of differences into one lens, we lose a lot of the precision of policy that might come from separating out those differences." Arguably, however, this is exactly what diversity mainstreaming challenges – the idea that differences *can* be separated out. Moreover, it refutes the erroneous assumption embedded in such an argument, that gender should remain the most important category of analysis. Without doubt, as long as GBA is used, the hegemony of gender will not be displaced and "the unique vulnerability of differently socially constructed groups of women and men will remain obscured" (Hankivsky 2005, 979). GBA, as an extrapolation of white, middle-class, heterosexual women, simply fails to illuminate the unique quality of women's as well as men's lives, or to address their problems in the context of policy. Thus, GBA cannot succeed in challenging the status quo because it "valorize[s] the very centre that is problematic to begin with" (Benhabib 1996, 44).

In comparison, the more comprehensive approach offered by diversity mainstreaming would have considerable transformative implications in all areas of policy, but in particular, in relation to issues such as HIV/AIDS, maternal and child mortality, reproduction, marriage and family, aging, interpersonal violence and trafficking, education, immigration, criminal justice, and labour/employment, all of which require an intersectional analysis to capture fully the diverse experiences of women, who cannot be statically categorized (Crenshaw 2000; DAW, OHCHR, and UNIFEM 2000; Hankivsky 2005). In the final analysis, diversity mainstreaming would operationalize the theoretical conception of intersectionality, providing what Rita Dhamoon has described as a "roadmap for policy with normative concerns for social justice" (quoted in Hankivsky 2005). In so doing, it brings to the foreground of policy analysis the necessary questions, information, data, and contextual considerations that are essential for understanding and responding to all the contours of systemic domination and discrimination, not just those attributable to a rigid category of gender.

Future Challenges

If mainstreaming is to succeed, that is, if it is to realize its potential for promoting social justice in the realm of public policy, a number of key issues will need to be addressed in relation to the essential pillars discussed in this chapter. First, mainstreaming strategies must become central to all government decision making and not remain the primary responsibility of SWC. Second, through funding and ensuring meaningful involvement, efforts should be made to re-energize the civil society participation of the Canadian women's movement, including the wide range of community-based and equity-seeking organizations. Most importantly, however, policy makers must have a much more sophisticated and nuanced approach to understanding inequality, oppression, and subordination. The ability to work in a diversity-inclusive fashion is necessary for disrupting the status quo, introducing new policy ideas, and effectively moving toward social justice. Unless the current GM approach, with its near-exclusive focus on equality between the sexes and its inadequate consideration of the intersecting factors of discrimination and oppression, is replaced by diversity mainstreaming, the future of mainstreaming as an effective policy tool will remain uncertain, and the skepticism and apprehension regarding this approach will persist.

NOTE

1 As of June 2005, the committee included representatives from Health Canada, Indian and Northern Affairs Canada, Canadian International Development Agency, Citizenship and Immigration Canada, Agriculture and Agri-food Canada, National Defence, Canadian Heritage, Canadian Mortgage and Housing Corporation, Statistics Canada, Privy Council Office, Finance Canada, and Social Development Canada and Human Resources and Skills Development Canada; the latter two are formally known as Human Resources Development Canada.

REFERENCES

Agnew, Vijay. 2003. "Gender and Diversity: A Discussion Paper." Status of Women Canada. Paper presented at Intersections of Diversity: Developing New Approaches to Policy and Research, Toronto.

Andrew, Caroline. 1984. "Women and the Welfare State." *Canadian Journal of Political Science* 17: 667-83.

Arneil, Barbara. 1999. *Politics and Feminism*. Oxford: Blackwell Publishers.

Bacchi, Carol. 1999. *Women, Policy and Politics: The Construction of Policy Problems*. London: Sage Publications.

Bakker, Isabella, ed. 1996. *Rethinking Restructuring: Gender and Change in Canada*. Toronto: University of Toronto Press.

Barry, Brian. 2001. *Culture and Equality: An Egalitarian Critique of Multiculturalism*. Cambridge, MA: Harvard University Press.

Bashevkin, Sylvia. 1989. "Free Trade and Canadian Feminism: The Case of the NAC." *Canadian Public Policy* 15(4): 363-75.

—. 2002. *Welfare Hot Buttons*. Toronto: University of Toronto Press.

Benhabib, Seyla. 1996. *Democracy and Difference: Contesting the Boundaries of the Political*. Princeton: Princeton University Press.

Bretherton, Charlotte. 2001. "Gender Mainstreaming and EU Enlargement: Swimming against the Tide?" *Journal of European Public Policy* 8(1): 60-81.

Brodie, Janine. 1996. *Women and Canadian Public Policy*. Toronto: Harcourt.

Burt, Sandra. 1995. "The Several Worlds of Policy Analysis: Traditional Approaches and Feminist Critiques." In *Changing Methods: Feminists Transforming Practice*, ed. Sandra Burt and Lorraine Code, 357-78. Toronto: Broadview Press.

Burt, Sandra, and Sonya L. Hardman. 2001. "The Case of Disappearing Targets: The Liberals and Gender Equality." In *How Ottawa Spends*, ed. Leslie A. Pal, 201-22. Don Mills: Oxford University Press.

Butler, Judith. 1990. *Gender Trouble*. London: Routledge.

Canada. Royal Commission on the Status of Women in Canada. 1967. Briefs to the Royal Commission on the Status of Women in Canada. Toronto: Micromedia Ltd. http://www.library.utoronto.ca/robarts/microtext/collection/pages/carylcos.html.

Carens, Joseph H. 2000. *Culture, Citizenship and Community: A Contextual Exploration of Justice as Evenhandedness*. New York: Oxford University Press.

Carlyle, Elizabeth. 2002. "NAC Attack: As Canada's Premier, Mass-Based Feminist Organization, the National Action Committee on the Status of Women, Fights for Its Life." *Canadian Dimension* 36(1): 14-16.

Carney, Gemma. 2004. "Researching Gender Mainstreaming: A Challenge for Feminist IR." Paper presented at the International Studies Association annual conference, Montreal, 17-20 March.

CIDA (Canadian International Development Agency). 1999. *CIDA's Policy on Gender Equality*. Hull, QC: Minister of Public Works and Government Services Canada.

Collins, Patricia Hill. 1990. *Black Feminist Thought: Knowledge, Consciousness, and the Politics of Empowerment*. New York: Routledge.

Council of Europe. 1998. *Gender Mainstreaming: Conceptual Framework, Methodology and Presentation of Good Practices.* Final Report of Activities of the Group of Specialists on Mainstreaming EG-S-MS. Strasbourg: Council of Europe.

Crenshaw, Kimberle. 1991. "Mapping the Margins: Intersectionality, Identity Politics, and Violence against Women of Color." *Stanford Law Review* 43(6): 1241-99.

—. 2000. *Background Paper for the Expert Meeting on Gender-Related Aspects of Race Discrimination.* Zagreb: Croatia.

CWGL (Center for Women's Global Leadership). 2004. *Background Briefing on Intersectionality.* Working Group on Women and Human Rights. http://www.cwgl. rutgers.edu/globalcenter/policy/bkgdbrfintersec.html.

DAW, OHCHR, and UNIFEM (United Nations Division for the Advancement of Women, Office of the High Commissioner for Human Rights, and United Nations Development Fund for Women). 2000. *Gender and Racial Discrimination: Report of the Expert Group Meeting. 21-24 November 2000.* http://www.un.org/womenwatch/daw/ csw/genrac/report.htm.

Dwyer-Renaud, Hélène. 2000. "Policy Making and Gender-Based Analysis: Tailoring a World for Both Men and Women." In *Made to Measure: Women, Gender and Equity.* Vol. 3, ed. Carol Amaratunga, 21-23. Halifax: Maritime Centre of Excellence for Women's Health.

Eaton, Mary. 1994. "Patently Confused, Complex Inequality and *Canada v. Mossop* (1994)." *Review of Constitutional Studies* 1: 203-45.

Einarsdóttir, Thorgerdur. 2003. "Challenging the Slow Motion of Gender Equality – The Case of Iceland." Paper presented at the fifth European Feminist Research Conference, Lund University, Sweden, 20-24 August.

Fraser, Nancy. 1997. *Justice Interruptus: Critical Reflections on the "Postsocialist" Condition.* London: Routledge.

Fraser, Nancy, and Linda Nicholson. 1990. "Social Criticism without Philosophy: An Encounter between Feminism and Postmodernism." In *Feminism/Postmodernism,* ed. L. Nicholson, 19-38. London: Routledge.

Galston, William A. 2002. *Liberal Pluralism: The Implications of Value Pluralism for Political Theory and Practice.* Cambridge: Cambridge University Press.

Greaves, Lorraine, Olena Hankivsky, Carol Amaratunga, Penny Ballem, Donna Chow, Marie De Koninck, Karen Grant, Abby Lippman, Heather Maclean, Janet Maher, Karen Messing, and Bilkis Vissandjée. 1999. *CIHR 2000: Sex, Gender and Women's Health.* Vancouver: British Columbia Centre of Excellence for Women's Health.

Hankivsky, Olena. 2005. "Gender vs. Diversity Mainstreaming: A Preliminary Examination of the Role and Transformative Potential of Feminist Theory." *Canadian Journal of Political Science* 38(4): 977-1001.

Hankivsky, Olena, and Marina Morrow, with Pat Armstrong, Lindsey Galvin, and Holly Grinvalds. 2004. *Trade Agreements, Home Care and Women's Health.* Status

of Women Policy Research. http://www.swc-cfc.gc.ca/pubs/pubspr/0662360565/
index_e.html.

Hannan, Carolyn. 2001. "Gender Mainstreaming – A Strategy for Promoting Gender
Equality: With Particular Focus on HIV/AIDS and Racism." Paper presented at the
NGO Consultation in preparation for the forty-fifth session of the Commission
on the Status of Women, NYU Medical Centre, New York, 6-16 March.

Haraway, Donna D., ed. 1991. *Simians, Cyborgs, and Women: The Reinvention of Nature.*
London: Routledge.

Haslanger, Sally, and Nancy Tuana. 2003. *Topics in Feminism (SEP).* http://
plato.stanford.edu/entries/feminism-topics/.

Hassanali, Soraya. 2000. *International Trade: Putting Gender into the Process. Initiatives
and Lessons Learned.* Ottawa: Status of Women Canada.

Health Canada. 2003. http://www.hc-sc.gc.ca/hl-vs/women-femmes/gender-sexe/policy-
politique_e.html.

Health Canada, with Ann Pederson, Olena Hankivsky, Marina Morrow, and Lorraine
Greaves. 2003. *Exploring Concepts of Gender and Health.* Ottawa: Women's Health
Bureau.

IDRC (International Development Research Centre). 2003. *Institutionalising Gender Equity Goals in the Policy Process.* Ottawa. http://www.idrc.ca/en/ev-42969-201-1-
DO_TOPIC.html.

Indian and Northern Affairs Canada. 1999. *Gender Equality Analysis Policy.* Ottawa. http://
www.ainc-inac.gc.ca/pr/pub/eql/eql_e.html.

Kartini International. 2001. *Final Report: Gender-Based Analysis On-line Dialogue.* Canadian Congress for Learning Opportunities for Women (CCLOW). http://www.
nald.ca/canorg/cclow/doc/fnal_rpt/cover_1.pdf.

Kukathas, Chandran. 1998. "Liberalism and Multiculturalism: The Politics of Indifference." *Political Theory* 26(5): 686-99.

Kymlicka, Will. 1989. *Liberalism, Community and Culture.* Oxford: Oxford University
Press.

—. 1995. *Multicultural Citizenship.* Oxford: Clarendon Press.

—. 1997. "Do We Need a Liberal Theory of Minority Rights?" *Constellations* 4(1): 72-87.

—. 2001. *Politics in the Vernacular: Nationalism, Multiculturalism, and Citizenship.* New
York: Oxford University Press.

Lahey, Kathleen. 2002. "Gender-Based Analysis in Law, Research, and Policy: Strategies
to 'Mainstream' Women's Equality." Materials prepared for gender workshops,
Canada-China Women's Law Project, Changchun and Beijing. http://qsilver.
queensu.ca/law/canchinaproject/genderaug3.htm.

Lorde, Audre. 1984. *Sister Outsider.* New York: Crossing Press.

Mazur, Amy G. 2002. *Theorizing Feminist Policy.* New York: Oxford University Press.

Mohanty, Chandra Talpade. 1997. "Under Western Eyes: Feminist Scholarship and
Colonial Discourses." In *The Women, Gender and Development Reader,* ed. Nalini

Visvanathan, Lynne Duggan, Laurie Nisonoff, and Brenda Wyss, 79-86. London: Zed Books.

Morrow, Marina, Olena Hankivsky, and Colleen Varcoe. 2004. "Women and Violence: The Effects of Dismantling the Welfare State." *Critical Social Policy* 24(3): 358-84.

Mullings, Leith. 2002. "The Sojourner Syndrome: Race, Class, and Gender in Health and Illness." *Voices* 6(1): 32-36.

Rankin, Pauline L., and Jill Vickers. 2001. "Women's Movements and State Feminism: Integrating Diversity into Public Policy." http://www.swc-cfc.gc.ca/pubs/pubspr/ 0662657756/index_e.html.

—. 2004. "Women's Movements and State Feminism: Integrating Diversity into Public Policy." In *Feminisms and Womanisms*, ed. Althea Prince and Susan Silva-Wayne, 43-51. Toronto: Women's Press.

Rawls, John. 1971. *A Theory of Justice*. London: Oxford University Press.

Raz, Joseph. 1994. "Multiculturalism: A Liberal Perspective." *Dissent* (Winter): 67-79.

Rebick, Judy. 1999. "Liberals Try to Sink NAC." *Herizons* 12(4): 31-32.

Rees, Teresa. 1998. *Mainstreaming Equality in the European Union: Education, Training, and Labour Market Policies*. London: Routledge.

Report of the Fourth World Conference on Women. 1995. WomenWatch. http://www.un.org/ womenwatch/confer/beijing/reports/plateng.htm.

Shaw, Jo. 2001. "European Union Governance and the Question of Gender: A Critical Comment." In *Symposium: Mountain or Molehill? A Critical Appraisal of the Commission White Paper on Governance*. Jean Monnet Working Paper No. 6/01. http://www. jeanmonnetprogram.org/papers/01/011901.html.

Slack, Jennifer Daryl. 1996. "The Theory and Method of Articulation in Cultural Studies." In *Stuart Hall: Critical Dialogues in Cultural Studies*, ed. David Morley and Kuan-Hsing Chen, 112-27. New York: Routledge.

Spelman, Elizabeth V. 1988. *Inessential Woman: Problems of Exclusion in Feminist Thought*. Boston: Beacon Press.

Spinner, Jeff. 1994. *The Boundaries of Citizenship: Race, Ethnicity, and Nationality in the Liberal State*. Baltimore and London: Johns Hopkins University Press.

Standing Committee on the Status of Women. 2004a. *Evidence*. Anu Bose, 30 November 2004, 1255.

—. 2004b. *Evidence*. Beth Phinney, 2 December 2004, s. 1255.

—. 2004c. *Evidence*. Beverly Jacobs, 2 December 2004, s. 1255.

—. 2004d. *Evidence*. Jennifer Dickson, 2 December 2004, s. 1235.

—. 2004e. *Evidence*. Joyce Hancock, 30 November 2004, s. 1105.

—. 2004f. *Evidence*. Liza Frulla, 23 November 2004, s. 1120.

—. 2004g. *Evidence*. Sheila Genaille, 2 December 2004, s. 1125.

—. 2004h. *Evidence*. Sungee John, 30 November 2004, s. 1155.

—. 2005a. *Evidence*. Florence Ievers, 10 February 2005, s. 1535.

—. 2005b. *Evidence*. Joan Atkinson, 22 March 2005, s. 1615.

—. 2005c. *Evidence.* Julie Delahanty, 22 February 2005, s. 1540.

—. 2005d. *Evidence.* Karen Green, 8 March 2005, s. 1530.

—. 2005e. *Evidence.* Pauline Rankin, 24 February 2005, ss. 1520, 1555, 1620.

—. 2005f. *Gender-Based Analysis: Building Blocks for Success. Report of the Standing Committee on Status of Women.* Ottawa: Communication Canada. http://www.parl.gc.ca.

SWC (Status of Women Canada). 1995. *Setting the Stage for the Next Century: The Federal Plan for Gender Equality (1995-2000).* Ottawa: Status of Women Canada.

—. 1998. *Gender-Based Analysis: A Guide for Policy-Making.* http://www.swc-cfc.gc.ca/pubs.

—. 2002. *Canadian Experience in Gender Mainstreaming.* http://www.swc-cfc.gc.ca/pubs/0662667352/200112_0662667352_1_e.html.

—. 2004a. *The 2004 Speech from the Throne Status of Women Canada: Gender Equality Review.* http://www.swc-cfc.gc.ca/pubs/sft2004/sft2004_1_e.html.

—. 2004b. *An Integrated Approach to Gender-Based Analysis: Information Kit. What Is GBA?* http://www.swc-cfc.gc.ca/pubs/gbainfokit/index_e.html.

Taylor, Charles. 1994. "The Politics of Recognition." In *Multiculturalism: Examining the Politics of Recognition,* ed. A. Gutmann, 25-74. Princeton: Princeton University Press.

—. 1998. "Living with Difference." In *Debating Democracy's Discontent,* ed. A.L. Allen and M.C. Regan, 212-27. Oxford: Oxford University Press.

—. 1999. "Democratic Exclusions (and Its Remedies?)." In *Citizenship, Diversity and Pluralism,* ed. A. Cairns, 265-87. Montreal and Kingston: McGill-Queen's University Press.

Teghtsoonian, Katherine. 1999. *Centring Women's Diverse Interests in Health Policy and Practice: A Comparative Discussion of Gender Analysis.* Halifax: Atlantic Centre of Excellence for Women's Health.

Verloo, Mieke. 2001. *Another Velvet Revolution? Gender Mainstreaming and the Politics of Implementation.* IWM Working Paper No. 5/2001. Vienna: Institut für die Wissenschaften vom Menschen.

Vickers, Jill. 1997. *Reinventing Political Science.* Halifax: Fernwood.

Vincent, Louise. 2003. "Current Discourse on the Role of Women in Conflict Prevention and Conflict Transformation: A Critique." *Conflict Trends* 3: 5-10.

Vlassov, Carol, and Garcia Moreno. 2002. "Placing Gender at the Centre of Health Programming: Challenges and Limitations." *Social Science of Medicine* 54: 1713-23.

Williams, Wendy. 2000. "Will the Canadian Government's Commitment to Use a Gender Based Analysis Result in Public Policies Reflecting the Diversity of Women's Lives?" In *Made to Measure: Women, Gender and Equity.* Vol. 3, ed. Carol Amaratunga, 74-82. Halifax: Maritime Centre of Excellence for Women's Health.

Woodward, Alison E. 2001. *Gender Mainstreaming in European Policy: Innovation or Deception?* Discussion Paper FSS 01-103. Berlin: Wissenschaftszentrum Berlin für Sozialforscung.

—. 2003. "European Gender Mainstreaming: Promises and Pitfalls of Transformative Policy." *Review of Policy Research* 20(1): 65-88.

Young, Iris Marion. 1990. *Justice and the Politics of Difference.* Princeton: Princeton University Press.

Yuval-Davis, Nira. 1997. *Gender and Nation.* London: Sage Publications.

7
Political Science, Race, Ethnicity, and Public Policy

Yasmeen Abu-Laban

The development of modern social sciences in the nineteenth century introduced the concepts of "state" and "society" into a shared academic lexicon, although these constructs have been appropriated and utilized in different ways both within and especially across disciplines. With respect to the discipline of political science, "the state" has served as a major orienting concept both historically and contemporaneously (Katznelson and Milner 2002, 26). This helps to explain the important role played by political scientists in the study of public policy, and the critical part they may continue to play in moving the multidisciplinary study of policy analysis in new and fruitful directions.

It is the contention of this chapter that, though the study of the state has been central to the agenda of political scientists, social diversity has been unevenly taken up in the consideration of issues pertaining to power, state processes, and public policy in Canada. In other words, the dominant examination of governance and its consequences by political scientists has tended to be shaped by a selective understanding of Canadian society. This in turn refracts a selective attention to history and in particular the variety of historical narratives that exist in contemporary Canada. These narratives show no signs of abating despite the intensity of such forces as globalization and regionalism evident in the early years of the twenty-first century, as well as the unfolding "war on terrorism."

The new century is characterized by profound change that is, arguably, on the momentous order of the industrial revolution. For the "fathers" of modern social science – Marx, Durkheim, and Weber – the great historical development of industrialization generated key ideas that guided social science, including political science, in the twentieth century (Abrams 1982); for us, the deepening of processes that affect the world, as captured in the notion of globalization, may well bring similar fundamentally momentous change. As such, globalization presents empirical and theoretical challenges to all those who study human life, and will inevitably engage both the social sciences and humanities in the years to come.

Despite the frequent use of the term "globalization" (and the prolifera-tion of related phrases such as "global village," "global civil society," "the in-formation revolution," "the computer age," "the glocal," and so on), some analysts question whether there is something really distinct going on today that warrants the term (Held et al. 1999, 5-7). The position I would forward is that though the social, technological, cultural, economic, and political processes identified with globalization may not be new in that "for many centuries, the agents of the world system continuously moved merchandise, humanpower and ideas across human borders and political barriers" (Roniger 1995, 260), what makes the current era unique, and what makes globaliza-tion a pertinent concept today, is the intensification and magnitude of these processes. Consequently, the processes associated with contemporary glo-balization (marked roughly from 1945) have spurred qualitative changes, trends, and modes of thinking unlike those of the past (Held et al. 1999).

For political scientists in particular, how globalization is challenging the autonomy of nation-states, as well as the salience of the nation-state system, are two of the most central questions of our time. Indeed, from the late 1980s, intrastate and interstate dynamics have been characterized by a velocity of change. The fall of the Berlin Wall, the clear end of the Cold War, and the collapse of the Soviet Union have taken place alongside growing regional integration in the European Union (EU). The European Union of fifteen countries enlarged in May 2004 to twenty-five, and further enlargement re-mains on the agenda. Consequently, analysts have increasingly looked not only to how member states affect policy at the European level, but also to how the EU influences the policies of member states (McCormick 1999; Hix 1999) and even potential member states (Lavenex and Uçarer 2002). In Canada the 1988 Free Trade Agreement with the United States expanded to the 1993 North American Free Trade Agreement (NAFTA) to include Mexico. These developments spurred new discussions about the impact of neo-liberalism on policy making in the three countries (Grinspun and Cameron 1993). The impact of globalization and continental regionalism on the state are all the more compelling because theories of the state, and of the relation-ship between state and societal forces, "provide the most unified focus for various fields within the discipline [of political science] as a whole" (O'Leary 1996, 632).

Added to this is the impact of the "war on terrorism" – a war defined by American president George W. Bush as one that has neither a temporal nor a spatial horizon, but that involves governments both nationally and internationally. The ongoing responses to the attacks in New York and Washington on 11 September 2001 have given rise to a slate of new policies across Western states (Freedman 2002; Salter, this volume) and new meaning to scholarship focusing on themes of American imperialism and empire (Parenti 2002).

Yet, as we grapple with the complex issues presented by the twenty-first century, it is unlikely that the intellectual baggage of the nineteenth century can be completely avoided – a point made by Charles Tilly (1984) many years ago in his criticism of how the concept of society has been treated by sociologists. Proscriptively, as Tilly has suggested, in invoking the concept "society," I do not think society should be treated as a thing, or a thing apart (ibid., 20-25). Prescriptively, I will argue that in order to come to terms with the new challenges portended by globalization, regionalism, and the ongoing war on terrorism, we need to rethink traditional definitions and modes of inquiry within political science, especially but not exclusively within Canada, that have served to give us a very narrow understanding of so-called Canadian society. Thus, it is only by retooling our focus, theoretically and conceptually, that we can begin to better understand the complexity of governance and public policy in contemporary Canada.

This argument has three major and interrelated components that will be treated in separate sections in this chapter. First, though political scientists in Canada have paid increasing attention in recent years to multiculturalism as an ideal and, to a lesser extent, as a policy, attending to public policy in a way that takes seriously ethnicity, language, and processes of racialization can and must go further.

Second, attending to public policy more fully requires political scientists to explicitly acknowledge the legacy of colonialism permeating all social relations, with potential reverberations even in the present. Only then will we have the potential to begin dealing with the significance of multiple, hybrid, and even shifting identities, as well as with the danger of essentialism. I use essentialism to refer to the common-sense perception that "each culture has a unique, fixed essence that can be understood independently of context or intercultural relations, and which makes an ethnic group act the way it does" (Modood 1997, 10). Specifically, the kind of essentialism that I consider dangerous is that which is neither a choice nor part of a legitimating discourse used by ethnic collectivities, but rather is imposed externally and connected to negative sanctions and discrimination (Schmidtke 2002, 276).

Third, in this era of globalization and the war on terrorism, the potential terrain that confronts public policy analysts is multi-layered and complex. We must continue to acknowledge the idea that public policy involves both what a state does and does not do, but also consider how there may be an internationalization of policy that has implications for racialization processes both nationally and internationally. If this is done, it is possible to go beyond the obvious – namely, the tendency by political scientists to conflate multiculturalism with all or much of what the state does in relation to race and ethnicity – and to better engage policy analysis with both Canadian history and the changes the twenty-first century presents and portends.

The Rise of the Study of Multiculturalism

The Royal Commission on Bilingualism and Biculturalism, formed by the Liberal government of Lester B. Pearson to respond to the resurgence of nationalism and an increasingly violent anti-colonialist movement in Quebec in the early 1960s, set the stage for what would eventually become Canada's multicultural policy. Multiculturalism came about because non-British, non-French, and non-Aboriginal Canadians – especially those of Ukrainian origin – challenged the symbolism of a bicultural and bilingual Canada. In response, in 1971 Prime Minister Trudeau introduced a policy of multiculturalism within a framework of English and French bilingualism.

The 1960s and 1970s also witnessed the emergence of the multidisciplinary field of ethnic studies, but from the outset, unlike scholars from other fields, political scientists were not heavily involved (Palmer 1977, 173). As a result, by the late 1980s Gilbert H. Scott (1989, 228) observed, in a paper tellingly entitled "Race Relations and Public Policy: Uncharted Course," that "thus far, the study of multiculturalism has been pursued mainly by sociologists, anthropologists and historians. Other social scientists such as political scientists have largely ignored the area."

It is against this backdrop that the decade of the 1990s is somewhat remarkable, as multiculturalism did appear on the agenda of Canadian political science in two ways. First, it came onto the agenda of constitutional politics. This was not simply because multiculturalism was entrenched in the Canadian Charter of Rights and Freedoms, but also because issues relating to multiculturalism were salient in debates over proposed constitutional amendments, such as the Meech Lake Accord (Cairns 1989). In addition, there was an explosion of work done by Canadian political theorists, including Charles Taylor (1992), Will Kymlicka (1995), and Joseph H. Carens (2000), which tackled themes relating to the politics of multiculturalism, recognition, and liberalism. Such work has been widely taken up, both nationally and internationally, and forms one of the major intellectual contributions of Canadians to the international field of political philosophy.

Yet, though liberal theorists have typically considered certain narratives about a wide range of groups (in Canada this has included French speakers, Aboriginal peoples, and recent immigrants), their work by itself has not transformed the manner in which political scientists conceptualize Canadian history and power relations. This is because the question driving much of this normative work concerns the limits of liberalism in light of the demands of minorities, and the limits of minority rights in light of liberalism. Consequently, this work has been strangely silent about the ways in which liberal thought itself has been tied to expressions of racism (Goldberg 1993) and, in particular, about the impact and legacy of colonialism (Abu-Laban 2002a). Significantly, theoretical work outside the liberal tradition which has engaged with the challenge of colonialism in considering multiculturalism (Day 2000; Mackey 2002) has not attracted many followers within Canadian political science.

This state of affairs may explain why political scientist Philip Resnick confidently presents his *European Roots of Canadian Identity* (2005, 7) as the outcome of viewing things "in a new light." In this book (ibid., 96), he advances the thesis that Canada has been shaped by its beginnings as an "offshoot of European colonization." Resnick writes, "Canada is not a blank slate to be reinvented with each new group of immigrants that arrives at our airports. Its underlying political and social values are intimately European-derived ones: peace, order, good government, constituted authority, political community, individual liberty, and citizen equality ... But the source from which this democratic tradition derives is Europe, and more broadly speaking, the western political tradition" (ibid., 61-62).

Of course, Resnick's assertion that notions of peace, political community, liberty, democracy, and the like are uniquely and essentially European is erroneous, as attention to indigenous traditions in North America, and their influence on European thinkers historically, readily shows (see, for example, Alfred 1999; Ladner 2003). In identifying Europe as *the* source of light, Resnick's approach is very familiar: it also appears in Samuel Huntington's (1996) "clash of civilizations" thesis, which claims that the struggle for democracy is essentially "European" and the reason for a purportedly permanent divide between "the West" and "the rest" (Abu-Laban 2001a). Yet, that Resnick (2005, 57-64) suggests that the power and influence of European values is ignored in many readings and discussions of multiculturalism is telling. This may indeed be the best testimony to the manner in which many normative accounts of multiculturalism have been disconnected from colonialism and history, and therefore from explicit consideration of power.

Additionally, for the most part neither constitutional nor normative liberal interventions systematically analyze the actual workings of multiculturalism policy in relation to the Canadian state (exceptions are Kymlicka 1998 and more recently his 2003 collaborative work with Keith Banting; the latter, which examines whether the adoption of multiculturalism policies leads to a less robust welfare state, uses cross-national data to suggest that this is not the case). Generally, multiculturalism as policy has primarily been left to the more empirically oriented accounts by political scientists. These include Leslie A. Pal's *Interests of State* (1993), which traces the programs relating to the status of women, official languages, and multiculturalism in the postwar period, and more recently Yasmeen Abu-Laban and Christina Gabriel's *Selling Diversity* (2002), which traces the impact of neo-liberalism on the policy as well as the way in which multiculturalism has, ironically despite cutbacks, become a model for the world – a notion increasingly asserted by Canadian policy makers.

Thus, by the early years of the twenty-first century, discussions of multiculturalism as an ideal and, to a far lesser extent as a policy, have come to stand for much of what the discipline in Canada has to say about race and ethnicity and public policy. Yet, this state of affairs is problematic. In Canada the federal policy of multiculturalism receives relatively little funding (just over $16 million in 2001). Thus, there are clearly more areas of state spending which could be addressed for their impact on citizens, including ethnocultural collectivities. Indeed, as a result of the 1988 Canadian Multiculturalism Act, all public sector departments are supposed to make decisions in light of the act's emphasis on equality (Frideres 1997, 102), yet there has been no academic analysis of the consequences of this. As well, public policy also involves what the state does not do – a point typically lost in the emphasis on multiculturalism, perhaps because the very term itself is actually rooted in Canada's 1971 federal policy.

Why political scientists have not systematically addressed a fuller range of policies and non-policies is related, arguably, to a failure to bring colonialism front and centre in considering Canada. If Canada's formation as a settler colony is acknowledged, and the impact of colonialism historically and contemporaneously is addressed, a different way of conceptualizing social relations and the significance of state policies and non-policies may emerge. As Stephen Steinberg (1995, 2-3) notes, for American sociologists of ethnicity, attention to colonialism explicitly directed researchers to consider the political and economic context more closely, so as to understand both how social inequalities have come to be and how they are sustained. Notwithstanding the importance of addressing multiculturalism as a policy, by itself such a focus is too narrow. And though the lively debate engendered by the examination of multiculturalism as an ideal has been important, this focus in its liberal variant does not attend to how social relations are sustained or potentially transformed by state action and inaction. Consequently, attention to colonialism, and its potentially varied legacies, can bring new ways of considering Canadian society, power relations between groups, and the role of the state.

Reconsidering Canadian Society and State

Unlike much of the liberal normative work done on multiculturalism and recognition, that by many Aboriginal scholars and those in the multi- and interdisciplinary field of Native Studies takes as a fundamental starting point Canada's formation as a settler society (Alfred 1999; Green 2001; Proulx 2000). Indeed, in the "white settler colony" controlled initially by the French and then by the British, racial, ethnic, class, and gender inequity and exclusion were foundational in social relations and state policies (Stasiulis and Jhappan 1995). In this way, identity was key to determining resources and belonging in the political community. The Canadian state played a central role in these processes through policies and practices that maintained the power and advantage of white males, especially those of British origin. This was overtly evident in immigration policies and in the treatment of the indigenous population (Abu-Laban 2001b). Thus, as Sherene H. Razack (2002, 6) notes, a focus on racial/ethnic hierarchies needs also to involve a focus on other hierarchies including class and gender, since "racial hierarchies come into existence through patriarchy and capitalism, each system of domination mutually constituting the other."

Yet, within the empirical Canadian political science tradition, the conventional tendency in the early decades following the Second World War was to define ethnic relations in Canada as relations between the French and the English. This remains apparent even in contemporary studies of voting where the categories are "French," "English," and some undifferentiated mass called "Other" (Abu-Laban 2002b). At the same time, despite the growing body of work on Aboriginal politics, colonialism as a frame for understanding Canada's history and contemporary social relations is not commonly engaged within the empirical work done in the political science discipline. This is readily apparent in the standard narratives provided in leading textbooks in Canadian politics, which ignore Aboriginal histories and colonialism in presenting political institutions and practices (Jhappan 1998).

More broadly, there remains real ambiguity about the place of race and ethnicity within political science, both in Canada (Wilson 1993) and internationally. As Rupert Taylor (1999) notes, the limited work that exists tends to treat "race" and "ethnicity" as "real" variables, rather than as the outcome of historically specific social processes.

If we take colonialism as a starting point for understanding all social relations in Canada, a more explicit consideration of history as well as the variety of historical narratives that exist in contemporary Canada would emerge in sharper relief. Thus, along with discussions of French-English politics, those of race and ethnicity would come to stand for the complex politics of Aboriginal peoples in Canada, as well as for non-British, non-French, non-Aboriginal Canadians, and their complex intersections with other forms of difference. Attention to colonialism as permeating all social relations, since it brings with it attention to diversity and complexity, may also provide an avenue for sidestepping essentialism.

Propelled by the interventions of minority women in Canada, new ways of understanding and theorizing about race and ethnicity were generated during the 1980s, especially within feminist scholarship. A key and important epistemological development concerns the emphasis on race, gender, and class oppression as linked and interlocking. What this has done is shift the lens from a unidimensional focus on gender, or race, or ethnicity, or class to a framework in which race, gender, and class, amongst other forms of difference, are integrated and seen to interact. This kind of approach carries the potential to consider a range of power relations in Canada, and can help to explore the complex and hybrid identities that can result from immigration and continual movement across state boundaries.

Not least, as Rupert Taylor (1999) also notes, political scientists need to pay attention to processes of racialization (that is, the historically and culturally specific ways in which some groups become seen as separate and are treated as inferior). Such a focus is especially pertinent in light of the kind of essentialism that underpins the call to profiling in the post–September 11 period, and examples in which state immigration and security personnel differentially targeted those perceived to be Muslim or Arab. Indeed, this has been one of many policy consequences across industrialized states after September 11 (see Freedman 2002).

In short, the acknowledgment of colonialism would not only make issues pertaining to Aboriginal politics more evident, but it might also encourage consideration of social diversity and related state processes in new ways. This is relevant to thinking about public policy beyond multiculturalism.

A New Agenda for Public Policy Research in Canada?

Given the points made above, what might an agenda for policy analysis in which colonialism, anti-essentialism, and processes of racialization and globalization are taken seriously look like? It would clearly be a broad agenda, but not necessarily unwieldy. In what follows, I use the existing Canadian and international literature to provide only a rough sketch of the complex and multi-layered terrain which policy analyses might potentially consider further.

One fundamental area to address in the realm of public policy is bureaucratic organization and racial/ethnic classification systems, both historically and today. As Alice Robbin (2000, 402) has written of the United States, "Official classification of 'race' and 'ethnicity' provides the bureaucratic justification for rules that establish the legitimacy of political action in the civil state (e.g., citizenship), embed individuals in a network of social relations (e.g., majority-status-minority status, property-owner-slave), allocate important social resources, and create both commitment to and deviations from social norms (e.g., miscegenation, slavery, multiculturalism, interracial marriage)."

Such a perspective is crucial for helping understand Canada's history as a settler colony in which gender, class, and race/ethnicity played a critical role in federal, provincial, and local policies concerning eligibility and ineligibility for public office and the franchise. Likewise, contemporaneously, there is no doubt that what the federal Canadian state does today in its spending and its bureaucracy continues to have much to do with being a colonial state.

English *and* French were not declared as official languages of the federal state until 1969, a fact that mirrors the power of those of British origin historically. In comparison with multiculturalism (adopted in 1971), considerably more money goes into promoting official languages, and indeed the area of multiculturalism has much less stature in the federal bureaucracy than bilingualism, which has been viewed as a reflection of the relative power of those of British and French origins in shaping Canada (Stasiulis 1988). The prioritizing of official languages, as opposed to other languages, including indigenous languages, is not accidental. As Kenyan writer Ngugi wa Thiong'o (1995, 443) has observed, the imposition of language is central in colonial practices: "to control a people's culture is to control their tools of self-definition in relationship to others."

It would be a mistake, however, to view official languages as being about the equivalent positioning of French and English. As Wilfrid Denis (1999) notes, about half of the money allocated to official bilingualism gets directed to English speakers in the province of Quebec, with French speakers outside Quebec not receiving as much money in comparison, largely because their relative class disadvantage makes them less able to access the same resources to mobilize and exert power. In other words, official bilingualism in practice has very much to do with the protection and promotion of the English language (Couture 1997). And this in turn relates to the colonial legacy and the relative power of those of British origin as compared to the French, as well as to other groups.

A cursory overview of Indian and Northern Affairs would also show that despite the emergence from the early 1970s of a discourse around "self-government" (Howlett 1994), the Indian Act, dating from 1876, continues to affect the culture and politics of Native communities in keeping with long-standing assimilationist goals of the state (Alfred 1999). As Kiera Ladner (2003, 49) puts it, "Through the *Indian Act*, Canada tells band governments and their citizens what they can and cannot do with respect to everything from birth (by determining band membership) to death (validating wills)." In this way, the band councils imposed by the federal state's Indian Act violate traditional forms of indigenous governance, as well as many treaties, and foster the conditions for the differential and sexist treatment of indigenous women in relation to membership (Green 2001).

As well, the ongoing role the state plays in identity construction itself, especially through the census, is pertinent to understanding public policy and the maintenance of, or challenges to, power relations. Although sociologists have traditionally looked at the questions and data relating to the census (see, for example, Sarkar 2003), this has not been an area of extensive discussion for political scientists. Yet the very questions that are asked on a census are inherently political since they influence the conception of "the population." For example, in France, the census asks no ethnic origin questions; one consequence of not asking, as Gérard Noiriel (1992) points out, is that the immigrant disappears from history. The limited research-based data on "race" or "ethnicity" also have implications in the realm of public policy: in France, there is no public policy expressly aimed at groups on the grounds of their ethnic/racial composition (Bleich 2000, 51). In contrast, in the United States, the census does ask about race and ethnicity; as a result, it "is inextricably bound up with the administrative needs of the contemporary welfare state" (Skerry 2002, 332). Consequently, analysts underscore how changes in research design in the 2000 American census to allow for a "multiracial" as opposed to a single response carried implications not only for identity (Herring 2004, 15) but also for public policy throughout all US federal agencies (Perlmann and Waters 2002, 1).

In Canada, an ethnic origin question is asked, but its design has shifted over time: since the 1986 census, a growing number of people have chosen multiple categories and even "Canadian" as their ethnic origin (most of those choosing "Canadian" appear to have formerly chosen either a single British origin or a single French origin) (Abu-Laban and Stasiulis 2000, 484). Because of this, there have been some in Canada arguing that the ethnic origin question should be removed, but this move would have other public policy consequences (ibid., 485-86). For example, Canada's federal policy of employment equity, enacted in 1986, depends on constructing so-called visible minorities, which is a category derived from the census' ethnic origin question.

Likewise, health policy – deemed to be in drastic need of both cultural and gender sensitivity in all levels of health services (Vissandjée et al. 2001) – depends heavily on census data (Rummens 2003). Although medicare is a provincial responsibility constitutionally, the fact that it is federally funded implicates both levels of government in how health care is experienced by diverse Canadians. Indeed, in light of the relevance of immigration in Canada, and the aging of the population, extrapolating from American research suggests that policy makers need to better consider the distinct experiences and attitudes of aging female immigrants when it comes to health care (Patterson 2004, 25-37).

Like the census, immigration policy, the concurrent responsibility of Ottawa and the provinces, has a clear, direct, and significant impact upon the population, and thus warrants sustained consideration. Since Confederation in 1867, about 16 percent of the Canadian population has been foreign-born. The 2001 Canadian census indicates that the percentage of immigrants in the population currently stands a little higher, at close to 20 percent. Immigration has been an area where the state has shaped the very nature of the political community. The overt discrimination in the policy of immigration, reflecting Canada's formation as a white settler colony, was removed in 1967. Since that time, immigration from countries outside of Europe has grown. Nevertheless, immigration selection criteria continue to have clear differential effects on immigrants by way of their gender, class, and geographic area of origin, and thus their race/ethnicity (Abu-Laban and Gabriel 2002). Indeed, over the past decade, Canada's selection criteria have arguably become more exclusionary (Abu-Laban 2004). Thus, Canada, like other Western industrialized countries, has erected new barriers to the flow of people, raising questions about both the anticipated and unanticipated consequences domestically and internationally of such a policy trend (Dale, LeMay, and Mariam 1994, 729-32). The practice of allowing non-citizens to enter the country as temporary or migrant labour, as opposed to extending citizenship to immigrants, is also an area that deserves ongoing investigation for its implications politically, socially, and economically.

Yet, traditionally, immigration policy has not been a major area of research for Canadian political scientists. Only in the post–Cold War period did this change somewhat, as migration has now begun to be defined, particularly by Western states, as an issue of security, and hence, of "high politics." Thus, international relations specialists such as Thomas Homer-Dixon (1991) have implicitly posited migration as a national security issue for Western states. Nonetheless, the range of policy questions that could be entertained by consideration of immigration go further. For example, why and how do certain migrants come to be defined as security threats, and with what consequences for citizenship policy? This is a particularly pertinent question, historically and in light of the contemporary "war on terrorism" and recent parliamentary discussion of revoking Canadian citizenship on security grounds.

Also relevant to consider in the context of the post–September 11 order are regionalism and the ongoing discussion between Canada and the United

States (and to a lesser extent between the US and Mexico) around "smart borders" (see Salter, this volume). In the case of Canada and the United States, "smart borders" carry the potential to harmonize aspects of immigration and refugee policy between the two countries, akin to the Schengen arrangement and Dublin Convention between countries of the European Union. Those who do get into Canada may experience a range of issues relating to the treatment of immigrants; some of these are addressed in the Metropolis Project, which has focused on the "integration" of newcomers. Although integration is seen to involve a wide range of processes, and thus policies, the Metropolis Project, which since 1996 has brought together academics, NGOs, and policy makers, has not been heavily represented by political scientists.

Issues relating to citizenship rights, and in particular to civil liberties for immigrants and minorities – especially those seen to be Arab or Muslim – also demand attention, given the rapid passage of Bill C-36 (Canada's anti-terrorist legislation) in 2001 (Roach 2003). Indeed, after September 11 many countries passed new anti-terrorist legislation, including the United States and Britain. Such legislation is one area that could be perceived as representing an internationalization of policy. American anti-terrorist legislation has carried specific implications for minorities and especially immigrants from certain countries (Cole 2002-03), as has its British counterpart (Fenwick 2002). As such, anti-terrorist measures constitute an emergent racialization process that carries regional dimensions in North America and Europe, as well as global dimensions.

Foreign policy is another area in which the implications of colonialism, Canada's diverse polity, and globalization may be discerned. However, one leading analyst of international relations maintains that Canadian foreign policy can be best explained independently of ethnic group mobilization: "Canadian foreign policy is founded on the need to resolve problems that are endemic to all modern industrial democracies. These problems concentrate around security and welfare needs, the two great aims of modern government. The interests that derive from these considerations relate to the interests of all Canadians, and not just the interests of persons who share particular ethnic attributes" (Holsti 1993, 150-51). Such an analysis fails to problematize Canadian foreign policy in relation to Canada's history as a settler colony. Indeed, the fact that today Canada is a member of both the Commonwealth and La Francophonie is indicative of the defining influence of both the British and the French in Canada.

Writing about the United States, Alexander DeConde (1992, x) notes that Americans of English/British origin have typically been excluded from analyses of ethnicity and foreign policy. Yet, his historical survey shows how members of this majority "created the national ideology" and "defined their stance in foreign relations as at the center of mainstream American culture" (ibid., 197). Although I do not suggest that ethnicity accounts for all foreign policy decisions in Canada, it is nonetheless the case that if a consideration of colonialism and power relations were factored in more explicitly, some patterns may be more easily discerned. The fact that, historically, Canada's foreign policy stance has both favoured and asserted independence from Britain (for example, under Prime Minister Laurier with the Boer War, King during the Second World War, and Pearson with the Suez crisis) may be viewed as both support for and resistance to the metropolis – a feature less apparent if colonialism is not taken up directly. Additionally, tensions between English-speaking and French-speaking Canadians regarding conscription during both world wars may be seen to reflect how foreign policy decisions relate to the playing out of power relations between groups within Canada. Today, the ongoing debate about whether Canadian foreign policy should support America, and/or Britain/Europe (Resnick 2005, 73-82), and/ or an internationalist citizenship which gives ethical consideration to global rights, obligations, and interests (Franceschet and Knight 2001) suggests how Canadian foreign policy can take varied directions. Which direction is taken in any given instance might well be viewed and experienced differently by distinct groups of Canadians precisely because, as a result of immigration, Canada now contains "the world" within its borders.

Flowing from the above discussion, the general point could be made that there is probably no public policy that does not have significant implications for distinct ethnocultural and racialized collectivities, even if it is not explicitly defined as a "cultural policy" (or as a "multicultural policy"). One especially pertinent example might be social policy, which, from residential schools to integrated social services, proved unable to provide Aboriginal children with security and options, while simultaneously preventing the transmission of their heritage (Armitage 1995, 236-38). Relatedly, there is probably no public policy that stands outside the influence of social context, and in Canada this social context has been shaped by race, ethnicity, gender, and class, amongst other variables. Some of these complexities have been captured in a particularly promising way, through the growing attention to the differential impact that the neo-liberal responses of Canadian policy makers to globalization have on specific and intersecting groups (Abu-Laban and Gabriel 2002; Brodie 2002; Jenson and Phillips 1996).

If we consider public policy as what the state does not do, there is also no doubt that non-policies carry differential consequences. Not having a national child care policy in Canada, for example, has specific ramifications for women, especially poor women, and particularly poor women without familial support structures, as would be the case for some recent immigrants. Moreover, because social policy in Canada has evolved largely in ways that value neither care as a practice nor the needs of those who give care (Hankivsky 2004), the consequences for women in general differ from those for female minorities. Thus, the interaction between state policy and non-policy feeds into the fact that, today, those who undertake the insecure and poorly remunerated care work in Canadian homes, as well as in hospitals and daycares, are frequently immigrant women from the developing world who lack Canadian citizenship (see, for example, Stasiulis and Bakan 2004).

Returning for a moment to the theme of the colonial legacy and differing historical narratives, I will point out another area in which the federal Canadian state has generally chosen not to act: this is in offering explicit apologies and redress to certain groups (James 1999). The three exceptions are the 1988 apology and redress offered to Japanese Canadians for internment during the Second World War, the 1998 apology and compensation offered to Aboriginal victims of sexual assault in residential schools, and the 2006 apology to Chinese Canadians for the head tax. Basically, however, the response to groups seeking redress from the Canadian state has been marked more by expedience than principle (Abu-Laban 2001b, 266). Nonetheless, given the history of inequalities and injustices pertaining to groups in Canada, given the power of the idea of restitution in Western legal thought (McKinney 2002), and given the facts that people have memories and groups nurture narratives (Abu-Laban 2001b, 266), redress claims are unlikely to disappear. This forms an important avenue for exploring non-policy in twenty-first-century Canada.

To summarize, then, as even this cursory overview suggests, there is much more than multiculturalism that could be discussed in the name of race, ethnicity, and public policy. Doing this successfully depends on the kind of historical sensitivity shown in much work in the multidisciplinary and interdisciplinary areas of ethnic studies and native studies which is making its way even further into the heart of political science. As the discipline claims the state and state-society relations as its guiding focus, this is a possible venture.

Conclusion

This chapter has shown that the discipline of political science has evolved over time to increasingly take on the challenge of multiculturalism. In the process, Canadian political theorists in particular have been at the forefront in assessing the limits and potential of the recognition of diversity in liberal democratic states such as Canada. Yet, this chapter also suggests that we can and should go further, both in the theoretical work which is engaged and in the manner in which empirical work is approached. This is especially important because the field of policy studies, though multidisciplinary, has been heavily influenced by political scientists.

The discussion suggests that new directions for public policy can begin to be entertained only when the starting assumptions are challenged. Taking seriously Canada's formation as a settler colony, and the varied legacies this may create when it comes to power, can lead to new ways of thinking about public policy that venture beyond multiculturalism. Taking seriously the manner in which both policies and non-policies touch our lives in differential ways also offers new promises. Not least, taking seriously the fact that research agendas do indeed evolve collectively over time means that political scientists, and therefore policy analysts, may increasingly be able to tackle the study of the state and public policy in a way that captures a fuller range of social relations and the shifting contexts from which they emerge. Political theorists have already made enormous contributions to the philosophical study of multiculturalism, and could do the same for the study of Canadian public policy, if they take on new directions. As globalization brings the world ever closer and capital, people, and ideas – in all their complexity – crisscross borders rapidly, Canadian political scientists have the potential to make a relevant contribution not only at home but abroad.

ACKNOWLEDGMENTS
For helpful comments on an earlier draft of this chapter, I thank the anonymous reviewers, Claude Couture, Michael Orsini, and Miriam Smith.

REFERENCES
Abrams, Philip. 1982. *Historical Sociology*. Ithaca: Cornell University Press.
Abu-Laban, Yasmeen. 2001a. "Humanizing the Oriental: Edward Said and Western Scholarly Discourse." In *Revising Culture, Reinventing Peace: The Influence of Edward Said,*

ed. Naseer Aruri and Muhammad A. Shuraydi, 74-85. New York and Northampton: Interlink Publishing.

—. 2001b. "The Future and the Legacy: Globalization and the Canadian Settler-State." *Journal of Canadian Studies* 35(4): 262-76.

—. 2002a. "Liberalism, Multiculturalism and the Problem of Essentialism." *Citizenship Studies* 6(4): 459-82.

—. 2002b. "Challenging the Gendered Vertical Mosaic: Immigrants, Ethnic Minorities, Gender and Political Participation." In *Citizen Politics: Research and Theory in Canadian Political Behaviour,* ed. Joanna Everitt and Brenda O'Neill, 268-82. Don Mills: Oxford University Press.

—. 2004. "Jean Chrétien's Immigration Legacy." *Review of Constitutional Studies* 9(1-2): 135-49.

Abu-Laban, Yasmeen, and Christina Gabriel. 2002. *Selling Diversity: Immigration, Multiculturalism, Employment Equity, and Globalization.* Peterborough: Broadview Press.

Abu-Laban, Yasmeen, and Daiva Stasiulis. 2000. "Constructing 'Ethnic Canadians': The Implications for Public Policy and Inclusive Citizenship." *Canadian Public Policy* 26(4): 477-87.

Alfred, Taiaiake. 1999. *Peace, Power, Righteousness: An Indigenous Manifesto.* Don Mills: Oxford University Press.

Armitage, Andrew. 1995. *Comparing the Policy of Aboriginal Assimilation: Australia, Canada and New Zealand.* Vancouver: UBC Press.

Banting, Keith, and Will Kymlicka. 2003. "Multiculturalism and Welfare." *Dissent* 50(4): 59-66.

Bleich, Erik. 2000. "Anti-racism without Races: Politics and Policy in a 'Colour-Blind' State." *French Politics, Culture and Society* 18(3): 48-74.

Brodie, Janine. 2002. "Citizenship and Solidarity: Reflections on the Canadian Way." *Citizenship Studies* 6(4): 377-94.

Cairns, Alan C. 1989. "Political Science, Ethnicity and the Canadian Constitution." In *Federalism and Political Community in Canada: Essays in Honour of Donald Smiley,* ed. David P. Shugarman and Reg Whitaker, 113-40. Peterborough: Broadview Press.

Carens, Joseph H. 2000. *Culture, Citizenship and Community: A Contextual Exploration of Justice as Evenhandedness.* Oxford: Oxford University Press.

Cole, David. 2002-03. "Their Liberties, Our Security: Democracy and Double Standards." *Boston Review* 27 (December-January): 1-17.

Couture, Claude. 1997. "Pierre E. Trudeau et Edward Said: Libéralisme et postcolonialisme." Paper presented at Colloque Multiculturalisme, constitutionalisme et citoyenneté, Centre culturel canadien, Paris, October.

Dale, Suzanne McGrath, Michael C. LeMay, and Al G. Mariam. 1994. "Breaching the Barriers: Migrating Ethnic Groups and Immigration Policy." *Southeastern Political Review* 22(4): 729-52.

Day, Richard. 2000. *Multiculturalism and the History of Canadian Diversity.* Toronto: University of Toronto Press.

DeConde, Alexander. 1992. *Ethnicity, Race and American Foreign Policy.* Boston: Northeastern University Press.

Denis, Wilfrid. 1999. "Language Policy in Canada." In *Race and Ethnic Relations in Canada.* 2nd ed., ed. Peter S. Li, 178-216. Don Mills: Oxford University Press.

Fenwick, Helen. 2002. "Responding to 11 September: Detention without Trial under the Anti-terrorism Crime and Security Act 2001." In *Superterrorism: Policy Responses,* ed. Lawrence Freedman, 80-104. Oxford: Blackwell.

Franceschet, Antonio, and W. Andy Knight. 2001. "International(ist) Citizenship: Canada and the International Criminal Court." *Canadian Foreign Policy* 8(Winter): 51-74.

Freedman, Lawrence, ed. 2002. *Superterrorism: Policy Responses.* Oxford: Blackwell.

Frideres, J.S. 1997. "Multiculturalism and Public Policy in Canada." In *Multiculturalism in Cross-National Perspective,* ed. Michael A. Burayidi, 87-112. Lanham: University Press of America.

Goldberg, David Theo. 1993. *Racist Culture: Philosophy and the Politics of Meaning.* Oxford: Oxford University Press.

Green, Joyce. 2001. "Canaries in the Mines of Citizenship: Indian Women in Canada." *Canadian Journal of Political Science* 34(4): 715-38.

Grinspun, Ricardo, and Maxwell A. Cameron, eds. 1993. *The Political Economy of North American Free Trade.* Montreal and Kingston: McGill-Queen's University Press.

Hankivsky, Olena. 2004. *Social Policy and the Ethic of Care.* Vancouver: UBC Press.

Held, David, Anthony G. McGrew, David Goldblatt, and Jonathan Perraton. 1999. *Global Transformations: Politics, Economics, Culture.* Stanford: Stanford University Press.

Herring, Cedric. 2004. "Skin Deep: Race and Complexion in the 'Color-Blind' Era." In *Skin Deep: How Race and Complexion Matter in the 'Color-Blind' Era,* ed. Cedric Herring, Verna Keith, and Hayward Derrick Horton, 1-21. Chicago: University of Illinois Press.

Hix, Simon. 1999. *The Political System of the European Union.* New York: St. Martin's Press.

Holsti, Kalevi J. 1993. "Ethnicity and Canadian Foreign Policy." In *Diasporas in World Politics: The Greeks in Comparative Perspective,* ed. Dimitri C. Constas and Athanassios G. Platias, 137-52. London: Macmillan Press.

Homer-Dixon, Thomas. 1991. "On the Threshold: Environmental Changes as Causes of Acute Conflict." *International Security* 16(2): 76-116.

Howlett, Michael. 1994. "Policy Paradigms and Policy Change: Lessons from the Old and New Canadian Policies towards Aboriginal Peoples." *Policy Studies Journal* 22(4): 631-49.

Huntington, Samuel. 1996. "The West Unique Not Universal." *Foreign Affairs* 75(6): 28-48.

James, Matt. 1999. "Redress Politics and Canadian Citizenship." In *The State of the Federation 1998: How Canadians Connect,* ed. Tom McIntosh and Harvey Lazar, 247-81. Kingston: Queen's University Press and the Institute of Intergovernmental Relations.

Jenson, Jane, and Susan D. Phillips. 1996. "Regime Shift: New Citizenship Practices in Canada." *International Journal of Canadian Studies* 14 (Fall): 111-36.

Jhappan, Radha. 1998. Comments given at the Roundtable Dialogue on "Identity Politics in Canadian Politics Teaching and Research." Canadian Politics Section of the Canadian Political Science Association, Congress of Social Sciences and Humanities, Ottawa, 31 May-2 June.

Katznelson, Ira, and Helen V. Milner. 2002. "American Political Science: The Discipline's State and the State of the Discipline." In *Political Science: The State of the Discipline,* ed. Ira Katznelson and Helen V. Milner, 1-26. New York: W.W. Norton and the American Political Science Association.

Kymlicka, Will. 1995. *Multicultural Citizenship: A Liberal Theory of Minority Rights.* Oxford: Oxford University Press.

—. 1998. *Finding Our Way: Rethinking Ethnocultural Relations in Canada.* Don Mills: Oxford University Press.

Ladner, Kiera. 2003. "Rethinking Aboriginal Governance." In *Reinventing Canada: Politics of the 21st Century,* ed. Janine Brodie and Linda Trimble, 43-60. Toronto: Pearson.

Lavenex, Sandra, and Emek M. Uçarer, eds. 2002. *Migration and the Externalities of European Integration.* Lanham: Lexington Books.

Mackey, Eva. 2002. *The House of Difference: Cultural Politics and National Identity in Canada.* Toronto: University of Toronto Press.

McCormick, John. 1999. *The European Union: Politics and Policies.* 2nd ed. Boulder: Westview Press.

McKinney, Tiffany M. 2002. "Reparation to Black America: A Legal Analysis." *Harvard Journal of African American Public Policy* 8: 19-37.

Modood, Tariq. 1997. "Introduction." In *The Politics of Multiculturalism in the New Europe,* ed. Tariq Modood and Pnina Werbner, 1-25. London: Zed Press.

Noiriel, Gérard. 1992. "Difficulties in French Historical Research on Immigration." In *Immigrants in Two Democracies: French and American Experience,* ed. Donald L. Horowitz and Gérard Noiriel, 66-79. New York: New York University Press.

O'Leary, Brendan. 1996. "Political Science." In *The Social Science Encyclopedia.* 2nd ed., ed. Adam Kuper and Jessica Kuper, 632-38. London and New York: Routledge.

Pal, Leslie A. 1993. *Interests of State: The Politics of Language, Multiculturalism, and Feminism in Canada*. Montreal and Kingston: McGill-Queen's University Press.

Palmer, Howard. 1977. "History and Present State of Ethnic Studies in Canada." In *Identities: The Impact of Ethnicity on Canadian Society*, ed. Wsevolod Isajiw. Canadian Ethnic Studies Association series, vol. 5, 167-83. Toronto: Peter Martin.

Parenti, Michael. 2002. *The Terrorism Trap: September 11 and Beyond*. San Francisco: City Light Books.

Patterson, Fiona M. 2004. "Policy and Practice Implications from the Lives of Aging International Migrant Women." *International Social Work* 47(1): 25-37.

Perlmann, Joel, and Mary C. Waters. 2002. "Introduction." In *The New Race Question: How the Census Counts Multiracial Individuals*, ed. Joel Perlmann and Mary C. Waters, 1-32. New York: Russell Sage Foundation.

Proulx, Craig. 2000. "Current Directions in Aboriginal Law/Justice in Canada." *Canadian Journal of Native Studies* 20(2): 371-409.

Razack, Sherene H. 2002. "Introduction: When Place Becomes Race." In *Race, Space and the Law: Unmapping a White Settler Society*, ed. Sherene H. Razack, 1-20. Toronto: Between the Lines.

Resnick, Philip. 2005. *The European Roots of Canadian Identity*. Peterborough: Broadview Press.

Roach, Kent. 2003. *September 11: Consequences for Canada*. Montreal and Kingston: McGill-Queen's University Press.

Robbin, Alice. 2000. "Administrative Policy as Symbol System: Political Conflict and the Social Construction of Identity." *Administration and Society* 32(4): 398-431.

Roniger, Luis. 1995. "Public Life and Globalization as Cultural Vision." *Canadian Review of Sociology and Anthropology* 32(3): 259-85.

Rummens, Joanna Anneke. 2003. "Ethnic Ancestry, Culture, Identity and Health: Using Ethnic Origin Data from the 2001 Census." *Canadian Ethnic Studies* 35(1): 84-112.

Sarkar, Eileen. 2003. "Introduction: Ethnicity in the Canadian Census." Special issue, *Canadian Ethnic Studies* 35(1): 1-4.

Schmidtke, Oliver. 2002. "Naïve Universalism." *Ethnicities* 2(2): 274-79.

Scott, Gilbert H. 1989. "Race Relations and Public Policy: Uncharted Course." In *Canada 2000: Race Relations and Public Policy*, ed. O.P. Dwivedi, Ronald D'Costa, C. Lloyd Stanford, and Elliot Tepper, 227-32. Guelph: Department of Political Studies, University of Guelph.

Skerry, Peter. 2002. "Multiracialism and the Administrative State." In *The New Race Question: How the Census Counts Multiracial Individuals*, ed. Joel Perlmann and Mary C. Waters, 327-39. New York: Russell Sage Foundation.

Stasiulis, Daiva K. 1988. "The Symbolic Mosaic Reaffirmed: Multiculturalism Policy." In *How Ottawa Spends: 1988-89*, ed. Katherine A. Graham, 81-112. Ottawa: Carleton University Press.

Stasiulis, Daiva, and Abigail Bakan. 2004. *Negotiating Citizenship: Migrant Women in Canada and the Global System.* London: Palgrave.

Stasiulis, Daiva, and Radha Jhappan. 1995. "The Fractious Politics of a Settler Society: Canada." In *Unsettling Settler Societies: Articulations of Gender, Race, Ethnicity and Class,* ed. Daiva Stasiulis and Nira Yuval-Davis, 95-131. London: Sage Publications.

Steinberg, Stephen. 1995. *Turning Back: The Retreat from Racial Justice in American Thought and Policy.* Boston: Beacon Press.

Taylor, Charles. 1992. "The Politics of Recognition." In *Multiculturalism and the Politics of Recognition,* ed. Amy Gutman, 25-73. Princeton: Princeton University Press.

Taylor, Rupert. 1999. "Political Science Encounters 'Race' and 'Ethnicity.'" In *Ethnic and Racial Studies Today,* ed. Martin Bulmer and John Solomos, 115-23. London and New York: Routledge.

Thiong'o, Ngugi wa. 1995. "Decolonising the Mind." In *One World: Many Cultures,* ed. Stuart Hirschberg, 428-37. Boston: Allyn and Bacon.

Tilly, Charles. 1984. *Big Structures, Large Processes, Huge Comparisons.* New York: Russell Sage Foundation.

Vissandjée, Bilkis, Morton Weinfeld, Sophie Dupéré, and Shelly Abdool. 2001. "Sex, Gender, Ethnicity and Access to Health Care Services: Research and Policy Challenges for Immigrant Women in Canada." *Journal of International Migration and Integration* 2(1): 55-75.

Wilson, V. Seymour. 1993. "The Tapestry Vision of Canadian Multiculturalism." *Canadian Journal of Political Science* 26: 645-69.

PART THREE

Discourse and Knowledge

8
Governmentality and the Shifting Winds of Policy Studies

Karen Bridget Murray

The role of the state in social and economic life is the cornerstone of *public* policy research, which uses the term "public" as a synonym for programs and activities funded by government tax revenues and undertaken by official institutions of power, such as legislatures, courts, and bureaucracies, generally referred to as "the state." This perspective underpins standard textbook definitions, which define power and politics in relation to what the state does or does not do. As Leslie A. Pal (1992, 2) puts it, public policy "is a course of action or inaction chosen by public authorities to address a given problem or interrelated set of problems."

In the latter years of the twentieth century, this focus was called into question as states began to more actively promote extra-state domains in areas once thought to be the appropriate purview of public action (Brock 2001; Kernaghan and Charih 1997; Wolfe and Gertler 2004). One manifestation of this shift was the growing emphasis placed on voluntary, non-profit, and philanthropic entities – "communities"[1] – as central domains in the design and delivery of services and resources to address issues of social and economic disadvantage (Hall and Reed 1998).

In Canada, this transformation took shape in the New Deal for Cities and Communities, the Social Union Framework Agreement, the Voluntary Sector Initiative, social economy programs, and a plethora of new provincial-level activities. Of course the role of community organizations in social welfare was not "new" (Procacci 1991; Valverde 1995; Walters 2004), but the growing centrality given to extra-state organizations in the social sphere was distinct. This change made it clear that new questions and approaches needed to be brought to bear in order to more fully grasp the political and governmental role of community organizations in social policy and administration (Graefe 2004; Rochefort, Rosenberg, and White 1998).

This chapter argues that Foucauldian-inspired studies of governmentality can provide a new approach in Canadian policy studies, especially with regard to the growing emphasis placed on communities as both objects and mechanisms of governing. In developing this argument, the chapter introduces key governmentality themes, comparing them to selected conventions of positivist-oriented welfare state scholarship and paying special attention to Canadian contributions. It highlights several examples of how governmentality lenses have been used to study the role of communities in governmental practices, including a concluding illustration that draws upon original research conducted in the Grandview Woodland area of Vancouver. As this chapter shows, studies of governmentality can illuminate facets of politics, power, and rule that mainstream approaches are incapable of bringing to light.

Governmentality

In a series of lectures at the Collège de France in 1978 and 1979, Michel Foucault coined the term "governmentality,"[2] a neologism of government and rationality (Foucault 1979b; Lemke 2001, 191). Governmentality refers to government, not as centralized in a single institution, set of institutions, or even a person or group, but rather as the outcome of a multitude of thoughts and practices that shape assumptions about what government is, how it should be exercised, by whom, and for what purposes. To better understand what Foucault meant by this neologism, it is worth sketching out some of his views on power and knowledge.

In his way of thinking, knowledge was fundamental to power; in fact, they were one and the same, a point that he captured by referring to the two as power/knowledge. In *Discipline and Punish* (1979a, 27), he wrote that "power produces knowledge (and not simply by encouraging it because it serves power or by applying it because it is useful) ... power and knowledge directly imply one another ... there is no power relation without the correlative constitution of a field of knowledge, nor any knowledge that does not presuppose and constitute at the same time power relations." Power is not something to be possessed; it is decentred, diffuse, heterogeneous, and ubiquitous. Actors may scheme, and competing ideas may circulate, but they are limited by what Foucault (1972, 31, 49) referred to as discursive practices, or discourses, which constitute parameters of what can be thought and spoken. For Foucault (1979a, 27-28; 1990, 83), no place exists outside of power: power is ubiquitous; it cannot be possessed or dispossessed; and the truth shall not, nor can it, set you "free."

For Foucault, power/knowledge, the discursive field, is constitutive and not simply repressive. As he (1980b, 119) put it, "What makes power hold good, what makes it accepted, is simply the fact that it doesn't only weigh in on us as a force that says no, but that it traverses and produces things, it induces pleasure, forms of knowledge, produces discourse. It needs to be considered as a productive network which runs through the social body, much more than as a negative instance whose function is repression." This productive dimension of power was seen by Foucault as a source of resistance. As he (1990, 101) wrote, "Discourses are not once and for all subservient to power or raised up against it, any more than silences are. We must make allowance for the complex and unstable processes whereby discourse can be both an instrument and an effect of power, but also a hindrance, a stumbling-block, a point of resistance and a starting point for an opposing strategy. Discourse transmits and produces power; it reinforces it, but also undermines and exposes it, renders it fragile and makes it possible to thwart." It cannot be reduced to ideological battles, the unmasking of falsehoods, or the revealing of truths: resistance permeates the discursive field.

His conception of power/knowledge shaped his understanding of government. For him (ibid., 136), "the state" was not the locus of power, but rather a historically specific domain. As he explained it, images of a centralized state, which permeate understandings about liberal forms of government, emerged from sovereign modes of rule, wherein the "sovereign exercised his right of life only by exercising his right to kill, or by refraining from killing; he evidenced his power over life only through the death he was capable of requiring." And, famously, Foucault (1980b, 121) stated that "What we need ... is a political philosophy that isn't erected around the problem of sovereignty, nor therefore around the problem of law and prohibition. We need to cut off the King's head." To be clear, Foucault did not mean that the state was irrelevant to the study of politics. Rather, he wanted to emphasize the capillary aspects of power/knowledge, as well as the multiplicity of institutions and practices that run through relations of power. The state, in this way of understanding, is just one sphere and not necessarily the primary one through which power relations emerge and take form (Gordon 1991, 48).

Two main analytical lenses were brought to bear in Foucault's analytics of power: biopower and genealogy. Biopower refers to the governmental interest in the regulation of individuals and populations. In *The History of Sexuality* (1990), he explained that biopower works on the human body as a machine, seeking to maximize its competencies while rendering it politically docile. At the level of the population, biopower aims to regulate biological processes, birth rates, and mortality rates. His interest in biopower stemmed from what he saw as a paradox within liberal forms of government. On the one hand, liberal forms of government hinge on a basic assumption: individual freedom, which theoretically imbues liberal subjects with freedom of choice about how to live. On the other hand, liberal forms of government also rest on capitalist economic forms; for market economies to grow, individuals must be both able (healthy, skilled, educated, etc.), and willing (law abiding, raising civic-minded children, participating in the workforce, etc.) to support larger economic aims. At the same time, social stability in all its forms was crucial for creating a context for the maximization of wealth. Foucault therefore saw two perennial governmental questions as integral to liberal forms of governing: How to govern without governing too much? And, how to ensure that individual freedom aligns with larger governmental objectives? Biopower provided the answer to these questions.

Foucault saw genealogy, the second main lens, as a way to examine the relationship between biopower and liberal forms of governing (Dean 1999). Genealogy is a mode of historical analysis that is focused on grasping how various types of knowledge and discourses shape widely held presuppositions about what government is, how it should be conducted, for whom, and to what ends. Foucault used genealogy to understand how different types of biopolitical knowledge, especially expert and scientific forms, legitimated particular ways of thinking about and acting upon liberal subjects, and how these changed over time (Foucault 1980c, 83). These knowledges, for Foucault (1980a, 55), formed part of a "materiality of power operating on the body," as well as on the thoughts, wishes, and beliefs of individuals, for which the "social body is their effect." For instance, expert knowledge was drawn upon in various ways and at various times to justify a whole range of endeavours: educators relied on knowledge about pedagogy; counsellors trusted theories of human nature; parents turned to parenting journals in determining how to raise their children; administrators drew upon organizational theory, and so on. These types of knowledge shaped norms about how best to live and for what aims (Chambon 1999, 52; Donzelot 1979).

For Foucault, the study of government was most appropriately undertaken by examining, in a genealogical way, how these knowledges shifted and changed, and how they connected with larger political processes. But he wasn't interested only in these predominant discourses: he also wanted to identify the struggles over knowledge, points of resistance, and openings for the reformulation of new ways of thinking about government. Foucault (1984, 82) did not reject the significance of unified theories or scientific knowledge, but he did want to bring into light alternative ways of knowing: "local, discontinuous, disqualified, [and] illegitimate knowledges." Genealogy allowed him to do that, but not as a way to erect new "truths." Rather, he aimed at "disturb[ing] what was previously considered immobile ... fragment[ing] what was thought unified; [and showing] the heterogeneity of what was imagined consistent with itself." Not synonymous with a particular class, institutional, or ideological position, genealogical studies of biopower show that constellations of discourse shape rationalities of government, hence the neologism *governmentality*.

Power, Politics, and Rule in Welfare Scholarship

The question of how governmentality-inspired studies differ from conventional welfare scholarship can be answered by contrasting how each analytical orientation conceives of the key triumvirate of knowledge, levels of analysis, and citizenship, and where power, politics, and rule figure in each of these themes. It is always dangerous to take up "a literature," and this chapter makes no claim to delineate the "tenets" writ large of either one. Nevertheless, discussions such as this do have a propensity to caricature, and the potential to offend is great. To be clear, the goal is simply to tease out some predominant analytical threads that show where these two broad approaches most starkly diverge.

First, a basic premise of mainstream welfare research is the positivist assumption that there is a decipherable "external world" of knowledge which can be examined for the purposes of drawing "valid inferences by the systematic use of well-established procedures of inquiry" (King, Keohane, and Verba 1994, 6). Their traditions are buttressed by the presupposition that a social sphere exists which can be known, studied, and acted upon in a way that is unsullied by politics; such research views some types of data and methods, and in particular social statistics and assessments modelled after randomized control trials, as neutral reflections of social realities. It is extremely relevant that the value of mainstream welfare research is almost exclusively measured by how well it speaks to the specialist audiences who read academic journals. Governmentality-inspired research does not escape these hierarchical tendencies, but nevertheless Foucault sought to challenge them by bringing into view knowledge that is routinely considered marginal, inconsequential, and illegitimate. This point is particularly salient in relation to how communities are studied in welfare scholarship, which will be taken up in the next section.

In their governmentality-inspired genealogy of the "new regionalism," Wendy Larner and William Walters (2002) provide a lucid example of some of the governmental implications of positivist welfare research. They show that the emergence of welfare liberal forms of governing, what they refer to as *social* modes of rule, and the economy to which they were tied, required the collection and tabulation of statistical and other forms of knowledge to calculate how best to maximize individual health and well-being. This knowledge presumed and augmented the Westphalian nation-state as a fundamental entity of power. How was this so? First, statistics and data were often generated by state institutions. Second, this knowledge provided the foundation for comparing different national indicators, such as economic growth, unemployment, poverty, and mortality rates, which then allowed for the ordering and ranking of countries (ibid., 401-5). Third, the terrains of economy and society produced by this knowledge became the foundations of mainstream welfare studies (Bonoli, George, and Taylor-Gooby 2000, chap. 1). These in turn defined economic management and social welfare policies as coterminous with the state. As Immanuel Wallerstein (2004) also points out, rather than being unbiased and neutral, such analyses were tilted toward specific ways of knowing which had major governmental ramifications, as Larner and Walters highlight: Foucault (1979a, 27-28) expressed a similar sentiment when he said that "the subject who knows, the objects to be known and the modalities of knowledge must be regarded as so many effects of [the] fundamental implications of power/knowledge." The chasm between positivist and governmentality-oriented research could not be wider than on their differing orientations toward knowledge. Studies of governmentality show that, as is the case with other ways of knowing, the presumed impartiality and neutrality of mainstream studies is imbued with biases which have governmental ramifications. Cloaked in all its legitimizing assertions of objectivity, positivism, like the emperor, has no clothes.

The question of knowledge also needs to be considered in terms of how mainstream approaches study the role of ideas in policy processes, and how they differ from Foucauldian-inspired analyses of discourse. The typical objective of ideas research, which often erroneously uses the terms "ideas" and "discourse" interchangeably, is to properly classify dependent and independent variables in causal relations of change (Kingdon 1984; White 2002), prediction being another mantra of positivist approaches. Ideas are sometimes conceptualized as justifications for the agendas of self-interested policy actors, or as resources for actors to choose from when navigating through periods of uncertainty. At other times, ideas are assessed in relation to how they shape political behaviour (Berman 2001; Braun 1999; Nahrath 1999). Almost always, "dominant" ideas are emphasized. Vandna Bhatia and William D. Coleman (2003, 717) have even gone so far as to classify some ideas as "dominant," others as "argumentative," and still others as "transformative." A great deal can be gained by considering the relative importance that political authorities and social actors accord to certain ideas (Stone 2002), but typologies do reinforce positivist presuppositions. It is also worth noting that even Frank Fischer's influential post-positivist analysis, *Reframing Public Policy: Discursive Politics and Deliberative Practices* (2003), differs significantly from Foucauldian-based approaches. Fischer (ibid., 41) defines discourse in terms of language, and construes discourse analysis as a theoretical undertaking. Studies of governmentality, by contrast, are not theories, but rather analytical orientations, and though they too are interested in how language mediates power, they also see discourse as inherent in practices, physical constructs, tacit effects, and silences.

A second area where conventional welfare research and studies of governmentality diverge concerns their views on the levels-of-analysis question. Welfare scholarship is typically divided into micro, meso, and macro levels, an analytical ladder that mirrors the hierarchical bureaucratic structures of power upon which the corpus was built. Micro-level lenses tend to be focused mainly on evaluating best practices, the congruence of policy objectives with implementation, or assessing unintended consequences. Research on the policy-making role of street-level bureaucrats excluded (Lipsky 1980), there is a lack of attention paid to the political and governmental implications of micro-level practices. Meso-level analyses, such as the influential works of Michael M. Atkinson and William D. Coleman (1989, 1992) and William Coleman and Grace Skogstad (1990), encompass analyses of policy systems, epistemic communities, networks, governance, and regime typologies (Boychuk 1998; Brodie 1997; Esping-Andersen 1990). Their primary aim is to theorize processes of, rationales for, and characteristics attendant upon public policy action (Howlett and Ramesh 1995). Meso-level studies have significantly enhanced policy research (McKeen 2004; Tuohy 1999), but, like their micro-level counterparts, they most often favour state-centred questions and themes. Typically, they (Howlett and Ramesh 1995, chap. 5) emphasize policy problems defined by political elites, public

authorities, and the "attentive public" (Pross 1986). As well, meso-level approaches sometimes study policy implementation undertaken by actors engaged in what is referred to as the "subgovernment," but weight their analyses
heavily toward questions pertaining to the role of the state. Given the preoccupation in mainstream research with assessing state-centred cause-and-
effect processes, it is not surprising that macro-level research, with important
exceptions (Esping-Andersen 1990), ranks at the pinnacle of influence in
this corpus (Pierson 1994). These studies have trained attention on broad
economic, social, and political patterns, such as those shaped by public spending, official political institutions, changing demographics, and the power of
social movements. Such indicators explicitly or implicitly treat local-level
processes as epiphenomena, as opposed to integral to wider governmental
frameworks. There might be sound analytical reasons for treating micro-,
meso-, and macro-level governmental processes in distinct ways, but conceptual borders, by design, leave out certain lines of investigation; it is no small
point that each of these three levels of analysis favours elite views (Howlett
and Ramesh 1995, chap. 3).

Studies of governmentality, by contrast, slice through micro, meso, and
macro domains of power. This is so because they aim, not to explain *why*
states act the way they do, but rather *how* individual-level and population-
level biopolitical forms take shape and what governmental implications flow
from them. They pose a series of interrelated questions: From where do policy
issues, public problems, or political classifications emerge? What types of
dilemmas do they raise? What techniques and mechanisms are brought to
bear to solve them? What aims are pursued, to what forms of knowledge are
they tied, and how have historical struggles played out across them? And, of
course, the paramount question: what types of political subjectivities do they
engender (Rose 1995)? These lines of investigation train attention on how
power, politics, and rule are interconnected with research and knowledge;
they break down and transcend conventional analytical hierarchies; and they
catapult the subject of politics to centre stage.

This brings us to the issue of citizenship, a third area where the two
intellectual orientations sharply contrast. In positivist approaches, questions
of citizenship have traditionally been addressed in terms of citizen-state relations that assume a self-evident liberal subject: the citizen. Although there
have been important departures from this assumption, which will be addressed further on in this chapter, the common point of entry for positivist
studies is Gøsta Esping-Andersen's widely cited work on welfare regimes, *The*

Three Worlds of Welfare Capitalism (1990). Esping-Andersen expanded on the ideas of Thomas H. Marshall (1992): in *Citizenship and Social Class*, a seminal study first published in 1950, Marshall had maintained that modern citizenship developed in three stages, one upon the other, from civil, political, and finally to social rights, as expressed through the modern welfare state. Esping-Andersen argued that modern welfare regimes were shaped by degrees of decommodification, defined in terms of the extent to which a person's life chances were independent from market forces. For him, as for Marshall and numerous scholars in Canada and elsewhere (Brodie 2003; Graham and Phillips 1997; Jenson 1997; Jenson and Papillon 2000; Jenson and Phillips 1996; Jenson and Saint-Martin 2003), decommodification was, in the main, determined by the state, which limits or confers social rights.

Although they do not deny the importance of citizenship's legal dimensions, studies of governmentality inspire a different orientation that stresses how knowledge and practice shape social classifications in terms of normalcy and deviance, and all manner of variations in between and across this dichotomy (Isin 2002; Isin and Wood 1999; Rose 1996). There is never one single division but rather multiple cleavages and dimensions. In the spheres of social welfare provisions, these sensibilities are generated through discursive practices that create idealized images about how people should behave, think, feel, act, and understand their place in the world. Those who fall short or interfere with such expectations become the targets of a whole swath of authoritative actions, such as addictions services, suicide counselling, rehabilitation, skills retooling, parenting workshops, and the like. These activities aim to reorient individual conduct toward acceptable standards, be they moral, emotional, mental, behavioural, spiritual, physical, or other such measure. The state does not dictate these norms or force people to abide by them (Donzelot 1979). To do so, of course, would be anathema to one of the basic tenets of liberal government, which rests on the assumption of individual freedom (Rose 1999). Instead, the shaping of individual conduct emerges from dynamic interplays between various discursive domains, both within and beyond official institutions of authority.

A thumbnail genealogical sketch of the emergence of the figure of the "single mother" illuminates several crucial features of governmentality-inspired studies of government: these include the focus on the role of knowledge and practices, both within and outside of the state, the integration of micro-, meso-, and macro-level governmental domains, and the central significance of shifting forms of political subjectivities in liberal forms of rule (Murray

2001, 2004b). The figure of the single mother was thrust to the fore of policy debates in Canada during the early 1990s, but its genealogy traces back to transformations of the late nineteenth century. Prior to that time, liberal forms of governing were based on a *classical liberal* sensibility which defined the market as a natural, functioning entity. In the face of major social and economic dislocations shaped by industrialization and urbanization, this classical sensibility proved problematic, and a nascent *welfare liberal* rationality began to emerge. These welfare mentalities of rule hinged on the view that judicious interventions in social and economic life could be justified as necessary to maximize, stabilize, and unleash "natural" human capabilities undermined by, yet simultaneously needed for, the "free" market. This shift toward welfare governance was brought about in part by the growing role of "community" entities, such as charitable, voluntary, and philanthropic organizations, which began regulating various problematic people. Single mothers were one such concern. Females flocking to urban centres for employment, especially those who found themselves pregnant and unmarried, starkly challenged established sexual mores and patriarchal, two-parent family norms which were considered fundamental to social order, a well-functioning market, and the development of the Canadian "nation."

This growing salience of welfare sensibilities began an unfolding of what would become over the twentieth century an ever-changing field of governmental practices aimed at single mothers. Religious sensibilities dominated until the 1920s; tenets of social work would then take hold; psychiatric knowledge ascended in significance in the 1940s and 1950s; finally, economic theories gained credence in the latter decades of the century. These governmental transformations, which sometimes explicitly divided single mothers into subclassifications according to race, ethnicity, age, religion, and class, legitimated various regulatory mechanisms and political goals. Religious leaders sought to save souls by providing religious counselling; social workers aimed at fostering good character through rehabilitation; psychiatric authorities hoped to address neurotic tendencies by employing Freudian techniques; and then welfare program dismantlers tried to engender individual economic self-sufficiency by "recommodifying" citizenship – removing any non-market-based solutions to poverty and social disadvantage. This most recent alteration revealed an emergent *neo-liberal* form of rule that had many similarities to classical approaches, except with greater emphasis on making sure that markets were unencumbered by "extraneous" public spending.

State interventions were sometimes brought to bear in these processes: illegitimacy and adoption laws, as well as Mothers' Allowance schemes, were created in the early 1920s; adoption laws were dramatically reformulated in the early 1950s; and the 1960s saw the development of new laws pertaining to reproduction and divorce. Throughout these years, the state also engaged in various other gendered income-security policies, and those at the end of the twentieth century were aimed at restricting entitlements to single mothers.

Casting a wider analytical net, this governmentality-inspired investigation shows that the state, though important, was nevertheless only one domain of governmental action, and at times not necessarily the dominant one. Training the lens on the diffusive dimensions of power also reveals that the changing contours of political subjectivity are of great consequence to power, politics, and rule. Far from being self-evident, the single mother was a deeply political, historically specific figure that illuminated different angles of liberal rule, which in turn hinged on politically salient norms – sexual, gender, racial, ethnic, religious, and class, all of which were inextricably tied to broader governmental goals, such as social stability, fiscal prudence, and the maximization of wealth.

As this genealogy of single mothers illustrates, studies of governmentality reject the assumptions of universal citizenship in mainstream welfare research. It would be remiss, however, not to acknowledge that some scholars working within positivist traditions have sought to do the same, but, like the proverbial square peg in the round hole, they don't fit. Such efforts are trying to wed studies of contingencies to analyses based on clearly defined measurement variables. This is not to deny the value of assessing the gendered implications of state programs, some of which have been particularly insightful and illuminating (Bashevkin 2002; Dobrowolsky and Jenson 2004; McKeen 2004; Newman and White 2006; Porter 2003). Rather, it is to point out that sometimes these analyses create other global classificatory schemes, such as "women," "men," and "children," which can also exclude or ignore the political import of race, ethnicity, class, sexual orientation, and other social divisions.

This type of problem appeared in the influential *States, Markets, Families,* by Julia S. O'Connor, Ann Shola Orloff, and Sheila Shaver (1999). Even though elsewhere Orloff (2003) chastised the "thinness" of "mainstream scholars' conceptions of gender," she nevertheless slips into essentialist tendencies herself. Anne Schneider and Helen Ingram (1993) were particularly

misguided in seeking to devise a "theory of the social construction of identity" by evaluating why certain "target populations" are "more powerful" than
others. In studies of governmentality, it is precisely groups considered "less
powerful" that are of particular interest. Those imaged as the outsiders, the
excluded, the disenfranchised, the troublesome, the difficult, and those feared
to be lurking in darkened corners illuminate the outlines, shifting and hazy,
between pathos and norm, bleak and bright (Rose 1996, 131).

Given that studies of governmentality focus on questions of "the how"
of government as opposed to "the why," it will come as no surprise that they
are criticized for their perceived failure to "locate, judge and denounce the
enemy" (Barry, Bell, and Rose 1995, 485). In Chapter 2 of this volume, Peter
Graefe (p. 24) makes this point when he argues that by eschewing "the burdens of explanation and causation," Foucauldian analyses pay "too steep a
price" for policy research aimed at "interven[ing] in the world." However,
comparing mainstream approaches with studies of governmentality turns
this criticism on its head. Positivist research, in fact, is implicated in the
reinforcement of problematic discursive assumptions based on hierarchical
norms that divide the privileged from the oppressed. Even activist-oriented
positivist research cannot escape the fact that it is in some senses hamstrung
out of the gate by ignoring or sidestepping the overlapping relationship of
power and knowledge. That positivist approaches tower over the field of welfare scholarship is therefore important, not because they show themselves to
be more insightful or rigorous than other research orientations, but because
they contribute to silencing, marginalizing, and delegitimizing other claims
to "truth." The growing salience of communities in governmental processes,
with their seeming novelty and inventiveness, is a chance to rectify this im-
balance. It is an opportune political moment to shift the winds of policy
research toward ways of knowing which have been relegated to the fringes of
welfare scholarship. The next section evaluates how governmentality-inspired
research might do just that.

Shifting the Policy Winds toward Communities

In conventional social policy research, the growing emphasis on communities has been examined from three main, often overlapping, vantage points.
First, some scholars, many working within the social movement tradition,
examine the role of community groups attempting to make claims upon the
state (Smith 2005). A second focus is on understanding how the boundaries
between the state and society are shifting, and the ramifications of these

changes on ministerial accountability and democratic participation (Banting 1999). A third line of inquiry concerns how public problems are addressed through various types of relationships or networks that include political authorities, experts, and citizens. This third area of research has generated an emerging subfield under the guise of governance studies, which is divided into descriptive and conceptual accounts of "what actually happened and how" (Phillips 2001) and prescriptive accounts about how "good" governance can be attained (Salamon 2002).

These differing analytical angles have led to numerous interpretations concerning the relationship between communities and the realignment of government. During the years of major public program cuts, many analysts equated the growing emphasis on communities as tantamount to a quantitative reduction in the role of the state. Especially among observers on the right of the political spectrum, the larger role for communities was seen as a welcome development that would not only reduce welfare expenditures, rein in welfare "cheats," and promote the traditional family, but also foster greater freedom and choice (Richards 1998). For many others on the left, this transformation was nothing more than an abdication of public responsibility for citizens, particularly those who were economically and socially marginalized (Shields and Evans 1998), although some also saw promise in what were hoped might be more democratic forms of administration in the wake of the flattening and streamlining of bureaucratic hierarchies (Albo, Langille, and Panitch 1993). Then attention turned to conceptualizing what came to be regarded as a governmental paradigm shift. This analytical regrouping arose from the recognition that governments, though altering priorities, had not reduced overall spending, as had initially been assumed (Andrew, Graham, and Phillips 2002; Bradford 2004; Brenner 2004; Howlett 2000; Jenson and Saint-Martin 2003; Peck and Tickell 2002). Despite the various dimensions of these debates, they shared the common inclination of remaining at a high level of abstraction in their assessments of the policy aspects of communities. Even though a nascent interest emerged aimed at assessing how communities were being shaped through governmental practices, these analyses nevertheless continued to be heavily state-centric, construing state interventions as marginalizing or silencing "authentic" community forms (Brock 2001; Laforest and Orsini 2005).

A discussion of the limits of the influential "social investment state" paradigm can further illuminate the insights to be gained by taking up governmentality themes. Denis Saint-Martin, who, along with Jane Jenson, has helmed this interpretation in the Canadian setting (Jenson and Saint-Martin 2003), expands upon the social-investment-state theory in Chapter 13 of this volume, so only two core themes will be highlighted here. First, the theory maintains that state policies have become increasingly future-oriented. Children are the emblem of this focus, the "ideal" citizen-workers of tomorrow, and the programmatic emphases are life-long learning and "active" citizenship, which together are aimed at promoting self-sufficiency and self-responsibility. Welfare state rationales are geared toward achieving equality in the present, but the goal of social investing is to foster the hope of equality in years to come. A second dimension of this paradigm is that new modes of governing are said to rest on a larger role for communities as domains for promoting social capital as an antidote to social exclusion. Social-investment-state theorists have said very little about what this feature means in practice. Now this relative silence might suggest that these theorists do not see communities as governmental terrains; alternatively, these theorists might deem the community dimensions of their theory as beyond the purview of welfare policy research grounded in the discipline of political science. This assumption, which may or may not exist, would nevertheless reinforce the dominant ways of knowing, which Foucauldian-inspired research would find problematic.

Although they may differ regarding epistemology, both social-investment-state scholars and researchers drawing upon governmentality themes seek to identify and grasp underlying rationales shaping the realignment of government. One important difference is that social investment studies, as the nomenclature suggests, focus on state-centred changes, whereas studies of governmentality cast a wider analytical net, paying close attention to the political significance of the community dimensions within emerging governmental schemes. Governmentality-influenced research would not juxtapose the state and community, but rather would analyze them in tandem as overlapping and interconnected discursive sites shaping new modes of rule. This field of questioning would attempt to ascertain the political and governmental salience of discourses and practices that seek to make communities tangible entities, and to identify the political subjectivities they engender (Cruikshank 1994; Ilcan and Basok 2004; Rose 1999). These analytical angles would be brought to the fore, not as a specific research template or method, but rather as an orientation to political investigation.

Three specific governmentality-inspired lines of scrutiny can shed light on dimensions of governing that are missed in social-investment-state research. A first area of attention would examine the presuppositions under-pinning official authoritative designs targeting communities (Procacci 1991, 152). A study of Canadian federal government programs (Murray 2004a) took up this issue and showed remarkably similar sensibilities across several policy spheres. The analysis highlighted a cross-cutting governmentality to mould communities toward regulating "problematic" people, generally people who just "hadn't made the grade" on the global political economy test. Pro-grams were aimed at shaping communities as technical or managerial units for addressing the unseemly side of global capitalism. To use a Marxist meta-phor, communities were in effect construed as clearinghouses for dealing with the lumpen proletariat. Another dimension at play was that the meas-ure of civic duty was defined in relation to a commitment to voluntarism and philanthropy (Ilcan and Basok 2004), which in a seemingly paradoxical way, could be made manifest only by the existence of poverty and disadvan-tage. But, then again, altruism assumes a border between giver and receiver, and in the realm of community activity this binary can serve a governmental aim by dividing "responsible" citizens from their anti-, sub-, and non-citizen counterparts (Rose 1999, 259). Applications of social-investment-state theory have shown none of this.

Street-level discourses can focus a second line of investigation into how communities are formed as perceptible fields amenable to and harnessed for governmental interventions. This dimension was addressed in a study con-ducted in the East Vancouver district of Grandview Woodland, in an area clustered around the Britannia Community Centre. This area is marked by high levels of economic and social disadvantage, making it a suitable focal point for examining the street-level dimensions of the realignment of gov-ernment. The research performed extensive document analyses and drew upon data from interviews conducted with twenty-seven people identified as hav-ing in-depth knowledge of local institutional changes in the latter years of the twentieth century and into the new millennium. In contrast to studies based on elite views, this research included community workers in its infor-mant pool, as well as individuals availing themselves of services and resources provided by organizations attempting to address issues of poverty and marginalization; the research, therefore, systematically sought to incorpo-rate forms of knowledge typically excluded from policy research. A main-stream welfare scholar would be quick to point out that findings from a single research site are not generalizable. However, generalization and grand-theorizing are not the point of Foucauldian-inspired studies such as this one in Vancouver, which treated the research site as a discursive terrain, and the interview findings as a set of indicators to identify, in the spirit of genealogy, changing power relations; in turn, these analytical steps served as lenses for assessing wider governmental dynamics and their effects, both explicit and tacit.

Taking up these street-level dimensions, the Grandview Woodland study found that established community networks had fractured, while simultaneously mandates and approaches being brought to bear had shifted. These changes were not a quantitative reduction in government, but instead a fundamental transformation in *how* individuals were being governed. They were certainly not antidotes to social exclusion: in fact, social exclusion itself was serving governmental purposes by carving out community as a tangible sphere which institutionalized disadvantage, normalized more extreme forms of poverty, and naturalized disenfranchisement. These discursive processes reconfigured citizenship norms, thereby calling into question, if not wholly refuting, some of the future-oriented assumptions which social-investment-state theories highlight. Although they were not the product of any single intent or grand plan, the community interventions identified in Grandview Woodland were shaping social inequalities in both implicit and overt ways. A growing body of research shows similar processes at play in other spatial contexts (Murray 2004a, 2004b; Murray, Low, and Waite forthcoming 2006). It is too soon to draw firm conclusions, but these similarities suggest a major realignment of discursive practices. Clearly, none of these dimensions would be decipherable in a state-centred study. More crucially, such an omission is akin to the further augmentation of the apparent ordinariness and acceptability of discourses on community which create and enhance political identities defined by social inequality.

A third line of inquiry might focus more centrally on examining how community interventions construe political identities. In Grandview Woodland, for instance, this governmentality lens showed that major changes were taking shape in relation to policies and practices aimed at children's health and well-being. Many programs were closed or rolled back, such as services for parents caring for children and resources for children with disabilities; in the case of the latter, access for some children was discontinued because parents could not or would not provide medical proof of their child's condition. These combined modifications in policy and practice were not simply a matter of benign neglect, but the outcome of deliberate interventions that determined which children would be entitled and which ones would not. If we set aside the important questions of intent and practical "realities," which are not the focus of studies of governmentality, we see how such transformations groom so-called citizen-workers of the future, by dividing the deserving from the undeserving and the "haves" from the "have nots." These were not exclusively class issues. Although obviously very much about economic status, these dimensions also traversed classificatory schemes shaped by race, ethnicity, and other social partitions. In the Grandview Woodland study, none of these cleavages were dictated by a centralized state. Even though official institutions of power were of enormous consequence, particularly with regard to program cuts, these emergent categories took shape through an intricate interplay that included a growing demand for services, a greater emphasis on community organizations, and contextually specific responses. No one would be naïve enough to think that local community activity would match idealized images in official policy programs, but it is significant that changing governmental images of "children" cannot be fully captured in a singular emphasis on broad-based state programs (Chen 2005). Canadian researchers have made internationally recognized contributions with regard to state-focused research on these matters (Dobrowolsky and Jenson 2004). However, many of the political dimensions of social categories can be captured only by examining the constellations of governmental effects apparent in street-level discursive shifts. Again, social-investment-state theories neglect these important processes.

These three lines of investigation reveal facets of governing which are obscured in studies of the social investment state. Although there are many other questions that a Foucauldian-influenced approach could also fruitfully address, such as points of resistance in community discourses, these three areas alone shed light on some of the explicit rationales, micro-level interactions, and tacit results taking shape under the mantle of *community*. These emerging forms of rule are of enormous consequence (Dean 1991; Polanyi 1963; Procacci 1991), and especially crucial to grasp in light of the resurgence of "poverty" as a major policy concern in the early years of the new millennium (Noël 2005; O'Connor 2002). An important part of this change is the presupposition that issues of poverty are best addressed by building community, an assumption which hinges on a biopolitical imperative to gain more knowledge on how to unleash community competencies (Murray 2004a). And, in a dramatic alteration from welfare sensibilities, the question of poverty has been redefined in terms of the *technical* question of how to harness communities better and more effectively, as opposed to the *political* dilemma of how to make social, economic, and political structures more just and equitable (Rochefort and Cobb 1993; Ruggeri Laderchi, Saith, and Stewart 2003). If these are not welfare or social investment elements, are they then aspects of a neo-liberal governmentality? The evidence indicates that this might be an appropriate assessment, as discourses on communities are augmenting, rather than undermining, individualist forms of political subjectivity, even while engendering new types of politically salient identities. This suggests that communities might mark out a new terrain for fostering what Jamie Peck and Adam Tickell (2002) refer to as the neo-liberalization of space. The full implications of what this might mean, however, are waiting to be examined.

Conclusion

This chapter has elaborated on how themes of governmentality might be applied in Canadian policy studies, especially to the study of communities in social welfare research. The chapter has shown that there are important limits to conventional positivist analyses which uncritically adopt dominant discourses. These limits are not benign: they are creating and solidifying problematic norms and ideals. To be sure, this is not to suggest that positivists should pack their bags and go home. The point is merely to propose that pressing the soft (or hard) spots of discourse is a way to make tactical use of the historical struggle over knowledge (Foucault 1980c, 83). When it comes to discursive categories that reinforce social, economic, and political inequalities, a governmentality orientation would seem particularly appropriate. Grasping and resisting problematic basic precepts, especially those valorized in official policy debates, *is* a political act aimed at creating new and less oppressive governmental forms. In the contemporary context, where boundaries of power, politics, and rule shift as we think, speak, and write, such endeavours are particularly apropos.

ACKNOWLEDGMENTS
A special thank you is extended to the interview informants who gave so generously of their time to participate in this research. The study benefited enormously from the research assistance of highly qualified researchers Michael Caverhill and Angela Waite, as well as from Margaret Condon of the Social Planning and Research Council of British Columbia, who conducted the interviews. The council's Michael Goldberg advised and contributed to the development of the research instruments and the choice of site.

I am indebted to Xiaobei Chen, Mariana Valverde, and David Wolfe, who offered important insights that made their way into this chapter; and thanks to both the editors and anonymous reviewers who provided immense support and advice in the shaping of this chapter. Errors are obviously my own. The empirical section is part of an ongoing project being undertaken with Caroline Andrew, Judith McKenzie, and Michael Orsini as co-applicants. Funding for this research, which is gratefully acknowledged, was obtained from the Canadian Institutes of Health Research (Grant Number: ROP-62676) and the Social Sciences and Humanities Research Council of Canada (Grant Number: 832-2002-0114).

NOTES

1   Part of the aim of this chapter is to destabilize essentialist images of various political categories, including "community." For the purpose of clarity, I will not repeat the quotation marks throughout the discussion.

2   There are many excellent overviews of Michel Foucault's ideas on governmentality. This section is heavily influenced by my readings of Mitchell Dean (1999), Colin Gordon (1991), Nikolas Rose (1999), Nikolas Rose and Peter Miller (1992), and William Walters (2000).

REFERENCES

Albo, Greg, David Langille, and Leo Panitch, eds. 1993. *A Different Kind of State? Popular Power and Democratic Administration.* Toronto: Oxford University Press.

Andrew, Caroline, Katherine A. Graham, and Susan D. Phillips. 2002. *Urban Affairs: Back on the Policy Agenda.* Montreal and Kingston: McGill-Queen's University Press.

Atkinson, Michael M., and William D. Coleman. 1989. "Strong States and Weak States: Sectoral Policy Networks in Advanced Capitalist Economies." *British Journal of Political Science* 19(1): 47-67.

—. 1992. "Policy Networks, Policy Communities and the Problems of Governance." *Governance* 5(2): 154-80.

Banting, Keith, ed. 1999. *The Nonprofit Sector in Canada: Roles and Relationships.* Montreal and Kingston: McGill-Queen's University Press.

Barry, Andrew, Vicki Bell, and Nikolas Rose. 1995. "Introduction." *Economy and Society* 24(4): 485-88.

Bashevkin, Sylvia. 2002. *Welfare Hot Buttons: Women, Work, and Social Policy Reform.* Toronto: University of Toronto Press.

Berman, Sheri. 2001. "Ideas, Norms, and Culture in Political Analysis." *Comparative Politics* 33(2): 231-50.

Bhatia, Vandna, and William D. Coleman. 2003. "Ideas and Discourse: Reform and Resistance in the Canadian and German Health Systems." *Canadian Journal of Political Science* 36(4): 715-39.

Bonoli, Giuliano, Vic George, and Peter Taylor-Gooby. 2000. *European Welfare Futures: Towards a Theory of Retrenchment*. Cambridge: Polity Press.

Boychuk, Gerald William. 1998. *Patchworks of Purpose: The Development of Provincial Social Assistance Regimes in Canada*. Montreal and Kingston: McGill-Queen's University Press.

Bradford, Neil. 2004. "Place Matters and Multi-level Governance: Perspectives on a New Urban Policy Paradigm." *Policy Options* (February): 39-44.

Braun, Dietmar. 1999. "Interests or Ideas? An Overview of Ideational Concepts in Public Policy Research." In *Public Policy and Political Ideas*, ed. Dietmar Braun and Andreas Busch, 11-30. Cheltenham: Edward Elgar.

Brenner, Neil. 2004. *New State Spaces: Urban Governance and the Rescaling of Statehood*. Oxford: Oxford University Press.

Brock, Kathy L. 2001. "Promoting Voluntary Action and Civil Society through the State." *ISUMA* 2(2): 53-61.

Brodie, Janine. 1997. "Meso-discourses, State Forms and the Gendering of Liberal-Democratic Citizenship." *Citizenship Studies* 1(2): 223-41.

—. 2003. "Citizenship and Solidarity: Reflections on the Canadian Way." *Citizenship Studies* 6(4): 377-94.

Chambon, Adrienne S. 1999. "Foucault's Approach: Making the Familiar Visible." In *Reading Foucault for Social Work*, ed. Adrienne S. Chambon, Allan Irving, and Laura Epstein, 51-81. New York: Columbia University Press.

Chen, Xiaobei. 2005. *Tending the Gardens of Citizenship: Child Saving in Toronto, 1880s-1920s*. Toronto: University of Toronto Press.

Coleman, William, and Grace Skogstad. 1990. *Policy Communities and Public Policy in Canada: A Structural Approach*. Mississauga: Copp Clark Pitman.

Cruikshank, Barbara. 1994. "The Will to Empower: Technologies of Citizenship in the War on Poverty." *Socialist Review* 23(4): 29-55.

Dean, Mitchell. 1991. *The Constitution of Poverty: Toward a Genealogy of the Liberal Governance*. London: Routledge.

—. 1999. *Governmentality: Power and Rule in Modern Society*. London: Sage Publications.

Dobrowolsky, Alexandra, and Jane Jenson. 2004. "Shifting Representations of Citizenship: Canadian Politics of 'Women' and 'Children.'" *Social Politics: International Studies in Gender, State and Society* 11(2): 154-80.

Donzelot, Jacques. 1979. *The Policing of Families*. New York: Random House.

Esping-Andersen, Gøsta. 1990. *The Three Worlds of Welfare Capitalism*. Cambridge: Polity Press.

Fischer, Frank. 2003. *Reframing Public Policy: Discursive Politics and Deliberative Practices*. Oxford: Oxford University Press.

Foucault, Michel. 1972. *The Archaeology of Knowledge and the Discourse on Language*, trans. A.M. Sheridan. New York: Harper and Row.

—. 1979a. *Discipline and Punish*. New York: Vintage Books.

—. 1979b. "On Governmentality," trans. Rosi Braidotti. *Ideology and Consciousness* 6(Autumn): 5-21.

—. 1980a. "Body/Power." In *Michel Foucault: Power/Knowledge: Selected Interviews and Other Writings 1972-1977*, ed. Colin Gordon, 55-62. New York: Harvester Press.

—. 1980b. "Truth and Power." In *Michel Foucault: Power/Knowledge: Selected Interviews and Other Writings 1972-1977*, ed. Colin Gordon, 109-33. New York: Harvester Press.

—. 1980c. "Two Lectures." In *Michel Foucault: Power/Knowledge: Selected Interviews and Other Writings 1972-1977*, ed. Colin Gordon, 78-108. New York: Harvester Press.

—. 1984. "Nietzsche, Genealogy, History." In *The Foucault Reader*, ed. Paul Rabinow, 76-100. London: Penguin Books.

—. 1990. *The History of Sexuality: An Introduction*. Vol. 1. New York: Vintage Books.

Gordon, Colin. 1991. "Governmental Rationality: An Introduction." In *The Foucault Effect: Studies in Governmentality*, ed. Graham Burchell, Colin Gordon, and Peter Miller, 1-52. Chicago: University of Chicago Press.

Graefe, Peter. 2004. "Personal Services in the Post-industrial Economy: Adding Nonprofits to the Welfare Mix." *Social Policy and Administration* 38(5): 456-69.

Graham, Katherine A., and Susan D. Phillips. 1997. "Citizenship Engagement: Beyond the Customer Revolution." *Canadian Public Administration* 40(2): 255-73.

Hall, Michael H., and Paul B. Reed. 1998. "Shifting the Burden: How Much Can Government Download to the Non-profit Sector?" *Canadian Public Administration* 41(1): 1-20.

Howlett, Michael. 2000. "Managing the 'Hollow State': Procedural Policy Instruments and Modern Governance." *Canadian Public Administration* 43(4): 412-31.

Howlett, Michael, and M. Ramesh. 1995. *Studying Public Policy: Policy Cycles and Policy Subsystems*. Oxford: Oxford University Press.

Ilcan, Suzan, and Tanya Basok. 2004. "Community Government: Voluntary Agencies, Social Justice, and the Responsibilization of Citizens." *Citizenship Studies* 8(2): 129-44.

Isin, Engin F. 2002. *Being Political: Genealogies of Citizenship*. Minneapolis: University of Minnesota Press.

Isin, Engin F., and Patricia K. Wood. 1999. *Citizenship and Identity*. London: Sage Publications.

Jenson, Jane. 1997. "Fated to Live in Interesting Times: Canada's Changing Citizenship Regimes." *Canadian Journal of Political Science* 30(4): 627-44.

Jenson, Jane, and Martin Papillon. 2000. "The Changing Boundaries of Citizenship: A Review and Research Agenda." In *Modernizing Governance: A Preliminary Exploration*. Paper published by the Canadian Centre for Management Development. http://dsp-psd.communication.gc.ca/Collection/SC94-75-2000E.pdf.

Jenson, Jane, and Susan D. Phillips. 1996. "Regime Shift: New Citizenship Practices in Canada." *International Journal of Canadian Studies* 14(Fall): 111-36.

Jenson, Jane, and Denis Saint-Martin. 2003. "Building Blocks for a New Welfare Architecture: Is LEGO the Model for an Active Society?" Paper presented at the Fourth International Conference on Social Security, Antwerp, Belgium, 4-7 May.

Kernaghan, Kenneth, and Mohamed Charih. 1997. "The Challenge of Change: Emerging Issues in Contemporary Public Administration." *Canadian Public Administration* 40(2): 218-33.

King, Gary, Robert O. Keohane, and Sidney Verba. 1994. *Designing Social Inquiry: Scientific Inference and Qualitative Research*. Princeton: Princeton University Press.

Kingdon, John. 1984. *Agendas, Alternatives and Public Policies*. Boston: Little Brown.

Laforest, Rachel, and Michael Orsini. 2005. "Evidence Based Engagement in the Voluntary Sector: Lessons from Canada." *Social Policy and Administration* 39(5): 481-97.

Larner, Wendy, and William Walters. 2002. "The Political Rationality of the 'New Regionalism': Towards a Genealogy of the 'Region.'" *Theory and Society* 31(3): 391-432.

Lemke, Thomas. 2001. "The Birth of 'Bio-politics': Michel Foucault's Lecture at the Collège de France on Neo-liberal Governmentality." *Economy and Society* 30(2): 190-207.

Lipsky, Michael. 1980. *Street-Level Bureaucracy: Dilemmas of the Individual in Public Services*. New York: Russell Sage Foundation.

Marshall, Thomas H. 1992. *Citizenship and Social Class*. London: Pluto Press.

McKeen, Wendy. 2004. *Money in Their Own Name: The Feminist Voice in Poverty Debate in Canada, 1970-1995*. Toronto: University of Toronto Press.

Murray, Karen Bridget. 2001. "Upsetting the Public-Private Divide: The Third Sector and the Governance of 'Single Mothers' in Twentieth-Century Canada." PhD diss., Political Science, University of British Columbia.

—. 2004a. "Do Not Disturb: Vulnerable Populations in Federal Government Policy Discourses and Practices." *Canadian Journal of Urban Research* 13(1): 50-69.

—. 2004b. "Governing 'Unwed Mothers' in Toronto at the Turn of the Twentieth Century." *Canadian Historical Review* 85(2): 253-76.

Murray, Karen Bridget, Jacqueline Low, and Angela Waite. Forthcoming 2006. "The Voluntary Sector and the Realignment of Government: A Street-Level Study." *Canadian Public Administration* 49(3).

Nahrath, Stéphane. 1999. "The Power of Ideas in Policy Research: A Critical Assessment." In *Public Policy and Political Ideas*, ed. Dietmar Braun and Andreas Busch, 41-60. Cheltenham: Edward Elgar.

Newman, Jacquetta A., and Linda White. 2006. *Women, Politics, and Public Policy: The Political Struggles of Canadian Women*. Toronto: Oxford University Press.

Noël, Alain. 2005. "The New Politics of Global Poverty." Paper presented at the Social Justice for a Changing World Conference, University of Bremen, Bremen, Germany, 10-12 March. http://www.uni-bielefeld.de/soz/personen/Leisering/pdf/Noel%20globale%20Armut.pdf.

O'Connor, Alice. 2002. *Poverty Knowledge: Social Science, Social Policy, and the Poor in Twentieth Century U.S. History.* Princeton: Princeton University Press.

O'Connor, Julia S., Ann Shola Orloff, and Sheila Shaver. 1999. *States, Markets, Families: Gender, Liberalism and Social Policy in Australia, Canada, Great Britain and the United States.* Cambridge: Cambridge University Press.

Orloff, Ann Shola. 2003. "Systems of Social Provision and Regulation." Paper presented at the Canadian Political Science Association annual meeting, Halifax, 31 May. http://www.cpsa-acsp.ca/paper-2003/orloff.pdf.

Pal, Leslie A. 1992. *Public Policy Analysis: An Introduction.* 2nd ed. Toronto: Nelson.

Peck, Jamie, and Adam Tickell. 2002. "Neoliberalizing Space." *Antipode* 34(3): 380-404.

Phillips, Susan D. 2001. "More Than Stakeholders: Reforming State-Voluntary Sector Relations." *Journal of Canadian Studies* 35(4): 1-22.

Pierson, Paul. 1994. *Dismantling the Welfare State? Reagan, Thatcher, and the Politics of Retrenchment.* Cambridge: Cambridge University Press.

Polanyi, Karl. 1963. *The Great Transformation.* Boston: Beacon Hill.

Porter, Ann. 2003. *Gendered States: Women, Unemployment Insurance, and the Political Economy of the Welfare State in Canada, 1945-1997.* Toronto: University of Toronto Press.

Procacci, Giovanna. 1991. "Social Economy and the Government of Poverty." In *The Foucault Effect: Studies in Governmentality,* ed. Graham Burchell, Colin Gordon, and Peter Miller, 151-68. Chicago: University of Chicago Press.

Pross, Paul. 1986. *Group Politics and Public Policy.* Toronto: Oxford University Press.

Richards, John. 1998. *Retooling the Welfare State: What's Right, What's Wrong, What's to Be Done?* Toronto: C.D. Howe Institute.

Rochefort, David A., and Roger W. Cobb. 1993. "Problem Definition, Agenda Access and Policy Choice." *Policy Studies Journal* 21(1): 56-71.

Rochefort, David A., Michael Rosenberg, and Deena White. 1998. "Community as a Policy Instrument: A Comparative Analysis." *Policy Studies Journal* 26(3): 548-69.

Rose, Nikolas. 1995. "Authority and the Genealogy of Subjectivity." In *De-traditionalization: Authority and the Self in an Age of Cultural Uncertainty,* ed. Paul Heelas, Paul Morris, and Scott Lash, 294-327. Oxford: Basil Blackwell.

—. 1996. "Identity, Genealogy, History." In *Questions of Cultural Identity,* ed. Stuart Hall and Paul du Gay, 128-49. Bonhill: Sage Publications.

—. 1999. *Powers of Freedom: Reframing Political Thought.* Cambridge: Cambridge University Press.

Rose, Nikolas, and Peter Miller. 1992. "Political Power beyond the State: Problematics of Government." *British Journal of Sociology* 43(2): 173-205.

Ruggeri Laderchi, Caterina, Ruhi Saith, and Frances Stewart. 2003. "Does It Matter That We Do Not Agree on the Definition of Poverty? A Comparison of Four Approaches." *Oxford Development Studies* 31(3): 243-74.

Salamon, Lester M. 2002. "The New Governance and the Tools of Public Action: An Introduction." In *The Tools of Governance: A Guide to the New Governance*, ed. Lester M. Salamon, 1-47. Oxford: Oxford University Press.

Schneider, Anne, and Helen Ingram. 1993. "Social Construction of Target Populations: Implications for Politics and Policy." *American Political Science Review* 87(2): 334-47.

Shields, John, and B. Mitchell Evans. 1998. *Shrinking the State: Globalization and Public Administration "Reform."* Halifax: Fernwood.

Smith, Miriam. 2005. *A Civil Society? Collective Actors in Canadian Political Life.* Peterborough: Broadview Press.

Stone, Deborah. 2002. *Policy Paradox: The Art of Political Decision Making.* Rev. ed. New York: W.W. Norton.

Tuohy, Carolyn Hughes. 1999. *Accidental Logics: The Dynamics of Change in the Health Care Arena in the United States, Britain, and Canada.* New York: Oxford University Press.

Valverde, Mariana. 1995. "The Mixed Social Economy as a Canadian Tradition." *Studies in Political Economy* 47(Summer): 33-60.

Wallerstein, Immanuel. 2004. *The Uncertainties of Knowledge.* Philadelphia: Temple University Press.

Walters, William. 2000. *Unemployment and Government: Genealogies of the Social.* Cambridge: Cambridge University Press.

—. 2004. "Some Critical Notes on 'Governance.'" *Studies in Political Economy* 73 (Spring-Summer): 27-46.

White, Linda A. 2002. "Ideas and the Welfare State: Explaining Child Care Policy Development in Canada and the United States." *Comparative Political Studies* 35(6): 713-43.

Wolfe, David A., and Meric S. Gertler. 2004. "Clusters from the Inside and Out: Local Dynamics and Global Linkages." *Urban Studies* 41(5-6): 1071-93.

9
Agenda-Setting and Issue Definition

Stuart N. Soroka

Agenda-setting and issue definition are certainly not new approaches to analyzing public policy. The origins of each were published over fifty years ago, and related theories played prominent roles in public opinion and political communications research throughout the late twentieth century. Interest in the analysis of agendas and issue frames as they pertain to policy making has increased markedly in recent years, however, primarily in US studies, but in research in Canada (and elsewhere) as well.

This chapter first reviews the policy literatures on agenda-setting and issue definition. The two are closely allied; indeed, both draw on some of the same influential authors. The literatures are distinguishable, however, and worth discerning from each other if only to highlight their strengths when combined. Having outlined the theories themselves, the chapter then presents an example of their use in explaining the development of federal environmental policy in Canada. Environment is a classic issue in the agenda-setting literature; in Canada, changing issue definitions probably played a role in federal environmental policy shifts. Indeed, much of environmental policy development in Canada relates to the changing salience and definition of the issue over time. This case is made below in more detail. First, however, we turn to the development of agenda-setting and issue definition as theories of the policy process.

Agenda-Setting
Agenda-setting is the study of issue salience – the relative importance of an issue on an actor's agenda. Moreover, it is the study of the rise and fall of issue salience over time, and of the relationships between actors' agendas. At a basic level, agenda-setting analysis seeks to draw empirical links between actors' agendas. As a literature, its more ambitious purpose is to track public issues and trace processes of political communication and policy development.

Agenda-setting is sometimes regarded as a "stage" in the policy process. Once prominent in the policy-making literature, "stages" models have the advantage of describing the policy-making process with relative clarity and simplicity. They portray the policy process as following a clear sequence of events: first, the agenda is set; then, policies are formulated, implemented, and finally evaluated (see, for example, May and Wildavsky 1978). The sequence makes the complicated process of policy development readily understandable; it bears little relation to reality, however (see, for example, John 1998; Sabatier and Jenkins-Smith 1993). Agenda-setting is evident throughout the policy process; indeed, formulation, implementation, and evaluation often occur simultaneously rather than sequentially, particularly for programs that are already under way. In the agenda-setting literature, it is not regarded as a stage in policy development. It is more accurately viewed as a critical, ongoing part of the entire policy-making process.

There are several key early works on policy agenda-setting. In perhaps the most widely cited example, Anthony Downs (1972) suggests that many public issues regularly move through a cycle of public interest – from a "pre-problem" stage through a period of increased attention to a decline in public interest.[1] Environment, Downs suggests, is one of these issues. Writing in the early 1970s, he saw a recent rise in attention to environmental issues and forecast its approaching decline. Trends during that period confirmed his expectations, and Downs' issue attention cycle has since been instrumental in illustrating the shifts in salience that many issues exhibit over time.

The weakness of Downs' work is its rather thin account of *how* issue salience changes. Other influential studies concentrate more on this fundamental question. In *The Semisovereign People* (1960), Elmer E. Schattschneider makes the case that much of politics is about competing elites managing and framing political conflict. Such conflicts are won and lost based on the way in which they are framed. Thus, a primary goal of political elites is to affect which issues are on the policy agenda, or, rather, the relative importance of issues. Similarly, Roger W. Cobb and Charles D. Elder's (1972) work on "agenda-building" focuses on both what kinds of issues are most likely to see changes in salience and definition over time, and what actors and processes facilitate these changes in salience. This examination of "issue expansion" and "issue containment," like that of Schattschneider, has an essentially pluralist view of politics in which interest groups, policy advocates, and mass media move issues onto, or keep issues off of, the public and policy agendas.

Succeeding research has examined both interrelationships between mass media, public, and policy agendas (examples include Flickinger 1983; Gilberg et al. 1980; Mayer 1991; Page and Shapiro 1983; Pritchard 1986, 1992; Wanta et al. 1989), for instance, and the relationship between issue salience and change in policy institutions (Peters and Hogwood 1985). (In Chapter 4 of the present volume, note the significance of agendas in citizen engagement.)

Prominent recent work includes John W. Kingdon (1995) on policy streams and Frank R. Baumgartner and Bryan D. Jones (1993) on punctuated equilibrium theory. Kingdon (1995) emphasizes the interactions between "problems, policies and politics." The problem or political "streams" can open "policy windows" – opportunities for advocates to push their issue onto the agenda. This process of agenda-setting is a critical component of policy development. Policy windows constitute the moment in which certain issues and/or policies are selected to receive attention from policy makers. And the varying attention to diverse issues over time is a critical component in determining how – and particularly when – policy change occurs. Attentiveness to issues is similarly critical in Baumgartner and Jones' punctuated equilibrium model of policy change. In this model, policy development is characterized by long periods of stability punctuated by brief periods of both increased issue salience and major policy change. In short, the relative salience of issues determines the potential for change.

Baumgartner and Jones make explicit the connection between agenda-setting in public policy and rational choice theories of political decision making. The punctuated equilibrium account in particular draws on the literature on policy incrementalism and bounded rationality in policy making (see Jones 1994; on incrementalism and bounded rationality, see for example, Lindblom 1968; Simon 1957; Rose and Davies 1994; Wildavsky 1986). In short, incrementalism is the product of individuals' limited capacity to process information. Decision making can thus be fully informed and attended to (that is, rational) in only a limited number of domains at any given time, if at all. Most pertinent to agenda-setting theory is the fact that attention is a finite resource – policy makers can pay attention to only a few issues at a time. The result is that most issues coast along, attracting little attention and experiencing only minor change. According to Baumgartner and Jones (1993), these issues are dealt with in policy subsystems, where issue experts come to define and perpetuate policies in a given domain. Intermittently, however, the public salience of certain domains increases and those issues consequently move to the top of the policy agenda. It is at this time that a policy subsystem or network is interrupted, policy-makers' attention to the issue increases, and new actors and ideas can contribute to policy making. Policy change is most likely to occur during periods of heightened issue salience.

That *public* salience tends to drive policy agendas is significant; it points to the other link between agenda-setting work and rational-choice-based accounts of policy making – the expectation that politicians are essentially office seeking. Motivated by their desire to be re-elected, politicians will both take an interest in public preferences and represent public concerns. This account of representatives' behaviour is most explicit in Downs' *Economic Theory of Democracy* (1957), but is also evident in voting-oriented studies in political economy (for example, Lewis-Beck 1988; Tufte 1978). In agenda-setting work, this is typically an implicit rather than explicit assumption. (For an explicit account, see Harrison 1996.) It is critical nevertheless – indeed, the connection between the public and policy-making agendas relies on it.

With these assumptions in mind, then, agenda-setting work suggests that exploring how issue salience changes over time is critical to our understanding of politics and policy making. In some issue domains, mass media and public opinion play a role in determining issue salience for policy makers. A more central component of Baumgartner and Jones (1993) – also evident in Cobb and Elder (1972) – is the consequent change in the individuals, groups, and ideas involved in policy making in a given domain. This change in policy actors is often linked to a shift in issue definition, and it is to the literature on issue definition that we now turn.

Issue Definition

Agenda-setting and issue definition are in one sense unlikely bedfellows. Agenda-setting is premised in large part on empirical rational-choice-inspired theories of policy making. Issue definition, however, finds its roots in constructionist or interpretivist – even anti-empirical – research strategies in political communications, emphasizing the importance of language and the subjective, manipulable descriptions that structure everyday politics. Nevertheless, the two approaches have been used in concert increasingly in recent years, drawing together notions of salience and definition, and capitalizing on a twofold epistemological perspective.

The literature on issue definition in public policy owes much to the scholarship of Murray Edelman. Edelman's (1985, 1988) work emphasizes the importance of symbols and language in policy making. Indeed, it portrays policy making as a kind of theatrical game aimed at placating or manipulating citizens. Policy makers can describe policies in a manner that simply confuses citizens and helps perpetuate their monopoly over certain domains, for instance. In fact, problems can be constructed in ways that inescapably support certain policies and outcomes. Edelman's work highlights the fact that the definition, or framing, of problems and policies is central in the policy-making process.

This constructionist account is echoed in philosophical work by J. Habermas (1970), for instance, and in policy-oriented research, from Harold D. Lasswell (1949) to Malcolm Spector and John I. Kitsuse (1977) and Pauline V. Rosenau (1993). Deborah Stone's (1989, 281; 1997) examination of the process by which issues "come to be seen as caused by human actions and amenable to human intervention" has been particularly influential. "Causal stories" attribute both blame and suffering, and thus are critical in policy development. Most importantly, they are subjective and contestable; actors consequently seek to control the story that leads to their desired policy outcome. Comparable themes are evident in David A. Rochefort and Roger W. Cobb's (1994) description of the "problem definition" approach. For example, how one defines the Los Angeles riots of 1992 – as an issue of race, law and order, or a general decline in morals – will have a significant effect both on how one understands the problem and suggests solutions. Similarly, the way in which problems with the British National Health Service (NHS) were defined was intimately linked to government policies focusing on institutional reorganization rather than fiscal investment (Soroka and Lim 2003). And in Chapter 15 of this volume, Matt James indicates the significance of framing and discourse in Canadian government responses to reparations claims and natural-disaster compensation. Policy instruments and outcomes are intimately linked to issue definitions.

Barbara J. Nelson (1984) draws on agenda-setting theory to describe how US policy making on child abuse was linked to the increased salience in media coverage in the 1960s. At the same time, she borrows from constructivist accounts of the policy process, suggesting that child abuse was constructed as an issue of "medicalized deviance." Corresponding policies were thus concerned primarily with medical treatment rather than punishment; because the issue was defined in terms of individual deviance rather than societal problems, the larger structural causes of child abuse were ignored. Policies were a function of the way in which the issue was defined *(issue definition)* when it rose to salience *(agenda-setting)* in the 1960s.

Nelson's work is emblematic of the ongoing link between agenda-setting and issue definition approaches. Indeed, the notion that both issue salience and problem definition are equally important to the development of public issues is echoed in the public-opinion-focused literature on agenda-setting.[2] And it is also evident in the aforementioned recent work on policy agenda-setting (especially Baumgartner and Jones 1993).

In spite of epistemological differences, then, agenda-setting and issue definition are quite complementary approaches. This is perhaps due to one principal similarity and defining feature of the two: in both, issues are a central unit of analysis. Indeed, this is what separates them from most other analytical frameworks in the study of public policy, and it is an important advantage of agenda-setting and issue definition as analytical strategies. The policy process can be viewed through a wide variety of lenses – class, networks, advocacy coalitions, or institutions, to name a few. The advantage of agenda-setting and issue definition is that issues are as much actual as they are theoretical – the unit of analysis in agenda-setting and issue definition research is the content of daily news stories, party platforms, and parliamentary debates. As a result, agenda-setting and issue definition approaches have helped establish links between the study of the policy process and analyses of media or public opinion, for instance. And the connection between academic policy analysis and real life is rarely so clear.

Most importantly, there is now a considerable body of research demonstrating that policy change is often linked to changes in issue salience and/or the redefinition of public issues. The strength of agenda-setting and issue definition strategies is further illustrated below, in a discussion of variations in Canadian federal environmental policy.

Federal Environmental Policy in Canada

A very brief account of federal environmental policy in Canada is as follows: The environment did not become a distinct legislative domain until the 1960s. From that time, federal legislative output in this field heightened during two periods. In the first, the late 1960s and early 1970s, some of the (still) most significant environmental bills were passed, including the Canada Water Act and the Clean Air Act. Few major environmental policies were introduced in the late 1970s and early 1980s, but a second period, the late 1980s to the early 1990s, saw the passing of the Canadian Environmental Protection Act and the Green Plan. The latter, a blueprint for the development of more comprehensive environmental programs in Canada, introduced a number of new and considerable spending programs. However, many Green Plan initiatives were scrapped only a few years later, as federal government budgets focused increasingly on deficit reduction. Subsequent environmental legislation does exist, but it has been much smaller in scope and significance, dealing with the regulation of fuels and hazardous materials, for instance.

Environmental policy has been central to the development of agenda-setting and issue definition approaches. The relevance of environmental issues is partly related to their lack of "obtrusiveness" or "prominence," since issues that we do not experience consistently and directly are probably more open than others to agenda-setting and issue definition effects.[3] To put it another way, when we experience something directly, our reliance on others for information concerning it diminishes. Most environmental issues – such as seal hunts in northern Canada or the depletion of the ozone layer – are largely unnoticeable for the vast majority of the population, however. Accordingly, as Downs (1972) was the first to suggest, environmental issues seem ripe for agenda-setting effects; certainly, they have been particularly prominent in the agenda-setting literatures on public opinion and/or policy making.[4] The fact that environmental issues can and have been variously defined also makes this policy domain a useful test case for issue definition approaches. Anders Hansen (1991), for instance, emphasizes the role of media sources, and particularly "cultural givens," in defining environmental issues.

In Canada, Kathryn Harrison and George Hoberg have greatly influenced the literature on agenda-setting for environmental issues.[5] An early piece (Harrison and Hoberg 1991) explores the significance of science and technology, and policy entrepreneurs – in this case, environmental groups – in setting the policy agenda for toxic substance regulation. In subsequent work, Harrison (2001) suggests that environmental policy advocates have refrained from highlighting the dioxin contamination of breast milk, despite its considerable health risks. This self-restraint on the part of environmentalists is attributable to a combination of fear that women will stop breastfeeding and general personal discomfort with the issue. The paper is important both as one of the few Canadian policy studies adopting an issue definition approach, and because it examines the role that cultural values can play in defining policy issues.

The remainder of this section further explores the importance of agenda-setting and issue definition for the development of environmental policy in Canada. For the most part, it draws on past work on the topic, but it also adds new analyses of aggregate data covering public opinion, government

STUART N. SOROKA

spending, and legislative activity. Two hypotheses are examined: first, change
in environmental policy is most likely to occur when the issue increases in
salience; second, change in environmental policy is coincident with a redefinition of environmental issues. The former is addressed in greatest detail; the
latter, much more complex than the former, is examined in a preliminary way
only. Still, the potential value of both agenda-setting and issue-definition-
based accounts is made clear.

Salience and Environmental Policy Change

The agenda-setting hypothesis is grounded in the simple assertion that policy
change is most likely to occur during periods of increased issue salience.
Issue salience for the public is most often measured in surveys, using the
"most important problem" (MIP) question – "What do you think is the most
important problem facing our country today?" The proportion of respondents
citing environmental issues, for instance, is taken to be a reasonable indication of the aggregate salience of those issues. A time series from 1972 to
2004 is shown in Figure 9.1; details of these data are given in the Appendix.

The time series shows a trend relatively well known in the environmental policy literature (see especially Harrison 1996) – a rise in the salience of
environmental issues in the early 1970s, followed by low levels of salience

FIGURE 9.1

Public opinion: Issue salience and spending preferences

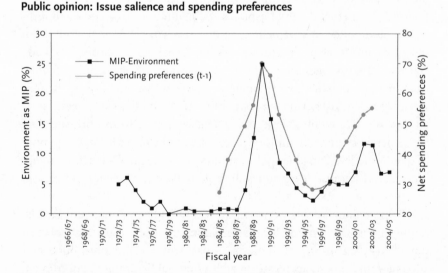

through the early 1980s and a second rise in the late 1980s and early 1990s. Thereafter, salience diminishes, except for a moderate rise near the end of the series, around the time of the Kyoto Convention on Climate Change.

Note that the salience of environmental issues actually began to increase during the 1960s, as is evidenced in part by J.W. Parlour and S. Schatzow's (1978) content analysis of newspapers dating from 1967-68.[6] However, because no pre-1972 public opinion data exist regarding the environment, Figure 9.1 does not detail the developments of the late 1960s. Still, the heightened salience in the early 1970s is revealed there, if only for its latter half. These, then, are the trends in issue salience against which policy measures will be compared.

But first, it is worth noting that there is a strong connection between the salience of environmental issues and public preferences for environmental spending during this period. A second series in Figure 9.1 shows these net public preferences for environmental spending from 1984 onward. They are measured using the question "Do you think the government should spend more, spend less, or spend the same amount on the environment?" (Again, details are in the Appendix.) The proportion citing "less" is subtracted from the proportion citing "more" to obtain a kind of "net" aggregate preference for increased spending on environmental issues. Although the measure is grounded in a desire for more (or less) spending, it can be broadly construed as a signal for more (or less) policy.

The two series track each other rather closely, suggesting that the (increased) salience of environmental issues in Canada is closely linked to (increased) spending preferences. This need not be true across all policy issues: heightened concern about unemployment may be positively or negatively linked to preferences for spending on employment insurance and retraining, for instance. Similarly, concern about taxation does not imply one particular direction in taxation preferences. Indeed, because salience and preferences can be positively or negatively related, policy agenda-setting focuses on the link between salience and policy change in *any* direction. Environmental issues are relatively unusual, then, in that the growth of issue salience is consistently and positively associated with a desire for more environmental policy.

The distinction between salience and preferences is nevertheless worth making, as it has substantive implications for analyses of policy change. A number of authors suggest that issue salience is an important mediating variable in the opinion-policy link (Jones 1994; Franklin and Wlezien 1997; Soroka 2003). In this view, though the public may always have policy preferences regarding an issue, these will matter most to policy makers when the issue is salient. Because only a limited number of issues can be given attention at one time, an issue of little salience may prompt little government responsiveness to public preferences. More salient issues may generate more policy responsiveness. (This has been found to be true across policy domains in Canada and elsewhere. See Soroka and Wlezien 2004, 2005.)

For our current purposes, the correlation between salience and policy preferences makes it hard to distinguish the effect of one over the other. It nevertheless suggests that there should be a particularly strong link between issue salience and policy activity.

It should not be surprising, then, that spending on environmental issues tracks quite nicely the shifts in issue salience. Federal spending figures are displayed in Figure 9.2; these data are described in the Appendix. The first panel shows levels of environmental spending over time, in constant 1992 Canadian dollars; the second panel shows yearly percentage changes in this series.

The second panel, showing percentage changes, makes the direction and magnitude of variation more clear. The figure shows that changes in federal spending move alongside the public opinion measures. Changes in environmental spending were greatest from the late 1980s through the early 1990s. The other period showing considerable change spans the late 1960s and early 1970s – like the former, this period too is identified as one of expanded interest in environmental issues. When policy is measured by federal environmental spending, a strong positive connection emerges between issue salience and policy change.

Environment is a shared jurisdiction; Figure 9.3 shows that the trends for federal spending are mirrored in those for consolidated federal, provincial, and municipal spending. The scale on the x-axis makes clear that consolidated spending is much greater than federal spending alone. Indeed, federal spending never makes up more than 18 percent of consolidated spending on the environment. Due to the addition of the provincial and municipal data, the figure does not show the same magnitude of year-to-year changes as does federal spending alone. Changes are evident, however. Compared to those in federal spending, shifts in consolidated spending in the early 1970s seem more dramatic, and changes in the early 1990s less so. Still, as in the federal series, these are the two periods during which change is most evident.[7]

Spending is just one measure of public policy, of course (see Soroka 2002a; Wlezien and Soroka 2003); a wide range of environmental policies

FIGURE 9.2

Federal government spending

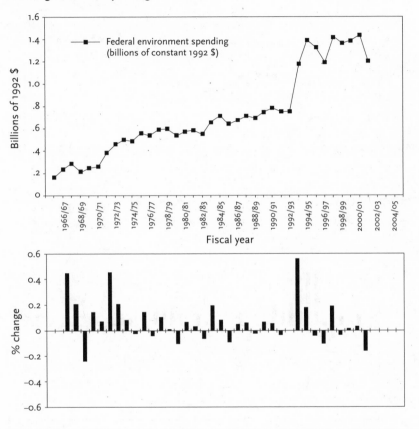

deals primarily with regulation that is at best only partly reflected in spending data. Accordingly, Figure 9.4 shows a time series based on federal environmental policy making. The data on environmental legislation are drawn from the Canadian EnviroOSH Legislation database, which is maintained by the Canadian Centre for Occupational Health and Safety (CCOHS). The database includes all federal and provincial Canadian health, safety, and environmental legislation, as well as critical guidelines and codes of practice. For the current purposes, only federal acts, statutes, and regulations are included in Figure 9.4; guidelines, codes, and bulletins are omitted, as is provincial legislation. Each item in the figure is coded by the year in which it was signed;

Figure 9.3

Consolidated federal, provincial, and municipal spending

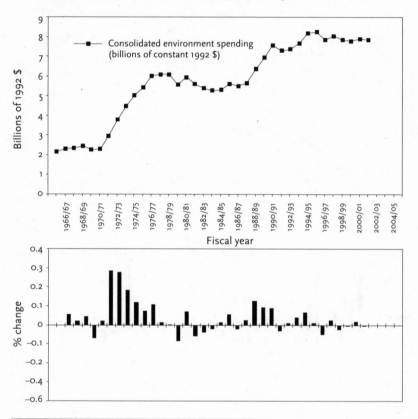

amendment years are not included. Data are shown from 1930; they are described in more detail in the Appendix.

One caveat: for these data, distinguishing purely environmental legislation from that having environmental relevance is very difficult. Bills dealing with endangered species are clearly environmental; bills legislating toxic substances have a quite different (business and industry) focus, but are for the most part environmental; bills regarding nuclear power can be environmentally motivated, and have environmental impacts, but are sometimes simply technical or scientific in scope. The line between legislation that is environmental and legislation that is not, in short, is hazy.[8] For the data used here, all items were subject coded, and acts, statutes, and regulations that were not even vaguely related to the environment were excluded. Many acts with marginal or tangential environmental content remain, however, with the consequence that some "noise" in the series can be only partly attributed to environmental policy making.

Nevertheless, the general trend in the legislative series supports the hypothesis that issue salience and policy change are connected. The time series falls into three periods: Until the late 1960s, relatively little federal legislation on environmental issues was enacted. In the early to mid-1970s, coincident with the first rise in public concern, the volume of federal legislation increased.[9] Legislation then decreased somewhat until the late 1980s.

The punctuations are not as clear as in the spending series, however. Perhaps more visible is a change in average yearly levels of environmental legislation over the three periods. On a year-to-year basis, the first panel of Figure 9.4 shows that the average from 1930 to 1967 is .5 per year, the average from 1968 to 1986 is 2.9, and the average from 1987 to 2003 is 10.8. The pace of environmental legislation visibly changes over the three periods, and the points at which this occurs coincide with the periods of heightened public salience.

This is even clearer when environmental legislation is viewed cumulatively rather than yearly. The cumulative measure (where the values for each year are added on incrementally), tracked in the second panel of Figure 9.4, again shows the three distinct periods, this time marked by changes in the rate of increase of the cumulative series (shown by dark lines on the graph). These changes have two possible explanations. One is that environmental legislation creates the need for more legislation; it creates bureaucracies and regulative bodies that then create the need for more legislation. As a consequence, this legislation will not exhibit the same kind of punctuations as those in the spending series. Rather, there will be shifts in the pace of legislation – the rate at which the volume of legislation increases. Another possibility attributes the trends in part to the capacity of government more generally. As government expands, it can (and does) do more. The pace of *all* legislation thus increases over time, and it is this trend that is evidenced in the environmental legislation seen here. In this account, the upward trend is not specific to environment, although it is certainly evident in this series.

In all likelihood, both accounts are at play here. Certainly, the rate of legislation gradually increased in the twentieth century. At the same time, shifts in the rate of increase in environmental legislation seem suspiciously coincident with periods of increased issue salience. In levels, and in changes

FIGURE 9.4

Federal legislative activity, all environmental issues

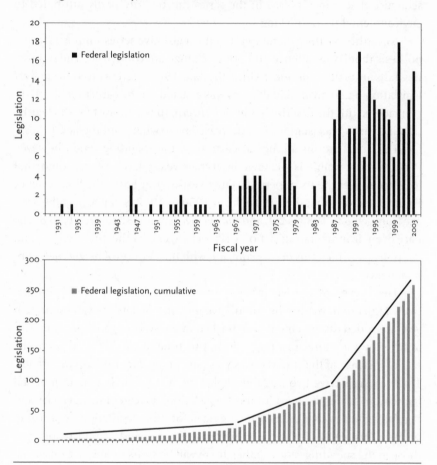

Fiscal year

in the cumulative series, there appear to be three periods of environmental policy making from the 1930s to the present, characterized by rising rates of increase over time and marked by the two periods of increased public issue salience.

It is worth noting that legislative output remains relatively high through to 2003, a time in which public concern about the environment is only moderate (see Figure 9.1). The legislative series is slightly misleading late in this period, however. First, it is clear from Figure 9.2 that spending does not increase substantially after the mid-1990s, suggestive of the nature of post-1995 legislation as compared with that of the early 1990s (which increased spending considerably). Also, the particularly high punctuation in 2000, shown in Figure 9.4, is a function of nine related regulatory items on nuclear power which had only tangential environmental content (and which fell under the supervision of the Ministry of Natural Resources).

The rather broad definition of environmental legislation used for the data in Figure 9.4 also tends to mask abrupt shifts in some of the more centrally environmental subtopics. Changes in the rate of legislation over time are clearer still when we look only at legislation dealing with pollution (categorized as air, water, and general) and wildlife protection, as tracked in Figure 9.5. This series ignores legislation on transportation, hazardous materials, and energy, among other subjects (see Appendix); although these do contain environmental components, they are perhaps not quite as clearly environmental as legislation focusing on pollution and wildlife. As Figure 9.5 reveals, even minor progress in legislation disappears completely throughout most of the 1980s. These central environmental concerns dropped entirely off the legislative agenda between the periods of increased public salience.

This and the preceding figures suggest a certain degree of representation by policy makers: attention to environmental issues and shifts in federal policy making tend to coincide with heightened public concern about the environment.[10] The trends illustrated above testify to the strong link between issue salience and policy change, as measured by both government spending and legislative output. They also demonstrate the significance of agenda-setting and issue salience in policy making.

Issue Definition and Environmental Policy Change

Thus far, we have spent little time on issue definition; nonetheless, its role in the evolution of Canadian environmental policy making is probably as important as that of agenda-setting. Admittedly, the preceding data speak less well to issue definition than to agenda-setting – issue definition accounts usually require more nuanced analysis than our aggregate data provide. Nevertheless, Figures 9.1 to 9.5 show quite distinct phases in federal environmental policy making. These, along with past work in the field, are at least suggestive of the issue definition account that follows.

Our explanation builds on work by Bob P. Taylor (1992), who distinguishes between pastoral and progressive environmental philosophies. In

FIGURE 9.5

Federal legislative activity, pollution and wildlife protection only

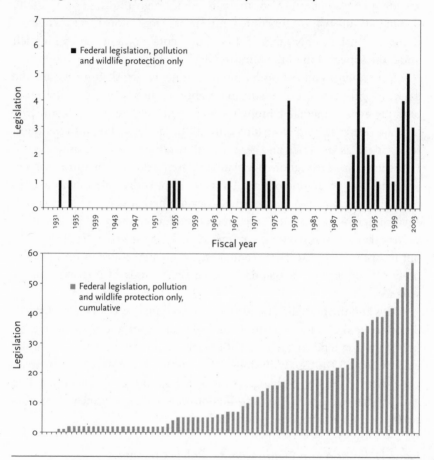

the former, the natural environment takes precedence over human welfare; in the latter, management of the natural environment is important primarily in order to facilitate human interests. Joseph F. Coughlin's (1994) analysis of transportation policy in the US draws directly on Taylor's theoretical work. He suggests that policy development in this domain has reflected two competing definitions of the problem: the first, an individualist, material view emphasizing individual mobility and economic health, has opposed the second, a communitarian, environmentalist stance stressing air quality, energy efficiency, and social equality. Corresponding policy responses vary from road construction (following from the individualist view) to investment in mass transit (following from the communitarian view). Different policies and outcomes are linked to relative predominance of one definition over the other.

This approach bears some resemblance to Harrison's (1996, 119) suggestion that environmental policy in Canada is salient only when economic affairs are not. Although it is true that public and policy agendas are limited, and that only a finite number of issues can top the agenda at one time, environmental matters seem particularly prone to decline as economic issues (re)surface. This trend is perhaps most clear in the quick demise of Green Plan proposals, which occurred in tandem with rising concern about budget deficits in 1993. It is also evident in longitudinal trends in the MIP series, which show that environmental issues are a high priority only when the economy is not.

Drawing on a combination of agenda-setting and issue definition, then, we may find our explanation in the ongoing competition between individualist and communitarian definitions of environmental problems. The former are not necessarily anti-environmental but rather environmental by primarily market-oriented means; the latter are environmental through strong regulation and coercion. The extreme cases are something like the following: individualist, material definitions present economic concerns as givens, and explore environmental solutions that will impact industry as little as possible; communitarian, environmental definitions present environmental concerns as paramount, and expect industry to adapt regardless of economic impact.

The history of Canadian environmental policy suggests that the individualist, material view has dominated. Michael Howlett's (2002) account of environmental policy instruments, for instance, is helpful in this regard. He suggests that environmental policy in the 1970s and 1980s was developed through cooperation between government and industry, and premised far more on compliance than coercion. There are hints in this work that environmental policy was indeed framed by concerns about economic rather than environmental health.

Similarly, the predominance of economic concerns in international environmental governance is evident in Steven Bernstein's (2001) discussion of "liberal environmentalism." Bernstein suggests that the notion that environmental protection is linked to development, rather than opposed to it, became pre-eminent in the mid-1990s. International norms and institutions now overwhelmingly support "sustainable development," privileging economic development and market forces as means of solving environmental problems.

In Canada, there are only two periods when this seems not to have been the case: the early 1970s and early 1990s, the two periods of increased public salience highlighted in the data from public opinion polls, the federal spending series, and federal legislation. It is during these periods that significant bills on pollution control and wildlife protection were passed (see Figure 9.5), perhaps emblematic of shifts in the balance of individual versus communitarian – or economic versus environmental – definitions.

Only further, more contextual work can speak to the extent to which changing definitions structured Canadian federal environmental policy making over the past fifty years. Nevertheless, the value of an issue definition perspective on environmental policy change in Canada is (hopefully) evident. Thus, it follows that we need to consider how the definition and salience of environmental issues change, and – more generally – how policy agendas are formed.

Conclusion

This chapter has outlined the agenda-setting and issue definition approaches to public policy, and demonstrated their use through a preliminary investigation of Canadian federal environmental policy. The two approaches are clear, but many questions remain regarding environmental policy.

First and foremost is how exactly the salience and definition of environmental issues change over time. That they do change is readily evident. In the early 1970s and early 1990s, environmental issues were much higher on the public agenda, and policy makers made more, and substantively different, environmental policy during these periods. Why this occurred is another matter, however, and one that relatively few authors have tackled to date.

A likely explanation implicates interest groups, focusing events, and mass media. Jeremy Wilson's (1992, 2002) analyses of environmental interest groups in Canada suggest that they have intermittently played a significant and direct role in environmental policy making, for endangered species legislation, for instance. Public protests staged by interest groups have served as "focusing events" (Birkland 1997), turning media attention and public concern toward environmental issues. And other focusing events, such as the 1989

Exxon Valdez oil spill, have probably been critical in shifting the salience and definition of environmental issues (Anderson 1991, 2002; Birkland and Lawrence 2002).

Both interest groups and focusing events are reliant on the mass media, of course, a political actor that plays a particularly conspicuous role in histories of the environment as a public and policy issue. Agenda-setting studies concerned with media–public opinion links have found that the media play a critical part in generating public concern about environmental affairs (for examples, see note 4). In the Canadian context, Soroka (2002a, 2002b) finds that media content leads both public opinion and policy measures on environmental issues.

The mass media are likely to be a significant source of change in the salience and definition of environmental issues, then, with one caveat: economic problems cannot be too prominent. Harrison's (1996) identification of the environment-economy trade-off in the MIP series makes this relatively clear, and the preceding section outlines an issue definition account that leads to similar conclusions. The salience of environmental issues changes over time; so too does the way in which they are defined; but both are restricted by the salience of economic issues. Attention is a limited resource.

This is perhaps the most significant assumption of agenda-setting research; it is also one of its major contributions to the study of public policy. Agenda-setting work suggests that attention, and thus capacity for policy change, is limited, and therefore the formation of policy agendas is a critical area of study. Issue definition research further suggests that the way in which issues are defined has an impact on whether they will appear on policy agendas, and – if so – how they will be addressed. Both perspectives are critical to our understanding of policy-making processes.

Appendix: Data Sources

Public Opinion

Results for the MIP question are drawn from commercial polls by Gallup, Environics, and Ipsos-Reid. Where more than one poll is available for a fiscal year, the reported value reflects the average result for all polls in that year. For further details on merging Canadian MIP data, see Soroka (2002a). Data on environmental spending preferences are from Environics. For further details on these data, see Soroka and Wlezien (2004).

TABLE 9.1

Environmental legislation database

INCLUDED ITEMS (ACTS, STATUTES, AND REGULATIONS)	260
Energy (alternative)	2
Energy (fossil fuels)	38
Energy (general)	11
Energy (nuclear)	24
Food and drug	4
General	13
Hazardous materials (pesticides)	6
Hazardous materials/toxic chemical	49
Hazardous materials/toxic chemical (explosives)	5
Health/disease	4
Indian environment/heritage	6
Mining	4
New substances	2
Other	4
Pollution (air)	1
Pollution (general)	4
Pollution (ozone)	2
Pollution (water)	7
Transportation (auto)	8
Transportation (dangerous goods)	6
Transportation (railways)	4
Transportation (shipping)	9
Water (general)	23
Weather	2
Wildlife protection (fish and fisheries)	5
Wildlife protection (forestry management)	2
Wildlife protection (general)	14
Worker safety/public hazards	1
EXCLUDED ITEMS	
Guidelines, codes, and bulletins[a]	61
Not environment[a]	71
Air safety	1
Employment	2
Worker safety/public hazards	40
TOTAL	364

a Note that these two categories are not mutually exclusive – an item can be excluded both because it is a guideline, code, or bulletin and is not related to the environment.

GOVERNMENT SPENDING

Current data from fiscal year (FY) 1988-89 are available from Statistics Canada. Another now discontinued Statistics Canada matrix contains functional spending data from FY 1965-66 to FY 1994-95. The functional definitions used by the former series differ slightly from those of the latter, so the two cannot simply be connected. Rather, the percentage difference from FY 1988-89 to FY 1987-88 is calculated based on the discontinued series, and this percentage change is then applied to the current series. This is repeated back to FY 1965-66. For further details on these data, see Soroka and Wlezien (2004).

FEDERAL LEGISLATION

The source of legislative data – the EnviroOSH database available from CCOHS – is described in the text. The following table shows details of the environmental legislative database used to create Figures 9.4 and 9.5. Data are available upon request from the author, at the Department of Political Science, McGill University.

ACKNOWLEDGMENTS

The author is grateful to the editors for comments, to Zachary Finkelstein for comments and aid with the legislative database, and to Terry Moore and Graham Lyttle at Statistics Canada for their help with Canadian budgetary data.

NOTES

1 Downs further suggests that issues featuring unobtrusiveness and the potential for dramatic presentation are most likely to experience these cyclical increases and decreases in attention, and that environment displays these two characteristics. Both are discussed further below; for a more detailed treatment of dramatism and obtrusiveness/prominence in agenda-setting, see Stuart N. Soroka (2002a).

2 Issue-framing studies are the public opinion equivalent of the policy research on issue definition. For reviews of the framing literature, see Shanto Iyengar (1996), Zhongdang Pan and Gerald M. Kosicki (1993). For an account of framing as an extension of agenda-setting, see Salma Ghanem (1997).

3 See, for instance, Downs (1972), Harold G. Zucker (1978), Soroka (2002a, 2002b). See also Sandra J. Ball-Rokeach and Melvin L. DeFleur (1976).

4 See, for example, Christine R. Ader (1995), T. Atwater, M.B. Salwen, and R.B. Anderson (1985), Joe Bob Hester and William J. Gonzenbach (1995), Michael B. MacKuen and Steven L. Coombs (1981), and Kim A. Smith (1987).

5   See also Sheldon Kamieniecki (2000).

6   Note, however, that media content and public opinion are not necessarily con-
    nected. See Soroka (1999).

7   It is also worth noting that federal spending as a proportion of consolidated spend-
    ing changes most during the two periods of heightened salience. This fits with
    Harrison's (1996) account of federal and provincial governments' environmental
    policy making during the period. She suggests that the federal government as-
    serted itself in the environmental domain only when public concern was high. It
    also notably supports Peters and Hogwood's (1985) hypothesis that institutional
    flux – here, in the form of federal-provincial relations – is greatest when issue
    salience is high.

8   Indeed, the same is true for spending. Above, we use spending categorized as
    environmental, and miss environmentally relevant spending on natural resource
    management, for instance.

9   Note that legislation, which can take months and often years to finalize, typi-
    cally lags behind public opinion and spending. Public opinion can change rather
    quickly; spending, though swifter than legislation in responding to opinion
    shifts, is nonetheless always one year behind, as budgets are set in the previous
    fiscal year.

10 They also coincide with public preferences for environmental spending. See Stuart
    N. Soroka and Christopher Wlezien (2004).

REFERENCES

Ader, Christine R. 1995. "A Longitudinal Study of Agenda Setting for the Issue of Envi-
    ronmental Pollution." *Journalism and Mass Communication Quarterly* 72(2): 300-11.

Anderson, Alison G. 1991. "Source Strategies and the Communication of Environmen-
    tal Affairs." *Media, Culture and Society* 13(4): 459-76.

—. 2002. "The Media Politics of Oil Spills." *Spill Science and Technology Bulletin* 7(1-2):
    7-15.

Atwater, T., M.B. Salwen, and R.B. Anderson. 1985. "Media Agenda-Setting with Envi-
    ronmental Issues." *Journalism Quarterly* 62: 393-97.

Ball-Rokeach, Sandra J., and Melvin L. DeFleur. 1976. "A Dependency Model of Mass
    Media Effects." *Communication Research* 3: 3-21.

Baumgartner, Frank R., and Bryan D. Jones. 1993. *Agendas and Instability in American
    Politics.* Chicago: University of Chicago Press.

Bernstein, Steven. 2001. *The Compromise of Liberal Environmentalism.* New York: Colum-
    bia University Press.

Birkland, Thomas A. 1997. *After Disaster: Agenda Setting, Public Policy, and Focusing Events.*
    Washington, DC: Georgetown University Press.

Birkland, Thomas A., and Regina G. Lawrence. 2002. "The Social and Political Meaning
    of the *Exxon Valdez* Oil Spill." *Spill Science and Technology Bulletin* 7: 17-22.

Cobb, Roger W., and Charles D. Elder. 1972. *Participation in American Politics: The Dynamics of Agenda-Building.* Baltimore, MD: Johns Hopkins University Press.

Coughlin, Joseph F. 1994. "The Tragedy of the Concrete Commons: Defining Traffic Congestion as a Public Problem." In *The Politics of Problem Definition: Shaping the Policy Agenda,* ed. David A. Rochefort and Roger W. Cobb, 138-58. Lawrence: University Press of Kansas.

Downs, Anthony. 1957. *An Economic Theory of Democracy.* New York: Harper.

—. 1972. "Up and Downs with Ecology: The Issue Attention Cycle." *Public Interest* 28(1): 38-50.

Edelman, Murray. 1985. "Political Language and Political Reality." *PS* 18(1): 10-19.

—. 1988. *Constructing the Political Spectacle.* Chicago: University of Chicago Press.

Flickinger, Richard. 1983. "The Comparative Politics of Agenda Setting: The Emergence of Consumer Protection as a Public Policy Issue in Britain and the United States." *Policy Studies Review* 2(3): 429-44.

Franklin, Mark, and Christopher Wlezien. 1997. "The Responsive Public: Issue Salience, Policy Change, and Preferences for European Unification." *Journal of Theoretical Politics* 9: 247-63.

Ghanem, Salma. 1997. "Filling In the Tapestry: The Second Level of Agenda-Setting." In *Communication and Democracy: Exploring the Intellectual Frontiers in Agenda-Setting Theory,* ed. M.E. McCombs, D.L. Shaw, and D. Weaver, 3-14. Mahwah, NJ: Lawrence Erlbaum Associates.

Gilberg, Sheldon, Chaim Eyal, Maxwell McCombs, and David Nicholas. 1980. "The State of the Union Address and the Press Agenda." *Journalism Quarterly* 57: 584-88.

Habermas, Jürgen. 1970. "Toward a Theory of Communicative Competence." *Inquiry* 13: 360-75.

Hansen, Anders. 1991. "The Media and the Social Construction of the Environment." *Media, Culture and Society* 13(4): 443-58.

Harrison, Kathryn. 1996. *Passing the Buck: Federalism and Canadian Environmental Policy.* Vancouver: UBC Press.

—. 2001. "Too Close to Home: Dioxin Contamination of Breast Milk and the Political Agenda." *Policy Sciences* 34(1): 35-62.

Harrison, Kathryn, and G. Hoberg. 1991. "Setting the Environmental Agenda in Canada and the United States: The Cases of Dioxin and Radon." *Canadian Journal of Political Science* 24(1): 3-27.

Hester, Joe Bob, and William J. Gonzenbach. 1995. "The Environment: TV News, Real-World Cues, and Public Opinion over Time." *Mass Communication Review* 22(1): 5-20.

Howlett, Michael. 2002. "Policy Instruments and Implementation Styles: The Evolution of Instrument Choice in Canadian Environmental Policy." In *Canadian Environmental Policy: Context and Cases.* 2nd ed., ed. Debora L. VanNijnatten and Robert Boardman, 25-45. Toronto: Oxford University Press.

Iyengar, Shanto. 1996. "Framing Responsibility for Political Issues." *Annals of the American Academy of Political and Social Science* 546: 59-70.

John, Peter. 1998. *Analysing Public Policy.* London: Continuum.

Jones, Bryan D. 1994. *Reconceiving Decision-Making in Democratic Politics: Attention, Choice and Public Policy.* Chicago: University of Chicago Press.

Kamieniecki, Sheldon. 2000. "Testing Alternative Theories of Agenda Setting: Forest Policy Change in British Columbia, Canada." *Policy Studies Journal* 28(1): 176-89.

Kingdon, John W. 1995. *Agendas, Alternatives, and Public Policies.* 2nd ed. New York: HarperCollins.

Lasswell, Harold D. 1949. "Style in the Language of Politics." In *The Language of Politics: Studies in Quantitative Semantics,* ed. Harold D. Lasswell, N. Leites and Associates, 20-39. New York: George Stewart.

Lewis-Beck, Michael. 1988. *Economics and Elections: The Major Western Democracies.* Ann Arbor: University of Michigan Press.

Lindblom, Charles. 1968. *The Policy-Making Process.* Englewood Cliffs, NJ: Prentice-Hall.

MacKuen, Michael B., and Steven L. Coombs. 1981. *More Than News: Media Power in Public Affairs.* Beverly Hills, CA: Sage Publications.

May, Judith V., and Aaron Wildavsky, eds. 1978. *The Policy Cycle.* Beverly Hills, CA: Sage Publications.

Mayer, Robert N. 1991. "Gone Yesterday, Here Today: Consumer Issues in the Agenda-Setting Process." *Journal of Social Issues* 47(1): 21-39.

Nelson, Barbara J. 1984. *Making an Issue of Child Abuse: Political Agenda Setting for Social Problems.* Chicago: University of Chicago Press.

Page, Benjamin I., and Robert Y. Shapiro. 1983. "Effects of Public Opinion on Policy." *American Political Science Review* 77: 175-90.

Pan, Zhongdang, and Gerald M. Kosicki. 1993. "Framing Analysis: An Approach to News Discourse." *Political Communication* 10(1): 55-75.

Parlour, J.W., and S. Schatzow. 1978. "The Mass Media and Public Concern for Environmental Problems in Canada, 1960-1972." *International Journal of Environmental Studies* 13: 9-17.

Peters, B. Guy, and Brian W. Hogwood. 1985. "In Search of the Issue-Attention Cycle." *Journal of Politics* 47(1): 238-53.

Pritchard, David. 1986. "Homicide and Bargained Justice: The Agenda-Setting Effect of Crime News on Prosecutors." *Public Opinion Quarterly* 50(2): 143-59.

—. 1992. "The News Media and Public Policy Agendas." In *Public Opinion, the Press, and Public Policy,* ed. J.D. Kennamer, 103-12. London: Praeger.

Rochefort, David A., and Roger W. Cobb. 1994. *The Politics of Problem Definition: Shaping the Policy Agenda.* Lawrence: University Press of Kansas.

Rose, Richard, and Phillip L. Davies. 1994. *Inheritance in Public Policy: Change without Choice in Britain.* New Haven: Yale University Press.

Rosenau, Pauline V. 1993. "Anticipating a Post-modern Policy Current?" *Policy Currents* 3: 1-4.

Sabatier, Paul A., and Hank C. Jenkins-Smith, eds. 1993. *Policy Change and Learning: An Advocacy Coalition Approach.* Boulder, CO: Westview Press.

Schattschneider, Elmer Eric. 1960. *The Semisovereign People.* New York: Holt, Rinehart and Winston.

Simon, Herbert. 1957. *Administrative Behavior.* 2nd ed. New York: Free Press.

Smith, Kim A. 1987. *Newspaper Coverage and Public Concern about Community Issues: A Time-Series Analysis.* Journalism Monographs 101. Columbia, SC: Association for Education in Journalism and Mass Communications.

Soroka, Stuart N. 1999. "Policy Agenda-Setting Theory Revisited: A Critique of Howlett on Downs, Baumgartner and Jones, and Kingdon." *Canadian Journal of Political Science* 32(4): 763-72.

—. 2002a. *Agenda-Setting Dynamics in Canada.* Vancouver: UBC Press.

—. 2002b. "Issue Attributes and Agenda-Setting by Media, the Public, and Policymakers in Canada." *International Journal of Public Opinion Research* 14(3): 264-85.

—. 2003. "Media, Public Opinion and Foreign Policy." *Harvard International Journal of Press and Politics* 8: 27-48.

Soroka, Stuart N., and Elvin Lim. 2003. "Issue Definition and the Opinion-Policy Link: Public Preferences and Health Care Spending in the US and UK." *British Journal of Politics and International Relations* 5(4): 576-93.

Soroka, Stuart N., and Christopher Wlezien. 2004. "Opinion Representation and Policy Feedback: Canada in Comparative Perspective." *Canadian Journal of Political Science* 37(3): 531-60.

—. 2005. "Opinion-Policy Dynamics: Public Preferences and Public Expenditure in the UK." *British Journal of Political Science* 35: 665-89.

Spector, Malcolm, and John I. Kitsuse. 1977. *Constructing Social Problems.* Menlo Park, CA: Cummings.

Stone, Deborah. 1989. "Causal Stories and the Formation of Policy Agendas." *Political Science Quarterly* 104(2): 281-300.

—. 1997. *Policy Paradox: The Art of Political Decision Making.* New York: Norton.

Taylor, Bob P. 1992. *Our Limits Transgressed: Environmental Political Thought in America.* Lawrence: University Press of Kansas.

Tufte, Edward R. 1978. *Political Control of the Economy.* Princeton, NJ: Princeton University Press.

Wanta, Wayne, Mary Ann Stephenson, Judy VanSlyke Turk, and Maxwell E. McCombs. 1989. "How the President's State of the Union Talk Influenced News Media Agendas." *Journalism Quarterly* 66(3): 537-41.

Wildavsky, Aaron. 1986. *Budgeting: A Comparative Theory of Budgeting Processes.* New Brunswick, NJ: Transaction Books.

Wilson, Jeremy. 1992. "Green Lobbies: Pressure Groups and Environmental Policy." In *Canadian Environmental Policy: Ecosystems, Politics, and Processes*, ed. Robert Boardman, 109-25. Toronto: Oxford University Press.

—. 2002. "Continuity and Change in the Canadian Environmental Movement: Assessing the Effects of Institutionalization." In *Canadian Environmental Policy: Context and Cases*. 2nd ed., ed. Debora L. VanNijnatten and Robert Boardman, 46-65. Toronto: Oxford University Press.

Wlezien, Christopher, and Stuart N. Soroka. 2003. "Measures and Models of Budgetary Policy." *Policy Studies Journal* 31(2): 273-86.

Zucker, Harold G. 1978. "The Variable Nature of News Media Influence." In *Communication Yearbook*, ed. B.D. Ruben, 225-45. New Brunswick, NJ: Transaction Books.

10

Scientists, Government, and "Boundary Work": The Case of Reproductive Technologies and Genetic Engineering in Canada

Francesca Scala

The birth of the first "test-tube" baby in 1976 represented the technological realization of an idea once confined to the imagination of science fiction writers – the conception of human life within the sterile confines of medical laboratories. One of the earliest and most popular literary depictions of this scenario is Aldous Huxley's 1932 *Brave New World*, which describes a futuristic society in which each person is conceived in a test tube rather than a mother's womb, and an authoritarian government controls every aspect of human reproduction. The successful birth of a child conceived through the technology of in vitro fertilization (IVF) not only exemplified scientific and technological advancements in contemporary reproductive medicine but also raised a number of ethical and social issues regarding the impact of these technologies on prevailing institutions and practices, such as reproduction, motherhood, parenthood, and the family.

Today, reproductive technologies and genetic engineering[1] are among the most contentious public policy issues facing governments in Europe and North America. In all countries, the debate on reproductive technologies in general has been polarized between, on the one hand, industry leaders and scientific researchers who espouse the scientific merits and benefits of these technological advancements, and, on the other hand, critics concerned with their social and ethical consequences. Governments are also faced with the challenge of regulating an increasingly international and competitive biotechnology industry, where companies are constantly searching for the most favourable regulatory climate (Fukuyama 2002).

Human biotechnology, therefore, offers an ideal research site for studying how science policy and the politics of science interact at different levels. At one level, the study of biotechnology policy contributes to our understanding of government agendas and decision-making processes in the development of scientific and technical research. At a broader level, it also provides an opportunity for exploring the interaction between science and power, the exercise of social control over knowledge, and the cultural authority of expertise in general (Cozzens and Woodhouse 1995). Drawing from the field of science and technology studies (STS), this chapter utilizes the concept of "boundary work" to examine the interaction among social and political actors, specifically the state, civil society, and the scientific community in negotiating their roles in governing the scientific enterprise. Boundary work is an important conceptual tool not only in STS but in policy studies in general, as it highlights how political and societal actors strive to shape the parameters of a debate and have their knowledge claims translated into the legitimate and authoritative voice on a policy issue. Essentially, it provides a conceptual lens for understanding contests over "insider" and "outsider" status of groups and individuals during policy deliberations. These are highly politicized struggles, for the "winners" ultimately determine the framing of issues and the policy responses that ensue.

This chapter explores these struggles in the area of Canadian policy on reproductive technologies and genetic engineering. More specifically, it examines the strategies, or "boundary work," employed by the scientific community to safeguard its autonomy and authority in the area of human biotechnology. First, the chapter introduces the concept of boundary work, focusing on the different strategies employed by expert organizations in their attempt to gain legitimacy and authority in an area of activity. It then provides a historical examination of human biotechnology policy in Canada and the conflict which ensued among government, civil society organizations, and the scientific-medical community. The chapter ends with a review of the recent federal legislation in this area and its implications for researchers in Canada.

Science, Policy, and Boundary Work

Conventional accounts of policy making have traditionally focused on the lobbying efforts of interest groups that strive to influence government action on behalf of their members. Financial and organizational resources, such as size, leadership, and access to decision makers, are said to be important determinants of whether a group fails or succeeds in influencing government policy. Within this framework, science policy is best understood as a result of interest-group competition, with the scientific community regarded as one among several lobby groups vying to exert influence on policy makers.

Although the scientific community may engage in lobbying activities, it is far from a typical lobby group. In society, science is accorded more power and authority relative to other forms of knowledge. There are several reasons for the privileged status of scientific knowledge in a policy debate. First, experts are expected to have special skills and policy-relevant knowledge derived from their training and professional membership. Second, as Stephen Brooks (1996) argues, experts have a symbolic and cultural role in our society, which characterizes them as the purveyors of moral truths. The third reason is related to the channels through which expert knowledge enters the policy process. Frequently, expert or scientific knowledge enters policy processes through formal institutional arrangements, such as policy research institutes or advisory commissions. This allows for greater inter- and intra-agency communication among experts and policy makers. Other forms of knowledge are usually marginalized from these formal channels.

The relationship between science and politics is therefore a unique one. Increasingly, science is inculcated into the day-to-day activities of policy making. As Clark Miller (2001, 482) explains, "Informed by science, concepts of objectivity, practices of knowledge making, objects of discourse and embodied expertise pervade the hallways, offices, and court rooms ... executive agencies, and the legal system, helping to make up the constitutional foundations of contemporary democracy." However, science and politics constitute different forms of life, with unique sets of institutions, social organization, practices, and discourses. For example, though objectivity and neutrality are said to inform the production of scientific knowledge, politics is primarily concerned with values and power. The manner in which science and politics are bridged in the area of policy making cannot fully be explained by models of interest-group politics and lobbying strategies.

A more fruitful theoretical framework for understanding science and technology policy is what STS scholars refer to as the "boundary work" between science and politics. Boundary work theories are used to explain how different disciplines, professions, and social organizations negotiate and maintain the boundaries that delineate their activities and spheres of influence and authority. These boundaries are not fixed or impermeable: rather, they are, as Thomas F. Gieryn (1983, 782) states, "ambiguous, flexible, historically changing, contextually variable, internally inconsistent, and sometimes disputed." The concept of boundary work contests the notion that scientific knowledge and experts enjoy a privileged status in society because of some quality inherent or essential to science. Instead, the cognitive authority of the scientific community is perceived as a product of its boundary work. In other words, scientific knowledge is also inherently political, as it involves conflicts over values and power.

Gieryn (1996) describes four different types of boundary work: monopolization, expansion, expulsion, and protection. Monopolization refers to the acceptance of certain knowledge claims as authoritative and authentic. When activities are labelled as science, individuals who are not scientists are automatically precluded from participating in this area of inquiry (Jasanoff 1990). Consequently, the distinction between science and non-science ensues. The second type – expansion – occurs when insiders broaden their sphere of influence and authority into areas that are already claimed by others. An example of this type of activity is what some feminist scholars refer to as the medicalization of reproduction, in which, during the early twentieth century, midwives were "displaced" by the newly emerging profession of obstetrics. The third type of boundary work, expulsion, occurs when members are rejected because they do not conform to the accepted principles and practices of the group. Here, real science is distinguished from fraudulent or "junk science," with the latter deemed illegitimate by insiders. This activity serves not only as a form of social control but as an "opportunity for corrective public relations campaigns, restoring among powerful constituencies elsewhere in society the belief that science on its own is capable of weeding out imposters" (Gieryn 1995, 422). The last type of boundary work, protection, occurs when scientists strive to safeguard their autonomy from external controls. This struggle for control is most evident in the boundary negotiations between science and politics (Jasanoff 1990). For example, the scientific community generally resists any effort on the part of legislators to determine its standard practices of care or its research agenda.

The issue of autonomy is especially important in the boundary negotiations between scientists and policy makers. Scientists have become influential actors in the policy-making process, by way of scientific advisory boards and regulatory agencies. Governments increasingly rely on the scientific community to advise them on technology and science policy. In this case, the challenge for the scientific community is to remain influential in the political sphere while still maintaining its autonomy vis-à-vis its own professional activities, such as setting its research agenda. Too close a relationship between scientists and policy makers can undermine the legitimacy and semblance of impartiality enjoyed by scientists in society. Conversely, a very distant relationship between the two can undermine their capacity to influence government decisions and access government funding for research projects (Gieryn 1996). From a political or democratic standpoint, a heavy reliance on experts in the formulation of science policy can effectively shut out from the process other societal groups who have an interest in a particular policy issue.

The central issue that defines boundary negotiations between science and policy is control. What control does the public have in scientific endeavours? What is the appropriate role of the government in defining the boundaries of scientific activities? How are disputes among scientists, political officials, and the public resolved on highly contested issues such as biotechnology policy? Deliberations on science and technology policy have generally been located away from public scrutiny and dominated by scientific knowledge and professional discourses (Abraham and Sheppard 1997; Fischer 1990). Through technology and science advisory boards and research councils, researchers and experts have been disproportionally represented in discussions of "scientific" issues that have broader social and ethical implications, such as embryo and stem cell research. The cognitive authority of scientists and experts in society has helped maintain their privileged status in the policy process, and, in turn, has served to frame socially relevant issues in narrow technical terms. As Anne Schneider and Helen Ingram (1997, 167) argue, science and professionalism can "commandeer an issue with important social value implications and transform it into a matter of elite scientific and professional concern. In such cases they define the issue, specify the goals, supply the assumptions, and rationalize the policy element choices."

The knowledge claims of the scientific community, however, do not go unchallenged. Interest groups, social movements, and other political actors often challenge the expertise of scientists, especially during scientific disputes and controversies. This is especially the case with what Giandomenico Majone (1989) terms "trans-scientific" problems, that is, issues which arise from technological or scientific developments but which cannot be resolved through the methods of scientific inquiry. For example, scientific evidence showing minimal risks associated with the building of a hazardous-waste site is often contested by neighbourhood groups and community leaders concerned with the quality of their environment. Although scientists may frame these problems in scientific terms, critics of science and technology see themselves engaged primarily in moral or ethical disputes (Nelkin 1987). It is during these disputes that "ambiguous knowledge claims, the authority of science and social movements, political power and vested interests have met in yet unre-solved conflict" (Jasanoff et al. 1995, 393).

The interplay between science, politics, and disputes arising from con-flicting knowledge claims is very much apparent in the area of biotechnol-ogy. While scientists engage in boundary work to safeguard their power and autonomy in this area, societal actors, such as religious and feminist groups, seek to reframe the debate in an effort to advance their agendas. Often lack-ing expertise in the area, policy makers, for their part, can be ill-equipped to make timely decisions on highly technical matters. Moreover, they must rec-oncile the public's demand for accountability and open deliberations with calls to safeguard the autonomy of the scientific community. These struggles would play themselves out in the development of Canadian policy on repro-ductive technologies and genetic engineering.

The Science/Policy Divide: Scientific Autonomy in the Development of Human Biotechnology

The origins of reproductive technologies and embryo research can be traced to the 1940s, when American scientists performed the first in vitro fertiliza-tion (IVF) procedure by mixing a viable egg with sperm donated by a medi-cal student. In the late 1960s, drugs to induce ovulation and increase the number of eggs per menstrual cycle were developed and soon made widely available (RCNRT 1993). In the 1970s, researchers in several countries devel-oped techniques to retrieve and fertilize an egg outside of the woman's body and transfer the resulting embryo into her uterus. In 1977, British research-ers successfully performed this procedure: Louise Brown, the first "test-tube" baby, was born in July of the following year. Embryo research developed concurrently with advances in IVF. Ovulation-inducement drugs resulted in the production of more eggs and embryos than were needed for assisted conception. Researchers were able to use the surplus embryos to conduct scientific research into genetic diseases and causes of infertility. However, it was not until the birth of Louise Brown that new reproductive technologies began to capture the imagination of both scientists and ordinary citizens alike. The once futuristic sci-fi tale of "test-tube" babies became a scientific reality and soon would become a widely accepted treatment for infertility.

In the early 1970s, research in infertility treatments, especially in the case of IVF, was highly experimental and its application was limited to over-coming infertility due to fallopian-tube obstruction. Moreover, procedures such as assisted or self-insemination took place in private settings, usually between doctors and their patients. Sperm donors were usually medical students affiliated with the hospital in which the procedure was performed (Farquhar 1996). In the years following the 1978 birth of Louise Brown, reproductive technologies were used as a means of overcoming a wide range of infertility problems. In the 1980s, infertility treatments were quickly incorporated into medical practice throughout the Western world and became regarded as routine procedures rather than as experimental treatments. As José Van Dyck (1995, 24) explains, "15 years after its first successful application, IVF [became] accepted both as a research discipline, a specialised medical field ('reproductive medicine') and as a common medical procedure." From in vitro fertilization to embryo research, the development and application of these technologies have been propelled by technological values and the positivist notion of "scientific progress."

Other social institutions also played a part in legitimizing the scientific community's ownership of the issue. The media, for instance, took a significant role in "normalizing" reproductive technologies and genetic engineering. While reproductive technologies were being transformed into routine medical practices they were also being depicted as revolutionary procedures in the popular media. Through mainstream movies, television dramas, and science fiction novels, scientific and media images of reproductive treatments became part of the public consciousness. Van Dyck (1995) contends that the positive depiction by scholarly scientific articles and news reports of reproductive treatments as both routine and revolutionary contributed to the general public's approval of the treatments and the medical-scientific community that surrounded them. According to Janice Raymond (1993) and Van Dyck, the cultural and media representations of reproductive technologies, for the most part, upheld the notions of scientific and technological progress and the promise of technological discoveries. News captions regarding "miracle babies" and a "reproductive revolution" romanticized technological and scientific research and depicted biomedical practitioners as both the guardians and transformers of human life. As Raymond (1993, 110) explains, "Reproductive and genetic engineering news is often covered as a series of dramatic events with the stress on technological miracle, magic, and mystique. Today, reproductive and genetic engineering has become a national symbol of progress, comparable to the space program of the 1960s and '70s."

The role of government in this area was minimal at best. In most countries, the boundary between science and politics in the area of human biotechnology was rigidly delineated. In Canada, reproductive technologies and genetic engineering were governed by the professional self-regulation of the scientific and medical communities. Consequently, decisions regarding re-search and standards of care were largely made outside of civil society, and outside of official policy arenas as well. Government guidelines for ethical genetic-engineering research were established by the Medical Research Council of Canada (MRC).[2] For example, the MRC determined voluntary guidelines on embryo research, allowing experimentation for non-therapeutic purposes on embryos that were between fourteen and seventeen days old. The guide-lines also recommended that research on embryos be permitted only to ad-vance knowledge on the causes and treatment of infertility, and that embryos not be created solely for research purposes (MRC 1987). These guidelines effectively left intact the local decision-making authority of research ethics boards. As a result, research ethics boards were free to determine how em-bryos were handled and stored and what kind of procedures to follow to obtain a donor's informed consent (RCNRT 1993). The lack of national stan-dards or monitoring of embryo research meant that decisions concerning the research were made outside of formal political institutions. The public had little information regarding what kind of research was being conducted in this area.

Challenging Scientific Authority: Canada's Royal Commission on New Reproductive Technologies

In the 1980s, the scientific community's authority in the area of reproductive technologies and genetic engineering was challenged by a number of social actors. Many groups representing different segments of civil society voiced their concerns regarding the lack of attention assigned to the social and moral implications of reproductive technologies. Religious groups were the earliest critics, arguing that reproductive technologies and embryo research trans-gressed natural law and undermined the dignity of the unborn. Religious organizations and their leaders publicly called for a ban on all forms of re-productive technologies, from assisted insemination and in vitro fertiliza-tion to surrogacy and embryo research (Farquhar 1996). In the mid- to late 1980s, feminist organizations and academics at the national and interna-tional levels forged a debate on the ramifications of reproductive treatments on the health and well-being of women (Stanworth 1987; Arditti, Klein, and Minden 1984). In 1987 Canadian feminist researchers and women's groups formed the Citizens' Coalition for a Royal Commission on New Reproduc-tive Technologies to bring attention to the social and ethical implications of these technologies for women, children, and the disabled.[3] The coalition, critical of the lack of public input on these matters, pressed the government to appoint a public inquiry to investigate them. Essentially, the coalition was asking the government to redraw the boundary of scientific research.

In response to the efforts of the Citizens' Coalition, the Royal Commission on New Reproductive Technologies (RCNRT) was appointed in 1989 under Part 1 of the Inquiries Act. It was asked to identify national policy needs and to develop policy recommendations in the area of reproductive technologies. The commission was to inquire into the medical and legal issues raised by these technologies, their implications for women's reproductive health and well-being, their social and legal arrangements, such as surrogacy, and "ownership" rights and economic and commercial considerations, such as research funding and marketing regulations (RCNRT 1993).

The commission's public hearings provided a forum for societal groups to express their opposition to reproductive technologies and embryo research. Most religious groups that participated in the hearings argued that reproductive technologies and embryo research constituted a threat to traditional family values and to the "dignity" of the unborn. They opposed treatments and procedures such as IVF and pre-natal diagnosis because these often resulted in the selective termination of embryos or fetuses. Referring to the embryo as the "unborn child," Catholic groups were among the most critical opponents of the use of surplus human embryos for research purposes. Dismissing the notion of "scientific progress," religious groups situated their position on reproductive technologies within a broader critique of technology and science. As a representative of a religious group stated during a hearing, "Contrary to a widely held view, however, science and technology do not always result in progress for everyone. One need only think of the disastrous consequence of many new industrial and medical techniques, not only on the environment but on human life and dignity" (Pentecostal Assemblies of Canada, RCNRT Public Hearings Transcripts, Toronto, 19-20 November 1990).

Feminist opposition to reproductive technologies and embryo research was embedded in a broader critique of science and medicine. Several women's organizations, including the National Action Committee on the Status of Women (NAC) and the federally funded Canadian Advisory Council on the Status of Women (CACSW), challenged the depiction of science as being free of concerns about values and power. Instead, they regarded science as inherently political, actively shaping gender relations and the distribution of power in society. The CACSW (1991, 4), for example, situated reproductive technologies within the broader over-medicalization of pregnancy and childbirth, which demonstrated "the divergence between women's interests and professional interests in matters of reproductive health." Rejecting the professional authority of medical-scientific experts in the area of reproductive technologies, feminist critics strove to shift the discourse of embryo research and reproductive technologies from a scientific matter to a women-centred issue. In the end, both religious and feminist groups called on the government to introduce a moratorium on these technologies. At the very least, they advocated that the federal government strictly regulate these activities.

Many in the medical and scientific communities engaged in boundary work to protect their autonomy and authority vis-à-vis reproductive technologies and engineering. They strongly opposed the creation of a regulatory body and the use of criminal sanctions. For example, the Medical Research Council of Canada questioned the need for legislation on embryo research and argued in favour of maintaining the existing voluntary system of professional self-regulation. Individual physicians and centres providing services such as genetic counselling, pre-natal diagnosis, and infertility treatments argued that existing ethical guidelines put in place by national professional bodies such as the Canadian Medical Association (CMA) and the Royal College of Physicians and Surgeons were sufficient safeguards against unethical or harmful practices. Of major concern was the preservation of medical authority in the area of pre-natal testing and genetic services. One medical institute advised the commission to recognize the autonomy of individual hospitals and professional medical organizations to devise their own set of guidelines (RCNRT 1993). This stance was reiterated by private fertility clinics. Several representatives of these clinics argued that government regulation targeting the field of reproductive technologies was discriminatory. For example, the Centre for Assisted Reproduction (CARE) maintained that practitioners working in private clinics were already governed by moral and ethical guidelines established by the medical professional bodies such as the CMA. Therefore, the application of special guidelines for reproductive health care constituted "professional discrimination and witch-hunting" (RCNRT, Public Hearings Transcripts, Toronto, 19-20 November 1990). In general, most scientists and medical practitioners depicted professional self-regulation as the panacea for any potential misuse of reproductive technologies.

The scientific and medical communities engaged in boundary work by distinguishing legitimate from illegitimate practices in the area of reproductive technologies. For example, scientists conducting research on embryos dissociated themselves from the more controversial aspects of the research, such as human cloning and eugenics. Characterizing their work as beneficial to society, they blamed the media for sensationalizing the potential risk of embryo research in creating a genetically superior "master race." Fertility specialists also sought to demarcate the boundaries between genetic research and infertility treatments such as IVF. They argued that they were being unfairly associated with the controversial risks posed by genetic engineering. As one intervenor stated, invoking a 1978 movie featuring Nazi eugenics, "Listen to patients with fertility problems and provide adequate funding to solve them. This has nothing to do with genetic engineering or *The Boys from Brazil*. Let us not throw the babies out with the bath water" (RCNRT, Transcripts of Public Hearings, Ottawa, 18-20 September 1990). Ultimately, the scientific and medical communities demarcated boundaries between acceptable and unacceptable research in an effort to maintain their expertise, authority, and autonomy in the field.

In 1993, the commission submitted its final report, *Proceed with Care*, to Parliament. The report's recommended prohibitions included the following: the commercialization of human reproductive materials and surrogacy arrangements; research involving ectogenesis (the creation of artificial wombs), cloning, the creation of human/animal hybrids; research on human embryos older than fourteen days; and creation of embryos for research purposes only. Criminal sanctions and financial penalties would be imposed on individuals and institutions that undertook these activities. Given that reproductive technologies, as a health issue, fell under provincial jurisdiction, the federal government could prohibit unsafe medical practices and scientific research under the Criminal Code only.

The royal commission also called on the federal government to create a national regulatory body, the National Committee on Reproductive Technologies (NCRT), to evaluate, monitor, and license reproductive technologies and practices across all provinces. It recommended that membership of each subcommittee reflect a diversity of professional backgrounds, expertise, and social experiences. The NCRT would comprise both experts and non-experts, with women making up at least half of the membership. Members would also have to represent the interests of other groups, including ethnic minorities, Aboriginal communities, the disabled, the infertile, and the economically disadvantaged. The committee would also include members who represented other areas of expertise, including ethics, law, and the social sciences (RCNRT 1993).

Bill C-47: Negotiating the Boundary between Science and Government

After the release of the commission's final report, the federal government continued to deliberate on the issue of human biotechnology, including genetic engineering and reproductive technologies. In 1995, it announced an interim moratorium on nine problematic applications of human reproductive and genetic technologies as the first phase in the development of an overall framework to regulate reproductive and genetic technologies. In 1997, the federal government introduced Bill C-47, An Act Respecting Human Reproductive Technologies and Commercial Transactions Relating to Human Reproduction. The stated goals of the act were to "protect the health and safety of Canadians" as well as "the dignity of all persons" in the area of reproductive technologies and genetic engineering. The act also aimed to ensure the "appropriate treatment of human reproductive materials outside the body" (Bill C-47 1997, cls. 3(a), 3(c)). It outlined a number of prohibitions that would have effectively limited the authority of researchers and practitioners in certain areas of reproductive technologies and genetic engineering. Some of these, such as genetic cloning and the fusion of human and animal zygotes and embryos, were already discredited by the scientific community. More contentious, however, were certain prohibitions in the area of infertility treatments and biotechnology research. For example, the act banned the commercialization of human gametes, effectively restricting the sale, purchase, and barter of ova, sperm, and embryos. The act also restricted certain practices that would potentially expand the autonomy of scientists in embryo research, namely, the maturation of ova outside the body for research purposes. Essentially, the act would criminalize these practices. Any individual who violated these prohibitions would face imprisonment and/or fines of up to $500,000 (Bill C-47 1997).

The use of criminal sanctions in the area of reproductive technologies and genetic engineering was criticized by the scientific community during parliamentary hearings on the bill. Several professional organizations and societies spoke out against the prospective legislation, arguing that it would undermine legitimate scientific research and medical practices. Moreover, it would also infringe on the autonomy of the medical and scientific community in determining standards of care and a research agenda. The Canadian Medical Association (CMA) (Parliamentary Hearings, Transcripts, 17 March 1997), for example, argued that the bill would "create major obstacles to the treatment of infertility and to legitimate scientific and medical progress. The proposed bill represents an unjustified intrusion of the government's criminal law power into the patient-physician relationship. The bill's focus on criminalization has the potential to create a chill on much needed research on reproductive and genetic technologies."

Other groups, such as the Canadian Fertility and Andrology Society (CFAS) and the Society of Obstetricians and Gynaecologists of Canada (SOGC), opposed the prohibitions on the grounds that they amounted to total control by the government. The CMA and the CFAS stated that the legislation focused too heavily on restrictions and not enough on the merits of reproductive technology. The SOGC criticized the legislation because it conflated controversial practices in genetic engineering, such as animal-human transfer of gametes, with more conventional infertility treatments (Easton 1998). These groups argued in favour of standards and regulations emanating not from government but from the traditional self-regulating bodies such as professional societies and research councils (ibid.). They asserted that any regulations introduced by the federal government should be consistent with the existing system of professional self-regulation.

The scientific and medical communities also criticized what they saw as the government's lack of consultation with relevant stakeholders in drafting the legislation. During the parliamentary hearings on the bill, the CFAS complained that, prior to the legislation's tabling for first reading, its representatives had not been consulted regarding its specifics. The organization argued that, because scientists and medical practitioners had not been involved in drafting the bill, several errors existed in the legislation. The non-involvement by "experts" ultimately undermined the legitimacy of the bill. As a representative of the CFAS (Parliamentary Hearings, Transcripts, 17 March 1997) stated, "This lack of consultation with experts in the field has resulted in serious shortcomings in the bill, both on the level of technical details and of overall design. One straightforward example is the failure of the bill to correctly define the term 'zygote.' If an expert in the area of human reproduction had reviewed this bill in its final stages, this error would not have slipped through."

Although Bill C-47 passed second reading in the House of Commons, it died on the Order Paper in 1997 due to a call for a federal election and growing dissatisfaction in the scientific and medical communities with what they perceived as the generally hostile tenor of the legislation. Following the publication of the commission's final report, the scientific and medical communities stepped up their "boundary work" in an effort to protect their professional autonomy and interest in the area of human biotechnology research.

The next section will examine the ways in which scientists worked to blur the line between science policy and industrial policy.

Blurring the Boundaries: Biotechnology and the Innovation Economy

After the failure of Bill C-47, Ottawa continued to consult stakeholders via a subcommittee of the Standing Committee on Health, and through Health Canada. Although religious groups continued to speak in terms of morality and ethics, the medical-scientific community advanced economic arguments in favour of embryo and stem cell research. One of the recurring themes to emerge from consultations with the medical-scientific community was the economic benefits of promoting Canada's research capacities in biotechnology. This theme was consistent with the Liberal government's Innovation Strategy, a set of federal initiatives introduced in the late 1990s and aimed at making the economy globally competitive by strengthening Canada's science and research capacity. The scientific-medical community constructed reproductive and genetic technologies, and in particular stem cell research, as the Western world's leading industry and a national symbol of progress. During this stage of the policy process, the boundary work of the scientific and medical communities focused on blurring the distinctions between science and industry policy in an effort to enhance the legitimacy of their research agenda vis-à-vis the government and the general public.

During the 1990s, researchers had pressured the federal government to invest more money in basic health research, especially in the area of biomedicine and genetics. In 1992, a network of concerned researchers and scientists founded the Coalition for Biomedical and Health Research (CBHR)[4] to push for greater funding in biomedical, health, and clinical research and to enhance public awareness of its economic and health-related benefits. In 1998, the organization submitted a brief to the House of Commons Finance Committee that explained how economic growth and productivity rested on innovative research and development in the health sciences. The CBHR argued that basic research in genetics yielded a high social rate of return by building human capital, creating employment and new technologies, and alleviating the economic burden of illness through the development of treatments and cures (CBHR 1998).

Another concern raised by the CBHR was the "brain drain" of Canada's "best and brightest" researchers to the United States, where career opportunities were more lucrative than in Canada. Several CBHR members approached members of the Liberal Party to discuss the need for increased funding in health research to prevent Canada's top scientists from leaving the country. As Liberal MP Carolyn Bennett explained at the time, "medical researchers ... were despondent that all our brightest and best young researchers were leaving the country. After years of cuts there was a perception that there was no future here. The American Howard Hughes grants were offering million dollar packages to Nobel track researchers. We had to fight back" (Bennett 2001). The researchers' efforts proved successful. The following year, during the January 1998 Liberal caucus meeting and before the impending budget, several MPs raised the issue of increased funding for health research. These interventions were successful in persuading the prime minister to introduce a number of initiatives to encourage health research in Canada. One of these was the creation of the Canadian Institutes of Health Research (CIHR) in 2000, which replaced the Medical Research Council of Canada. The new agency's main objective was to "excel, according to internationally accepted standards of scientific excellence, in the creation of new knowledge and its transition into improved health for Canadians, more effective health services and products and a strengthened health care system" (Bill C-13 2000, cl. 4). Interestingly, the newly appointed president of the CIHR, Dr. Alan Bernstein, was also a founding member of the CBHR and chair of a consortium known as the Toronto Biotechnology Initiative, which aimed to create a downtown research park.

One of the CIHR's main objectives was to promote biotechnology in Canada, especially research related to the genome project.[5] In the early 2000s, the federal government, through the CIHR and Industry Canada, announced a number of programs to promote genomic research, including a $160 million grant to Genome Canada, an agency whose mandate is to develop and fund a genomic research strategy in Canada. These initiatives were part of Ottawa's Canadian Biotechnology Strategy (CBS), a long-term plan to promote the highly profitable biotech industry in Canada. The CIHR was also assigned authority to devise guidelines and standards for embryo and stem cell research. As prospective legislation was being examined and debated in Parliament, the agency announced guidelines that would allow stem cell research on aborted fetuses and on embryos left over at fertility clinics. The announcement of the CIHR's guidelines and Ottawa's subsequent funding of stem cell research projects drew criticism from a number of sources, including religious groups, opposition parties, and some members of the Liberal Party. Critics argued that elected representatives, rather than a funding agency, should be deciding on policy guidelines (Harper 2002). They accused the government of circumventing Parliament in order to prevent MPs from speaking out against the issue.

Despite strong opposition from members of Parliament and religious organizations, the medical-scientific community was able to protect its authority in the area of embryo research by blurring the boundaries between industry and science. By focusing on the economic potential of basic scientific research, the scientific community safeguarded its authority in research matters while still bridging the gap between science and politics. As David H. Guston (1999, 291) explains, "the attempt to move the intellectual and other products of research from the laboratory into commercial and other uses – is almost by definition 'boundary work,' in that it involves simultaneously demarcating research from other activities while attempting to bridge the demarcation as efficiently as possible."

The object of this boundary work is represented by Ottawa's 1998 Canadian Biotechnology Strategy, which was generated in a climate of state restructuring and privatization that favoured market and private investments. Desiring to remain competitive in the new global economy, Canada's "neo-liberal" state strove to create an environment that would attract foreign investment and encourage economic growth. It regarded biotechnology as a key industry in this attempt, one with the potential to provide strong economic growth and employment levels. Permissive policies on human biotechnology were therefore deemed necessary if Canada wished to maintain its leading position in an increasingly competitive and international industry. As Francis Fukuyama (2002, 11) explains, "Globalization and international competition in biomedical research ensure that countries that hobble themselves by putting ethical constraints on their scientific communities or biotechnology industries will be punished."

The creation of the CIHR and the Canadian Biotechnology Strategy represents what Henry Etzkowitz and Andrew Webster (1995) view as the obliteration of the boundary between science policy and industrial policy due to the merging of their distinct institutional efforts and the mediation of the intellectual property system. Basic scientific research is being translated into commercial opportunities, as public-private partnerships emerge to foster technology transfer and generate financial rewards. The continuing blurring of industry and science policy may change the intellectual and research role of scientists, as they strive to capitalize on the commercial application of their scientific inquiries (ibid.).

Bill C-6: The Assisted Human Reproduction Agency as a Boundary Organization

In May 2004, the federal government passed Bill C-6, the Assisted Human Reproduction Act. Unlike Bill C-47, which noted Ottawa's "grave" concerns regarding reproductive technologies and genetic engineering, Bill C-6 (2004, cl. 2) set a more positive tone: the first principle outlined in its second clause states that "the benefits of AHR [assisted human reproduction] and related research can be most effectively secured when appropriate measures are taken for protecting and promoting human health, safety, dignity and rights." Other principles included recognizing the health and well-being of women and children vis-à-vis research and practices in this area, upholding the principle of informed consent in the use of the technologies, the non-commercialization of human gametes, and the preservation and protection of human individuality and the integrity of the human genome (Bill C-6 2004).

The bill created two categories of activities: the first, "prohibited activities," is banned; the second, "controlled activities," can be carried out only in conformity to the legislation and regulatory framework. Like Bill C-47, the legislation prohibits certain controversial activities, such as inter-species transplantation, sex selection, ectogenesis, reproductive and therapeutic cloning, germ-line genetic modification, and the purchase, sale, and barter of human ova and sperm (ibid.). It also forbids the creation of embryos for research purposes, but this restriction has a qualification which stipulates that embryos can be created for research purposes if they aid in "improving or providing instruction in assisted reproduction purposes" (Bill C-6 2004, cl. 5(1)(b)). Although this prohibition constitutes a restriction on stem cell research in Canada, it does allow greater flexibility than did Bill C-47, which did not contain this qualification.

The bill also established the Assisted Human Reproduction Agency, a regulatory body intended to oversee a number of activities. These include licensing individuals and institutions working in genetic engineering and reproductive technologies, inspecting AHR clinics and research laboratories, advising the minister of health of recent developments in the area, and maintaining a personal health registry containing health reporting information. In terms of composition, the new agency was to draw from relevant areas of expertise in appointing its members. Clause 26 of the bill states, "The membership must reflect a range of relevant backgrounds and disciplines." Unlike the royal commission report, which recommended that a regulatory agency comprise both experts and non-experts as members, Bill C-6 calls for members of the regulatory agency to be recruited from relevant fields of expertise – scientific expertise.

Although members of the new regulatory agency will probably be specialists in the field, this does not mean that the scientific community was completely successful in protecting its autonomy. As a regulatory body, the Assisted Human Reproduction Agency will have to negotiate between political judgments and directives, on the one hand, and scientific processes of assessment, on the other. As Sheila Jasanoff (1993, 145) explains, regulatory agencies are contested sites where science and policy judgments intermingle, especially when "scientists are confronted with issues labeled as 'trans-science,' 'science policy' or 'at the frontiers of scientific knowledge.'" In addressing issues that draw upon both facts and values, the regulatory agency will need to be cognizant of the political context and the concerns of other relevant actors. Consequently, the boundary between policy and science will have to be constantly negotiated as the political realities of science policy confront new developments in scientific research.

Conclusion

The concept of boundary work is an important one for the study of public policy for a number of reasons. First, it recognizes that the authority and legitimacy of groups, such as experts, are not embedded in objective conditions but rather are socially constructed. The question of social standing, therefore, becomes highly contested in policy making. Second, expert organizations, such as scientists, engage in a number of different strategies to distinguish themselves from others in an effort to protect their sphere of activity. This can have important consequences for whose "voices" are included during policy deliberations. Third, the concept of boundary work draws our attention to the political nature of the scientific enterprise and the use of scientific research in policy making. The divide between science and policy or between facts and values is therefore an artificial one at best.

This chapter examined the concept of boundary work within the context of Canadian policy on reproductive technologies and genetic engineering to uncover the struggles involved in framing debates on policy issues. It revealed how the scientific community engaged in a number of different types of boundary work to safeguard its autonomy and authority in this highly contested area. Early on, the community sought to limit the involvement of government and the general public in determining the standard practices of care for reproductive technologies and the research agenda on stem cells. It argued that government legislation was dangerous to the scientific enterprise and indeed unnecessary, given that professional guidelines were already in place on these matters. During this time, the scientific community's boundary work focused on establishing a distinct separation of science and policy. Later on, however, the community would work toward blurring the boundary between science and policy by framing the issue of stem cell research as an economic imperative, one that was crucial to the development of Canada's biotechnology industry. The Liberal government's Biotechnology Strategy, along with the universal discourse of the new knowledge economy, provided the scientific community with an opportunity to highlight the commercial and economic benefits of genetic engineering. Against this backdrop, critics who wished to frame the debate on moral and ethical grounds were at a clear disadvantage.

NOTES

1 The term "reproductive technologies" is used to identify a category of biomedical practices and procedures used to assist conception and pregnancy. New reproductive technologies include in vitro fertilization, surrogacy, egg donation, therapeutic donor insemination, and embryo freezing and transfer. "Genetic engineering" refers to the alteration of genetic material of cells or organisms to enable them to make new substances or perform new functions.

2 The MRC has since been replaced by the Canadian Institutes of Health Research (CIHR).

3 Disability groups were concerned that pre-natal diagnosis techniques to detect fetal abnormalities were being used for the purpose of deciding to abort a pregnancy.

4 CBHR's members included individual scientists and health researchers as well as organizations such as the Association of Canadian Medical Colleges, the Royal College of Physicians and Surgeons of Canada, and the Canadian Institute of Academic Medicine.

5 Genomics is the science of deciphering the genetic codes of humans, animals, plants, and pathogens.

REFERENCES

Abraham, John, and Julie Sheppard. 1997. "Medicine's Control." *Science, Technology and Human Values* 22(2): 139-67.

Arditti, Rita, Renate Duelli Klein, and Shelley Minden, eds. 1984. *Test-Tube Women: What Future for Motherhood?* Boston: Pandora Press.

Bennett, Carolyn, 2001. "Investment in Research Shows Grits Ahead of Public Opinion." *Hill Times*, 12 March, 27.

Bill C-6, *An Act Respecting Human Reproduction and Related Research*, 3rd Sess., 37th Parl., 2004 (referred to the House of Commons for 3rd reading 3 March 2004).

Bill C-13, *The Canadian Institutes of Health Research Act*, 36th Parl., 13 April 2000.

Bill C-47, *An Act Respecting Human Reproductive Technologies and Commercial Transactions Relating to Human Reproduction*, 2nd Sess., 35th Parl., 1996-97.

Brooks, Stephen. 1996. "The Policy Analysis Profession in Canada." In *Policy Studies in Canada: The State of the Art*, ed. Laurent Dobuzinskis, Michael Howlett, and David Laycock, 65-90. Toronto: University of Toronto Press.

CACSW (Canadian Advisory Council on the Status of Women). 1991. *Brief to the Royal Commission on New Reproductive Technologies*. Ottawa: Canadian Advisory Council on the Status of Women.

CBHR (Coalition for Biomedical and Health Research). 1998. "Building on Canada's Brain Power: The Canadian Institutes of Health Research: Brief Submitted to the House of Commons Finance Committee."

Cozzens, Susan, and Edward Woodhouse. 1995. "Science, Government, and the Politics of Knowledge." In *Handbook of Science and Technology Studies*, ed. Sheila Jasanoff, Gerald Markle, James Petersen, and Trevor Pinch, 533-53. Thousand Oaks: Sage Publications.

Easton, Megan. 1998. "Infertility Treatment: Lack of Consensus Plagues an Unregulated Field." *Canadian Medical Association Journal* 158(10): 1345-48.

Etzkowitz, Henry, and Andrew Webster. 1995. "Science as Intellectual Property." In *Handbook of Science and Technology Studies*, ed. Sheila Jasanoff, Gerald Markle, James Petersen, and Trevor Pinch, 480-505. Thousand Oaks: Sage Publications.

Farquhar, Dion. 1996. *The Other Machine: Discourse and Reproductive Technologies*. New York: Routledge.

Fischer, Frank. 1990. *Technocracy and the Politics of Expertise*. Newbury Park: Sage Publications.

Fukuyama, Francis. 2002. *Our Posthuman Future: Consequences of the Biotechnology Revolution*. New York: Farrar Straus and Giroux.

Gieryn, Thomas F. 1983. "Boundary-Work and the Demarcation of Science from Nonscience: Strains and Interests in Professional Ideologies of Science." *American Sociological Review* 48: 781-95.

—. 1995. "Boundaries in Science." In *Handbook of Science and Technology Studies*, ed. Sheila Jasanoff, Gerald Markle, James Petersen, and Trevor Pinch, 393-443. Thousand Oaks: Sage Publications.

—. 1996. "Policing STS: A Boundary-Work Souvenir from the Smithsonian Exhibition on 'Science in Everyday Life.'" *Science, Technology and Human Values* 21(1): 100-15.

Guston, David H. 1999. "Stabilizing the Boundary between US Politics and Science: The Role of the Office of Technology Transfer as a Boundary Organization." *Social Studies of Science* 29(1): 87-111.

Harper, Tim. 2002. "Stem Cell Research Worries MPs; Call for the Vote on Reproductive Technology Bill." *Toronto Star,* 12 March, A6.

Jasanoff, Sheila. 1990. *The Fifth Branch: Science Advisors as Policy Makers.* Cambridge: Harvard University Press.

—. 1993. "Procedural Choices in Regulatory Science." *RISK: Health, Safety and Environment* 4: 143.

Jasanoff, Sheila, Gerald Markle, James Petersen, and Trevor Pinch. 1995. *Handbook of Science and Technology Studies.* Thousand Oaks: Sage Publications.

Majone, Giandomenico. 1989. *Evidence, Argument, and Persuasion in the Policy Process.* New Haven: Yale University Press.

Miller, Clark. 2001. "Hybrid Management: Boundary Organizations, Science Policy, and Environmental Governance in the Climate Regime." *Science, Technology and Human Values* 26(4): 478-500.

MRC (Medical Research Council of Canada). 1987. *Guidelines on Research Involving Human Subjects.* Ottawa: Minister of Supply and Services Canada.

Nelkin, Dorothy. 1987. "Controversies and the Authority of Science." In *Scientific Controversies,* ed. H. Tristram Engelhardt Jr. and Arthur L. Caplan, 283-93. New York: Cambridge University Press.

Raymond, Janice. 1993. *Women as Wombs: Reproductive Technologies and the Battle over Women's Freedom.* San Francisco: HarperCollins Publishers.

RCNRT (Royal Commission on New Reproductive Technologies). 1993. *Final Report – Proceed with Care.* Ottawa: Minister of Government Services Canada.

Schneider, Anne, and Helen Ingram. 1997. *Policy Design for Democracy.* Lawrence: University Press of Kansas.

Stanworth, Michelle, ed. 1987. *Reproductive Technologies: Gender, Motherhood, and Medicine.* Minneapolis: University of Minnesota Press.

Van Dyck, José. 1995. *Manufacturing Babies and Public Consent: Debating the New Reproductive Technologies.* Basingstoke: Macmillan.

11

Between Respect and Control: Traditional Indigenous Knowledge in Canadian Public Policy

Frances Abele

Somewhat tentatively, institutions of Canadian public policy have begun to invite "traditional knowledge," or "traditional Indigenous knowledge," into the circle of policy development and decision making. The invitation is by no means open-ended: to date, traditional knowledge is welcome mainly where social, physical, or environmental disturbances affect Indigenous populations, or where a policy directly involves Indigenous people as a group. Academic discussion extends the invitation somewhat more broadly, though attention to traditional knowledge does not extend very far beyond scholars who work directly on Indigenous issues.[1]

In this chapter, I consider some implications of the current opening to traditional knowledge, and particularly, whether the invitation to traditional knowledge will lead to better public policy decisions and greater social justice. To do this, I will situate the concept of "traditional knowledge" in the context of two great world historical processes that converge today in the institutions of Canadian government: democratization and imperialism.

The starting point for this discussion is the insight that a profound transformation in the form of economy and society in which people make their living and their lives lies at the heart of the contrast between "traditional" and other kinds of knowledge. All over the world, "traditional knowledge" has been distinguished at the moment when a people's way of making a living is challenged or displaced by modern industrial capitalism, with all its formidable power to invade, isolate, commercialize, exploit, and render universally marketable. Isolating and labelling "traditional knowledge" often accompanies the incorporation of this category into the global economy (as in the practice of corporate "bio-prospecting" among holders of traditional knowledge); in other cases, the label "traditional knowledge" appears when Indigenous peoples begin to be incorporated into contemporary political systems (through requirements that public decision makers take traditional knowledge into account) or contemporary administration (in health care or more generally).

Another way of making the same point is to note that without the concept of "modernity," it is not possible to make sense of "traditional." The concept of traditional knowledge is a modern artifact. But it is a *real* artifact, with material as well as ideological consequences. Certain knowledge *is* particular to all societies, arising from long experience of a given terrain and from the many small discoveries about the world that every human society makes, interprets, and saves for subsequent generations. Shared interpretations are built of epistemological premises, ethical principles, empirical generalizations, human experiences, and collective reflection and analysis of all of this, over generations.

In this chapter, I will use these ideas to comment on some practical aspects of the role of Indigenous peoples' traditional knowledge in the development of public policy and the making of public decisions in Canada. There is both a beneficent and a malevolent aspect to these efforts – a tension between respect and control that is as old as colonialism.

The argument proceeds in four stages. The first section provides some definitions and a clarification of the specific areas of focus in this essay. The second traces briefly the participatory logic that has led to attention in Canada to traditional knowledge. In the third section, I describe Canada's public policy approach to traditional knowledge in the context of some important global events and trends. Finally, I conclude by specifying the challenges that participatory logic has posed.

Exclusions and Definitions

The issues discussed here are extraordinarily complex, and I hope only to make some progress toward contextualization, simplification, and analysis. My mission entails many exclusions: the now vast international literature on intellectual property rights and traditional knowledge, the relationship between Indigenous peoples' knowledge and "science" (frequently rendered in quotation marks), the vital discussion of how the courts and jurisprudence have operated to define the place of traditional knowledge in political life, and the matter of whether it is sensible to speak of more than one kind of science or way of knowing. All of these are relevant, but they are not treated here. I will also ignore debates among anthropologists about what constitutes Indigeneity, and whether all pre-industrial peoples, or none, might be so labelled.[2] Instead, this chapter uses the understanding of "Indigenous" common in North America: "Indigenous peoples" refers to the many and varied existing societies descended from those which were established here when Europeans came to trade and then to settle, about five hundred years ago.

The term "public policy" is used to refer to the entire field of research, analysis, and traditions of authoritative decision making – ideas, institutions, and practices – that comprise the ground upon which citizens in a modern democracy meet to deal with issues of common concern. Most importantly for this examination, "public policy" includes the regulatory decision-making process, an arena in which traditional knowledge has been given some space, albeit awkwardly.

For the purposes of this discussion, traditional knowledge is that which well-educated[3] members of these Indigenous societies have: it is the knowledge particular to the society's own history, language, culture, and economic, political, and social practices. Very commonly, different aspects or fields of Indigenous knowledge are held by various members of an Indigenous society; also common has been the oral communication of such knowledge. Increasingly, though, it is being translated into English and other European languages, codified, and even made public through the Internet.[4] Much traditional knowledge is in principle interculturally communicable, but may not be entirely accessible to those who do not speak the appropriate language.

The current academic literature on traditional knowledge contains many generalizations about the shared qualities of the traditional knowledge of various Indigenous peoples. Commonly, this generalized Indigenous knowledge is contrasted to a generalized version of "Western" knowledge, or "Western science," an enterprise that often leads to the production of dichotomized lists of opposing characteristics.[5] I doubt that this is a useful way to proceed, particularly in public policy, but debunking this approach is not relevant to the argument I am making here.

Some conceptual distinctions can be offered. The various terms for traditional Indigenous knowledge (traditional ecological knowledge, TEK, traditional knowledge, Indigenous knowledge) are used in similar ways, and each can refer to quite a range of kinds of knowledge, depending upon the practical context. In the secondary literature and public discussion, it is possible to distinguish at least three different understandings of the term Indigenous knowledge, allowing for intertwining and some overlap. Each of these implies different consequences for the incorporation of Indigenous people's knowledge, insights, and perspectives in "mainstream" public policy.[6]

First, traditional knowledge can refer to a distinctive political and social perspective and set of interests, rooted in shared history. This meaning of the term refers to a people's shared way of understanding human life, identifying problems, and approaching social resolution. This shared understanding arises naturally as people live together in society over many generations, and when confronted by a similar challenge from outside, they will tend to defend their interests or respond to opportunities in similar ways. Though people may be "coming from the same place" analytically, they will certainly not be unanimous or infallible. Traditional knowledge understood in this sense is akin to that which is tapped in many forms of citizen consultation and participation. In fact, it is relatively easy to see that Indigenous knowledge understood as a perspective and a set of particular social interests can and should be engaged in public consultations and political decision making. If a favourable setting is provided (perhaps including translation and adequate time for discussion), it seems likely that integration of this kind of Indigenous knowledge is technically feasible – as long as varying positions and the normal range of disagreement concerning fact, judgment, and predicted outcomes are taken into account. In principle, something like traditional knowledge in this sense can probably be tapped by public hearings in which translation and sufficient time are made available, as was the case during the Mackenzie Valley pipeline hearings (discussed below).

Second, traditional Indigenous knowledge sometimes means local knowledge, the specific empirical knowledge garnered from the long use of a particular place and built up socially, passed on to subsequent generations, and available to be shared. Local knowledge is specific, empirically testable, and capable of explanation in segments. The premises and priorities of this kind of Indigenous knowledge may differ from those of other knowledge forms in a discussion, but in principle, given a forum in which perspectives can be adjusted on both sides, it seems able to be shared with scientists and policy makers, and ultimately tested for validity. Anecdotal experience to date suggests that Indigenous knowledge in its aspect as local knowledge is most easily shared among local-knowledge experts and those with scientific or other academic training. For example, caribou hunters and caribou biologists might share information and compare predictions regarding animal behaviour.

Arguably, the third meaning of the term traditional Indigenous knowledge includes but is greater than the two just mentioned. Traditional knowledge sometimes refers to an ethical-epistemological-cosmological understanding of how to live in the world and how best to be human, as well as of one's responsibilities to others and to the world. This entails understanding the relations among all things and making no sharp distinctions between humans, animals, birds, waters, land, mountains, and so on. It is difficult to write about this kind of knowledge in English or any modern language because the concepts and distinctions embedded there differ from those informing Indigenous knowledge. Furthermore, many Indigenous ethical and cosmological traditions hold that the forms of knowledge I have just distinguished should not be separated. Arriving at even a basic understanding of these themes requires extended study and reflection – not because the concepts are difficult, but because they are so different.[7] It is from within this last understanding that many Indigenous peoples (such as the Deh Cho Dene of the Northwest Territories) have hesitated to negotiate so-called land claims agreements or modern treaties with the Crown. They have done so out of a sense of responsibility: the Creator has given them responsibility for a particular territory, and they did not see that they had the right to negotiate this away.[8]

Even a casual observation of the Canadian experience with "including" traditional Indigenous knowledge indicates how difficult it is for Indigenous ethical and epistemological understandings to guide or inform public policy decisions. The institutions through which these decisions are made are built for a different purpose, and many of them are explicitly designed to exclude moral or philosophical considerations. Good illustrations of this may be found in the changes that may, or may not, be brought to territorial administration by the introduction of traditional knowledge policies to guide bureaucratic behaviour. Although the three senses of the term "traditional Indigenous knowledge" can be separated for the purposes of discussion, it is much more difficult to distinguish them in practice – though naturally it is in practice that the different senses of the term matter most. It is also "in practice" that we may discover the consequences of the analytical distinctions themselves. To help illuminate this aspect, I turn now to consider the large historical processes that have brought the discussion to this point.

Participation and Assimilation, Respect and Control

In this part of the chapter, I examine the common history of Europe and North America to outline, very briefly, the possible origins of the measures undertaken in Canadian public policy to take account of Indigenous peoples' traditional knowledge. In this way, I hope to create a context for understanding some current policy conundrums and posing some questions for further consideration.

Ultimately, government acceptance of the idea that the understanding and opinions of Indigenous peoples had to be consulted in public policy making is due to the post–Second World War mobilization of the Indigenous peoples themselves. Their struggle coincided with that of other reforming social movements of the period. The political processes engendered by these movements generally resulted in more democratic and consultative public policy processes, and they produced the conditions under which Indigenous peoples' views about their own interests could no longer be ignored.[9]

For example, after the 1974-76 Berger Inquiry into the construction of the Mackenzie Valley pipeline, it was no longer politically possible for decisions about major new development projects to be conducted without effective consultation of the people who lived in the affected area. The Berger Inquiry made special efforts to ensure that Indigenous people's involvement was effective, by travelling to the predominantly Dene, Métis, and Inuvialuit communities to hear submissions, by providing funding to non-governmental organizations to enable community preparations for participation, and by furnishing translation, so that people could testify in their strongest language. All of these measures ensured good quality of local involvement, doubtless informed by what would today be labelled "traditional knowledge" – a term which appears in neither the inquiry's transcripts nor its report. Judging from the inquiry's procedures and report, it seems that Thomas Berger and his staff took for granted that the specific knowledge and perspectives of Indigenous peoples could be understood if efforts at clear communication were made, and they took for granted that such information was material to their decisions. In the same spirit, the federal government provided intervenor funding to the representative Aboriginal organizations of the time to permit them to undertake research, develop analyses, and consult with the people they represented.

In subsequent hearings concerning development projects, procedures were formalized and to some extent tightened up, but the Berger Inquiry entrenched the precedent that hearings would be held before major development projects ensued, and that these would be conducted in such a way as to ensure wide public participation. The elaborate public consultation process now used for environmental assessment (with its references to traditional knowledge) follows the Berger Inquiry precedents. Similar methodologies (and other more conventional means, such as plebiscites) are now used in much of northern Canada for other decision-making processes concerning political and economic development.

If we take the long view, it is possible to place these developments in the lengthy trajectory of democratization that began, perhaps, with the Chartists' efforts to expand the franchise beyond men of property to include all men, and then the suffragettes' struggle to extend the franchise to all women citizens. The vote was not extended to members of First Nations (at least not to those registered as "Indians" in federal records) until 1959. The struggle for the franchise, and subsequently for a meaningful role in public decision making between elections, has been a great movement of many parts, one occurring in most of the nation-states that have originated during the last two hundred years. In Canada, oppressive and authoritarian measures directed at Indigenous peoples have been gradually reformed, in response to sustained pressure from Indigenous people aided by the democratic logic of these historical struggles that is larger than any particular historical conjuncture. Canadian institutions have moved from exclusion and oppression to cautious electoral inclusion to solicitation of opinion and advice, and are now contemplating the possibility that the analytical premises upon which all the preceding reforms were based might be reconsidered.

The trajectory and logic of democratization and inclusion run counter to another great process of recent human history, commonly known as European imperialism. Although there is no space here even to sketch its history, the phenomenon is perhaps sufficiently well understood to sustain some generalizations.[10] When Europeans encountered the societies of what are now called North and South America, they faced immediate problems of survival and diplomatic relations. As they pursued their objectives (plunder, trade, appropriation of land, and ultimately settlement), they had to come to terms with the civilizations already in place in the "New World." How the rulers and explorers, missionaries and settlers from Spain, Portugal, France, and England did so is a long and complicated tale, but eventually, due to the spread of communicable diseases, warfare, and the force of superior numbers, the Creole societies and imperial centres attained effective control of the Americas. As they did so, they defined a new subordinate role for the surviving members of the Indigenous nations. In Canada, this entailed registering the members of First Nations on a government-held list, controlling the activities of the members of these nations with respect to social, cultural, and political life, and attempting to assimilate them into the greater population through the forced schooling of children removed from their parents, and through various economic and political sanctions. If Indigenous nations could not be eliminated by assimilation, they were to be confined to "reserves," at once protected and controlled, primarily through the federal Department of Indian Affairs and Northern Development, and its predecessors. Although the liberation movements and political activism of the late twentieth century rendered this policy direction illegitimate, the feature of external bureaucratic control remains deeply entrenched in Aboriginal-state relations. Today, no Canadian political leader would argue for the control of Indigenous nations or the assimilation of Indigenous people, but the institutions through which Indigenous peoples and individuals interact with the rest of Canadian society express control which, though more subtle, is equally significant.[11] Democratization and imperialism, respect and control – these strong forces bracket the theory and practice of traditional knowledge in the public policy process.

Traditional Knowledge in Contemporary Institutions

According to one commentator, the term "Indigenous knowledge" was introduced by Robert Chambers and his development studies group at the University of Sussex in about 1979. Apparently, the first published use of the term dates from 1980.[12] The official and academic literature of the 1980s contains a wide international discussion of the terms "traditional knowledge" (TK), "traditional environmental knowledge" (TEK), "Indigenous knowledge," and variants. The 1987 Brundtland World Commission on Environment and Development refers to the concept. Later, with the 1992 United Nations Convention on Biodiversity,[13] came a huge increase in initiatives to protect, document, and distribute such knowledge – often explicitly responding to anticipated loss of specific bodies of Indigenous knowledge as its bearers were integrated into the world industrial economy.[14]

International "bio-prospecting" by large corporations has grown in the fields of traditional knowledge held by hundreds of Indigenous peoples, and in response there have been significant attempts to regulate this (Greene 2004; Sillitoe 1998). An important regulatory aspect has been the legal definition of Indigenous traditional knowledge as the intellectual property of particular Indigenous societies: once prospecting occurs, ownership and an attempt to prevent theft of knowledge must be established by a regime of property rights. This glum consequence is probably a practical, self-protective necessity for the Indigenous societies who are the object of this commercial attention. It has also probably begun to change the way in which people in those societies understand their heritage.[15]

In a concomitant global trend, traditional Indigenous knowledge has played an instrumental role in the service of environmental advocacy and conservationism. Prompted by the efforts of environmental activists to engage them in international advocacy to protect their homelands and way of life, Indigenous peoples may revise the way in which they see themselves and what they know, and they may begin to present themselves differently to the world.[16]

In Canada, though the term traditional knowledge came into use at about the same time as elsewhere, the direct economic potential of the knowledge itself has received relatively little attention. Similarly, until very recently, the concept of intellectual property, with all the resulting legal implications, has rarely been invoked. Instead, probably due to the strength and form of Indigenous political mobilization in Canada, the main emphasis has been upon finding ways for public administration and key regulatory and public policy decisions to take account of, and in some cases to rely upon, traditional knowledge. Federal and territorial government institutions, a royal commission, and non-governmental organizations have all been involved.[17]

A number of small Indigenous organizations focus on retrieval, preservation, and teaching of Indigenous knowledge and heritage. One of the oldest is the Dene Cultural Institute, established in 1987 "to assist Dene to maintain and strengthen [their] distinct culture ... [concentrating] on coordinating research and education activities that protect and promote Dene culture, language, spirituality, heritage, tradition and customs" (Dene Cultural Institute n.d.) Such organizations are usually well rooted in Indigenous communities, with support from elders and leaders, but they are poorly funded. Nevertheless, they have acted as "bridging" institutions, capable of community development internally and, externally, providing services of interpretation and information. They are in this sense, potentially at least, very important to the public policy process, despite the mismatch between their level of resources and the need for their work.

In 1993, a Traditional Knowledge Policy was adopted by the Government of the Northwest Territories (1993, s. 1): "The Government of the Northwest Territories recognizes that the aboriginal peoples of the Northwest Territories have acquired a vast store of traditional knowledge through their experience of centuries of living in close harmony with the land. The Government recognizes that aboriginal traditional knowledge is a valid and essential source of information about the natural environment and its resources, and the relationship of people to the land and to each other, and will incorporate traditional knowledge into government decisions and actions where appropriate."

The policy (ibid., s. 4) defines traditional knowledge as "knowledge and values which have been acquired through experience, observation, from the land or from spiritual teachings, and handed down from one generation to another." The policy is to be implemented in the design and delivery of all government programs and services. Responsibility for "preservation and promotion of traditional knowledge lies with aboriginal people," and "is best preserved through continued use and practical application" (ibid., s. 2). The government is required to support and track research in traditional knowledge (ibid., ss. 5, 6).

The policy's definition of traditional knowledge as including "values ... from spiritual teachings" sparked a minor controversy in the national magazine *Policy Options* and in some other discussions,[18] but this had no apparent material consequences in the Northwest Territories. Because the question has not been researched, it is difficult to determine whether the Traditional Knowledge Policy has changed government practices, but certainly it was of symbolic importance in acknowledging general acceptance of the relevance of Indigenous societies to territorial government.

In 1999, division of the old Northwest Territories created two new territories. The 1993 Traditional Knowledge Policy remained in force with respect to the new Government of the Northwest Territories, which now has jurisdiction over the western half of the old territory. In the east, the new Government of Nunavut adopted a similar policy, though it was expressed somewhat differently. Inuit Qaujimanituqangit (roughly, the Inuit way of life) "encompasses all aspects of traditional Inuit culture including values, world-view, language, social organization, knowledge, life skills, perceptions and expectations" (Inuit Tapirisat of Canada 1999, 1). As a matter of policy, it is intended to influence all aspects of the work of the Government of Nunavut, from relations among staff to policy and program development and implementation to relations between the state and the citizenry. It is not meant to displace the practices embodied in the imported institutions (from Canadian governments, and ultimately, from Europe), but rather to complement them.[19]

To date, these two governments are the only Canadian governments to adopt broad-brush policies directing public institutions to take traditional knowledge into account. Various federal regulatory processes, however, mention the term. For example, the Canadian Environmental Assessment Act (CEAA) (1992, s. 16.1) notes, "Community knowledge and aboriginal traditional knowledge may be considered in conducting an environmental assessment." *The Consolidated Information Requirements for the Environmental Assessment and Regulatory Review of a Northern Gas Pipeline Project through the Northwest Territories* (NPEIARCC 2002, s. 1.0) maintains that "Traditional knowledge should be incorporated to the extent possible into the baseline and assessment of impacts to each component of the bio-physical, social, cultural and economic environment." The *Canadian Handbook on Health Impact Assessment* includes a chapter on Aboriginal health and traditional knowledge, which is directed in part to supporting CEAA deliberations (Health Canada 2003).

The use of traditional knowledge in these decision-making arenas has both economic and political implications. Thorough implementation of the Northwest Territories and Nunavut governmental policies regarding traditional knowledge will require ingenuity, sustained experimentation, institutional and individual learning, and, very probably, considerable expenditures. A perhaps somewhat comparable initiative is that concerning official bilingualism, a policy that, over the last generation, has transformed the language of work in the federal public sector. To date, the resources devoted to implementing bilingualism at the federal level far outweigh those applied in proportionate fashion in the territorial governments to realizing the traditional knowledge policies. Nor is there much indication that the policies have actually changed any major policy outcomes. Nevertheless, the policies remain and general popular support for them does not appear to be waning.

More direct effects can be noted in the now common expectation that proponents in hearings related to non-renewable resource development (at least in federal jurisdictions such as the territories) will incorporate traditional knowledge in their submissions. This requirement (as in, for example, the Canadian Environmental Assessment Act) creates a need to gather traditional knowledge from its holders, to repackage and communicate it, and ultimately to integrate it with other sources of information. The pressures created by these statutory requirements have led some Indigenous peoples to develop their own traditional knowledge policies and to affirm their intellectual property as well, in order to assert their responsibility for it and to control its possible misuse. Most recently, the Deh Cho Dene of the southern Mackenzie Valley, facing extreme development pressure and high researcher as well as environmental impact, have drafted a traditional knowledge policy to guide those who would conduct research with them.[20]

Yet another arena in which traditional knowledge has provided advice and information is in the operations of the many co-management bodies established by modern treaties. Agreements negotiated by the Inuit of Nunavut, the Gwichin and Inuvialuit of the Northwest Territories, and many others provide for the establishment of joint management boards: comprising individuals appointed by the treaty signatories and the relevant government authorities, these regulate human activities as they may affect the wildlife, lands, and resources of the settlement areas. A general operating principle of such boards is that knowledge drawn from hunters, trappers, and other traditional users of the land, and from the natural sciences, will be used in the boards' deliberations and decision making. Thierry Rodon's careful empirical study of the operation of five such boards considered whether they best fit one of four interpretive models: "la cooptation," "la transaction," "l'autonomie," and "le malentendu" (2003, 144-47). He found elements of each of these models present in different degrees, and that the power relations embedded in the institutions themselves had a major influence.[21] His general conclusion is perhaps most relevant here: "En effet, la pratique de la cogestion influence les acteurs qui y participent. Pour les chasseurs autochtones, c'est l'occasion de se familiariser avec les processus administratifs occidentaux, mais surtout de se former une vision de la participation politique dans le système. Parallèlement, les fonctionnaires des agences publiques pourraient s'ouvrir aux valeurs et à la vision du monde des Autochtones. Ce phénomène fait partie du processus de transaction qui pourrait s'établir avec le temps si les jeux de pouvoir ne favorisent pas les processus de domination. L'expérience de cogestion est encore jeune et ses potentialités ne sont pas épuisées"[22] (ibid., 288).

The final sentence of Rodon's study, which points out the relative shallowness of experiences with building traditional knowledge into public decisions, is apposite to all of the cases considered in this chapter. To extend his questioning, we can consider a further initiative – the Royal Commission on Aboriginal Peoples (RCAP) – one of merit because it was intended, from the beginning, to synthesize Indigenous perspectives and understanding with those available generally in history and social science.[23] The royal commission was enjoined to consider exhaustively all aspects of the relationship between Indigenous peoples and the rest of Canada. The commission itself was structured so as to favour cross-cultural conversations, with four Aboriginal and three non-Aboriginal commissioners, women and men, all experienced in public life but born of the differing cultures of Mi'kmaq, Dene, Métis, Inuit, Québécois, and western Canadian. This somewhat essentialist approach to cross-cultural synthesis was mirrored in the commission's staff, which in all units carefully balanced Aboriginal and non-Aboriginal people and regions of the country. In this institutional mortar, the goal was to reconsider Canadian history and current circumstances in a manner that fairly reflected and accurately synthesized the versions of those who were well educated in Aboriginal traditions and those of the mainstream.

The royal commission's *Ethical Guidelines for Research* (RCAP 1994) contained some features that had not been seen before in a government document.[24] All research conducted for the commission was required to comply with the guidelines, which were "developed to help ensure that ... appropriate respect is given to the cultures, languages, knowledge and values of Aboriginal peoples, and to the standards used by Aboriginal peoples to legitimate knowledge" (ibid., 1). The guidelines specifically required researchers to respect orally transmitted knowledge (and beyond collecting it, to validate it in appropriate ways), to view previously published research with caution (because it might not have permitted Aboriginal people to correct misinformation), and to "conscientiously address themselves to the following questions" (ibid.):

- Are there perspectives on the subject of inquiry that are distinctively Aboriginal?
- What Aboriginal sources are appropriate to shed light on those perspectives?
- Is proficiency in an Aboriginal language required to explore these perspectives and sources?
- Are there particular protocols or approaches required to access the relevant knowledge?
- Does Aboriginal knowledge challenge in any way assumptions brought to the subject from previous research?
- How will Aboriginal knowledge or perspectives portrayed in research projects be validated?

In addition, the commission organized a process of peer review for research, one intended to involve both the Aboriginal and scholarly communities.[25]

In part because it has concluded and because the results of its deliberative process are published in a five-volume final report (RCAP 1996), the
Royal Commission on Aboriginal Peoples is a useful case to consider. Even a
cursory reading of the report reveals that the drafters made extraordinary
efforts to take into account Indigenous peoples' perspectives on key questions. The voluminous and comprehensive final report is not amenable to
summary, but its main message is deceptively simple. Charged with considering all aspects of Aboriginal-Canada relations, the commission focused its
recommendations on the basic principles of a "renewed relationship": mutual
recognition, mutual respect, sharing, and mutual responsibility.[26] As Alan
Cairns (1999) has noted, the analytical premise of the report is that there are
two "parties" to the discussion (hence its use of the word "mutual"), rather
than many, though the report does recognize the great differences in history
and circumstances among the Indigenous peoples of Canada and the society
built of settlers. The report also pays relatively little attention to the ways in
which the cultures from either side of the discussion are intermingled,
through, for example, shared citizenship, intermarriage, and interpersonal
neighbourliness.

If, for the purposes of this analysis, we see the logic informing RCAP as
generally paralleling that of the co-management boards studied by Rodon
(2003), we can draw conclusions that are somewhat similar to his. In RCAP,
it did prove possible to implement a research agenda that incorporated unprecedented official respect not only for the content but also for the guiding
principles of Indigenous peoples' knowledge.[27] On the other hand, the commission itself, its operating principles, languages of work, and the power
relations built into its structures were all firmly expressive of what Rodon
calls "les processus administratifs occidentaux."

The aspiration to forge a common understanding of the world by fusing
knowledge as currently understood by well-educated Indigenous people and
by academics, did not end with RCAP. It is alive today in research programs
funded under the Community-University Research Alliances (of the Social
Sciences and Humanities Research Council) and the Natural Science and
Engineering Research Council's Northern Research Chairs programs, among
others. The extent to which these are genuine epistemological partnerships –
and indeed, whether it makes sense to speak in these terms at all – are matters
for further study.

Whatever is the case with respect to the research community, Canadian
public policy institutions have absorbed the imperative to engage Indigenous

communities in discussion, to invite their participation in decision making, and to seek (though not always to find) means of analytical synthesis. In this process may be found elements of both participation and assimilation, respect and control.

Analyzing the Fate of Traditional Knowledge in Public Policy

In a limited way, Canadian public policy has opened to the possibility that Indigenous peoples might have particular knowledge and particular perspectives, otherwise unavailable, that are inherently valuable and material to public decision making and public governance. As mentioned above, this opening may be linked to the gradual democratization of public institutions, a long process occurring in nation-states everywhere in a manner particular to the institutional legacy and balance of social forces over time. Canadian experiences with traditional knowledge are dissimilar to the broad international trends that have emphasized the commercial extraction and development of Indigenous peoples' knowledge, and the protection of their interests by redefining their knowledge as a matter of private intellectual property. Little of this has occurred in Canada to date, though if past experience is a guide, the international trend will soon find its Canadian expression. For the moment, though, four areas of development, or experimentation, can be identified.

First are the ambitious aspirations of territorial governments to reshape bureaucratic behaviour, both in terms of internal staff relations and in the relationship between the bureaucracy and the public, so that these will express and sustain the evolving Indigenous societies. Certainly, public bureaucracies around the world do vary to some extent, and we may say they carry an ethnic inflection or express cultural difference. Successful examples of fundamental, conscious redesign are rare, however.

A second and related area of interest is the prospect (barely glimpsed) that Indigenous people might bring fresh insight and energy to policy development, not only by adding specialized knowledge to the discussion, but also by changing the institutions and the practices through which policy is developed. To date, the changes implemented in Canada have been largely symbolic (as in the growing practice of opening public events with smudging[28] and prayer by an Indigenous elder) or somewhat essentialist (in the engagement of Indigenous individuals to provide "an Aboriginal perspective"). With these beachheads in place, the next phase may be more thorough institutionalization of Indigenous ways of framing issues and making decisions.

Third, efforts are being made to rely upon syntheses of science and traditional knowledge regarding natural forces in wildlife or environmental behaviour, so as to know how to guide human interventions. Finally, we have seen important attempts to develop a common public understanding of shared history and current circumstances, based upon the widest possible range of human experience and interpretation, with no cultural perspectives systematically privileged.

In none of these four areas can we yet draw anything resembling solid conclusions based upon analyzed experience or even controlled experimentation. Of the four, the experiments with reshaping bureaucracy along different cultural lines are of most recent vintage; to my knowledge, no synthetic studies exist regarding the extent to which, over time, the premises of Indigenous epistemology might alter those of Canadian democracy and decision making.

In the end, we are left with a few searching questions. First, is traditional knowledge a separate category, a field of human endeavour comparable or parallel to science? Societies that are fully absorbed into contemporary industrial capitalism (or "modernity"), commonly differentiate between scientific knowledge and "common sense," historical knowledge, superstition, social science, religious ideas, and fictional stories. Although scientific knowledge is available to all, those who produce it are trained in its fundamental techniques, logical analysis, and empirical testing. We consider something to be "scientifically proven" only if it has been developed in such a way as to sustain independent testing and rigorous scrutiny. Scientific conclusions must also be universally applicable: Boyle's law holds true in Oxford, Toronto, and Yellowknife. In this sense, the development of scientific knowledge is an activity which lies outside the daily lives of most people, however much they may rely upon its conclusions and products; it is fundamentally an abstract, impersonal enterprise.

Such is not quite the case for what is labelled, in modern language and for modern purposes, "traditional knowledge." Certainly, local knowledge can be empirically tested – though, quintessentially, local knowledge need only be local. What is known about a particular ecosystem in northern Saskatchewan is neither expected nor required to apply in northern Quebec. Similarly, traditional knowledge involving a political or social perspective can be validated, explored, elaborated, or investigated – though in the process eventually the unity of understanding and evidence will probably be disturbed by the rules for scientific evidence. On the other hand, the ethical, epistemological, and cosmological ideas that give meaning to and sustain local knowledge and a particular perspective cannot be validated in remotely the same way. One can determine whether a particular account of cosmological knowledge is faithful to what people in a society take to be true, but one cannot determine whether the cosmological ideas themselves are compatible with science, or facts. This is not a particularly surprising conclusion (many important aspects of human life are not "verifiable" in a scientific way), but it probably means that cosmological ideas which differ from those governing existing social institutions will be "read out" of public policy decisions most of the time. What would be the results for modern democratic institutions, and for traditional knowledge itself, if they were not?

If modern institutions constitute a kind of social filter (built out of a particular social and political trajectory, for a particular way of life), they will tend to select some ideas (from local knowledge perhaps) while rejecting others (as, for example, those concerning the behaviour of animal herds).[29] Typically, too, traditional knowledge that does find its way into the policy process (in any one of the four ways listed above) will be written, not oral. It will be codified, not taught by experience. And it will be expressed in a language other than the one in which it was developed.

Finally, we may wonder to what extent understanding follows experience. Will the inclusion of Indigenous people as representatives in public decision making lead ultimately to a reconsideration of the forms of decision making themselves, so that instead of mainly symbolic and selective participation, a synthesis of old and new practices actually changes an aspect of Canadian public life? Or conversely, and as many would predict, will participation lead to absorption and assimilation of Indigenous difference?

In raising these questions, I pass no judgments on outcomes. Perhaps traditional Indigenous knowledge is now so transformed by language loss, urbanization, and changes in people's livelihoods that worrying about its fate in the policy process is not sensible. Some of the legacy of the original North American societies will find its way into how we live; the rest will pass from memory, as has so much of human experience. Or perhaps, if we learn how to institutionalize respect for those great traditions, we will change Canadian democracy for the better.

FRANCES ABELE

ACKNOWLEDGMENTS
Katherine Graham, Les Pal, Susan Phillips, Michael Prince, Thierry Rodon, and Peter
Usher generously provided comments to make this a much better chapter. Thierry Rodon
kindly translated a passage from his book. I would like to thank also Steve Augustine,
Ethel Blondin-Andrew, Tony Buggins, Elsie Casaway, and Phoebe Nahanni for opening
the doors of understanding over many years, and as always George Kinloch for intellectual challenge and companionship.

NOTES

1 Important conferences on these themes include the First Nations, First Thoughts
  Conference, Centre of Canadian Studies, University of Edinburgh, 5-6 May 2005,
  http://www.cst.ed.ac.uk/2005conference/archiveA-M.html, and Integrating Science, Technology and Traditional Knowledge in Today's Environment, University
  of Saskatchewan, September 2003. A third, a Summer Institute at the University
  of Saskatchewan on "postcolonial Indigenous thought," resulted in Marie Battiste
  and James Henderson (2000). A premise of Fikret Berkes and Carl Folke (2002,
  123) is that "all societies have their own science." I was able to find only one
  Canadian text in public policy or Canadian politics in which traditional Indigenous
  knowledge was mentioned (Pal 2005); nor did I locate any academic articles on
  this topic. Thierry Rodon (2003), Paul Nadasdy (1999, 2003), and Graham White
  (2005) provide excellent analyses of traditional knowledge in the regulatory and
  claims negotiations processes. On the role of scientists and other researchers, see
  Bielawski (1984) and Cruikshank (1981).

2 The defining role of jurisprudence in public policy, in this field above all others,
  requires separate consideration. Excellent sources include Asch (1997), and Dara
  Culhane (1998). A rich and thoughtful discussion of the question of Indigenous
  identity is James R. Miller (2004, 1-51); see also Bartholomew Dean and Jerome
  M. Levi (2003), Adam Kuper (2003), and for the roots of this question in European thought, Karen Ordahl Kupperman (1995).

3 Some important issues concerning publication and public discussion are elided
  in the use of the term "well educated." Indigenous societies, of course, all had and
  have social means of education and intellectual development. Like all other human societies, they use a variety of specific practices or indicators to identify the
  "well educated" – that is to say, those people who are respected for what they
  have learned and understood and can contribute. See Marlene Brant Castellano,
  Lynne Davis, and Louise Lahache (2000) and Marie Battiste and Jean Barman
  (1995).

4 See the contrasting discussions in Sharon Venne (1997), Kiera Ladner (2003),
  and Alaska Native Science Commission (n.d.).

5 Such a list appears in the Health Canada (2003) chapter on Aboriginal health
  and traditional knowledge. This list, though more substantive and subtle than

many, involves a great deal of unsubstantiated overgeneralization (where is the research to support its claims?) and it certainly obscures the common characteristics of all traditions of human knowledge. For yet another perspective, see Battiste and Henderson (2000).

6 I would like to acknowledge Peter Usher's help in understanding these distinctions – though he may not agree exactly with the construction I have put on our conversations.

7 See Ladner (2003) and Nadasdy (2003) for excellent reflections on this kind of "knowledge" (a term Nadasdy hesitates to use because it is too compartmentalizing) and on the process of learning about it.

8 I thank Phoebe Nahanni for helping me to understand this point. See also Nadasdy (2003, chap. 6).

9 A summary explanation of this process appears in Frances Abele (2001).

10 For more detailed treatments of the subject, see Barbara Arneil (1996), Kupperman (1995), James Tully (1980, 1993), Ellen Meiksins Wood and Neal Wood (1997), and Ellen Meiksins Wood (2003).

11 For further discussion, see Rodon (2003), Nadasdy (2003), and White (2005).

12 The information here is based on D. Michael Warren (1998); the book in which the term first appeared is David Brokensha, Denis M. Warren, and Oswald Werner (1980). This general chronology is confirmed in Roy Ellen, Peter Parkes, and Alan Bick (2000).

13 The United Nations Convention on Biodiversity, ratified in 1992 in the wake of the Rio de Janeiro UN Conference on the Environment and Development, regulates "bio-prospecting" – commercial or philanthropic efforts, always by well-funded outside organizations, to discover and distribute Indigenous peoples' traditional knowledge; on this and the other themes mentioned in this paragraph, see Shane Greene (2004), Paul Sillitoe (1998), and the comments that follow their articles in *Current Anthropology*. Useful and fairly comprehensive websites include http://www.ik-pages.net/ and http://www.nufficcs.nl/ciran/ikdm.

14 Greene (2004, 226) notes that "A key objective of ... [the] Convention was to create a formal regime of access to biological resources and benefit from sharing from their use."

15 J. Peter Brosius (2000) provides an interesting discussion of this process in Asia. With respect to Canada, Nadasdy (2003) demonstrates the force and form of resistance to this.

16 David Anderson (2004) discusses this shift in post-Soviet Russia.

17 Just as this essay traces the path of traditional knowledge in public policy institutions, another might examine its parallel but distinctive fate in jurisprudence, where it has been variously ignored, disrespected, and – in a limited fashion – accepted. See Culhane (1998).

18 For *Policy Options*, see Fikret Berkes and Thomas Henley (1997), Albert Howard and Frances Widdowson (1996, 1997), and Marc G. Stevenson (1997). For other sources, consult Abele (1997) and Stephanie Irlbacher (1998). A very useful consideration of varying scholarly approaches, with attention to their practical consequences as well as their epistemology, is George Wenzel (1999).

19 See also Government of Nunavut (1998); Annis May Timpson (2006) has studied the implementation of Inuit Qaujimanituqangit (IQ), noting the many practical difficulties that face any such broad effort at organizational change. In her admittedly early assessment of the IQ experiment, she stresses the importance of workplace use of Inuktitut, the Inuit language, in ensuring the successful implementation of the policy. On the general objectives of the Government of Nunavut, see Jack Hicks and Graham White (2000).

20 For more information about the Deh Cho Dene, see http://www.dehcho firstnations.com. At the time of writing, the Deh Cho Dene policy had been drafted but, pending internal approval, not yet made public.

21 Nadasdy (1999) makes a similar argument.

22 "Co-management affects its participants. For Aboriginal hunters, it is an opportunity to become familiar with Western administrative practices and the needs and values of government employees. At the same time, Western administrators have a chance to better understand Aboriginal values and worldviews. In time, this could lead to a transaction process if the balance of power does not favour the establishment of a domination process. In Canada, co-management experiences are still recent and their potential has not yet been exhausted."

23 The concrete examples offered in this section are meant to be illustrative, not exhaustive. I have chosen instances that I believe are sufficiently varied to be interesting, and sufficiently important to merit our sustained examination, but am aware that equally interesting experiments are underway in all parts of Canada. Think, for example, of the progress of development in the Nisga'a and adjoining territories in British Columbia, where education and new political institutions are rooted in Nisga'a traditions but being adapted to contemporary federalism and public administration.

24 The guidelines were unusual in public policy but not in academia: indeed, they were based on best practices in the social sciences, particularly anthropology.

25 *Ethical Guidelines for Research* also includes requirements concerning research protocol agreements with communities, the use of advisory committees, informed consent, and other provisions.

26 RCAP (1996, vol. 1, 675-97) contains a concise explanation of these principles, as well as comment regarding ways and means.

27 This statement is based upon my own observation, the 210 research studies that were completed and published, and the commission's final report, which is avail-

able for all to examine. The difficulties with implementing the research program of the commission along the lines specified in *Ethical Guidelines* were considerable, and remain to be studied systematically.

28 Smudging is a ritual involving the burning of certain herbs by an elder or other practitioner to create a cleansing smoke. Symbolically, those who participate seek clear vision, hearing, speech, and thoughts.

29 Nadasdy (1999) describes exactly this process with respect to interaction between hunters and scientists concerning the understanding of animal behaviour.

REFERENCES

Abele, Frances. 1997. "Traditional Knowledge in Practice." Editorial in *Arctic* 50(4): iii-iv.

—. 2001. "Small Nations and Democracy's Prospects: Indigenous Peoples in Canada, Australia, New Zealand, Norway and Greenland." *Inroads* 10: 137-49.

Alaska Native Science Commission. n.d. *What Is Traditional Knowledge?* http://www.nativescience.org/.

Anderson, David. 2004. "Nationality and 'Aboriginal Rights' in Post-Soviet Siberia." In *Circumpolar Ethnicity and Identity*, ed. Takashi Irimoto and Takako Yamada, 111-45. Senri Ethnological Studies 66. Osaka: National Museum of Ethnology.

Arneil, Barbara. 1996. *John Locke and America: The Defence of English Colonialism.* Oxford: Clarendon Press.

Asch, Michael, ed. 1997. *Aboriginal and Treaty Rights in Caanda: Essays on Law, Equality, and Respect for Difference.* Vancouver: UBC Press.

Association of Canadian Universities for Northern Studies. 1982. *Ethical Principles for the Conduct of Research in the North.* Ottawa: Association of Canadian Universities for Northern Studies. http://www.acuns.ca.

Battiste, Marie, and Jean Barman, eds. 1995. *First Nations Education in Canada: The Circle Unfolds.* Vancouver: UBC Press.

Battiste, Marie, and James (Sa'ke'j) Henderson. 2000. *Protecting Indigenous Knowledge and Heritage: A Global Challenge.* Saskatoon: Purich.

Berkes, Fikret, and Carl Folke. 2002. "Back to the Future: Ecosystem Dynamics and Local Knowledge." In *Panarchy: Understanding Transformations in Human and Natural Systems*, ed. Lance H. Gunderson and C.S. Holling, 236-70. Washington, DC: Island Press.

Berkes, Fikret, and Thomas Henley. 1997. "Co-management and Traditional Knowledge: Threat or Opportunity?" *Policy Options* 18(2): 46-48.

Bielawski, Ellen. 1984. "Anthropological Observations on Science in the North: The Role of the Scientist in Human Development in the Northwest Territories." *Arctic* 37(1): 1-6.

Brokensha, David, Dennis M. Warren, and Oswald Werner, eds. 1980. *Indigenous Knowledge Systems and Development.* Washington, DC: University Press of America.

Brosius, J. Peter. 2000. "Endangered Forest, Endangered People: Environmentalist Representations of Indigenous Knowledge." In *Indigenous Environmental Knowledge and Its Transformations: Critical Anthropological Perspectives,* ed. Roy Ellen, Peter Parkes, and Alan Bick, 293-318. Amsterdam: Harwood Academic.

Cairns, Alan. 1999. *Citizens Plus: Aboriginal Peoples and the Canadian State.* Vancouver: UBC Press.

Castellano, Marlene Brant, Lynne Davis, and Louise Lahache, eds. 2000. *Aboriginal Education: Fulfilling the Promise.* Vancouver: UBC Press.

Cruikshank, Julie. 1981. "Legend and Landscape: Convergence of Oral and Scientific Traditions in the Yukon Territory." *Arctic Anthropology* 17(2): 67-93.

Culhane, Dara. 1998. *The Pleasure of the Crown: Anthropology, Law and First Nations.* Burnaby: Talonbooks.

Dean, Bartholomew, and Jerome M. Levi, eds. 2003. *At the Risk of Being Heard: Identity, Indigenous Rights, and Postcolonial States.* Ann Arbor: University of Michigan Press.

Dene Cultural Institute. n.d. "Who Are We?" http://www.deneculture.org/whoarewe.htm.

Ellen, Roy, Peter Parkes, and Alan Bick, eds. 2000. *Indigenous Environmental Knowledge and Its Transformations: Critical Anthropological Perspectives.* Amsterdam: Harwood Academic.

Environmental Assessment Act, S.C. 1992, c. 37.

Government of the Northwest Territories. 1993. *Policy 52.06: Traditional Knowledge.* Yellowknife: Government of the Northwest Territories. http://www.gov.nt.ca.

Government of Nunavut. 1998. *Inuit Qaujimanituqangit.* Iqaluit: Department of Sustainable Development.

Greene, Shane. 2004. "Indigenous People Incorporated? Culture as Politics, Culture as Property in Pharmaceutical Bioprospecting." *Current Anthropology* 45(2): 211-37.

Health Canada. 2003. *The Canadian Handbook on Health Impact Assessment.* http://www.hc-sc.gc.ca/hecs-sesc/ehas/publications/canadian_handbook.

Hicks, Jack, and Graham White. 2000. "Nunavut: Inuit Self-Determination through a Land Claims and Public Government." In *Nunavut: Inuit Regain Control of Their Lands and Their Lives,* ed. Jens Dahl, Jack Hicks, and Peter Jull, 30-117. Copenhagen: International Work Group for Indigenous Affairs.

Howard, Albert, and Frances Widdowson. 1996. "Traditional Knowledge Threatens Environmental Assessment." *Policy Options* 17(9): 34-36.

—. 1997. "Traditional Knowledge Advocates Weave a Tangled Web." *Policy Options* 18(3): 46-48.

Inuit Tapirisat of Canada. 1999. *Towards an Inuit Qaujimajatuqangit (IQ) Policy for Nunavut: A Discussion Paper.* Ottawa: Inuit Tapirisat of Canada.

Irlbacher, Stephanie. 1998. "Using Aboriginal Traditional Knowledge in a 'Modern' Bureaucracy: The NWT Experience." Yellowknife. Ms. available from the author.

Kuper, Adam. 2003. "The Return of the Native." *Current Anthropology* 44(3): 389-95.

Kupperman, Karen Ordahl. 1995. *America in European Consciousness 1493-1750.* Chapel Hill: University of North Carolina Press.

Ladner, Kiera. 2003. "Governing within an Ecological Context: Creating an AlterNative Understanding of Blackfoot Governance." *Studies in Political Economy* 70: 125-57.

Miller, James R. 2004. *Lethal Legacy: Current Native Controversies in Canada.* Toronto: McClelland and Stewart.

Nadasdy, Paul. 1999. "The Politics of TEK: Power and the 'Integration' of Knowledge." *Arctic Anthropology* 36(1-2): 1-18.

—. 2003. *Hunters and Bureaucrats: Power, Knowledge, and Aboriginal-State Relations in the Southwest Yukon.* Vancouver and Toronto: UBC Press.

NPEIARCC (Northern Pipeline Environmental Impact Assessment and Regulatory Chairs' Committee). 2002. *The Consolidated Information Requirements for the Environmental Assessment and Regulatory Review of a Northern Gas Pipeline Project through the Northwest Territories.* http://www.neb.gc.ca/NorthOffshore/Mackenzie/northerngasinforeq_e.pdf.

Pal, Leslie A. 2005. *Beyond Policy Analysis: Public Issue Management in Turbulent Times.* Toronto: Nelson.

RCAP (Canada, Royal Commission on Aboriginal Peoples). 1994. *Ethical Guidelines for Research.* Ottawa: Royal Commission on Aboriginal Peoples.

—. 1996. Report of the Royal Commission on Aboriginal Peoples. 5 vols. Ottawa: Ministry of Supply and Services.

Rodon, Thierry. 2003. *En Partenariat avec L'Etat: Les Expériences de Cogestion des Autochtones du Canada.* Saint-Nicolas: Les Presses de l'Université Laval.

Sillitoe, Paul. 1998. "The Development of Indigenous Knowledge: A New Applied Anthropology." *Current Anthropology* 39(2): 223-35.

Stevenson, Marc G. 1997. "Ignorance and Prejudice Threaten Environmental Assessment." *Policy Options* 18(2): 25-28.

Timpson, Annis May. 2006. Expanding the Concept of Representative Bureaucracy: The Case of Nunavut. Manuscript available from the author.

Tully, James. 1980. *A Discourse on Property: Locke in Contexts.* Cambridge, UK: Cambridge University Press.

—. 1993. *An Approach to Political Philosophy.* Cambridge, UK: Cambridge University Press.

Venne, Sharon. 1997. "Understanding Treaty 6: An Indigenous Perspective." In *Aboriginal and Treaty Rights in Canada: Essays on Law, Equality, and Respect for Difference,* ed. Michael Asch, 173-207. Vancouver: UBC Press.

Warren, D. Michael. 1998. "Comment on P. Sillitoe." *Current Anthropology* 39(2): 244-45.

Wenzel, George. 1999. "Traditional Ecological Knowledge and Inuit: Reflections on TEK Research and Ethics." *Arctic* 52(2): 113-24.

White, Graham. 2005. "Culture Clash: Traditional Knowledge and Euro-Canadian Governance Processes in Northern Claims Boards." Paper presented at First Nations, First Thoughts, Centre for Canadian Studies, University of Edinburgh, 6 May. http://www.cst.ed.ac.uk/2005conference/.

Wood, Ellen Meiksins. 2003. *Empire of Capital.* New York: Verso.

Wood, Ellen Meiksins, and Neal Wood. 1997. *A Trumpet of Sedition: Political Theory and the Rise of Capitalism, 1509-1688.* Washington Square: New York University Press.

12
Framing Environmental Policy: Aboriginal Rights and the Conservation of Migratory Birds

Luc Juillet

Over the years, the study of the influence of discursive politics on public policy has gained important ground (Fischer 2003). Although this new attention paid to discursive dynamics and processes has generated some insightful treatments of environmental policy (such as Dryzek 1997; Fischer 2000; Hajer 1995; Liftin 1994), it has not been common in the study of Canadian environmental policy. Instead, in explaining the evolution of Canadian policy regarding the conservation of wildlife, scholars have tended to focus on the interplay of interest groups and state actors, the influence of intergovernmental relations, and the impact of bureaucratic politics.

Without disputing the importance of those factors, this chapter seeks to illuminate Canadian conservation policy through an analysis of discursive politics. It will focus on a significant controversy regarding Aboriginal waterfowl hunting during the spring season, tracing the evolution of policy from 1916 to the mid-1990s. In particular, it will show that this controversy turned on a conflict between two distinctive discursive frames which prevented a change in environmental policy for many years. Ultimately, the dispute was resolved after changes in the broader constitutional environment significantly altered the context of conservation policy making, thereby effectively redefining the terms of the debate. In the end, this case study illustrates the importance of discursive politics in the making of Canadian environmental policy; but it also demonstrates how the discursive struggles around environmental policy are embedded and enmeshed in the broader conflicts about the nature of the Canadian polity.

Discursive Politics and the Aboriginal Waterfowl Hunting Rights Controversy

At the turn of the twentieth century, expanding scientific knowledge of bird ecology prompted concern regarding several North American bird species.

With the extinction of some important species, the conservation of birds became a salient political issue. In particular, the decline of bird populations due to excessive harvesting by market hunters (who killed the birds for restaurants and milliners) caused alarm on both sides of the Canada-US border. In the US, the sympathetic Roosevelt administration, the young conservation movement, and the powerful farm lobby (concerned with the decline of insectivorous birds that acted as a natural pest control mechanism for crops) joined ranks to press for the adoption of federal conservation measures (Dorsey 1998, 165-237). In Canada, a nascent conservation bureaucracy similarly pushed the federal government to take action, also stressing the economic benefits that insectivorous birds represented for the agricultural industry (Dorsey 1998, 189-90; Foster 1998, 120-48).

The main result of these political efforts was the ratification of the US-Canada Migratory Birds Convention (MBC) in 1916, an international treaty that became the bedrock of bird conservation policy in both countries. The keystone of this conservation regime was a ban on the killing of non-game migratory birds and severe restrictions on the harvesting of game birds, including a ban on the hunting of waterfowl during the spring breeding season. Although in recent years the debates have largely turned to issues of habitat protection, biodiversity, and endangered species legislation (see Beazley and Boardman 2001; Boardman 2002; Boyd 2003, 164-210), the regulation of waterfowl hunting remains an important element of Canadian conservation policy. Given that millions of ducks and geese are harvested every year in North America, hunting regulations remain essential to the sustainability of their populations.

However, though it was hailed as a major success in conservation policy, the MBC also constituted a significant irritant for Aboriginal nations, especially those living in the northern part of the continent and whose traditional lifestyle significantly depended on waterfowl hunting (Wagner and Thompson 1993). Since its inception, Aboriginal peoples argued that the spring ban violated their hunting rights and represented a historical injustice preventing them from preserving their traditional lifestyles. For some northern communities, it also hindered their capacity to lawfully satisfy their spiritual, socio-cultural, and economic needs, which required the hunting and consumption of ducks and geese in the spring and summer (Condon, Collings, and Wenzel 1995; Scott 1987; Stairs and Wenzel 1992). Accordingly, Aboriginal nations pressed the federal government to modify its conservation policy in order to recognize their right to harvest waterfowl throughout the year. Only in the mid-1990s, when the spring hunting prohibition was at last lifted for Aboriginals, was the policy controversy finally resolved.

To explain the history of this controversy, as well as the nature and timing of the changes in federal policy, I examine the discursive politics that surrounded the issue.[1] Policy problems do not impose themselves as indisputable facts which can be recognized through observation. In an essential dimension of politics, actors construct them through arguments and other rhetorical devices (Fischer 2003). In this perspective, discursive politics can be defined "as a struggle for discursive hegemony in which actors try to secure support for their definition of reality" (Hajer 1995, 59). In the context of policy making, discursive politics can take the form of a confrontation between competing policy frames. By weaving a selection of facts, beliefs, and values into a plausible prescriptive narrative, these policy frames, or storylines, allow actors and publics to reduce the complexity of policy problems, ascribe meaning to problems and events, and crudely assess possible policy alternatives. The more dominant a frame becomes, the more successful it will be in shaping the terms of the policy debate and, consequently, the content of policy. For this reason, opposing discourse coalitions (sets of actors loosely brought together by their general, if potentially imperfect, adherence to a common storyline which underscores their political action) will work to impose their own storyline as the dominant frame of reference on a specific policy issue (Hajer 1995, 65-66).

How specific storylines or frames come to dominate a particular policy field or how frame shifting occurs over time must be uncovered through a contextualized empirical analysis of specific policy controversies (Fischer 2003, 145). Previous studies, however, have isolated the following factors as aids to the success of frames: credibility (that is, internal consistency, congruence with mutually recognized "facts"), "acceptability" (whether they can be perceived as necessary or beneficial by elites and publics with differing interests), "discursive affinity" (their capacity to be understood and believed as plausible by actors with differing and imperfect knowledge of a complex issue), the level of trust in the actors that support and advocate them, the degree of access that their supporters have to policy-making arenas, and their congruence with the broader normative environment in which they are articulated or with the culture of decision-making elites (see, for example, Bernstein 2000; Browne and Keil 2000; Campbell 2002; Fischer 2003; Hajer 1995; Honneland 2004; Morgan 2004).

It is important to note that approaches emphasizing the influence of discourse do not negate the importance of interests and institutions in social explanations. But, in the perspective of discursive politics, the interests of actors are not conceptualized as a set of given and fixed preferences to be pursued through instrumental strategic action: they are rather "intersubjectively constituted through discourse" (Hajer 1995, 59). In other words, it is through dialogue with other actors – the discursive "construction of reality" through dialogue – that actors come to understand and define the nature of their interests (Campbell 2002, 33-34). Given that discursive exchanges and practices are constitutive of actors' interests, actors can strategically engage in the production of frames or storylines, which, if they succeed in imposing themselves, will have a direct impact on the terms of the debate and the content of policy. Framing, or the construction of storylines in public debate, is a strategic act used to further actors' interests, but one that can also work by leading other actors to redefine their own interests in light of a new understanding of reality. In sum, discourse is not just a tool to be used strategically to advance or counter predetermined interests: it has transformative potential.

Similarly, discursive struggles do not take place in a vacuum. In particular, they occur in the context of existing institutional practices (Hajer 1995, 60-61). The polity as a whole and particular policy fields are constituted by an often dense collection of norms that have been institutionalized through social practices, including the use of state authority. These institutions serve to structure and guide the behaviour of social actors. Moreover, from the perspective of discursive politics, they are in a dialectical relation with the discourses of social actors. In constructing storylines in an effort to generate trust, bolster credibility, and ensure congruence with their normative environment, discourse coalitions mobilize these institutionalized norms. In return, when discourses become hegemonic and affect the content of policy, they contribute to the institutionalization of new norms that have a resilience of their own. In sum, the institutional and normative context of policy making is the product of discursive politics, but it is also a constraint and an instrument in the development of successful storylines.

Under this heuristic framework, the history of the controversy regarding Aboriginal waterfowl hunting rights can be divided into three periods. From the inception of the spring ban to the 1970s, the debate was marked by conflict between two distinctive frames or storylines. In one, the prevailing coalition of environmentalists and conservation authorities posed the issue as a disagreement between special-interest politics and sensible science-based wildlife management; it advocated in favour of retaining the spring ban. In the other, Aboriginal nations articulated a counter-discourse calling for an end to the ban and presenting the issue as one of justice, historical rights, and national affirmation. The period following this era of stalemate, from the mid-1970s to the 1990s, saw a significant discursive shift by conservation authorities. During this time, they sought to reframe the controversy as one of equity for northern communities; consequently, they attempted to grant exceptions for those communities. However, this attempt was a failure, in large part because this new frame was in dissonance with the broader normative context of Canadian constitutional politics. Finally, the current period began in the early 1990s with the landmark recognition of the limited right of Aboriginal peoples to hunt waterfowl throughout the year for subsistence purposes, subject to appropriate conservation measures. In good part, this historic shift in policy was made possible by an authoritative court decision that reframed the policy problem by restating the relationship between bird conservation and Aboriginal rights. By altering the legal landscape, this new frame changed the terms of the debate, forced the policy actors involved to rethink both their interests and strategies, and eventually permitted a resolution of the controversy. These three periods in the evolution of waterfowl conservation policy are now examined in turn.

Inter-Frame Conflict: Aboriginal Justice and Canadian Conservation Policy

The inter-frame conflict that characterized the first sixty years of the controversy opposed two distinctive narratives concerning the nature of the MBC and its associated ban on spring hunting. For conservation authorities and environmentalists, the MBC was one of the few great successes of conservation policy and environmental diplomacy. Hailed at the time of its ratification as "the most important and far-reaching measure ever taken in the history of bird protection" (Dorsey 1998, 232), its provisions are largely credited for having averted the dramatic decline in several bird species that was presaged early in the century (Wagner and Thompson 1993). It was recognized as an essential component of the modern conservation policy framework that has ensured, by and large, the sustainability of bird populations on the continent. As such, it stood as a rare demonstration that, in environmental policy and diplomacy, parochial self-interest could be set aside for the successful preservation of our common natural heritage.

According to this view, the ban on spring waterfowl hunting was an important component of a science-based wildlife management (Canadian Nature Federation and International Council for Bird Protection 1991; Canadian Wildlife Federation 1992). The sustainability of bird populations depends in no small measure on their ability to migrate to their northern breeding grounds and reproduce during this crucial period of the year. To the protection of habitat, sound environmental policy adds the requirement that birds be protected from hunters during this sensitive time. It should be stressed that most environmentalists do not advocate an end to recreational or subsistence waterfowl hunting. Eschewing a concern for animal rights or the integral preservation of nature, they seek rather to ensure the sustainability of bird populations by preserving their natural habitat and by ensuring that the number of birds killed annually does not threaten the reproductive capacity of the species. In this perspective, the ban on spring hunting was not the mere triumph of a romantic love of wildlife: it represented the logical outcome of a rational science-based management of wildlife resources that should not be compromised by interest-based politics or blind acquiescence to Aboriginal demands (see, for example, Keith and McMullen 1992, 15). In this narrative, the MBC was a triumph of science and ecological sensitivity over politics. Yielding to Aboriginal interests by eliminating the spring hunting ban in the name of treaty and historical rights would be a step backward, a return to the days when market and recreational hunters irresponsibly resisted the protection of the birds during their reproductive season.

Rejecting this "science over politics" frame, Aboriginal nations demanding an end to the spring hunting ban framed the problem in terms of respect for historical rights and special needs. For them, the ban was merely the product of a broader colonial policy by the Canadian state, which had failed to live up to its promises and treaty obligations (ibid., 100). Aboriginal demands for the recognition of their hunting rights were essentially demands for the respect of their status as distinct nations who retained these rights in particular historical circumstances. Moreover, by constraining their capacity to lawfully engage in their traditional way of life, the ban was perceived in part as an instrument of assimilation and a denial of identity. As such, it was not a mere issue of distributive politics or a simple matter of scientific management of bird populations: it was a matter of justice and national affirmation.

This way of framing the issue meant that Aboriginal nations also demanded to be exempted from federal hunting regulations, including annual harvest quotas (ibid., 110). With respect to their special rights, several

Aboriginal nations argued that they should be allowed to regulate themselves. Relying on their own traditional knowledge, as well as scientific management techniques, Aboriginal communities themselves would ensure that their harvesting did not threaten the sustainability of waterfowl populations (see, for example, Innu Nation 1992). In other words, the "justice and national affirmation" frame used by Aboriginal nations implied that conservation was a second-order objective, highly valued by these nations but nevertheless subsumed under the overarching values of justice and self-determination for Aboriginal peoples.

For much of the history of conservation policy, this inter-frame conflict resulted in a "dialogue of the deaf," with conservation authorities, environmentalists, and Aboriginal leaders talking past each other, fundamentally disagreeing on the terms of the debate. Aboriginal peoples suffered from some important disadvantages in the policy debate. They were generally poorly organized for political activity and they represented a marginal electoral constituency. They had limited access to the policy-making arena. As a result, their voice was barely audible, a definite disadvantage in imposing their own storyline regarding the spring ban. Moreover, when legal challenges were launched in the 1960s, Canadian courts merely confirmed the predominance of government environmental regulations over Aboriginal rights, depriving Aboriginal nations of another lever of policy change.[2] At that time, such incongruence with the dominant legal norms in the field of conservation policy vastly discredited their claims.

The fact that the two opposing discourse coalitions saw the spring hunt controversy in such different terms made a constructive dialogue impossible and the resolution of the controversy improbable. During this period, the waterfowl hunting rights controversy was not simply a case of distributive politics in which, using a mutually recognized frame of reference, opposing parties disagreed about the fair and appropriate allocation of resources. The disagreement rested largely on a fundamental difference in the very definition of the issue and, consequently, in the terms used in the debate over potential solutions. In this context, especially given the relatively weak voice of Aboriginal peoples in Canadian politics at the time, the ban on Aboriginal spring hunting remained firmly in place. In the narrow field of wildlife conservation, where the debate took place for the first sixty years of on-and-off controversy, the storyline proposed by Aboriginal nations had no significant resonance with other policy actors, including government authorities. The language of historical rights and national affirmation was clearly at odds with the dominant discourse on sustainability and science-based environmental management. In this context, demands for rights recognition were heard largely as self-interested demands for a bigger share of public resources and as an attempt to "corrupt" science-based wildlife management with interest-based politics.

Failing to Reframe the Controversy: The Search for Equitable Northern Access

The discursive politics of the spring hunting controversy changed significantly in the mid-1970s. During those years, a more vocal Aboriginal movement, fuelled by rising Aboriginal nationalism, seized the opportunity provided by government plans to further exploit northern natural resources located on contested ancestral lands to demand adequate recognition of their rights (Abele 1987, 314-16; Nichols 1999, 305-8). With regard to the spring hunting controversy, the signature of the James Bay and Northern Quebec Agreement in 1975 proved to be the most consequential. In this case, the Cree of northern Quebec sufficiently hindered government plans to develop hydro-electric projects on their territory to force the negotiation of the first modern treaty in Canada. Amongst the array of concessions won by the Cree was a commitment from federal authorities to seek a change to conservation laws to recognize their right to hunt waterfowl throughout the year (see Article 24.14.2 of the agreement). This formal commitment to the Cree, as well as fears that the new Aboriginal activism around hunting rights might generate clashes with non-Aboriginal hunters in other northern communities, triggered a shift in the federal government's position on the spring harvest.[3] Without completely conceding Aboriginal claims regarding the illegality of the spring ban, federal authorities were now advocating a change in policy that would permit greater flexibility toward northern Aboriginal communities.

However, before they could change domestic policy, Canadian authorities had to overcome some obstacles.[4] First, following their turnabout, they faced opposition from their former allies in the environmental movement, who still feared that a breach in the spring ban could be detrimental to waterfowl populations.[5] To further complicate matters, as Ottawa began to raise the possibility of a limited spring harvest, some provincial governments, especially in the west, voiced their opposition. Not only would an Aboriginal spring hunt be ecologically dangerous, it would also be unfair to non-Aboriginal hunters, including those in the territories and the northern parts of the provinces who also relied heavily on the land for their livelihood. If a limited spring harvest were permitted, the provinces argued, it should apply equally to Aboriginal and non-Aboriginal hunters.[6]

Second, because the ban had its roots in the MBC, the American government must agree to change the bilateral conservation treaty before Canadian policy could be changed. On this score, though federal authorities could be persuaded, lifting the ban on spring hunting was adamantly opposed by a group of US senators (whose agreement was constitutionally required in order for the US to ratify the proposed treaty modification) with close ties to environmentalists and recreational hunters from the Midwest states. Concerned about conservation and the interests of American recreational hunters, these senators made it clear that they would use their influence in the senatorial Foreign Relations Committee to veto a change to the bilateral convention (Juillet 2000, 131-32).

In order to overcome these obstacles, federal authorities explicitly attempted to reframe the spring hunting controversy. Setting aside the question of Aboriginal rights, they presented the issue in terms of the need to ensure equitable access to waterfowl resources for all northern residents. Under the terms of the MBC, the spring ban extended from 10 March to 1 September. This meant that northern communities were often completely prevented from hunting waterfowl because, due to their migratory timing, most species visited the North within this time frame only. As a result, the government argued, the real problem was to ensure better access to all northern residents, whether or not they belonged to a First Nation.[7] In this perspective, federal conservation authorities proposed that the international treaty, and associated domestic legislation, be amended to allow them to vary the dates of the hunting season without restrictions. They would then use their discretion to open a tightly regulated spring season for all northern residents who depended on waterfowl resources for their subsistence, when and where scientific estimates of bird populations would warrant it.[8] From Ottawa's viewpoint, the "equitable northern access" scenario would both deal with stakeholders' concerns for justice (northern Aboriginal and non-Aboriginal hunters would get their "fair and equal share" of the harvest and their subsistence needs would be met) and respect the imperatives of conservation (the regime would still be firmly based on scientific evidence and the harvest could be curtailed to ensure the sustainability of the resource).

However, this attempt at reframing the issue failed to resolve the controversy. Part of the failure was due to the inability of federal authorities to convince environmentalists and American legislators that the proposed change represented an adequate compromise between justice and conservation. In particular, environmentalists believed that, once a spring harvest was allowed, the Canadian government would be unwilling or unable to adequately enforce regulations, for fear of creating difficulties with the more vocal Aboriginal nations.[9] As a result, science-based wildlife management would progressively give way to political expediency as the foundation of waterfowl conservation policy. Moreover, the problem was compounded by the fact that the Canadian government seemed to lack credibility. Before it wanted to secure access to northern natural resources and placate Aboriginal nationalism, it had consistently argued that an Aboriginal spring harvest would be detrimental to waterfowl populations. By suddenly changing narrative, it could appear to be a "manipulative framer" (Campbell 2002, 28), concealing its true motives and attempting to reframe the problem purely to advance other interests. As relayed by the environmental lobby, these fears of a politically charged and poorly regulated spring harvest served to consolidate the American Senate's opposition to amending the MBC.[10] Eventually, even the US Department of State became convinced that it would not be able to secure congressional approval for the amendment proposed by Canada (Juillet 2000, 131-32).

Although these difficulties abroad were important, domestic politics proved fatal for Ottawa's proposal. The key problem was that the "equitable northern access" storyline proved to be in dissonance with the emerging normative context of Canadian constitutional politics. As it moved into the early 1980s, the debate over Aboriginal hunting rights was overtaken by the larger issue of constitutional reform. In particular, the negotiations regarding the Constitution Act, 1982, resulted in the entrenchment of Aboriginal and treaty rights in section 35. Although the nature of those rights originally remained rather indeterminate, it was clear from the outset that their constitutional recognition would have significant implications for hunting rights and conservation policy.

In this context, the equitable northern access storyline seemed dramatically out of synch with the emerging norms of Canadian constitutional discourse. First, the government was proposing to limit the spring hunt to northern Aboriginal communities, though the constitutional recognition of Aboriginal rights was obviously not limited to the North. Second, conservation authorities proposed to allow a limited spring harvest as a privilege, through their discretionary power and depending on their assessment of the resource. This limited harvest would also be tightly regulated and it would not be reserved to Aboriginal hunters. In other words, the "equitable northern access" storyline framed the spring harvest as an issue of privilege for northern residents, to be granted by the state when and where it deemed it warranted, as opposed to an issue of constitutional rights for Aboriginal peoples throughout Canada. For this reason, the new frame did not win the adhesion even of Aboriginal nations. But, more significantly, by the mid-1980s, this line of thinking was no longer in keeping with the dominant norms of Canadian constitutional discourse. As a result, noting this incompatibility of language and norms, the Canadian government ordered its conservation authorities to abandon their "equitable northern access" proposal.

Shifting the Context: *Sparrow* and the New Conservation Policy

If the broader normative context of constitutional politics and law proved to be a constraint on policy change during the 1980s, by the early 1990s, it actually provided the impetus for the successful modification of conservation policy with regard to the spring waterfowl harvest. The most important development was the *Sparrow* decision rendered by the Supreme Court in 1990.[11] Although lower courts had begun in the late 1980s to spell out the consequences of the Constitution Act, 1982, for waterfowl hunting rights,[12] the decision by the highest court provided a more definitive and important statement on how to deal with Aboriginal hunting rights in the context of conservation policy.

Sparrow involved infractions to fisheries regulations, but in acquitting the Aboriginal defendant in the case, the Supreme Court confirmed that section 35 of the Constitution Act, 1982, conferred a constitutional status to the wildlife harvesting rights of Aboriginal peoples. As such, where these rights existed, they trumped government statutes, except when these laws pursued a "valid legislative objective" that could justify limiting the exercise of Aboriginal rights. The court explicitly cited conservation and resource management as "uncontroversial" examples of such valid objectives. However, even in situations where Aboriginal rights were lawfully curtailed, the protection of the Crown's honour required that conservation policy adhere to specific norms in its dealings with Aboriginal peoples. In particular, such measures must be shown to be truly necessary for conservation, and their design must minimize the extent to which the rights were restricted. In practice, these principles meant that the government could limit the hunt by invoking conservation reasons but that, if hunting were permitted, Aboriginal harvesting for food and ceremonial purposes must always receive top priority in allocating the resource, given that these communities have a unique constitutional claim to wildlife harvesting.

It is difficult to overstate *Sparrow*'s impact on the spring hunting controversy. First, through its authoritative statement, the court legitimized the historical claims of Aboriginal nations. Although the court reasserted the ultimate predominance of conservation laws over Aboriginal rights (a victory for environmentalists and conservation authorities), it also affirmed the constitutional status of Aboriginal hunting rights, placing a much higher burden on the state for their curtailment and giving priority to Aboriginal nations in the allocation of wildlife resources. In debates regarding conservation policy, it was now much more difficult to devalue the claims of Aboriginal nations by simple reference to the normative preponderance of sustainability and scientific management. It also became difficult to disqualify the claims as mere self-interested, unreasonable demands for a bigger share of public natural resources, since those claims now also translated credibly into an exhortation to respect the norms of the constitution and the rule of law.[13]

Moreover, in practical terms, the spring ban had clearly become incompatible with the new priority accorded to Aboriginal hunters. Due to the priority status of First Nations, any ban on Aboriginal hunting for food and ceremonial purposes, regardless of duration or date of application, would be legal only if all hunting by non-Aboriginals was also prohibited throughout the year. In other words, even if scientific reasons did justify special protective measures during the breeding season, it would remain illegal to prohibit Aboriginal nations from exercising their rights to subsistence harvesting during this period while allowing Canadian non-Aboriginal hunters to kill over a million birds during the rest of the year. If conservation measures were needed, the new framework established by the Supreme Court required that subsistence harvesting by Aboriginal peoples be the last category of hunting to be curtailed. In this context, it became obvious that the spring ban would eventually be declared unconstitutional with regard to Aboriginal hunters because it did not afford sufficient priority to Aboriginal subsistence hunting.[14] And if the spring ban was declared to be unconstitutional, conservation authorities and stakeholders faced the prospect of an uncontrolled Aboriginal spring harvest with potentially damaging consequences for the sustainability of waterfowl populations.

As we can see, though the court's decision in itself did not settle the spring harvest controversy, it significantly reframed the terms of the debate.

It partly validated Aboriginal claims and enhanced the status of their storyline in the spring hunt debate. Furthermore, by changing the normative and legal backdrop of the controversy, it forced several policy actors to reconsider the nature of their interests. Once it became clear that the ban would have to be terminated, environmentalists and American authorities who opposed a spring harvest considered that their interests would now be best served by ensuring that an inevitable Aboriginal spring harvest would be carefully monitored and controlled. Their strategic interests no longer lay in blocking amendments to the MBC and changes in domestic policy. They now consisted of ensuring that a new policy, though favourable to Aboriginal interests, would still ensure the conservation of waterfowl resources, without excessively penalizing non-Aboriginal (especially American) hunters. These changes reframed the debate, which progressively came to focus on how Aboriginal rights could best be integrated into a reformed conservation regime.

Between December 1990 and the end of 1995, this debate occurred through a series of difficult discussions in multi-stakeholder consultations, bilateral meetings with Aboriginal nations and provincial governments, and international negotiations with American interests. An international agreement recognizing the special rights of the Aboriginal peoples of Canada to harvest waterfowl throughout the year for food and ceremonial purposes was finally concluded in 1995.[15] It came into effect after it was approved by the US Senate in 1997. Canadian domestic policy was also modified. The rights of Aboriginal nations to hunt waterfowl throughout the year for subsistence purposes are now recognized, as is their priority status compared to other users should the annual harvest be limited for reasons of conservation. Moreover, in order to ensure that Aboriginal hunters are well integrated into the continental conservation regime, federal authorities are also committed to a new collaborative approach in waterfowl management, including the use of joint regulatory bodies, such as wildlife co-management boards, where Aboriginal nations are well represented.

It is important to note that the coalition of actors who defended the final settlement reflected a major shift in the politics of waterfowl conservation. Some environmental groups which had strongly opposed an Aboriginal spring harvest in the 1970s and 1980s, such as Ducks Unlimited, not only supported the new policy but even participated actively in lobbying American senators in favour of the 1995 agreement.[16] Similarly, officials involved in the consultations leading to the new policy observed a real shift in the discourse of environmentalists and recreational hunters concerning Aboriginal rights. The legitimacy of such rights and the importance of subsistence hunting practices for Aboriginal communities were more widely recognized than they had been in the 1970s and 1980s.[17] With varying degrees of enthusiasm or resignation, a broad consensus seemed to have emerged on the need to acknowledge the special rights and circumstances of Aboriginal nations, especially in the North, and on the possibility of doing so without jeopardizing the conservation of waterfowl species. In this respect, there is no doubt that the credibility and standing of the Supreme Court, and its authoritative statement in *Sparrow*, powerfully contributed in progressively forging this consensus.[18]

Conclusion: Constitutional Norms, Discursive Politics, and Policy Change

The chapter illustrates how the evolution of environmental policy depends significantly on the discursive politics surrounding environmental problems and controversies. "Ecological conflicts are not inherent in the physical facts of environmental change" (Hajer 1995, 264): instead, they depend in important ways on the discursive dynamics that construct them and reshape them through time. Hence, the analysis of discursive politics is important to shed light on the nature of government responses to environmental challenges. In particular, understanding how some discursive frames or storylines come to dominate a policy field and how changes in the discursive environment occur through time should be important preoccupations for environmental policy scholars.

In this case, I have shown that much of the history of the Aboriginal waterfowl hunting rights controversy has been marked by a conflict between two discourse coalitions presenting very distinct storylines about the ban on spring harvesting. These conflicting frames led policy actors to perceive and present Aboriginal demands for an exemption from the spring ban in very different terms. And, within the narrow confines of the conservation policy field, the Aboriginal narrative about the need to redress a historical injustice and recognize historical rights was largely discredited, as it clashed with the dominant norms of science-based wildlife management. Poorly organized politically, relatively absent from public and institutional forums, and with little economic or legal leverage, Aboriginal peoples' counter-frame was unable to shake the dominant normative order of conservation policy. As a result, their claims went unanswered and the spring ban remained firmly entrenched in the institutional practices of conservation policy.

The analysis then considered two historical attempts at reframing the controversy. The first instance, a conscious effort by conservation authorities to redefine the debate as an issue of equitable access to waterfowl hunting for northern communities, failed to fundamentally alter the terms of the controversy. It came as a result of an extraneous shift in the socio-economic realm: the combination of the rise in Aboriginal nationalism and the desire of the Canadian state to fuel its economic development through further exploitation of northern natural resources situated on contested Aboriginal territories. Some Aboriginal nations, such as the Cree, used this newfound leverage to break up the dominant discourse coalition of environmentalists and conservation authorities, and to force the federal government to find a way to reconcile Aboriginal claims with conservation imperatives. The "equitable northern access" storyline was then the result of an interested, conscious attempt by Ottawa to reframe the controversy in a way that could reconcile the counter-discourse of Aboriginal national affirmation with the dominant discourse of science-based management. The failure of this attempt to reframe the debate is testimony both to the enduring nature of discursive frames underpinning the positions of actors and to the crucial importance of the broader normative context of the conservation policy debate. As we have shown, the dissonance of the "equitable northern access" frame with the emerging language and norms of Canadian constitutional politics regarding Aboriginal rights eventually destroyed the credibility of this new storyline.

The discursive shift that eventually allowed for the resolution of the Aboriginal waterfowl hunting controversy came as an unintended effect of a broader shift in the norms and discourse of Canadian constitutional politics. The entrenchment of Aboriginal and treaty rights in the 1982 constitutional law, and the subsequent Supreme Court *Sparrow* decision on Aboriginal fishing rights bolstered the credibility of the "Aboriginal national affirmation" storyline and created credibility problems for the "science versus politics" frame, which had dominated the debate for decades. More importantly, by casting serious doubts on the constitutionality of the Aboriginal spring hunting ban, it also had the effect of reframing the controversy: the question was no longer whether Aboriginal claims for justice ought to be accommodated by the conservation regime, but rather how the accommodation could best be achieved while ensuring the sustainability of the resource and the adequate regulation of Aboriginal subsistence harvesting. In this new context, conservation authorities, environmentalists, and even American actors had to reconsider their strategic interests. The combined result of these developments was to bring previous opponents toward a common frame of reference and, even if reluctantly, a necessary compromise. Ultimately, it rendered possible a change in conservation policy.

NOTES

1　The term "controversy" is used here as defined by Donald Schön and Martin Rein (1994, 3-4), that is, to designate a policy dispute which occurs between different frames, as opposed to one that is contained within a mutually accepted frame. The latter, termed a disagreement, can possibly be resolved through references to facts.

2　The most important decision in this regard is probably *Sikyea v. The Queen*, [1964] S.C.R. 642.

3　Author interview with Anthony Keith, former director of the Migratory Birds Branch at the Canadian Wildlife Service, 16 October 1998.

4　For a detailed analysis of these developments, see Luc Juillet (2000, 2005).

5　See, for example, a 1982 memorandum by Anthony Keith, then director of the Migratory Birds Branch at the federal government's Canadian Wildlife Service. In it, Keith stated that the Canadian Wildlife Federation, an environmental group, intended to "bring down" the proposal to modify the ban and that it should be treated "strictly as an opponent." Anthony Keith, memorandum, "Discussion on the Protocol to Amend the MBC," 10 February 1982, official records of the Canadian Wildlife Service.

6　An illustration of their stance may be taken from the Wildlife Ministers' Conference of 1981, at which the western provinces expressed their opposition to the proposal: the Government of Manitoba suggested that it was willing to take the federal government to court to block the changes to the ban.

7　Author interview with Anthony Keith, former director of the Migratory Birds Branch, Canadian Wildlife Service, 16 October 1998.

8　This proposal was eventually translated into a protocol of amendment to the MBC; though it was signed in January 1979, it was never ratified by the two countries.

9　See, for example, the 1982 Keith memorandum "Discussion on the Protocol to Amend the MBC."

10　See, for instance, the letter by K.A. Brynaert (Canadian Wildlife Federation) to the Director of the US Fish and Wildlife Service, dated 15 April 1982. Official records of the Canadian Wildlife Service.

11　*R. v. Sparrow*, [1990] 1 S.C.R. 1075.

12   The two important decisions on the matter were *Flett* and *Arcand*. See *R. v. Flett,* [1989] 4 C.N.L.R. 128 and *R. v. Arcand,* [1989] 2 C.N.L.R. 110.

13   Author interview with Gregory Thompson, former director of the Migratory Birds and Wildlife Conservation Branch at the Canadian Wildlife Service, 10 November 1998.

14   Ibid.

15   The Protocol between the Government of Canada and the Government of the United States of America Amending the 1916 Convention between the United Kingdom and the United States of America for the Protection of Migratory Birds in Canada and the United States was signed on 14 December 1995.

16   Author interview with Gregory Thompson, former director of the Migratory Birds and Wildlife Conservation Branch at the Canadian Wildlife Service, 10 November 1998.

17   Author interview with Robert F. Keith, Canadian Arctic Resources Committee and coordinator of the federal government's multi-stakeholder consultation process in 1992, 20 November 1998.

18   Ibid.

REFERENCES

Abele, Frances. 1987. "Canadian Contradictions: Forty Years of Northern Political Development." *Arctic* 41(4): 310-20.

Beazley, Karen, and Robert Boardman, eds. 2001. *Politics of the Wild: Canada and Endangered Species.* Don Mills: Oxford University Press.

Bernstein, Steven. 2000. "Ideas, Social Structure and the Compromise of Liberal Environmentalism." *European Journal of International Relations* 6(4): 464-512.

Boardman, Robert. 2002. "Canada's Threatened Wildlife: Civil Society, Intergovernmental Relations, and the Art of the Possible." In *Canadian Environmental Policy: Context and Cases.* 2nd ed., ed. Debora L. VanNijnatten and Robert Boardman, 299-320. Don Mills: Oxford University Press.

Boyd, David. 2003. *Unnatural Law: Rethinking Canadian Environmental Law and Policy.* Vancouver: UBC Press.

Browne, David, and Roger Keil. 2000. "Planning Ecology: The Discourse of Environmental Policy Making in Los Angeles." *Organization and Environment* 13(2): 158-205.

Campbell, John. 2002. "Ideas, Politics, and Public Policy." *Annual Review of Sociology* 28: 21-38.

Canadian Nature Federation and International Council for Bird Protection. 1991. "Migratory Birds Amendments." Submission to the workshop to amend the Migratory Birds Convention Act of 1916. Official records of the Canadian Wildlife Service.

Canadian Wildlife Federation. 1992. "Recommendations of the Canadian Wildlife Federation to Environment Canada regarding Spring Hunting Amendments to the Migratory Birds Convention." Submission to the workshop to amend the Migratory Birds Convention Act of 1916. Official records of the Canadian Wildlife Service.

Condon, Richard G., Peter Collings, and George Wenzel. 1995. "The Best Part of Life: Subsistence Hunting, Ethnicity and Economic Adaptation among Young Adult Inuit Males." *Arctic* 48(1): 31-46.

Dorsey, Kurkpatrick. 1998. *The Dawn of Conservation Diplomacy: U.S.-Canadian Wildlife Protection Treaties in the Progressive Era*. Seattle and London: University of Washington Press.

Dryzek, John. 1997. *The Politics of the Earth: Environmental Discourses*. Oxford: Oxford University Press.

Fischer, Frank. 2000. *Citizens, Experts and the Environment: The Politics of Local Knowledge*. Durham, NC: Duke University Press.

—. 2003. *Reframing Public Policy: Discursive Politics and Deliberative Practices*. Oxford: Oxford University Press.

Foster, Janet. 1998. *Working for Wildlife: The Beginning of Preservation in Canada*. 2nd ed. Toronto: University of Toronto Press.

Hajer, Maarten. 1995. *The Politics of Environmental Discourse: Ecological Modernization and the Policy Process*. Oxford: Clarendon Press.

Honneland, Geir. 2004. "Fish Discourse: Russia, Norway, and the Northeast Arctic Cod." *Human Organization* 63(1): 68-77.

Innu Nation. 1992. "Amendments to the Migratory Birds Convention: The Innu Nation's Perspective." Brief submitted to the Consultation Workshop to Amend the Migratory Birds Convention of 1916, Goose Bay, Newfoundland, 16-18 March.

Juillet, Luc. 2000. "Domestic Institutions and Non-state Actors in International Governance: Lessons from the *Migratory Birds Convention*." In *Grounding Globalization: Relations and Levels of Power in the Global Era*, ed. T. Cohn, S. McBride, and J. Zimmerman, 125-41. London: Macmillan and St. Martin's Press.

—. 2005. "National Institutional Veto Points and Continental Policy Change." In *New Institutionalism: Theory and Analysis*, ed. André Lecours, 276-96. Toronto: University of Toronto Press.

Keith, R.F., and J. McMullen. 1992. *Report on Workshops to Amend the Migratory Birds Convention of 1916*. Ottawa: Canadian Arctic Resources Committee.

Liftin, Karen. 1994. *Ozone Discourses: Science and Politics in Global Environmental Cooperation*. New York: Columbia University Press.

Morgan, Rhiannon. 2004. "Advancing Indigenous Rights at the United Nations: Strategic Framing and Its Impact on the Normative Development of International Law." *Social and Legal Studies* 13(4): 481-500.

Nichols, Roger L. 1999. *Indians in the United States and Canada: A Comparative History*. Lincoln: University of Nebraska Press.

Schön, Donald, and Martin Rein. 1994. *Frame Reflection: Toward the Resolution of Intractable Policy Controversies.* New York: Basic Books.

Scott, C.H. 1987. *The Socio-economic Significance of Waterfowl among Canada's Aboriginal Cree: Indigenous Use and Local Management.* Technical Publication No. 6. Cambridge: International Council for Bird Protection.

Stairs, Arlene, and George W. Wenzel. 1992. "I Am I and the Environment: Inuit Hunting, Community and Identity." *Journal of Indigenous Studies* 3(1): 1-12.

Wagner, Murray W., and Gregory Thompson. 1993. "The Migratory Birds Convention: Its History and the Need for Amendment." *Northern Perspectives* 21(2): 2-6.

PART FOUR

Risky Subjects

13
From the Welfare State to the Social Investment State: A New Paradigm for Canadian Social Policy?

Denis Saint-Martin

> I would like to make yet one more appeal for a strong family
> and child-centred strategy for welfare state reconstruction.
> A revised social model requires a future-oriented perspective,
> and must therefore focus on those who will become tomorrow's
> adults. When goals for the future are defined in terms of
> maximizing Europe's competitive position in the world
> economy, the need to invest in today's children becomes
> obvious.
>
> — ESPING-ANDERSEN 2000, 31

In 1999, while he was reflecting on the past twenty years of social policy in Canada, Michael J. Prince (1999, 154) wrote that, "in the current post-deficit period ... we are witnessing the very early steps of a paradigm shift." Although we are still in the midst of this transition, and the future is still uncharted, we have now accumulated sufficient distance and knowledge from recent research in comparative social policy to be able to discern the broad contours of this newly emerging paradigm. What is this new paradigm and what does its adoption entail for the future of Canadian social policy and politics? These are the questions that I address in this chapter. Of course, such an exercise is full of traps, as it requires taking on the role of clairvoyant more than that of historian, in using the fluctuating ideas, policies, and discourses of present actors rather than analyzing the fixed events of the past. In the following pages, I argue that a social investment strategy of post-industrial welfare state reform is currently unfolding in Canada and replacing the social protection paradigm of the postwar era. The chapter compares and contrasts the two approaches. The conclusion for now is that the development of the social investment model is less likely to mobilize class identities than was the case in the postwar welfare state. Its implementation appears more likely to intensify the politicization of differences dealing with non-economic issues.

Toward a New Social Architecture

If, in the post-1945 era of the Golden Age, social and economic policy was based on relatively coherent and identifiable models, this is no longer the case today. The model that is presently emerging in North America and Western Europe is certainly not inspired by Keynesian ideas that encourage governments to run budgetary deficits in order to stimulate demand during periods of economic stagnation. At the same time, it would be false to claim that the new model relies solely on the laissez-faire theories of classical economists such as Friedrich Hayek. Although John Keynes was by no means responsible for the expansion of the welfare state that is sometimes linked to his name, his theories placed increasing responsibility for economic performance on the state's shoulders. His attacks on the priority that classical economics attached to a balanced budget helped to loosen a fiscal constraint that stood in the way of more generous social programs. In fact, the rejection by a growing number of political actors of the more radical ideas associated with both Keynes and Hayek probably constitutes the most solid indicator of a change in the field of social and economic policy (Albrow 1997; Garrett 1998; Giddens 1994).

The sense that a "new social architecture" is needed to deal with the various challenges that now face the welfare state is based on many factors. A defining characteristic of the current era is the coexistence of social conditions which are in many ways "new" with welfare states which are in many respects decidedly "old" (Pierson 2001). There is often a considerable "mismatch" between emerging social risks and the array of social policies inherited from the postwar era. The various aspects of this mismatch constitute an important dimension of the redesign agendas in contemporary welfare states. But though there is a growing recognition that existing policies may be inadequate, no clear blueprint for a new "regime" has yet emerged. This, in turn, leads to the view that experimentation is needed: that experimentation at the community, local, or regional levels may prove important, and thus that devolution or decentralization is appropriate (Saint-Martin 2004). Although the study of welfare states is opening up to include the micro and meso levels, such experimentation is not entirely new. In Chapter 8 of this volume, Karen Bridget Murray suggests that governmentality has long recognized the importance of linking the micro, meso, and macro levels into analysis. But though incorporating micro and meso levels of analysis is new to welfare state studies, it is a task fraught with some difficulty, according to Peter Graefe (Chapter 2, this volume), requiring ingenuity on the part of researchers to illustrate the textured linkages between the various levels. The need for experimentation with other levels is accompanied by some disenchantment with traditional forms of policy making and regulation, as well as a belief that more flexible approaches which stress problem solving are necessary. At the same time, there is a desire to give all stakeholders a voice in reforms to ensure both the legitimacy and effectiveness of new policies.

Of course, the search for a new social model, or a new social architecture, does not take place in a vacuum. Over the postwar decades, nations have built divergent kinds of welfare regimes; these arrangements have a structuring effect on which kinds of adaptation strategies can and will be pursued. But despite important institutional and political differences, policy communities in Canada and elsewhere are facing similar problems created by changes in productive organization, employment patterns, and household/family structures. How are they to redesign or recalibrate established welfare programs and expenditures to cover changing distributions of social risk between generations and genders across the life cycle in response to demographic pressures such as population aging and increasing female labour-force participation? How can they reconcile work and family life, in light of rising levels of women's paid employment, whose importance for economic growth and welfare state sustainability is widely acknowledged, but which requires expanded provision of complementary caring services for children and the aged, whether through public or private channels?

Thus, we see various models unfolding before our eyes rather than one single model for all nations. But attention to diversity should not make us blind to patterns of similarity. In Europe, as in Canada, and almost regardless of the welfare regime to which nations belong, governments are increasingly focusing on investing in the early years and children more generally. Even in those places that have long had generous family programs and explicit family policies, there is new attention to children. In these policy circles, this shift is considered an optimal anchor for the redesign of their welfare regimes, a broader event occurring everywhere in the European Union and North America. Many of the principles of redesign are similar, with attention going to human capital, "investments" for the future, life-long learning, activation, and so on. It is these signs of convergence that lead me to speak of a shift from the Keynesian welfare state to the social investment state (SIS).

Convergence does not mean uniformity, however. For different actors, the social investment model means different things. It is thus more accurate to talk about a *varieties of social investment model*. Convergence in this context does not refer to a narrowing of differences between countries; nor does it suggest that institutions and policies are becoming more like those already existing in one country (the idea of *Americanization* for instance) (Kitschelt et al. 1999, 438). Rather, I use it to imply that there is movement toward a new configuration comparable in scope to that of the Keynesian welfare states of the post-1945 decades.

From the "New Right" to the "Third Way"

We are presently living in a moment of political questioning comparable to the 1970s, during which most advanced industrial societies began to break from the social consensus that was constructed after the Second World War around the Keynesian welfare state (Rosanvallon 1995). The diffusion of monetarist ideas and the election of political leaders such as Thatcher, Reagan, and Mulroney, who professed a strong faith in the market, signalled the emergence of neo-liberalism and individualism (Krieger 1986; Levitas 1986). This ideological movement manifested itself differently from one country to another (Pierson 1994). But everywhere, state intervention and public expenditure were denounced as obstacles to entrepreneurship and as disincentives to individual initiative (Brown 1988). Critics argued that the resources transferred from the productive economy into unproductive social expenditures were inimical to economic prosperity. The belief that social spending was in conflict with economic growth became increasingly widespread.

But in the mid-1990s, with the switch from right-of-centre toward nominally left-of-centre governments, this typically Anglo-Saxon, New Right conception of social welfare has been challenged by "Third Way" ideas (Blair 1998; Finlayson 1999; Giddens 1998). In Canada, even if former prime minister Jean Chrétien has been described as a "Third Way leader" who pursued "a rhetoric on welfare reform that sounded more balanced and more compassionate than that of [his] conservative predecessors" (Bashevkin 2002, 21), his government never showed any desire to return to postwar Keynesian economic strategies. Fiscal conservatism is effectively always present, with most governments continuing to pursue or to implement policies that seem to be greatly inspired by neo-liberalism. However, this is not to say that they uncritically accept the socially disembedded vision of the market according to which *there is no such a thing as society,* as Thatcher suggested during the 1980s. Governments and political parties have instead entered into a new stage, identifying the negative aspects of strict versions of neo-liberalism (Segal 1997).

Today, increasing pressure is exerted on governments to account for the long-term social consequences of the economic liberalization policies they have pursued since the 1980s (Canada 1999; Maxwell 1996). Although these policies perhaps achieved general economic growth, they put the social body under increasing stress. The persistence of high levels of unemployment, the polarization of incomes, and the intensification of social exclusion sustained an increasingly strong sentiment of insecurity in the population (Canadian Council on Social Development 1999). In response to the political dis-enchantment resulting from the unbridled pursuit of measures favouring heightened market competition, the "social" – the issue of living together – has recently returned as a preoccupation for governments (OECD 1998). Concerns about social cohesion and deteriorating social indicators have led in the past few years to the appearance of a number of alternative rationales for state intervention and collective social provision. In this context, terms such as the social investment approach or social investment state have begun to circulate in policy and academic circles and are advocated as a new design or blueprint for successfully linking social and economic concerns. It is also in this context that new concepts such as "social capital" (Putnam 1993) and "social exclusion" (Paugam 1996), or, in French, *disqualification sociale* (Castel 1995), have appeared. That this vocabulary surfaced at this precise point in history was not due to chance. To use Karl Polanyi's notion (Polanyi 1944), each period of *great transformation* produces its own new concepts that indi-viduals invent in order to describe the changes which suddenly appear in structures and social realities. One cannot change paradigms without having words to describe the novelty.

Table 13.1 describes, in ideal-typical form, the broad contours of the social investment paradigm. The rest of this chapter discusses the key fea-tures of the social investment model and their impact on both policy and politics.

From Social Spending to Social Investment

Soon after its 1997 re-election, during the Throne Speech, the Chrétien government affirmed its resolution and willingness, in the future, to pursue

Table 13.1

The social investment paradigm

	Welfare state	Social investment state
Formative events	The past, the Depression, Second World War	The future, new knowledge economy
Emblematic figure	Father-worker	Child (future worker)
Criteria of integration	Employment	Employability
Type of capital	Finance	Social-human
Basic cohesion	Social justice	Inclusion/social principles
Goal of social policies	Protection against	Facilitate integration into the market
Conception of risk	As danger	As opportunity
Conception of security	Social safety net	Trampoline
Delivery mechanisms	Bureaucracy	Partnership

a "balanced approach of social investment and prudent financial management" (Canada 1997, 3). Although most of us were already familiar with the notion of "prudent financial management" associated with the program of deficit fighting pursued by Ottawa since the 1980s, the same could not be said for the idea of "social investment."

In their *Canadian Public Policy*, G. Bruce Doern and Richard W. Phidd (1992, 106) suggest that "the expenditure process involves controversy over social versus economic priorities and over whether certain subsidies are an 'investment' or 'welfare.'" The social investment state (SIS) radically challenges this vision. In the past, the right and the left supposed that a separation existed between society and market. For the left, social rights were intended to protect the individual against the risks of the economy and the market. On this basis of the separation of society and market, the right subsequently was able to set the market against society, suggesting that the former was being stifled by policies aiming to preserve the cohesion of the latter. Today, however, research increasingly demonstrates that the quality of social relations and networks have determinant effects on economic prosperity, health, and productivity (Kawachi and Kennedy 1997; Knack and Keefer 1997). And it is principally in light of this information that the social investment approach takes all its significance. Although, for the New Right social policy represented an obstacle to economic development, in the SIS it becomes a tool for economic development. The distinction between social policy and economic policy becomes blurred.

The term social investment state was coined by Anthony Giddens in his *The Third Way* (1998), which envisions a "new partnership" in the assignment of welfare function to families, markets, and states. In this book, Giddens calls for a SIS that develops an entrepreneurial culture, offering protection in a way that encourages risk taking and opens possibilities. The social investment approach provides a view of social policy as "productivist" and investment oriented, rather than distributive and consumption oriented.[1] This is expressed in policies that seek to shift the emphasis in social policy from consumption and maintenance-oriented programs to those that invest in people and enhance their capacity to participate in the productive economy (Midgley 2001).

Social Investment as a Future-Centred Form of Policy Intervention

The formative event in the construction of the welfare state was the war, and moreover, the Great Depression of the 1930s, with its mass dislocation and widespread economic and social insecurity for entire populations. The key goal of the postwar welfare state was security. The basic aim was to develop a system that would provide protection against the risks inherent in modern life – unemployment, disability, illness, and poverty in old age (Banting 1997, 265). This quest for greater security pervaded the Marsh Report (Marsh 1943), which laid down the intellectual foundations for the postwar social agenda in Canada.[2] Marsh (ibid., 17) summed up the case for the welfare state as follows: "The general sense of security which would result from such programs would provide a better life for the great mass of people and a potent antidote to the fears and worries and uncertainties of the times. The post-war world would not have to be anticipated with fear." The objective was to create a "better world ... for those who were victims of unemployment, of destitution, of insufficient medical care during the periods of crisis prior to the war" (ibid., 12). In other words, the welfare state sought to find a way to avoid repeating the great misery of the past, as well as to offer a minimum of support to those who were the actors in this past: the elderly, whose situation, although not perfect, had greatly improved in the postwar years.

Although the raison d'être for the postwar welfare state can easily be found in the past, the same cannot be said for the SIS. By definition, the idea of investment is entirely oriented toward the future. Investing is like sowing seeds: it is something – an effort, an expenditure – that one does in the present in hopes of a positive future return. Ideologically and politically, the justification for the SIS is found in the future. The SIS is an institutional and political form centred around the future

- by its link with the knowledge economy, whose birth it wishes to facilitate;
- by its focus on the child, the future worker of this new economy and the central figure around which social policy is reconstructed;
- and finally, by the notion of investment, which implies the hope for a profit, a future gain.

Thus, a notion of *time* underpins the social investment approach concerning the role of the state, one developed in response to neo-liberalism's delegitimation of social spending. The results produced by an investment are located in the *future*, whereas consumption (called an "expense" by accountants) is something that occurs in the *present*. For state spending to be effective, and therefore worthwhile, it must not simply be consumed in the present, to meet current needs: it must be an investment that will pay off and reap rewards in the future.

This conception of time has significant consequences for the design of social spending. In an "investment-driven" welfare regime, any measures of generous and innovative spending must be justified in future-oriented terms. Thus, spending may legitimately go to supporting and educating children, because they clearly hold the promise of the future; to promoting health and healthy populations because they pay off in lower future costs; to reducing the probability of future costs of school failure and crime, again with a heavy emphasis on children; and to fostering employability, so as to increase future labour-force participation rates.

These notions of the time horizon of public spending are quite different from those that informed the postwar welfare state. It was focused on the present. Therefore, spending could be legitimately justified by its consequences in the present. The primary business of the state was to assure equality and social justice to all its citizens. For example, efforts to increase gender equality were seen as both legitimate and necessary, a notion which has virtually disappeared in the current context.

An investment model also implies that social expenditures should have a payoff, a return on investment. Investments are generally undertaken to make profits, but some generate more profits than others. Therefore, investors will inject the most money where they think that profits are likely to be highest. When transplanted into the social policy realm, the investment idea sends varying messages regarding the social categories to which it is applied (or not applied). In other words, investments in some groups are likely to be more profitable than in other groups. Social policy is thus likely to construct an image or representation that reflects the expected profitability of the group in which money is invested. I will return to this idea below, in discussing the politics of age.

From Social Justice to Social Cohesion

It is important to underline that, unlike the welfare state, the SIS is not principally founded on the objectives of social justice and equality. The dichotomy that guides its actions is not that of equality/inequality, but instead social inclusion/exclusion (Levitas 1996). In the postwar welfare model, the market exists exterior to society, whose cohesion is constantly threatened by the disintegrative effects of the economy. In the SIS model, the border between society and market is blurred and porous; in this sense, active participation in the economy is the key to integration in society. Central to this approach is the notion that, at the beginning – that is, at the point of entry into the market – everyone has an equal chance to participate in economic life.

The postwar welfare state was based on the promise of equality for all "here-and-now." In contrast, the SIS emphasizes equality of life chances, which address questions of distribution of opportunities, resources, and capabilities. In the SIS, equality is redefined as inclusion, and inequality as exclusion. The goal of social policy is to fight against long-term social exclusion – to break the cycle of entrapment. In the social investment approach, low wages and poor jobs, as temporary deprivations, do not of themselves pose a serious problem: they do so only if individuals become trapped in those circumstances. As Gøsta Esping-Andersen (1999, 182) argues, "temporary deprivation is unimportant if it does not affect our life chances."

Thus, rather than focusing on equity now, the SIS seeks to provide equality of opportunity for *future* success. This new conception of equality goes hand in hand with the type of child-centred policy strategy that we find at the heart of the SIS. Social investment means that state actions should be preventive rather than curative; thus, greater emphasis is put on early interventions to ensure better-quality child care and early education for young children – the future bearers of human capital. The programs and policy instruments of the SIS will also differ from those of the welfare state. The postwar welfare regime sought to achieve equality through redistributive cash transfers, but the SIS focuses more on services. Investment implies that money go into services designed to improve the employability and future productivity of people. "Passive" cash transfers are transformed into "active" measures, most of which have a strong service dimension. Although state bureaucracies still take care of the cash transfer part of social policy, third-sector organizations are increasingly involved in the delivery of "social investment services" (day-care, training, and so forth).

Security as the Capacity to Change

The goal of the SIS is "to develop a society of responsible risk takers" (Giddens 1998, 100). This indicates a change in the conception of security. The "old" welfare state emphasized protecting people *from* the market. The emphasis of SIS policies, by contrast, is on integrating people *into* the market. In this context, the goal of social policies is no longer to protect people from economic disruptions in their lives. Rather, in the global era, security comes from the capacity to change; hence the emphasis on investing in human capital and life-long learning as the surest form of security in the modern world. Instead of investing in stability – as the notion of "social security" embedded in the postwar welfare state implies – the SIS invests in change. This entails a work life punctuated by frequent job changes and constant retraining.

Social investment turns largely on attempts to deal with new social risks. If, in the postwar years, social risks were addressed via the decommodification of wage earners, in the post-industrial era, new social risks are dealt with through recommodification. Using a mix of incentives and support measures, new social investment policies aim at keeping as many as possible in the labour market. Unlike the policies of the postwar welfare state, they do not attempt to reduce wage-earner dependence on the labour market. Instead, they focus on making the lives of commodified workers more bearable. Thus, they "make work pay" and provide measures such as tax credits, child care, and maternity and parental leave so as to reconcile work and family life, and improve the situation of commodified workers. One of the key issues involved in the politics of social investment is the extent to which commodification should be subsidized. Because it can be seen as enhancing employment among certain groups (women and the low-skilled, for instance) and as fostering the development of human capital, such subsidization is not perceived solely as a burden on the wealth-producing economy.

From Social Safety Net to Trampoline

In the social investment perspective, the role of social policy is no longer to offer protection against inherent risks in the market economy, but instead to give individuals the tools they need to improve their employability – to give them the means to *individually* confront the changes in the constantly transforming global economy. This is exactly what the Canadian government argued when it reformed unemployment insurance in the mid-1990s, suggesting that, "In the past, social security aimed above all to provide money and to support individuals in need. That is no longer sufficient. We must invest in the future of Canadians to aid them in the acquisition of the skills that they need to prosper in the economy of today" (Canada 1994, 21).

In the postwar welfare model, the inherent risks in the market economy were *social* in the sense that they could affect virtually everyone, not only the poor. In consequence, security against risks was also social, the responsibility of society as a whole, and thus universal in the sense of protecting the greatest possible number of citizens against misery and poverty. Today, the conceptions of risks and security inherited from the postwar welfare model have been radically redefined. The SIS opts resolutely in favour of an entrepreneurial conception of risk. Risk is no longer perceived as a danger, something to evade, but as an opportunity – an opportunity to ameliorate a situation. Citizens must learn to become responsible risk takers; in this, the role of the SIS is to encourage the development of an entrepreneurial culture by offering protections against risks that are taken.

As Keith Banting (1997, 270) once suggested, what one observes "is the transition between two conceptions of security: from security as protection *from* change, to security as the capacity *to* change." In this perspective, the role of the state consists of appropriately arming individuals who are exposed to the competitive and unpredictable world of globalization – supplying them with the means to acquire better training for their integration into the market. Thus, emphasis is placed on the necessity of "investing in people" as the most solid and safe form of investment. In the global economy, social transfer dollars intended to counteract the business cycle are commonly used to purchase imports instead of to maintain domestic employment levels; as a result, they tend to leak out of the economy. Unlike social transfers, social investments in people and infrastructure remain at home.

Child-Centred Policies

In November 1996, the OECD held a high-level conference of ministers and senior officials titled "Beyond 2000: A New Social Policy Agenda." The conference concluded with a call for a "social investment approach for the future of the welfare state." According to the OECD, the social investment approach provides a useful framework for priority setting in an environment where major increases in fiscal burden are unacceptable. "Such an approach implies greater investment in children and young adults, as well as the maintenance of human capital over the life course" (OECD Newsletter 1997, 7).

Social investment is primarily about human capital formation. And since the expected results of investments are located in the future, the SIS is also very much children-centred: the child is presented as the future citizen-worker around which social policy is being reconfigured. In the SIS, "children matter because human capital formation matters" (Myles and Quadagno 2000, 27).

This view is variously described as a "child-centred strategy for welfare state reconstruction" (Esping-Andersen 2000, 31), the "investing in children paradigm" (Jenson 2001, 107), or what Theda Skocpol (2000, 17) calls "child-focused liberalism." In this vision, children are investments with potentially important subsequent payoffs, both in terms of human capital formation and as a way to combat family poverty by facilitating the entry of women into the labour market – enabling women to *decommodify* themselves, in Ann Shola Orloff's terms (1993).

In the social investment model, children come to the fore, to the "heart of our choices," not only because they have present needs, but also because our actions concerning them will have consequences for the future. Because this regime pays such attention to positive outcomes for children, early childhood initiatives, quality child care, and so on become important policy instruments. Although all parents are assumed to be responsible for themselves and for earning their living by their own labour – gone is the option of full-time parenting, except for those who can afford it – it is nonetheless legitimate to help parents realize these investments. The regime envisions a partnership with parents, one in which both the community and the parents are responsible for investing in children. For instance, in a framework document entitled *Our Children ... Today's Investment, Tomorrow's Promise*, the Government of Nova Scotia described why, in its view, it made sense "to invest in the early years as an economic strategy ... The fiscal argument for investing in early childhood programs has gained momentum. Recent shifts in economic policy emphasize open economies and require a well-educated and flexible labour force in order to compete globally. Therefore, it is vital that we support and value children today in order to ensure their futures ... We can no longer consider the needs of young children solely as the private responsibility of their parents. Policies and systems that support families must reflect the new realities of family life" (Province of Nova Scotia 2001, 8).

The Knowledge Basis of the Social Investment State

The knowledge base of experts who focus on the potential contribution of early childhood initiatives to the well-being of all children has played a key role in constructing the social investment model. For instance, the federal, provincial, and territorial governments agreed in January 1997 to work together to develop the National Children's Agenda, a comprehensive strategy to improve the well-being of Canada's children. The National Children's Agenda has been justified by "strong evidence, including scientific research, that what happens to children when they are very young shapes their health and well-being throughout their lifetime. Science has proven what we have intrinsically known all along – healthy children grow into healthy, successful adults, who will shape our future" (National Children's Agenda 1997).

The "science" referred to here, which is now finding its way into policy, is derived from neurobiology, developmental psychology, and population health research. As one Canadian observer recently noted, "the rediscovery, in the policy world, of the role of early childhood as a lifelong determinant of health, well-being and competence [...] has occurred because issues of early childhood development began to be expressed in a credible vocabulary for modern society – the vocabulary of science" (Hertzman 2000, 16).

In Canada, much of the knowledge focusing on the importance of the early years has been produced and disseminated by the Canadian Institute for Advanced Research (CIAR). The CIAR is a think-tank founded in 1982 by a group of academics and business people as a private-sector initiative. It is now headed by Chaviva Hosek, former director of policy and research in the Prime Minister's Office during the Chrétien years.

J. Fraser Mustard, the CIAR's founding president and a medical scientist, has been described as an "intellectual activist" who has long been involved in neuroscience and children's health research (Greenspon 1999, A7). As head of the CIAR, Mustard acted as a "policy entrepreneur" and established various channels of communication with federal and provincial policy makers to disseminate knowledge about the importance of investing in the early years. For instance, in 1995 Mustard made a presentation to the Ontario

Conservative caucus a few months before that party was elected to a majority government. After becoming premier of Ontario, the Conservative leader appointed Mustard to the Premier's Council on Economic Renewal (an advisory body) and asked him to review the research on the life-long impact of childhood development (Mustard, McCain, and Bertrand 2000, 76).

Mustard's response was the Early Years Study, which involved several researchers from across Canada, as well as community-based organizations and government agencies, such as Human Resources and Development Canada and Statistics Canada. The study used data from the National Longitudinal Survey of Children and Youth (NLSCY). Begun in 1994 and funded by the federal government, the NLSCY is the most comprehensive survey ever undertaken in Canada.[3] The survey is conducted by the federal department of Human Resources and Development Canada, which is responsible for "ensuring that the data and research results are used to advise policy" (Brink and McKellar 2000, 111).

In 1999, Mustard and his co-author published the results of their work, a report entitled *Early Years Study* (Norrie McCain and Mustard 1999). This cited research evidence showing that spending which was devoted to early childhood produced higher returns than spending allocated to later stages of the life cycle. Significantly, it recommended a comprehensive child development strategy and called on all levels of government to invest in children. While the Ontario government was appointing a task force to implement the *Early Years Study* key recommendations, a great deal of policy experimentation was taking place in the early childhood area. Ottawa promised to increase the Canada Child Tax Benefit to $9 billion a year by 2004 and to double maternity and parental leave to one year under the Employment Insurance Program. At the same time, Quebec was establishing a fee of $5 per day for child care and Manitoba was developing a new Healthy Child Initiative, with new investments in pre- and post-natal nutrition and parent-child centres.

The Politics of Age

Clearly, children are now seen as having the highest rates of profitability for social investments. A consensus has recently emerged among economists that investments in early childhood are the most cost-effective. In contrast, controversy exists regarding the cost-effectiveness of "second-chance" interventions to promote educational attainment among high-school dropouts, welfare recipients, and other disadvantaged workers. For instance, various studies suggest that adults past a certain age and below a certain skill level make poor investments (Council of Economic Advisors 1997; Danziger and Waldfogel 2000). Others have emphasized the higher returns of early investment relative to those at later ages. Rates of expected profitability in the SIS are thus obviously linked to age.

The social investment model thus tends to politicize cleavages or identities that are related to age. The politics of class that underpinned the postwar regime is now being replaced by a new politics of intergenerational warfare and inequalities. Of course, this is not to suggest that the politics of age is "real" in any objective or positivist sense, but simply that it is created by social investment policies. This is a clear example of how policies shape politics (Pierson 1993). Social policy debates these days are notable for concentrating on the retired elderly versus children (Skocpol 2000). The development of old-age pensions has been at the heart of the postwar welfare state (Pierson 1994, 54). In all Western countries, most old-age pensions are delivered by governments; as a result, the modern welfare state has become a "welfare state for the elderly" (Myles 1989).

If the postwar welfare state was distinctly skewed in favour of the elderly, the new social investment model tends to favour children and youth. Social investment in daycare, or in job training for the young and even the middle-aged, can be expected to bring a return. But the yield on investments in older workers and retirees, for whom social expenditures are "passive" and represent pure consumption, will be zero or negative. As already noted, there are "implicit disadvantages of a 'social investment' model for the elderly" (Myles and Street 1994, 8). In this model, the elderly risk being characterized as bad investments and thus undeserving of support.

As Theda Skocpol argued for the US context, social policy debates these days are notable for concentrating on the elderly versus the young. Advocates are especially likely to disagree regarding the merits of public programs for the retired elderly versus those of efforts to aid poor children. Today, as Skocpol (2000, 16-17) explains,

> socially minded liberals tend to presume that expensive and
> inclusive new social programs are impossible. Many try, instead,
> to appeal to public sympathy by arguing that children should be
> helped as a separate category. Advocacy groups ... believe that
> upper-middle class and corporate support is most likely to be
> forthcoming for social programs framed as "saving children" or

"investing in America's future" ... Public initiatives aimed at children seem like the surest bets at a time when the terms of public
debate on fiscal fundamentals and the overall scope of government have been ceded to conservatives ... But child-focused
liberalism is not a bold position.

Conclusion

Making definitive statements about a work in progress, such as the SIS, is a
risky enterprise. In essence, it is an exercise in futurology, as the model which
is currently producing the post-deficit world is still not clearly identifiable;
nor, probably, will its form be fixed for years to come. What is certain, however, if the description of the SIS provided above is not completely incorrect,
is that it does not correspond with a non-interventionist model. Without
doubt, it has integrated many elements of neo-liberalism. However, in the
hands of governments that are situated more or less at the centre of the political spectrum, the social investment approach aims to inspire a new legitimacy for social policy intervention – social action that, as we have seen, will
henceforth be closely tied to the objectives of economic policy.

The SIS finds the source of its intervention in the knowledge economy
and the figure of the child – the future worker who must be prepared for the
arrival of the new economy. In focusing its actions on the child, the SIS encourages the increased politicization of linked identities – less for social class,
as with the welfare state – but more for age and gender, given the work of
women and the reconfiguration of the family unit. In part, it is around these
personal identities and issues which are linked to way of life, that the lines of
political contestation between the left and the right are now being drawn.
Paradoxically, if the SIS was born of the convergence of partisan positions
regarding the free market, its implementation is likely to intensify the
politicization of disagreements concerning non-economic issues.

NOTES

1   For recent discussions on this topic, see Paul Bernard and Sebastien Saint-Arnaud
    (2003), Alexandra Dobrowolsky (2002), G. Esping-Andersen (2002), Jane Jenson
    and Denis Saint-Martin (2002, 2003a, 2003b), and Ruth Lister (2003, 2004).
2   Its author, Leonard Marsh, a McGill University sociologist, is sometimes described
    as the "father of social security" in Canada.
3   For useful information regarding the NLSCY, see the Human Resources Develop-
    ment Canada's website at http://www.hrdc-drhc.gc.ca.

REFERENCES

Albrow, Martin. 1997. *The Global Age.* Stanford: Stanford University Press.

Banting, Keith. 1997. "The Internationalization of the Social Contract." In *The Nation State in a Global/Information Era,* ed. Thomas J. Courchene, 255-85. Kingston: John Deutsch Institute for the Study of Economic Policy.

Bashevkin, Sylvia. 2002. *Welfare Hot Buttons: Women, Work, and Social Policy Reform.* Toronto: University of Toronto Press.

Bernard, Paul, and Sebastien Saint-Arnaud. 2003. "Redefining Needs, Risks and Resources: Towards a Social Investment State in Canada." Paper presented to the Canadian Social Welfare Policy Conference, Ottawa, 15-17 June.

Blair, Tony. 1998. *The Third Way: New Politics for a New Century.* London: Fabian Society.

Brink, Satya, and Susan McKellar. 2000. "NLSCY: A Unique Canadian Survey." *Isuma: Canadian Journal of Policy Research* 1(2): 111-15.

Brown, Michael K., ed. 1988. *Remaking the Welfare State: Retrenchment and Social Policy in America and Europe.* Philadelphia: Temple University Press.

Canada. 1994. Human Resources Development. *Improving Social Security in Canada: A Discussion Paper.* Ottawa: Supply and Services Canada.

—. 1997. Office of the Governor General. *Discours du trône ouvrant la première session de la trente-sixième Législature du Canada.* Ottawa: Public Works and Government Services.

—. 1999. Parliament. *Rapport final sur la cohésion sociale* [Comité sénatorial permanent des affaires sociales, des sciences et de la technologie]. Ottawa: Sénat du Canada.

Canadian Council on Social Development. 1999. *Personal Security Index 1999: How Confident Are Canadians about Their Economic and Physical Well-Being?* Ottawa: Canadian Council on Social Development.

Castel, Robert. 1995. *Les métamorphoses de la question sociale.* Paris: Gallimard.

Council of Economic Advisors. 1997. *The First Three Years: Investments That Pay.* Washington, DC: Council of Economic Advisors.

Danziger, Sheldon, and Jane Waldfogel. 2000. *Investing in Children: What Do We Know? What Should We Do?* CASE Paper No. 34. Centre for Analysis of Social Exclusion, London School of Economics, London.

Dobrowolsky, Alexandra. 2002. "Rhetoric versus Reality: The Figure of the Child and New Labour's Strategic 'Social Investment State.'" *Studies in Political Economy* 69: 43-73.

Doern, G. Bruce, and Richard W. Phidd. 1992. *Canadian Public Policy: Ideas, Structure and Process.* Scarborough: Nelson Canada.

Esping-Andersen, Gøsta. 1999. *Social Foundations of Postindustrial Economies.* New York: Oxford University Press.

—. 2000. "A Welfare State for the 21st Century." Report to the Portuguese presidency of the European Union, prepared for the Lisbon Summit. http://www.nnn.se/seminar/pdf/report.pdf.

—. 2002. *Why We Need a New Welfare State*. London: Oxford University Press.

Finlayson, Alan. 1999. "Third Way Theory." *Political Quarterly* 70(3): 271-79.

Garrett, Geoffrey. 1998. *Partisan Politics in the Global Economy*. Cambridge: Cambridge University Press.

Giddens, Anthony. 1994. *Beyond Left and Right: The Future of Radical Politics*. Cambridge: Polity Press.

—. 1998. *The Third Way: The Renewal of Social Democracy*. Cambridge: Polity Press.

Greenspon, Edward. 1999. "A Year in the Life of the Canadian Family." *Globe and Mail*, 11 September, A7.

Hertzman, Clyde. 2000. "The Case for an Early Childhood Development Strategy." *Isuma: Canadian Journal of Policy Research* 1(2): 11-18.

Jenson, Jane. 2001. "Canada's Shifting Citizenship Regime: Investing in Children." In *The Dynamics of Decentralization*, ed. T.C. Salmon and M. Keating, 107-24. Montreal and Kingston: McGill-Queen's University Press.

Jenson, Jane, and Denis Saint-Martin. 2002. "Building Blocks for a New Welfare Architecture: From Ford to LEGO™?" Fostering Social Cohesion Working Paper No. 4, presented at the annual meeting of the American Political Science Association, Boston, 1 September.

—. 2003a. "From the Welfare State to the Social Investment State? Making Sense of Social Policy in Canada." Paper presented to the Canadian Social Welfare Policy Conference, Ottawa, 31 August-2 September.

—. 2003b. "New Routes to Social Cohesion? Citizenship and the Social Investment State." *Canadian Journal of Sociology* 28(1): 77-99.

Kawachi, Ichiro, and Bruce P. Kennedy. 1997. "Health and Social Cohesion: Why Care about Income Inequality?" *British Medical Journal* 314: 1037-40.

Kitschelt, Herbert, Peter Lange, Gary Marks, and John D. Stephens. 1999. *Continuity and Change in Contemporary Capitalism*. Cambridge: Cambridge University Press.

Knack, Stephen, and Philip Keefer. 1997. "Does Social Capital Have an Economic Payoff?" *Quarterly Journal of Economics* 112(4): 1251-88.

Krieger, Joel. 1986. *Reagan, Thatcher and the Politics of Decline*. New York: Oxford University Press.

Levitas, Ruth. 1986. *The Ideology of the New Right*. Cambridge: Polity Press.

—. 1996. "The Concept of Social Exclusion and the New Durkheimian Hegemony." *Critical Social Policy* 46: 5-20.

Lister, Ruth. 2003. "Investing in the Citizen-Workers of the Future: Transformations in Citizenship and the State under New Labour." *Social Policy and Administration* 37(5): 427-43.

—. 2004. "New Policy Directions in OECD Countries: The Emergence of the Social Investment State." Speech for Exploring New Approaches to Social Policy: PRI Conference, Ottawa, December.

Marsh, Leonard. 1943. Canada. *Report on Social Security for Canada.* Toronto: University of Toronto Press.

Maxwell, Judith. 1996. *Social Dimensions of Economic Growth.* Eric John Hanson Memorial Lecture Series, vol. 8. Edmonton: University of Alberta.

Midgley, James. 2001. "Growth, Redistribution and Welfare: Toward Social Investment." In *The Global Third Way Debate,* ed. Anthony Giddens, 157-71. Cambridge: Polity Press.

Mustard, J. Fraser, Margaret McCain, and Jane Bertrand. 2000. "Changing Beliefs to Change Policy: The Early Years Study." *Isuma: Canadian Journal of Policy Research* 1(2): 76-80.

Myles, John. 1989. *Old Age in the Welfare State.* Lawrence, KS: University Press of Kansas.

Myles, John, and Debra Street. 1994. *Should the Economic Life Course Be Redesigned?* Working Paper Series, Pepper Institute on Aging and Public Policy, Florida State University.

Myles, John, and Jill Quadagno. 2000. "Envisioning a Third Way: The Welfare State in the 21st Century." *Contemporary Sociology* 29(1): 22-38.

National Children's Agenda. 1997. "Background Information on the National Children's Agenda." http://socialunion.gc.ca/nca/nca1_e.html.

Norrie McCain, Margaret, and J. Fraser Mustard. 1999. *Early Years Study.* Toronto: Ontario Children's Secretariat.

OECD. 1998. *Cohésion sociale et mondialisation de l'économie.* Paris: OECD.

OECD Newsletter. 1997. *Beyond 2000: A New Social Policy Agenda.* Paris: OECD.

Orloff, Ann Shola. 1993. "Gender and the Social Rights of Citizenship." *American Sociological Review* 58(3): 303-28.

Paugam, Serge. 1996. *L'exclusion, l'état des savoirs.* Paris: La découverte.

Pierson, Paul. 1993. "When Effect Becomes Cause: Policy Feedback and Political Change." *World Politics* 45: 595-628.

—. 1994. *Dismantling the Welfare State?* Cambridge: Cambridge University Press.

—. 2001. *The New Politics of the Welfare State.* New York: Oxford University Press.

Polanyi, Karl. 1944. *The Great Transformation.* Boston: Beacon Press.

Prince, Michael J. 1999. "From Health and Welfare to Stealth and Farewell: Federal Social Policy, 1980-2000." In *How Ottawa Spends: Shape Shifting – Canadian Governance toward the 21st Century,* ed. Leslie A. Pal, 151-96. Don Mills: Oxford University Press.

Province of Nova Scotia. 2001. *Our Children ... Today's Investment, Tomorrow's Promise.* Halifax: Communications Nova Scotia.

Putnam, Robert. 1993. *Making Democracy Work: Civic Traditions in Modern Italy.* Princeton: Princeton University Press.

Rosanvallon, Pierre. 1995. *La nouvelle question sociale.* Paris: Seuil.

Saint-Martin, Denis. 2004. *Coordinating Interdependence: Governance and Social Policy Redesign in Britain, the European Union and Canada.* CPRN Social Architecture Papers, Research Report F/41. Ottawa: Canadian Policy Research Networks.

Segal, Hugh. 1997. *Beyond Greed: A Traditional Conservative Confronts Neoconservative Excess.* Toronto: Stoddart.

Skocpol, Theda. 2000. *The Missing Middle.* New York: W.W. Norton.

14
Canadian Post-9/11 Border Policy and Spillover Securitization: Smart, Safe, Sovereign?

Mark B. Salter

The traditional narrative of "the longest undefended border in the world" has undergone a powerful symbolic and administrative transformation since the 9/11 terror attacks. Conditioned by the asymmetrical relationship with the US and the new global atmosphere of anxiety, the Canadian government forged a new border policy to meet the various demands of its largest trading partner, its domestic and international constituencies, and its own liberal population. The new policy was expressed in the Smart Border Accord (SBA) of 2001 and the National Security Strategy (NSS) of 2004, both of which will be examined below. The approaches enshrined in the SBA and the NSS were restated in *Borderline Insecure,* a report produced by the Senate Committee on National Security and Defence (2005). Following precedents established by the SBA and the NSS, this recommended a major reorganization of the border function away from the collection of customs duties and toward the provision of security. Although it focused needed attention on the issue of the border, the report did not address some of the larger connected issues of document security, the dynamics of examination at the border, or the spillover effects of securitization, all of which had arisen from the implementation of the SBA and the NSS.

The border plays a significant role in symbolic, governmental, and legal spheres, and represents a key locus of national anxieties concerning identity, immigration, security, crime, health, and terror (Salter 2003). The security function of the Canadian border played a minor role in the Canadian and American public imagination until its weaknesses were exposed in 1999 by the thwarted millennium bomber Ahmed Ressam and by the 9/11 attacks. Ressam, caught while entering the US from Canada at Port Angeles, Washington, was on his way to detonate a car bomb at Los Angeles International Airport; he has since come to represent a failure of the Canadian border, police, immigration, and judicial systems (Neff, Wilson, and Bernton 2001).

A number of prominent policy analysts and scholars have questioned whether border security has increased since the terror attacks (Clarkson 2003; Drache 2004; Laxer 2003). Although the border represents a "line in the sand" which purports to be defensible, the realities – a global trade and transport system, a global telecommunications network, and a global finance web – undercut this narrative (Andreas 2003; Flynn 2004). An increase in border security spending does not necessarily serve national security, foster economic interests, or deter terrorists (Salter 2004).

This chapter adopts a method of discourse analysis, highlighting the ways in which political problems are framed in public speech. In short, discourses are specific linguistic patterns (persistent metaphors, structures, and narratives) that "construct social realities," rather than finding them whole, and which define, enact, and fix a specific pattern of social relations (Milliken 1999, 229). A contextual analysis places language and metaphor within its signifying system. For example, "fuddle duddle," Pierre Trudeau's infamous 16 February 1971 utterance, gains meaning only when we understand the rules of the House of Commons and the conventions governing *Hansard*, which declined to transcribe the two-word profanity Trudeau had directed at opposition MPs. Similarly, Deputy Prime Minister Anne McLellan (2005a) was able to equate SARS, BC forest fires, and an electrical blackout with international terrorism because of an emerging discourse of Canadian security that equated all threats in terms of their targets, rather than their origins. We now see an "all-hazards approach" to border security, typified by the mission of the Ministry of Public Safety and Emergency Preparedness (MPSEP) "to ensure the collective security and safety of Canadians, and to ensure that we are prepared to deal with any emergency, be it man-made or natural" (McLellan 2005b).

In addition, performing a kind of micro-analysis of the metaphors deployed in a particular discourse is as important as examining the broad structure of language (Chilton 1996, 195). Traditional border discourses rely on hydraulic metaphors: floods of immigrants, security leaks, channels of entry, and borders as dams against oceans and tides. The most consistent contemporary metaphor of Canadian border security is managerial: risk and risk management. In a discourse that differs markedly from that of national defence, the MPSEP and the Canadian Border Services Agency (CBSA) are described as developing "integrated border management" (McLellan 2005b).

This chapter employs a contextual analysis of the public and policy discourse of border policing. It provides an overview of contemporary border policy, substantiating the fundamental symbolic shift from the aspirations for a border open to trade toward a strategy of security and risk management. I argue that the "securitization" of the border leads to the spillover of securitization into other realms of public policy: health and immigration/refugee policies in particular. In the adoption of a risk-management strategy, border functions are delocalized, which has led to preventative surveillance of the entire population rather than of criminal elements alone. Because the policy cannot achieve its goal of perfect security, Canadian authorities have adopted the tactic of conspicuous consumption of policing for the benefit of a chiefly American audience, which allows mollification of our largest trading partner while resisting compromise on the core values of Canadian policy.

Borders and Discourse

The manner in which various actors, including governmental actors, structure problems in discourse can condition what policies appear to be possible to policy makers and their public constituency (Pal 2001, 104-6). Differing descriptions of a political problem, whether as chiefly administrative, economic, social, cultural, or judicial, will yield vastly differing outcomes. I focus specifically on the process of the "securitization" of border policies, or how a particular policy area is defined as "a *security* issue" (Buzan, Wæver, and de Wilde 1998).

Though often subsumed under analyses of trade or cultural policies, the border is understudied as its own proper site of public policy. It is particularly important for policy analysts as it represents the limits of the state and often represents an exceptional case of law and policy. If we view the border as the demarcation between "our" economy and the global economy, we will attempt to exclude foreign goods or dismantle trade barriers according to our economic model. If we perceive the border as the demarcation between "our" culture and other cultures, we will monitor the transmission of cultural products across the boundary – hoping for more exports than imports. If we think of the border as chiefly territorial, we will focus on the drawing of the actual line. If we conceive of the border in terms of political economy, we will be concerned with how capital and class determine the movement of goods and people, and vice versa. A traditional political scientist might consider the border in terms of the rise or decline of state sovereignty. If the national border is described as an "open door," this will have important implications for the facilitation of travel – the border is permeable. If the national border is framed as a protective wall, policy responses will tend toward exclusion – the border is impermeable.

Border studies is dominated by anthropology and sociology, which explore the ways in which the arbitrary border is constructed, reified, and subverted by local patterns of culture, economics, and politics (Donnan and Wilson 1999). Within these studies, there are few discussions of how governments themselves administer the border between nations, which is a missed opportunity for policy analysts. Josiah McConnell Heyman (1995, 2001) and Janet A. Gilboy (1991) are exceptional in their examination of the bureaucratic procedures of admission and exclusion at the border, but focus exclusively on the American-Mexican border. Geneviève Bouchard and Barbara Wake Carroll (2002) have provided a framework for understanding "discretion" within a Canadian context, but do so with reference to immigration only. In border studies, and in policy studies which happen to take in the administration of the Canadian border, there is a monopoly of the national category of analysis, with lip service paid to the globalization of public policy in terms of comparative studies or bilateral considerations. We see *in practice* the bleeding, leaching, and erosion of the boundary between public policy and foreign policy. Thus, border policy needs to be studied afresh, if we are to truly understand how policies are crafted in response to international as well as domestic factors.

In Canada, current border policy is defined in terms of security. The logic of security differs from that of the provision of public goods. Invoking a security threat frees rhetorical and public resources for defence. When an issue is defined as one of security, greater public and rhetorical resources become available, and public discussion of different policy options can be foreclosed (Wæver 1998). In a fundamental way, security lies outside the normal logic of politics; in the face of existential threats, extraordinary policies are necessary (Williams 2003). The process of securitization yields a hurried policy that often excludes or limits public debate. Once securitized, a policy solution is always reactive and already too late because the threat has already evaded non-security policy. However, securitization is not an uncontested process: defining an issue as one of security requires some degree of public acquiescence.

Smarter Is Safer: Canadian Border Policy

Canadian border administration has shifted from the strategy of good neighbours toward one of risk management. This strategy is implemented through the delocalization of border functions, the use of technology to discern safe from dangerous travellers or goods, and the surveillance of the general population. In this, two major Canadian policy initiatives, the Smart Border Accord (SBA) and the National Security Strategy (NSS), have played a key role.

Risk management has become a leitmotif of public administration, one which "dominates the language of governance" to the extent that "the fear of risk pervades nearly every policy debate" (Policy Research Initiative 2002, 1-2). Risk management entails the use of statistics "to estimate the probable harm to persons and environment resulting from specific types of substances or activities" (Leiss 2001, 10). As Ulrich Beck (1999, 50) argues, the notion of "risk" entails the taming of dangers and specifically the acceptance of dangers as an unavoidable part of industrial society. Thus, when border policing is assessed in terms of risk, "one does not *start from* a conflictual situation observable in experience, rather one *deduces* it from a general definition of the dangers one wishes to prevent" (Castel 1991, 288, emphasis in original). Thus, the solution to danger is the management of risk. For example, the danger inherent in highway driving is normalized through traffic regulations which create an acceptable rate of injuries and deaths; other, perhaps safer, options of mobility are not investigated (Packer 2003).

In the specific case of border security, the problem of terror is not defined as having a cause that can be addressed: instead, terror is perceived as a risk which inevitably arises in an open and prosperous society, one that can be managed by technology, surveillance, and policing. The weakness of such an approach is that risk management always chases its own failures: each succeeding risk profile will be generated only after the system has failed to expect the unexpected. For example, before 9/11, no risk profile existed to describe the types exemplified by Jose Padilla, Timothy McVeigh, Ted Kaczynski, John Allen Mohammed, or Lee Boyd Malvo. Furthermore, the continual expansion of risk-group identification does not render society safer, but serves to increase the populations under surveillance and the invasiveness of that surveillance. Risk management becomes a system to justify the constant expansion of policing and surveillance.

THE SMART BORDER ACCORD
Cross-border intercourse is vital to both the United States and Canada, though clearly the former holds both an economic and a political advantage in this relationship. Thus, after 9/11 and in response to American alarm about border security, Canadians framed the Smart Border Accord (SBA), with its

thirty-point Smart Border Action Plan (SBAP), which was signed in December 2001 (Kitchen 2004). The SBA was intended to make the border more discerning by guaranteeing "the secure flow of people, the secure flow of goods, secure infrastructure, and information sharing and coordination in the enforcement of these objectives" (DFAIT 2001). The Canadian government aimed to increase the porosity of the US border to legitimate business and desirable travellers, while making the border impermeable to criminal and terrorist threats. The chief strategy of the SBA was risk management, with the following logic: border agencies should devote most of their resources to the least desirable travellers and riskiest cargo and should not spend time hampering safe travellers or cargo. Thus, technology would be used to police "safe travellers," freeing the border police to deal with dangerous travellers. As Deborah Waller Meyers (2003, 13) describes the American response, the government is "emphasizing the role of intelligence and focusing resources on high-risk or unknown travelers, rather than wasting energy on the known, frequent travelers." This poses the border policing problem in terms of knowledge, to which the solution will be surveillance (the state gathering of knowledge) and information management (technology and coordination).

The primary tactics of border risk management, as expressed in the SBA, are delocalization of the border function, general surveillance of the population, and technological solutions to the problem of information and pathology. In delocalization, the border function (differentiating between desirable and undesirable travellers) is transferred away from the state's territorial limit in terms of space and time (Flynn 2002). This is achieved through the preclearance of people and goods, or so-called upstream examination. Along the Canada-US border, this preclearance takes three forms: information exchange, extra-territorial borders, and low-risk facilitation. For example, information regarding airline passengers is now exchanged between border agencies while planes are still airborne (Bennett 2004). US security posts have been established inside Canadian territory. Thus, while they are still in the Vancouver, Toronto, Ottawa, or Montreal airports, and before they even board their planes, America-bound travellers are inspected and admitted into the US. The Container Security Initiative plays the same role for cargo shipments from Vancouver, Montreal, and Halifax. Facilitation programs such as NEXUS and SMART allow for voluntary prescreening of frequent travellers. Applicants provide personal information in advance of their border crossing so as to gain preclearance from US officials; their submitted data, which contain more information (criminal and financial records) than is normally submitted at the border itself, are compared to existing profiles and records. Within the NEXUS and SMART programs, enhanced biometric (body measurement) data and document security deter identity fraud. A similar program exists for frequent cargo shippers. The private sector has been induced with the promise of easier border crossings to police itself by providing increased information and certifying its own safety. In this way, the delocalization of the border and the surveillance of the general population converge.

Surveillance regimes attempt to gather information on the population and, in doing so, to assess risk. Surveillance and risk management go hand in glove: "surveillance is the means whereby knowledge is produced for administering populations in relation to risk" (Lyon 2001, 6.) Of course, no surveillance regime is perfect. The spectre of the unknown haunts every surveillance system: the irreducible gap between the record and the reality can be held at bay only by an increase in information. With growing surveillance of the population, the disciplining of society takes on a much larger ambit – wider areas of social life are policed. As David Lyon (ibid., 1) suggests, this expansion of police powers is achieved under the discourse of "if you have nothing to hide, you have nothing to fear," which stands as a signal triumph of securitization. In the case of the war on terror, because terrorists do not form public groups for the promotion of terror, we see in Canada the surveillance of charity organizations, financial transactions, advocacy groups, educational institutions, communications, consumption, and so on (Roach 2003, 38-55).

One actualization of surveillance at the border, in addition to the usual closed-circuit television, one-way glass, and inspections, is the identity document. Passports, "tamper-proof" visas, permanent resident cards, and the like connect individuals to groups to records. The new Canadian permanent resident cards and passports, designed to be tamper-proof, include many biometric identifiers. Biometrics, the measurement of the body, attempts to identify individuals by recording their unique fingerprints, hand geometry, and retinal scans (Zureik with Hindle 2004). It provides a key technology in reducing information about a person to a single, stable, permanent, knowable identity, one which will always trump any other identity a traveller might present; it is a central component of the SBA.

Crucial to the success of biometrics and surveillance in monitoring and identifying the population are new technologies which process information and assist policing. The government use of technology to fix the problem of security appeals to both public and bureaucratic audiences in terms of reliability and efficiency. The SBA relies on information processing. The Computer Assisted Passenger Screening system (CAPS II), which assigns air passengers a risk score based on characteristics such as when their ticket was bought, how it was paid for, and the origin/destination, has recently been abandoned in the United States as a result of privacy concerns, but new systems are under development (Bennett 2004). Cross-border information sharing was paralleled by initiatives within Canada's borders: a substantial proportion of the federal funding made available by the 2001 Anti-terrorism Initiative went toward upgrading the interoperability of domestic police databases (Office of the Auditor General 2004, 19-21). Jason Ackleson (2003) and Peter Andreas (2000) illustrate how American bureaucracies used the political capital made available by terror and immigration crises to increase their budgets. This lesson is equally applicable to Canadian bureaucracies, as suggested by the Office of the Auditor General (2004, 10). The Canada Customs and Revenue Agency, Citizenship and Immigration Canada, and the RCMP all used funds from the Anti-terrorism Initiative to fund projects that had been on the books for some time, such as the Real Time Identification Project, which allows for the sharing of information amongst government agencies. With new technology, border agents will be able to correlate biometric information (such as facial scans, retinal scans, hand geometries, or fingerprints) with government records (such as criminal records, customs and visa information, intelligence information, and so on) (Baratto 2003, 17).

In sum, the SBA illustrates the shift toward a strategy of risk management wherein government resources are devoted to delocalization of the border function, surveillance, and technological fixes. As discussed below, the securitization of the border has a significant effect, both on the bureaucracies which implement it and in the spillover of securitization into traditionally non-security areas of domestic policy.

THE NATIONAL SECURITY STRATEGY
A major initiative of Paul Martin's incoming Liberal government in late April 2004 was the release of Canada's first National Security Strategy – Securing an Open Society (SOS). This was framed as a strategic response to a number of recent and historic events, including the 11 September 2001 terror attacks, the SARS outbreak, the 2003 blackout in Ontario, and the Madrid and Air India bombings, which necessitated a new kind of policy statement. The Martin government had already generated organizational innovations – the

creation of MPSEP, a Cabinet Committee on Security, Public Health, and Emergencies, and a national security advisor to the prime minister.

The first-ever Canadian National Security Strategy reconciled the tensions of American security demands with the Canadian public's desire to retain sovereignty: "we have addressed these [recent] threats to our society in a way that has strengthened the open nature of our country – open to immigrants from around the world and respectful of difference among us. Our prosperity is directly linked to this openness and to our ability to flourish in an increasingly interdependent world" (Privy Council Office 2004, iii). Thus, those liberal values that Canadians hold dear are described as the solution to the problem of contemporary insecurity. This entails a radical shift from traditional state-oriented geopolitics. Scholars of foreign policy and international relations would be surprised to see that interstate war is no longer listed as a chief threat to Canadian security. In its place, the threat environment is described as terrorism, proliferation of weapons of mass destruction, failed and failing states, foreign espionage, natural disasters, critical infrastructure vulnerability, organized crime, and pandemics (ibid., 6-8). Equating natural disasters and epidemics with terror has a double effect: it securitizes both the environment and health, and it naturalizes terror and organized crime. Terror is likened to the weather or disease – something with which Canada must live and cope. It is not a preventable danger. Furthermore, because these terror threats are global, Canada's response must be multilateral. Neither global warming nor terror, in this reading, can be dealt with by Canada alone. Canada's multilateral strategy depends on both international action and international perceptions. A crucial part of Canada's *international* reputation will lie in perceptions regarding the country's *domestic* action. In the post-9/11 global environment of risk management and perception management, the Canadian state must *be* seen both domestically and internationally to be acting on these threats. Part of its role in the war against terror is the policing of its domestic population – just as the role of a responsible global citizen involves environmental controls. However, this internationalization of domestic policing is a relatively new phenomenon, with a number of important spillover effects.

Border security is identified as a central plank in SOS. Many of the pioneering goals set by the SBA are restated in the NSS, including the delocalization of policing the border and the sharing and coordination of information for international cargo and passengers. In particular, the strategy of risk management is reinforced and the tools of surveillance and technology are allocated greater priority. The evolution of the Canada Public Safety Information Network (CPSIN) represents the convergence of these trends: surveillance, technology, and spillover. Led by the Integration Justice Information division of MPSEP, the CPSIN represents a partnership between Canada Customs and Revenue Agency, Citizenship and Immigration Canada, Correctional Service of Canada, Department of Justice, Department of the Solicitor General, National Parole Board, RCMP, Treasury Board Secretariat, Statistics Canada, Canadian Centre for Justice Statistics, and CSIS to facilitate the electronic sharing of information (IJI 2003). The border security section goes further than information sharing, and identifies immigration, refugee, and visa policies as vital aspects of the regime. This represents an expansion of the border security agenda. The correlation of foreign intelligence, passport and immigration data, and domestic criminal records provides a schema by which immigration inspectors, on the front lines at the border, attempt to discriminate between the safe and the dangerous – and allow entry into the domestic, safe space of Canada.

SOS also indicates increased investment in the governmental documentation which undergirds the surveillance regime. Passport reform, expanded visa investigations, and the new permanent resident card all link individuals to government records. This kind of hyper-documentation represents an effort by governments to know the mobile population. By hyper-documentation, I mean that each record is connected to other records (as in Internet hypertext), but also that information is gathered at incredible speed from disparate databases.

This brief description of the National Security Strategy reveals that the trends identified in the Smart Border Accord have a significant commitment of governmental rhetorical and political resources. For the remainder of this chapter, I will examine two unintended consequences of border securitization: the spillover, or inadvertent, securitization of domestic fields of public policy and the investment in border policing in the face of structural weaknesses in the anti-terror regime.

SECURITIZATION AND SPILLOVER

A number of Canadian policy makers have adopted the language of risk and risk management. It tracks neatly with the neo-liberal rhetoric of efficiency and the propensity for technical fixes to social problems. The threats represented by the war on terror are among the most difficult to manage. As a result, terror threats and risk management chase each other to increase their purview, yielding greater and greater realms of surveillance and security. This happens in terms of transnationalization of domestic issues and the securitization of non-security areas (Clarkson 2003, 75). This spillover has implicated a number of domestic public spheres in foreign policy. For example, membership in certain ethnic or religious groups, active participation in charity organizations, financial transactions, and particular travel histories are now grounds for extended questioning at the American border (Salter 2004, 85). Policy areas that adopted the rhetoric of risk management, such as those concerning immigration, refugees, and health, have also been "securitized" by the SBA and SOS.

The Refugee and Immigration System

Within American public discourse, the failures of border police to halt smuggling or illegal migration across the forty-ninth parallel are due primarily to the core weakness of Canadian "liberal" policies in terms of refugee adjudication and drug and immigration laws (Seper 2003a). As Athanasios Hristoulas (2003, 30) reports, "The U.S. media has portrayed Canada as a hotbed for terrorist activity. Special emphasis has been placed on Canada's refugee laws, which purportedly allow terrorists to operate within the country with relative ease." This discourse supports and is supported by the false belief that some of the 9/11 terrorists entered the US via the Canadian border (Haglund 2003, 678). In response, the Canadian government has tightened its immigration laws and revamped its refugee claimant process, without compromising the core liberal values upon which this hospitality rests. A significant aspect of these visible reforms is the signing of a "safe third country" agreement, which provides that refugees must claim asylum in the first "safe" country through which they pass (Meyers 2003, 12). More importantly, the Canadian government has had to promise to increase its policing of refugee claimants who are having their cases adjudicated or are under deportation order. Canada's domestic policing of refugees is now an transnational issue. Although immigration activist groups have raised the alarm, the mainstream media have accepted the securitization of the refugee regime with few qualms (*National Post* 2004).

Public Health

With the inclusion of pandemics as a threat to Canada, I contend that health policy – and particularly public health policy – is in the process of being securitized. Thomas S. Axworthy (2005, A17) illustrates the discourse: "The greatest threat to the lives of Canadians is the spectre of disease, especially a pandemic. Public health is now an intrinsic part of national security." The securitization of public health is by no means complete, however, and thus, more than is the case for refugee and immigration policy, it offers room for public resistance. SARS, HIV/AIDS, and BSE are now considered as inevitable risks of Canada's open society. In response to the recent SARS epidemic, the Canadian state reacted with the same mechanisms of risk management that it would have applied to a terror threat. World Health Organization immunization certificates (health passports) and quarantines attempted to upstream health inspections traditionally performed at the border. At airports, new kinds of technological surveillance, including heat sensors to detect fevers, attempted to fix the problem of invisible viral or microbial invaders. This is reminiscent of the Immigration and Refugee Protection Act of 2002, which allows for the exclusion of HIV/AIDS-positive immigrants if they pose a threat to public safety or public health or will be an "excessive burden" on the Canadian health system. That the cross-border movement of disease is not confined to humans was recently illustrated by the "mad cow" BSE outbreak, which closed the border to Canadian beef. This new plague discourse makes public health equivalent to public safety, enabling the same kinds of exclusions, incarcerations, and surveillance that Canadians have accepted in the war against terror. The logic underlying the securitization of health cannot improve health – defining disease as a security threat does not help policy makers act more expeditiously or efficiently. However, it does serve to make the security issue a problem which demands an immediate solution, providing an incentive for bureaucrats to securitize more of their mandate.

Three crucial dangers exist in this kind of spillover securitization. First, securitization increasingly results in the declaration of "emergencies," states which evoke some important, though little studied, legal paradoxes. Recent theoretical work inspired by Carl Schmitt examines the way that a declaration of a "state of emergency" can lead to an accrual of executive powers that is a precursor to anti-democratic politics (Agamben 2005; Butler 2004). As can be seen in the USA Patriot Act or the detainment of prisoners at Guantánamo Bay, a government can take extraordinary measures in the face of an emergency. Although Canada's provincial and federal laws clearly lay out the dynamics of emergency management, there has been insufficient consideration in policy or scholarly circles of the declaration and ending of emergencies. Trudeau's justification for his invocation of the War Measures

Act in 1970 was a terrorist threat. He warned that acceding to the terrorist demands would mean "we would be facing the breakdown of the legal system, and its replacement by the law of the jungle. Freedom and personal security are safeguarded by laws; those laws must be respected in order to be effective" (Trudeau 1970). Yet the War Measures Act specifically suspends the law in order to be effective. Its replacement, the current Emergencies Act (R.S. 1985, c. 22 (4th Supp.)), has not been challenged on this point, and this paradox informing states of emergency has not been analyzed. As government policy defines threats, those things which cause emergencies, in terms of their targets rather than their origins, we see aspects of public policy subsumed under security considerations. For example, if forest fires are seen as arising from forest conditions and a catalyst, resources will be allocated proportionately to prevention and prediction. If forest fires are seen as a threat to forests, the focus will be on fire fighting. If terrorism is seen as a result of motive and opportunity, resources will be allocated proportionately to prediction and prevention; but if terrorism is seen as a threat to Canadian society, the focus will be on border protection and policing.

Second, when an issue is defined as an emergency, public debate is often foreclosed. As in the invocation of the War Measures Act, a state of emergency comes into existence only when it is *declared*. Thus, as Giorgio Agamben (2005) argues, this assertion of fact erases the law, including laws regarding freedom of debate, because the law is suspended during a state of emergency. Paradoxically, and ironically, the erasure of law is accomplished by the law itself. For example, *Borderline Insecure*, the recent Senate Committee on National Security and Defence (2005, 60) report, argued that addressing problems at the Windsor-Detroit border "requires war-time urgency."

Third, when a risk-management strategy is adopted as the solution to security deficits, bureaucracies increasingly use surveillance to add to their knowledge of the factors. However, they will widen and deepen the scope of surveillance regardless of whether doing so has any effect in decreasing risk. Greater surveillance does not lead to less risk or the perception of less risk. Since 9/11, though the amount of information collected on entrants to the United States has increased exponentially, no terrorists have been detected at the American border. The degree of surveillance of risky populations and in dangerous spaces (such as airports) has also increased dramatically, with little result. In short, if the response of a government to a perceived security threat takes place within a risk-management strategy, greater surveillance is the most frequent outcome. In the Canadian context, this has become salient through the Maher Arar inquiry and the reports of the national privacy commissioner. Although the Office of the Auditor General (2004) and the Senate Committee on National Security and Defence (2005) have both reported on the issue of intelligence gathering and investigation at the border, there has been no scholarly analysis of this problem.

Conspicuous Consumption of Borders

In post-9/11 border policy, risk management and perception management are key objectives of the government. In this section, I show that the lack of material effects of border policy leads to the need for perceptual effects: the lack of security creates the need for conspicuous consumption of policing. Of course, no policy can effect its direct aim. Health policy does not cause health. Anti-terror policies do not stop terror. Similarly, border security policy cannot guarantee security. Because this dilemma seems newly discovered by policy makers, it is important to lay out precisely the impact of these imperfect policies in terms of discretion and technological weaknesses.

When a traveller petitions to enter a state, he or she abdicates all national rights (except basic human rights, I would argue); the application of sovereign power at the border is absolute. The ability of a border official to read the intentions of any particular traveller is severely limited. Initial, or primary, inspections take between 30 and 120 seconds. In that time, officials must verify the authenticity of the document, input the data from the passport and visa, and gauge the intention of the traveller (Gilboy 1991, 578-80). Immigration inspectors face enormous bureaucratic pressure to handle an immense caseload. Secondary inspections are more extensive, but inspectors are often sanctioned if they "secondary" too many suspicious travellers. Even sustained inquisition may not enable a state to determine a terrorist's intentions. Richard Reid was interrogated by French police on two consecutive days for nearly seven hours but still boarded a United Airlines flight with explosives in his shoe. Since 9/11, greater allowances have been made for inspection, but the underlying structure remains the same: ultimately, only The Shadow knows what evil lurks in the hearts of men.

Bouchard and Wake Carroll's (2002) study of "discretion" in Canada's immigration system provides us with a conceptual framework for distinguishing policy as written from policy as enforced. For example, a Customs and Border Services Agency inspector must not only assess the validity and authenticity of identity documents at the border, but also exercise discretion as to the validity of the traveller's narrative in determining whether a secondary examination is warranted. Bouchard and Wake Carroll argue that agent discretion provides vital flexibility and interpretation in the immigration system while simultaneously undermining the integrity of that system. A just system must balance procedural justice, which argues against discretion as unequal procedure, and substantive justice, which requires discretion for equal results. Risk assessment requires discretion because no agent can ever possess all the information regarding an immigrant. Conversely, because discretion can generate uninformed decisions, thereby increasing risk, it must be rejected. This fundamental uncertainty at the moment of policing renders the mobility of people a constant and irreducible danger.

The government's reliance on technology as a replacement (or supplement) to examination also has drawbacks. In keeping with risk-management strategy, database technology identifies risk factors rather than the experience of danger. In both American and Canadian cases, Ackleson (2003, 65-67) shows that the adoption of technology has capitalized on the new resources made available by the securitization of the border – even as that technology is unproven. As Zureik and Hindle (2004, 134) conclude, as Canada adopts the "techno-administrative" methods of the US, the danger exists that surveillance technologies will be broadened to "society generally, [especially] the poor, marginal, and vulnerable people," with no concurrent decrease in danger.

The Office of the Auditor General report on the 2001 Anti-terrorism Initiative (2004) pointed to a number of weaknesses in the system: the lack of an overall national strategy, the allocation of funds for pre-existing projects rather than for purpose-built projects, the inefficiency of inter-agency communication, and the lack of long-term vision. However, the auditor general supported the strategy of risk management, even while acknowledging the technical, bureaucratic, and cultural restrictions on the success of this strategy. In essence, risk management will always be shutting the barn door after the horse has escaped. The shibboleth of complete security against clandestine agents has been tempered in policy circles by the more realistic measures of risk management and threat containment. As US Customs and Border Patrol Commissioner Robert Bonner has stated, "If the goal is to stop every terrorist, every illegal alien, every drug smuggler, then we have set ourselves up for failure. But the goal is to gain substantial control of the border, to make it far more difficult to illegally enter the United States. And that we can do" (Seper 2003b, A1). Against the image of complete protection, the stated American policy goal is substantial control. The response of the Canadian

bureaucracies to their failures has been to increase the visibility of their policing. Because they cannot guarantee security, they aim to guarantee the perception of security.

Policy makers receive two conflicting sets of priorities from foreign and
domestic stakeholders. American policy makers have pushed for continental
security, advocating closer control of immigration and the tracking of na-
tionals. Canadians support close cooperation with the US on border security
issues, but are reluctant to either integrate into a North American union or
capitulate immigration and visa policy to American foreign policy dictates.
Canadians are willing to cooperate on border security – but view this issue as
separate from immigration and national defence (Citizenship and Immigration Canada 2000, 17). This is diametrically opposed to the post-9/11 American perception, as illustrated in the structure and purpose of the Department
of Homeland Security, the USA Patriot Act, and the Library of Congress (2003)
report. To further complicate this, Canadians – in a trend that reflects Canada's weak status in the bilateral relationship – are more anxious regarding
American disapproval than are Americans concerning Canadian disapproval.
In a March 2003 poll, half of the Canadian respondents believed that the
Canada-US relationship had worsened; 53 percent of Americans polled felt
there was no change (Citizenship and Immigration 2000, 11). In an Ipsos-
Reid poll of the previous year, more than three-quarters (81 percent) of Ameri-
cans felt very or moderately confident that Canada would help in the
Homeland Security border regime, but Canadians appeared to wonder
whether their government could in fact match this effort. When asked whether
"Canadian immigration and refugee rules" or "U.S. Immigration and Border
Security" were responsible the decreased confidence in US-Canada border
security, 72 percent of Americans blamed the pre–Homeland Security border regime, rather than Canadian policies (only 15 percent); 43 percent of
Canadians blamed Canadian immigration and refugee policy (which they
were unwilling to change), and only 32 percent cited the US border regime
(Privy Council Office 2002, 30).

The bureaucratic and symbolic logic of border policing by both American and Canadian agencies leads to a conspicuous increase in policing, though
not an actual increase in protection. The rubric of conspicuous consumption
adds depth to this analysis. As Thorstein Veblen (1902, 86-87) comments,
"One's neighbors, mechanically speaking, are often socially not one's neighbors, or even acquaintances; and still their transient good opinion has a high

degree of utility. The only practicable means of impressing one's pecuniary ability on these unsympathetic observers of one's everyday life is an unremitting demonstration of the ability to pay." Without wishing to unduly strain the metaphor, I will point out that, because Canada cannot impose the kind of surveillance or immigration policies which America desires, it must impress its neighbour by demonstrating an ability to pay for increased border security. Canada, which is not a superpower, relies a great deal on America's good opinion. Thus, risk management is coupled with perception management – and Canadian policing is performed for an American audience.

Conclusion

Too often subsumed under questions of identity, culture, and trade, and dominated by national or comparative analytical frames, the border is a much-neglected site in public policy studies. Policy analysts need to develop a framework that integrates foreign and domestic policy with the complex of security policies in which the border figures so prominently. This chapter has made a start at the attempt: using discourse analysis, which is attentive to both material and perceptual aspects of public policy, it has identified the logic of policy actions by showing that particular constructions of problems both enable and necessitate specific solutions. The concept of securitization brings this issue to the fore in a number of areas. Securitization of policy poses dangers – to border policy itself, of course, but also to that regarding refugees, immigration, and health. Securitization facilitates the use of emergency or extraordinary powers and the subsequent removal of policy issues from public debate. Policy analysis in this area is dominated by questions of immigration, economics, and security. In the current climate, we see the security aspect of the border coming to dominate the others. The securitization of border studies, and the spillover securitization of other areas of public policy, should be of greater concern to analysts. I argue that we are seeing increased restriction of everyday freedoms – including those of mobility and privacy – in exchange for a false promise of security. Risk management is condemned to chase its own failures. The unreliability of discretion and confession cannot be corrected by biometrics or technology. We should not accept surveillance and terror as necessary aspects of Canadian society when we might choose policies that seek to address insecurity at its root by desecuritizing terror. In short, terrorism is described in Canadian policy as one vector of threat to the Canadian way of life – but a threat that can be managed like others: "Terrorist threats, illegal migration, organized crime, and the introduction of previously unknown diseases, such as SARS and the avian flu, all pose serious threats to our way of life" (McLellan 2005c). By directing public perceptions to the targets rather than the origins of threats, we confine ourselves within a closed circle – always reacting, always late, always in a state of emergency. We must move beyond cold comparisons of migration numbers or budget allocations and heated expressions of indignation or panic when the border fails. The border should be a vibrant area of public debate and policy analysis. Nor should border studies simply end with the frontier. A longer, globalized view is necessary if we are to treat border security as a discrete but interconnected nexus of public policies with attendant local, provincial, national, regional, and global integrations.

REFERENCES

Ackleson, Jason. 2003. "Securing Through Technology? 'Smart Borders' after September 11th." *Knowledge, Technology, Policy* 16(1): 56-74.

Agamben, Giorgio. 2005. *State of Exception*, trans. Kevin Attell. Chicago: University of Chicago Press.

Andreas, Peter. 2000. *Border Games: Policing the U.S.-Mexico Divide*. Ithaca: Cornell University Press.

—. 2003. "Redrawing the Line: Borders and Security in the Twenty-first Century." *International Security* 28(2): 78-111.

Axworthy, Thomas S. 2005. "Public Health Should Be Job 1: Thomas S. Axworthy Says Canada Should Lead the World in Fighting Pandemics." *Toronto Star*, 29 May, A17, Ontario edition.

Baratto, Luigina. 2003. "Free and Clear: Securing the Canada-U.S. Border." *IJI@Work* 2(1): 17-18.

Beck, Ulrich. 1999. *World Risk Society*. Malden, MA: Polity.

Bennett, Colin. 2004. "What Happens When You Book an Airline Ticket (Revisited): The Computer Assisted Passenger Profiling System and the Globalization of Personal Data." Paper presented at State Borders and State Policing, Queen's University, 21 August.

Bonner, Robert C. 2003. *Securing America's Borders While Safeguarding Commerce*. Heritage Lecture No. 796. Washington, DC: Lexis-Nexis Academic.

Bouchard, Geneviève, and Barbara Wake Carroll. 2002. "Policy-Making and Administrative Discretion: The Case of Immigration in Canada." *Canadian Public Administration* 45(1): 239-57.

Butler, Judith. 2004. *Precarious Life: The Powers of Mourning and Violence*. New York: Verso.

Buzan, Barry, Ole Wæver, and Jaap de Wilde. 1998. *Security: A New Framework for Analysis*. Boulder: Lynne Rienner.

Castel, Robert. 1991. "From Dangerousness to Risk." In *The Foucault Effect: Studies in Governmentality*, ed. Gordon Burchill, Colin Gordon, and Peter Miller, 281-99. Chicago: University of Chicago Press.

Chilton, Paul A. 1996. "The Meaning of Security." In *Post-realism: The Rhetorical Turn in International Relations*, ed. Francis A. Beer and Robert Hariman, 193-216. East Lansing: Michigan State University Press.

Citizenship and Immigration Canada. 2000. *Canada-United States Accord on Our Shared Border: Update 2000*. Ottawa: Minister of Public Works and Government Services Canada.

Clarkson, Stephen. 2003. "The View from the Attic: Toward a Gated Continental Community?" In *The Rebordering of North America: Integration and Exclusion in a New Security Context*, ed. Peter Andreas and Thomas J. Biersteker, 68-89. New York: Routledge.

DFAIT (Department of Foreign Affairs and International Trade). 2001. "Smart Border Declaration." Ottawa, 12 December. http://www.dfait-maeci.gc.ca/anti-terrorism/declaration-en.asp.

Donnan, Hastings, and Thomas M. Wilson, eds. 1999. *Borders: Frontiers of Identity, Nation, and State*. Oxford: Berg.

Drache, Daniel. 2004. *Borders Matter: Homeland Security and the Search for North America*. Halifax: Fernwood.

Flynn, Stephen E. 2002. "America the Vulnerable." *Foreign Affairs* 81(1): 60-75.

—. 2004. *America the Vulnerable: How Our Government Is Failing to Protect Us from Terrorism*. New York: HarperCollins.

Gilboy, Janet A. 1991. "Deciding Who Gets In: Decisionmaking by Immigration Inspectors." *Law and Society Review* 25: 578-80.

Haglund, David. 2003. "North American Cooperation in an Era of Homeland Security." *Orbis* 47(4): 675-90.

Heyman, Josiah McConnell. 1995. "Putting Power in the Anthropology of Bureaucracy: The Immigration and Naturalization Service at the Mexico-United States Border." *Current Anthropology* 36(2): 261-87.

—. 2001. "Class and Classification at the U.S.-Mexico Border." *Human Organization* 60(2): 128-40.

Hristoulas, Athanasios. 2003. "Trading Places: Canada, Mexico, and North American Security." In *The Rebordering of North America: Integration and Exclusion in a New Security Context*, ed. Peter Andreas and Thomas J. Biersteker, 24-45. New York: Routledge.

IJI (Integrated Justice Information). 2003. "Charter: Canada Public Safety Information Network (CPSIN)." http://www.psepc-sppcc.gc.ca/publications/ingrat_justice/CpSIN_Charter_e.pdf.

Kitchen, Veronica M. 2004. "Smarter Co-operation in Canada-US Relations?" *International Journal* 59(3): 693-710.

Laxer, James. 2003. *The Border: Canada, the U.S. and Dispatches from the 49th Parallel.* Toronto: Doubleday Canada.

Leiss, William. 2001. *In the Chamber of Risks: Understanding Risk Controversies.* Montreal and Kingston: McGill-Queen's University Press.

Library of Congress (LaVerle Berry, Glenn E. Curtis, John N. Gibbs, Rex A. Hudson, Tara Karacan, Nina Kollars, and Ramón Miró). 2003. *Nations Hospitable to Organized Crime and Terrorism.* Federal Research Division, Library of Congress. Washington, DC: Library of Congress.

Lyon, David. 2001. *Surveillance Society: Monitoring Everyday Life.* Philadelphia: Open University Press.

McLellan, Anne. 2005a. "On the First Anniversary of Securing an Open Society: Canada's National Security Policy." Speech delivered at the meeting of Women in Defence and Security in Canada, Ottawa, 11 May. http://ww2.psepc-sppcc.gc.ca/publications/Speeches/2005/20050511_e.asp.

—. 2005b. "Senate Committee on National Security and Defence, Culture, Border Security and Infrastructure." Ottawa, 11 April. http://www.psepc-sppcc.gc.ca/publications/Speeches/2005/20050411_e.asp.

—. 2005c. "The Subcommittee on Public Safety and National Security: Review of Bill C-26 an Act to Establish the Canadian Border Services Agency." Ottawa, 1 February. http://www.psepc-sppcc.gc.ca/publications/Speeches/2005/20050201_e.asp.

Meyers, Deborah Waller. 2003. "Does 'Smarter' Lead to Safer? An Assessment of the US Border Accords with Canada and Mexico." *International Migration* 41(4): 5-44.

Milliken, Jennifer. 1999. "The Study of Discourse in International Relations: A Critique of Research and Methods." *European Journal of International Relations* 5(2): 225-54.

National Post. 2004. "Editorial: Making Canada Safer." 29 April, A19.

Neff, James, Duff Wilson, and Hal Bernton. 2001. "Few Resources Spent on Guarding Canada Border." *Seattle Times*, 23 September, A1.

Office of the Auditor General. 2004. "Chapter 3: National Security in Canada – The 2001 Anti-terrorism Initiative." In *Report of the Auditor General of Canada*, 1-50. Ottawa: Minister of Public Works and Government Services Canada.

Packer, Jeremy. 2003. "Disciplining Mobility: Governing and Safety." In *Foucault, Cultural Studies, and Governmentality*, ed. Jack Z. Bratich, Jeremy Packer, and Cameron McCarthy, 135-61. Albany: SUNY Press.

Pal, Leslie A. 2001. *Beyond Policy Analysis: Public Issue Management in Turbulent Times.* Scarborough: Nelson Thomson Learning.

Policy Research Initiative. 2002. "A New World of Risk." *Horizons: Policy Research Initiative* 5(3): 1-2.

Privy Council Office. 2002. *Trends in the Public Environment* 2(4). Ottawa: Communications and Consultation Secretariat.

—. 2004. "Securing an Open Society: Canada's National Security Policy." Ottawa: Minister of Public Works and Government Services Canada.

Roach, Kent. 2003. *September 11: Consequence for Canada*. Montreal and Kingston: McGill-Queen's University Press.

Salter, Mark B. 2003. *Rights of Passage: The Passport in International Relations*. Boulder: Lynne Rienner.

—. 2004. "Passports, Security, Mobility: How Smart Can the Border Be?" *International Studies Perspectives* 5(1): 71-91.

Senate Committee on National Security and Defence. 2005. *Borderline Insecure: Canada's Land Border Crossings Are Key to Canada's Security and Prosperity. Why the Lack of Urgency to Fix Them? What Will Happen If We Don't*. Interim Report by the Senate Committee on National Security and Defence. http://www.senate-senat.ca/borders.asp.

Seper, Jerry. 2003a. "Drug Smugglers Turn to Northern Border: Illegal Trade Soars to Meet U.S. Demand." *Washington Times*, 9 December, A01, final edition.

—. 2003b. "Guarding America's Border, Understaffed Patrol Must Balance Safety, Free Trade." *Washington Times*, 8 December, A01, final edition.

Trudeau, Pierre Elliott. 1970. "Notes for a National Broadcast by the Prime Minister." 16 October. http://collections.ic.gc.ca/discourspm/anglais/pet/1610970e.html.

Veblen, Thorstein. 1902. *The Theory of the Leisure Class: An Economic Study of Institutions*. New York: Macmillan.

Wæver, Ole. 1998. "Securitization and Desecuritization." In *On Security*, ed. Ronnie D. Lipschutz, 46-86. New York: Columbia University Press.

Williams, Michael C. 2003. "Words, Images, Enemies: Securitization and International Politics." *International Studies Quarterly* 47: 511-31.

Zureik, Elia, with Karen Hindle. 2004. "Governance, Security, Technology: The Case of Biometrics." *Studies in Political Economy* 73: 113-37.

15
The Permanent-Emergency Compensation State: A "Postsocialist" Tale of Political Dystopia

Matt James

Social policy expresses moral commitments, giving concrete shape to hege-monic views about the boundaries of community membership and even the relative worth of different groups and communities. Stated famously in Thomas H. Marshall's (1964) classic work on the welfare state, this maxim about social policy's diagnostic value demands renewed attention at a time when egalitarian redistribution is in decline.

The moral commitments embedded in neo-liberal distributive policies seem clear enough. In Canada, a decade of cuts to unemployment insurance and social assistance has reinforced "the absolute authority of the employer" while stigmatizing "welfare recipients as not deserving of public support" (Mullaly 1994, 84; Clarkson 2002, 412). This is no temporary state of affairs. As Denis Saint-Martin reports in Chapter 13 of this volume, a "social protec-tion paradigm" framing income security as a key responsibility of the whole political community has given way to a much leaner conception of the "so-cial investment state." Indeed, several years after the replacement of the fed-eral budget deficit with a string of surpluses, Leslie A. Pal (2001, 324) notes that "spending instruments are being used cautiously and often in the form of 'boutique' programs without major expenditures commitments."

But the story of citizenship in the age of neo-liberalism is not simply one of contraction and decay. The advanced capitalist democracies exhibit a long-run trend toward increased respect for group difference, of which Canada's same-sex marriage legislation and decision to protect gays and les-bians from hate propaganda are two recent examples ("MPs Vote" 2003). Indeed, the trend toward respect for difference has helped to sustain interest in Marshall's optimistic account of citizenship's evolutionary growth during what would otherwise be adverse times. Thus, critical theorist Axel Honneth (1995, 179) invokes Marshall's view, suggesting that social movement struggles for recognition are pushing Western citizenship toward "radically expand[ed] relations of solidarity."

This chapter explores the apparent contradiction just sketched by drawing on critical theorist Nancy Fraser's (1997) analysis of our "'postsocialist' condition." Neither celebration of ideology's end nor Marxist jeremiad, Fraser's account targets the reigning sensibility of an age that combines the near-abandonment of hopes for transformative economic change with increased receptivity to cultural and discursive recognition for historically marginalized groups. In Fraser's view, the emblematic problem of the "postsocialist" age is that this relatively new politics of recognition is serving to displace older commitments to egalitarian redistribution. However, rather than hectoring recognition seekers to "wait for the revolution," Fraser (2000, 2001) reacts to the apparent problem by advocating more harmonious combinations of recognition and redistribution as visions of social justice.

Fraser's analysis is at the heart of a lively "recognition versus redistribution" debate (Fraser and Honneth 2003). The debate tends to pit defenders of recognition politics (for example, Butler 1997; Young 1997) against those who view the emphasis on difference as a major culprit in the diminished contemporary fortunes of egalitarian redistribution (for example, Barry 2001; Rorty 2000). This chapter follows a different path. Taking a cue from recent empirical work devoted to understanding the interplay between recognition and redistribution in specific areas of political life (Hobson 2003; Van Parijs 2004; cf. Tully 2000), it seeks to open a window on what I call the changing moral contours of contemporary Canadian citizenship. The chapter does so by exploring two novel areas of political claims making from a Canadian perspective: reparations for historical injustices and compensation in the wake of natural disasters.

An important new species of recognition politics, demands for reparations from victims of historical injustices confront policy makers with new and often vexing challenges. These demands are also behind a telling semantic shift that seems to encapsulate key aspects of the "postsocialist" condition. Formerly defined as indemnities that defeated parties in military conflict were obliged to pay the victors, reparations are now understood as acts of compensation for past wrongs extended by states or institutions to victim groups that are often quite weak in conventional political resources. As sociologist John Torpey (2001, 2003b) argues, this change suggests both a profound underlying transformation in popular views of what counts as a repairable injustice and a corresponding enlargement of the polity's sense of responsibility toward particular sorts of victims.

However, Canada's past history of constitutional turmoil has created an unfavourable environment for groups seeking historical redress. After offering a brief introduction to the reparations phenomenon, this chapter explains how the practice of negotiating reparations for historical wrongs first emerged during the 1980s as an aspect of Canada's broader attempt at constitutional reconciliation and renewal. But as the chapter goes on to show, Ottawa's fear of the roving populist anger toward "special interests" and "identity politics" that defined the 1992 Charlottetown referendum result (Johnston et al. 1996) has led to a new intransigence on reparations. The few offers of redress to be found in the post-Charlottetown era can generally be characterized as rare gestures of minimal contrition and negligible expense extracted under pain of legal action or international embarrassment.

After discussing the new intransigence on redress as an expression of Ottawa's post-Charlottetown policy of constitutional avoidance, the chapter then turns to examine a related policy area that appears to be in a stage of ascendancy – natural-disaster compensation. In part, this ascendancy reflects the heightened political importance of disaster compensation at a time when disasters are increasing in frequency and growing in cost. Yet despite mounting costs, and in strong contrast to demands for historical redress, disaster compensation attracts no discernible criticism or even much in the way of public scrutiny. To explain this phenomenon, which constitutes a significant instance of what Stuart N. Soroka (Chapter 9, this volume) would identify as a change in "issue definition," I stress the ease with which publics are able to connect the deserving innocence of suffering natural-disaster victims with some precipitating, catastrophic event. I suggest further that compensating such innocent victims in the wake of obvious tragedy fills an ideological and emotional void created by the neo-liberalization of the Canadian welfare state.[1]

The chapter concludes by sketching an improbable yet potentially instructive future scenario. This is a scenario of political dystopia, characterized by the combined impact of climate change, the fiscal regressivity of disaster compensation, and a growing bias toward helping only "innocent" victims – victims whose plight does not challenge consciences, excite the neo-Victorian bugbears of effort and thrift, or impugn the past actions of the dominant society. This dystopia is the "permanent-emergency compensation state."

Redress Politics: A Brief Overview

Defined by the United Nations as responses to past wrongdoing that combine symbolic processes of apology with material compensation (United Nations Commission on Human Rights 2000, 10), reparations has arrived as an object of academic study. Indeed, a 24 June 2004 search of peer-reviewed journals in the Academic Search Elite database yielded ninety-six entries under the keyword "reparations." Reparative campaigns have emerged to target a growing range of injustices, including the trans-Atlantic slave trade, the Nanking massacre, American slavery and Jim Crow, Japan's "comfort women system," the Holocaust, South African apartheid, and the serial wrongs done to the world's indigenous peoples (Barkan 2000; Brooks 1999; Torpey 2003a).

The complexly unresolved history of Canada's multi-ethnic and multinational society also creates an important setting for what I have called "redress politics" (James 1999). The list is long: the "head tax" imposed on Chinese immigrants; the repression of the Doukhobors; the unjust rejection of the Sikh migrants aboard the *Komagata Maru*; the internments of Japanese, Italian, Ukrainian, and German Canadians; the litany of injustices experienced by First Nations, Métis, and Inuit; the slavery and official racism affecting various groups of African Canadians; the failure to admit Jewish refugees during the Second World War; the deportation of the Acadians – all have sparked redress claims (ibid.).

The basic point of departure for Canadian discussions of redress politics is the Japanese Canadian Redress Agreement of 1988 (Kobayashi 1992; Miki 2003). Following an effective campaign by the National Association of Japanese Canadians, the agreement provided an official apology from Prime Minister Brian Mulroney for the wrongful Second World War internment, which affected approximately twenty-three thousand individuals, and offered $21,000 in individual compensation to each living survivor. It also established a $12 million community development fund under the supervision of the National Association of Japanese Canadians and earmarked $24 million for the creation of the Canadian Race Relations Foundation. Finally, the agreement instituted a process for restoring Canadian citizenship to individuals and descendants of individuals whose citizenship was revoked during the internment operations, while pledging similarly to erase the criminal records of those convicted of resisting the internment order.

Redress advocates and critics alike view the Japanese Canadian Redress Agreement as a precedent. Where the former praise a historic milestone on the route to a more just and self-reflective society (Kobayashi 1992), the latter see the first in a stampede of attempted raids on the national treasury leaving a trail of divisive battles over bygone events (Dafoe 1994). Undoubtedly, the agreement's $412,908,000 price tag (Canada 1997) has played some role in encouraging a "compensation queue" (Simpson 1994). But the critics can take comfort in knowing that their view has largely prevailed. In December 1994, Liberal heritage minister Sheila Finestone announced her department's policy of refusing to compensate redress-seeking groups. Rejecting the very notion of historical redress, Finestone (Canada 1994a) stressed Ottawa's determination to "invest in the future" rather than "attempt to address the past." The stand has not seriously been challenged by either the 2005 Acknowledgment, Commemoration, and Education program, or that program's replacement, the Community Historical Recognition Program instituted in 2006 by the incoming Conservatives. Both federal programs reject serious negotiations concerning the dominant society's contemporary reparative responsibilities in favour of scattered depoliticized acts of national "commemoration"; and both programs reject funding anti-racism initiatives in favour of offering grants in support of groups promoting "racial harmony" (James 2006a).

Redress Politics and Constitutional Politics

The pioneer in using redress politics as a window on Canadian citizenship is Alan C. Cairns. Cairns sees an important link between the focus of formal constitutional politics on large-scale institutional change and that of redress politics on transforming the nation's stock of narratives and symbols. As he explains, both sorts of politics seek to reshape the parameters within which future civic relationships and self-understandings will develop. Accordingly, Cairns (1995, 28) presents redress politics as a dimension of constitutional politics: as "a different constitutional reform agenda ... [whose] achievement requires a revisiting of the past. This activity may be variously described as cultural-constitutional, or societal-constitutional. It involves the efforts of yesterday's outsiders to be fully and positively included in society's view of its past and present." By encompassing redress politics, Cairns' perspective underscores the capacious ambition of Canada's post-Charter constitutional politics: a blizzard of competing efforts to refashion political community. It also recommends viewing the trajectory of Canadian redress politics against that of the formal constitutional debate.

Associated with the demands of Japanese, Chinese, and Ukrainian Canadians, the first major wave of Canadian redress claims followed the 1982 entrenchment of the Charter of Rights and Freedoms. The addition of judicial review of citizen rights to the constitutional order furnished a dramatically authoritative contrast between historical patterns of Canadian public policy and the country's new founding principles (ibid., 22). Thus, the Chinese Canadian redress movement began in 1983 when Dak Leon Mark appeared at his Vancouver East MP's office, brandishing his head-tax certificate and demanding recompense on the ground that the tax contravened the equality guarantees in the new Charter (Chinese Canadian National Council 1988). This dynamic had been foreshadowed at four different sets of parliamentary hearings between 1950 and 1981 on the question of a national bill of rights. On each occasion, equality-seeking witnesses seized on the official focus on entrenching equality rights as an opportunity for promoting a more informed awareness of the discriminatory treatment meted out in the past (James 2006b).

The second wave of redress politics, in which citizens of Italian, German, Jewish, and Indian descent joined the earlier claimants, coincided with the 1987-92 debates over the Meech Lake and Charlottetown Accords. It was defined by an ultimately fruitless process of collective redress negotiations between the various claimant organizations and the federal multiculturalism ministry. These negotiations broke down in 1993 when Conservative multiculturalism minister Gerry Weiner declared that the country's fiscal situation made paying significant amounts of financial compensation impossible ("Hefty Price Tag" 1993, A12). A year later, Finestone's "invest in the future" announcement shut down negotiations entirely.

Although Japanese Canadian redress undoubtedly encouraged similar demands, the broader constitutional context also shaped the second wave of claims. As historians Franca Iacovetta and Robert Ventresca (2000, 383) note, Prime Minister Brian Mulroney's views on constitutionalism and historical redress virtually inverted those of his predecessor. Pierre Trudeau not only despised the decentralizing politics of constitutional brokerage; he also told redress claimants on several occasions that we can "only be just in our own time."[2] By contrast, it took Mulroney just three days at Meech Lake in 1987 to broker a deal that proposed to confer special constitutional status on Quebec (the infamous "distinct society" clause) in return for the decentralization of federal powers. And two years later, with the deal's unpopularity shading into full-blown constitutional crisis, Mulroney turned to collective redress negotiations as a way of mollifying Canadians of Chinese, German, Indian, Italian, Jewish, and Ukrainian descent. These were the same communities whose lead organizations had been waging a vigorous assault on Meech's ill-starred "distinct society" proposal, arguing that it denigrated the commitment to multiculturalism and slighted the contributions of ethnocultural minorities.[3]

Excepting Chinese Canadians, who made head-tax redress the subject of a high-profile but ultimately unsuccessful legal case (Dyzenhaus and Moran 2005), and Ukrainian Canadians, who persuaded Ottawa to establish commemorative plaques at various internment sites, Finestone's 1994 announcement silenced the remaining second-wave claimants. Yet the immediate post-Charlottetown period saw a third wave of redress claims: the federal Department of Indian and Northern Affairs began to face mounting calls to redress Canada's devastating residential schools policy and the coercive 1950s relocation of two Inuit communities to the High Arctic (James 2001, 64-68).

In 1996 the affected Inuit negotiated a $10 million trust fund, a deal which rejected their calls for apology and required them formally to accept that the relocation planners had acted with "honourable intentions." In 1998, Indian and Northern Affairs Minister Jane Stewart issued a Statement of Reconciliation and established a $350 million "healing fund" in an attempt to provide redress to residential school survivors. Although declaring that the federal government was "deeply sorry" for the sexual and physical abuse suffered by many students, Stewart resisted calls to apologize for the intentions behind the policy and for its ongoing effect on Aboriginal communities. Liberal prime minister Jean Chrétien's failure to apologize or even to appear at the press conference announcing the initiative also attracted criticism.

In retrospect, the High Arctic relocation trust fund and Statement of Reconciliation seem like end-of-an-era echoes of Canada's high days of constitutional politics. Their sheer existence was a product of Chrétien's unwanted inheritance from the Charlottetown era: the Royal Commission on Aboriginal Peoples, which Mulroney had established in 1991 as a time-buying signal of future federal action on the constitutional grievances of Métis, Inuit, and First Nations. Furthermore, the relatively low cost and careful vigilance on the implications of apology that characterized the Arctic relocation and residential schools initiatives also reflected Ottawa's determination to resist the sort of bold reconciliatory moves that might excite the populist outrage known euphemistically as "constitutional fatigue." Accordingly, in a decision emblematizing the new post-Charlottetown constitutional approach, the Chrétien government ignored the royal commission's emphasis on speedy, comprehensive self-government negotiations, offering truncated responses to the commission's more specific calls for residential schools reparations and High Arctic relocation redress instead (Canada 1994b, 163-64; Canada 2004f, chap. 10).

This approach to Aboriginal redress issues is a relatively undiscussed demonstration of the federal government's broader post-referendum policy of constitutional deflection and disengagement. Harvey Lazar (1998, 28, 4, 9) describes the policy as follows: hoping for "emotions ... to cool," Chrétien put "major constitutional reform into the political deep freeze" while deploying "one at a time ... legislative or administrative solutions" whenever particular unity problems became impossible to ignore. Assessing the contemporary state of reparations politics in Canada will demonstrate the policy's continued impact on Ottawa's approach to matters of historical redress.

Redress Politics: The Contemporary Canadian Scene

The current federal approach to redress alternates between outright refusal and stealthy avoidance, punctuated by the occasional positive response grudgingly extended in the face of legal action or awkward controversy.[4] For instance, in 1994 the federal government refused to redress or apologize for the Chinese head tax, then began desultory talks with the Chinese Canadian National Council after the commencement of litigation in the case of *Mack v. Attorney General of Canada*, only to abandon negotiations in September 2002 when the Ontario Court of Appeal ruled that the plaintiffs had failed to disclose a reasonable cause of action (Chinese Canadian National Council 2004).[5]

For its part, the federal government's recent commemorative acknowledgment of the Acadian deportation demonstrates how international embarrassment can prompt a temporary departure from Ottawa's alternating policy of refusal and avoidance. Although the package did not include an apology or financial compensation, on 10 December 2003 Intergovernmental Affairs Minister Stéphane Dion issued a Royal Proclamation recognizing "the historical fact of the [1755-63] Acadian deportation" (Canada 2003b). On the same subject, Heritage Minister Sheila Copps announced that, starting in 2005, 28 July would be marked as "A Day of Commemoration of the Great Upheaval" (Canada 2004a). In this case, Queen Elizabeth's October 2003 visit to New Brunswick had provided a crucial focal point for Acadian demands. Soon after the queen's visit, during which at least one heckler had shouted, "Give back the land you stole from my ancestors in 1755," Buckingham Palace and the federal Cabinet began secret discussions that led Ottawa to issue the proclamation on the queen's behalf (Boswell 2003, A5).

The prospect of international embarrassment may also have prompted what appears to be Ottawa's vaguely favourable reaction to a recent United Nations report. In March 2004, Doudou Diène, the United Nations special rapporteur on racism, reported on his fact-finding visit to Canada, calling "for an intellectual and ethical strategy which could respond adequately to the deep emotional and psychological experience of discrimination and encourage attitudes to evolve towards a [deeper] form of multiculturalism" (United Nations Commission on Human Rights 2004). As one potential instance of such a strategy in action, Diène urged redress for the 1964-67 destruction of Halifax's historic Africville community and relocation of its residents. The federal heritage department and the Government of Nova Scotia have since commenced what seem to be serious discussions with the Africville Genealogy Society on the matter (MacKinlay 2004, 8).[6] Although Diène also recommended head-tax redress, the insistence of the Chinese Canadian National Council on a minimum of $23 million compensation (the amount collected under the tax, without interest or inflation) founders against what appears to be Ottawa's equal determination to avoid spending significant sums on redress.

The residential schools file is a revealing example of a piecemeal response offered reluctantly in the face of litigation followed by positive action after an awkward controversy. Aboriginal leaders have pressed consistently for a public inquiry into the operation and legacy of the schools and for a broad-gauged compensatory response to the racist policy that the schools were designed to effect: the cultural extinction of Aboriginal peoples. For years, Ottawa refused to accept these demands, preferring to focus instead on minimizing the financial impact of the *Baxter* class action suit, in which over ten thousand former residential schools students sought approximately $12 billion in damages for their experiences of physical and sexual abuse. To this end, the office of Indian Residential Schools Resolution Canada was charged with establishing an alternative dispute resolution process, with $1.7 billion earmarked for the settlement of individual abuse claims (Assembly of First Nations 2004). Ottawa also spent considerable energy, achieving mixed results, in seeking to persuade the churches which ran the schools in its name to agree to share some of these alternative settlement costs (Canada 2003a). However, following strong pressure from the federal opposition parties, reports of suicides among survivors frustrated by an unresponsive dispute-resolution process, and blistering attacks from Native elders at parliamentary committee hearings on the issue, in November 2005 the federal

Liberal government agreed to expedite the claims of elderly survivors, to provide enhanced compensation, and to initiate some form of "truth and reconciliation" forum on the schools, including an official apology (Assembly of
First Nations 2006).

In summary, the federal government's post-Charlottetown engagement
with redress issues has been reluctant and episodic. To use psychologist and
redress expert Brandon Hamber's helpful distinction (2004; cf. Abu-Laban
2001), Ottawa avoids processes of *reparation:* broad, negotiated ensembles of
explicitly interlinked acts oriented toward transforming historically unjust
relations. Instead, it seeks to defuse particular controversies with low-profile,
scattered instances of *reparations.* In this approach, Ottawa appears motivated
not only by fiscal caution but also by distaste for any initiative redolent of
the community-refashioning dangers of constitutional politics.

Yet when we consider the extraordinary braking impact of Canada's recent constitutional history, the sheer persistence of reparative demands is
also striking. In a country suffering such a chronic case of constitutional
hypersensitivity syndrome, their survival – to say nothing of their capacity to
attract the occasional positive response – suggests the presence of a powerful
underlying momentum keeping redress on the national agenda.

Citing Torpey (2001, 2003b), I suggested earlier that redress politics points
to an important transformation in our view of what counts as a repairable
injustice and a corresponding enlargement of our sense of responsibility toward particular sorts of victims. Obvious acts of racism or colonialism committed against discrete groups are seen, at least potentially, as injustices that
engage communal duties of atonement and repair. This is a positive development. But its coexistence with the decline of egalitarian redistribution makes
it important to ask about the "postsocialist" context in which it takes place.
The key question is whether the decline of redistribution and the rise of
redress movements are products of a larger underlying trend. This trend re-
shapes the moral contours of contemporary Canadian citizenship, combining a new sensitivity to past racist policies that unjustly harmed the innocent
with an indifference toward those whose suffering seems either to lack the
requisite "innocent" quality or to have been caused by market forces.

But focusing on Canada's recent constitutional experience has also served
to highlight the difficulties that redress claimants face when the dominant
society acquires a well-honed aversion to country-changing deeds of contrition. Perhaps further insight can be gained by considering a different type of

reparative claims making, one that attracts the sympathy commanded by discourses of innocence while escaping the burdens that often plague so-called special interests: victim compensation in the wake of natural disasters.

Situating Disaster Compensation

As Canada's recent forest fires, floods, and an unprecedented ice storm may suggest, the processes associated with global warming appear to be contributing to an increase in the sort of extreme weather events that make disaster compensation necessary (Dore and Etkin 2000). At the same time, the political importance of disaster compensation is growing. Keenly aware of the television media's obsessive interest in spectacular calamities, elected officials descend upon disaster sites, don the requisite photo-friendly emergency gear, and then pledge their dedication to ensuring maximum compensation for the victims: a phenomenon that a skeptical American observer calls the "disaster racket" (Beinart 1997).

In a recent conversation, my colleague Jeremy Wilson gave these developments an arresting label. Referencing sociologist and Third Way policy guru Anthony Giddens' call for a new, "social investment state" (1998; cf. Jenson and Saint-Martin 2003; Saint-Martin, Chap. 13, this volume), Wilson wondered whether we might speculate about a potential future "permanent-emergency compensation state" instead: a neo-liberalized welfare state, seeking to confine its assistance to the truly "deserving," ignoring the victims of market-driven politics (Leys 2003), while becoming increasingly preoccupied with compensating the growing ranks of natural-disaster victims that global warming is expected to create. I now want to consider what light this scenario might shed on the changing moral contours of contemporary Canadian citizenship. But first, a preliminary comparison with the politics of historical redress is in order.

In situations where the event or policy is widely understood as unjust, and the victim community supports the claim, groups seeking historical redress appear to face two key barriers. The first is the difficulty of demonstrating a sufficiently straightforward link between present-day suffering and some earlier catastrophic episode. For example, Rhoda E. Howard-Hassmann (2004) argues that the chances of success will diminish once the passage of time begins to cloud the causal relationship between the past event and the group's contemporary plight. As Howard-Hassmann (ibid., 824) reports in a powerful comparative study of reparations, "it is much easier to effect change when facts are about recent events, and apply to a finite number of living, identifiable individuals ... than to effect change when the facts are about a seemingly infinite number of unknown people, many generations of whom are long dead."

Groups seeking historical redress face more than the broadly evidential problems stemming from the passage of time. Because the culpability of a victimizing agent is an important element in historical redress claims, the movement must also achieve political or legal success in affixing responsibility to its target (ibid., 826). This second criterion can be important even in cases of relatively recent injustices. For instance, Michael Orsini's (2002) analysis of Canada's tainted-blood scandal shows how the bitter debates around compensating persons infected with hepatitis C hinged on differing interpretations of the scope of federal responsibility for the fiasco.

Therefore, launching a successful historical redress claim appears to require demonstrating convincing linkages between the harm suffered, a precipitating policy or event, and the contemporary responsibility of the actor said to be answerable for the harm. Other things being equal, these requirements will tend to be less burdensome when there is a relatively short intervening time frame between the wrongful policy or act and the redress claim.

For further clarification, we can envision a field distinguishing redress for past injustices from disaster compensation on two dimensions. One dimension is the presence or absence of a victimizing agent; the other is the length of time between the relevant event and the claim. Historical redress involves the presence of a victimizing agent and a relatively lengthy intervening time frame. By contrast, disaster compensation lacks a victimizing agent and has a fairly short intervening time frame. Orsini's topic, compensation for victims of medical wrongdoing, involves the presence of a victimizing agent but may entail slightly lengthier intervening time frames, as some years may pass before the nature of the wrong comes to light and victims are able to seek compensation. These considerations are rendered visually in Figure 15.1.

Both of the relevant considerations, intervening time frames and the question of the victimizing agent, favour disaster-relief claimants. First, extremely short intervening time frames make it easy to link disaster losses to a discrete precipitating event. Second, claimants are not required to identify or, still less, do battle with a victimizing agent in the wake of what the insurance companies call "acts of God." This second consideration is particularly important. It means more than noting that disaster compensation claims

Figure 15.1

Distinguishing historical redress, medical compensation, and disaster compensation

Victimizing agent

Historical redress		Medical compensation	
			Disaster compensation

No victimizing agent

(Past on left vertical axis, Present on right vertical axis)

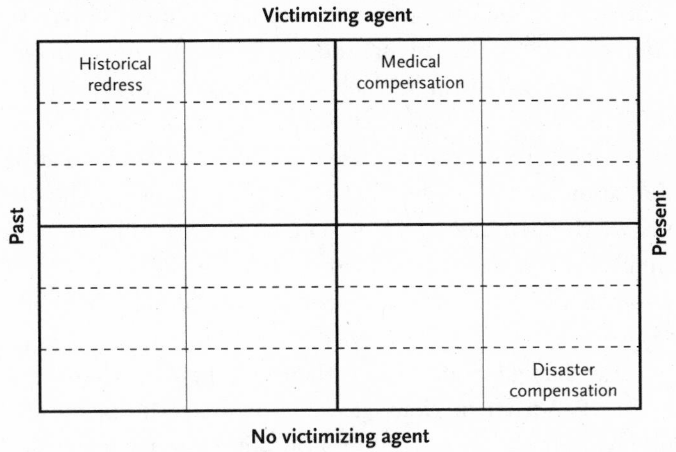

evade the ubiquitous institutional reluctance to own the misdeeds of predecessor incarnations. Because they arise from "acts of God" rather than from, say, injustices of racism or colonialism, they also avoid threatening the prestige and self-image of the dominant society. Thus, disaster-relief claims may fare well in a political climate averse to both the confrontational stresses of constitutional-cum-identity politics and the expenditure of public funds on the evidently less-than-innocent.

Disaster Relief in Canada

Expenditures under Ottawa's Disaster Financial Assistance Arrangements (DFAA) have risen sharply since the early 1990s. Established in 1970, and administered by the Office of Critical Infrastructure Protection and Emergency Preparedness, the DFAA establish an automatic, escalating cost-sharing formula that leaves most of the specific decision making about compensation to provincial governments (see Canada 2004d).

Following a natural disaster or emergency, individuals and businesses are typically required to submit their damage claims to their municipality. Municipalities then submit these claims and their own infrastructure costs to provincial governments, which are responsible for determining the levels and targets of compensation. Once a province's eligible disaster expenses exceed $1 per capita of its population, the DFAA formula is triggered. Eligible expenses include costs of emergency and recovery operations, infrastructure repair and replacement, and compensation for uninsured losses incurred by businesses and individuals. Once the $1 per capita floor is reached, the next $2 per capita in costs elicit federal compensation at 50 percent of submitted eligible provincial expenses. The next $2 per capita attracts compensation at the rate of 75 percent of provincial expenses, and any further expenses are compensated at 90 percent. In practice, this means that relatively small disasters are left to individual municipalities and provinces, with Ottawa taking a proportionately greater role as the financial magnitude of the disaster rises.

Even after the figures are converted into 2004 dollars (Canada 2003c), it is clear that DFAA payments have grown immensely. During the 1970s, total expenditures were just over $240 million. Although payments declined to about $142 million for the 1980s, disbursements during the 1990s rose to almost $978 million. And payments for the first three years of the current decade have already reached approximately $410 million – almost three times the total amount spent during the entire 1980s. Although there is as yet no clear trend showing expenditures rising as a percentage of GDP, disaster relief has certainly held its own, rising from 0.003 percent during the 1980s to 0.014 percent for the 1990s.[7] In contrast, total Canadian government expenditures on income-security programs have actually fallen as a percentage of GDP, from a high of 13.51 percent in 1992 to 10.05 percent in 2002.[8]

It should also be noted that the DFAA figures underestimate disaster and emergency expenditures. For instance, health emergencies such as Toronto's SARS outbreak do not qualify for DFAA assistance. In addition, a variety of federal agencies, departments, and ministries offer ad hoc compensation payments that fall outside the DFAA's purview. The Canadian Food Inspection Agency, Agriculture Canada, Health Canada, Western Economic Diversification, FedNor, Industry Canada, FedQ, the Atlantic Canada Opportunities Agency, the Department of National Defence, and the Department of Finance have all transferred disaster-relief funds to other levels of government, businesses, and individuals.[9] Finally, the DFAA figures do not include provincial or municipal expenditures that were either ineligible under the federal guidelines or too small to trigger the cost-sharing formula.

The Risk Society and Canada's Welfare State

To think about the import of the rising profile of disaster compensation for Canada's welfare state, it is useful to draw on social theorist Ulrich Beck's (1992) notion of the "risk society." Although there is considerable debate about Beck's approach (Adam, Beck, and Van Loon 2000), scholars agree that the risks on which a society chooses to focus will reveal much about its fears and priorities. Thus, geographer Kenneth Hewitt (2000, 334-35) argues that the growing preoccupation with disaster risks at a time of redistributive decline illustrates society's mounting indifference toward the hazards that low-income people face in capitalism.

Also useful is the focus of anthropologist Mary Douglas on risk awareness and identification as bases of social order and control: a focus conveyed by her classic titles *Purity and Danger* (1966) and *Risk and Blame* (1992). Sociologist Alan Scott has taken this emphasis on the broadly political function of risk in a particularly helpful direction. Discussing the case of environmentalism in Germany, Scott (2000, 41-42) maintains that the pressing sense of hazard that characterizes contexts of elevated risk consciousness may be a potent tool for mobilizing collective sentiments of social solidarity. The Western media and public response to the December 2004 Asian tsunami suggests that Scott's point may also apply at the global level. Indeed, the case of Hurricane Katrina in the United States – in which the initial incompetent response was followed by widespread public furor, the replacement of key officials, expressions of presidential contrition, and dramatic increases in aid – suggests that natural disasters can prompt even right-wing Republican regimes into actions of solidarity across lines of class and race. I now want to suggest that this diagnostic focus on the political significance of risk can help us to think about key changes in the contemporary Canadian welfare state.

Notwithstanding the ongoing debate about the magnitude of social policy retrenchment in advanced capitalism (Hacker 2004), it is clear that neo-liberal ideology and governance are altering Canadian social policy. One important development is the increasing hardship visited on the welfare state's least popular clients: unemployed persons and able-bodied indigent people (Doern, Maslove, and Prince 1988, 155). Thus, the 1995 cancellation of the Canada Assistance Plan eliminated the automatic fifty-fifty cost-sharing formula that once shielded welfare recipients from provincial attack, while a series of punitive alterations has sharply reduced the generosity and scope of the federal Employment Insurance program (Hurtig 1999; McBride and Shields 1997).

As these developments might suggest, social policy discussion seems increasingly influenced by discourses of innocence and desert. For instance, Canadian politicians of all stripes trumpet their commitment to a new national pharmacare program at a time when health care expenditures are already consuming well over 30 percent of most provincial budgets (Maioni 2002, 93). The imperative to help only deserving, "innocent" victims has certainly had a profound effect on anti-poverty campaigners, who focus increasingly on the plight of poor children in a tactical response to the demonization of poor children's parents (Chen 2003).

Yet at the same time, the growing involvement of the senior levels of government has made disaster relief a new element in Canada's welfare state. Since the 1960s, as Figure 15.2 shows, the pattern of disaster-relief contribution has been completely reversed. Whereas the vast majority of disasters prior to the 1960s drew aid from municipalities and private charities, with virtually no federal or provincial spending, the opposite is now true: the

FIGURE 15.2

Disaster and emergency relief contributions

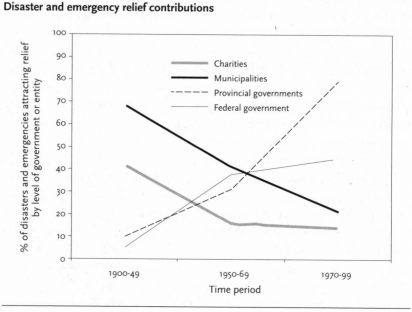

senior levels of government have taken over the financial side of disaster relief almost entirely.

Two developments are likely to heighten the federal role in particular. First, the profile of the Office of Critical Infrastructure Protection and Emergency Preparedness, the main national body responsible for disaster relief, seems set to rise with its recent transfer from the Department of National Defence to the new Ministry of Public Safety and Emergency Preparedness (Canada 2004e) – itself a response to the political importance of emergency management in the wake of the 9/11 attacks (Henstra 2003; see Salter, this volume). Second, provincial complaints about the DFAA's failure to cover a sufficiently wide range of emergency situations have prompted an ongoing program review that seems likely to result in an expansion of the DFAA (Nuutilainen 2002).

Innocence and Solidarity: Four Canadian Disasters

To further explore the political significance of disaster compensation, the following section looks briefly at political response and discourse in the wake of four Canadian natural disasters: the Edmonton tornado of 1987 (27 killed, $665,483,000 in estimated costs), the Montreal flood of 1987 (2 killed, $86,729,000 in estimated costs), the Saguenay floods of 1996 (10 killed, $1,722,343,000 in estimated costs), and the 1998 ice storm in eastern Ontario, Quebec, and New Brunswick (28 killed, $5,410,184,000 in estimated costs). Excepting instances of drought and crop failure, which I leave aside as primarily commercial emergencies with distinctive mechanisms of compensation, these cases, which represent a mix of regions, population centres, and linguistic contexts, are among the most costly Canadian natural disasters of the 1980s and 1990s (see Canada 2004b).

A key theme is what appears to be a diminishing skepticism toward disaster relief claims. In the case of the 1987 Edmonton tornado, Alberta public safety minister Ken Kowalski threatened fraud charges against the authors of "outrageous damage claims" ("Tornado Claims" 1987, F9). Similarly, after the 1987 Montreal flood, Quebec supply and services minister Gilles Rocheleau warned victims, "We are not an insurance company ... It's not Father Christmas passing by" (in Scott and Harris 1987, A1). Public officials in the late 1990s struck a different tone. After the 1996 Saguenay floods, Quebec premier Lucien Bouchard proclaimed, "I think we're going to beat the speed record in terms of putting the [disaster-relief] program in place" (in Thompson 1996a, A1). As one news report noted, Bouchard's response "raised questions of fairness and hopes of increased compensation among victims of previous natural disasters" (Thompson 1996b, A3). When asked about the mounting relief costs of the 1998 ice storm, Prime Minister Jean Chrétien expressed the new mood perfectly: "It's not my biggest preoccupation" (in Bryden 1998, A1).

A related theme is the growing personal attention that politicians pay to disaster victims. In the case of the 1987 Edmonton tornado, Prime Minister Mulroney visited the disaster site only because he was already in Edmonton making a scheduled announcement about the Western economic diversification program (Fisher 1987, A9). No federal or provincial officials visited the areas affected by the 1987 Montreal flood – indeed, Mayor Jean Doré left on holidays the day after the event (Norris and Semenak 1987, A1). By contrast, Prime Minister Chrétien and Premier Bouchard both took high-profile tours of the Saguenay in 1996; communities hit by the ice storm also saw veritable parades of visiting officials, including Chrétien, Quebec premier Bernard Landry, and Ontario premier Mike Harris.

Disaster response also seems increasingly important as a ritualized means of promoting social cohesion. As one columnist rather pointedly noted, the 1996 Saguenay floods, which came on the heels of 1995's near-miss sovereignty referendum, "provided an opportunity for other Canadians to show Quebecers ... that the national solidarity of which Bouchard so often speaks is not confined within Quebec's borders" (Macpherson 1996, A21). Thus, maverick Calgary MP Jan Brown drove a truck across the country to deliver donated relief goods to the Saguenay, proclaiming, "this is from us in the West" (in "Calgary MP" 1996, A3).

But the phenomenon goes beyond the post-referendum response to the 1996 Saguenay floods. For example, Premier Harris toured communities hit by Ontario's 1998 ice storm to praise the "unprecedented selflessness" of volunteers, saying, apparently at more than one stop, "I'm going to ask you when you see someone you know who was there when their community needed them, who may not be here today, I will ask you to tell them that Mike says thanks to them, too" (in Egan 1998, C1). Or as federal finance minister Paul Martin enthused in the wake of the ice storm, "Canadians have demonstrated ... that in times of crisis this country comes together. It is that deep feeling of mutual help and tremendous mutual affection that I think is one of the strongest ties in the land" (in Authier 1998, A4). The recent BSE crisis, SARS outbreak, and 2003 forest-fire season in British Columbia have all provided similar platforms for this sort of political ceremony and rhetoric.

Therefore, just as income security is beginning to revisit its classical liberal position as a matter left to markets and charities, natural disasters find an elevated status as risks to be borne collectively by the whole political community. Dominant conceptions of innocence, desert, and civic harmony appear to be key in the process. Politicians see disaster compensation as a chance to display conspicuous compassion, while governments view disaster response as an opportunity to stoke citizen emotions of solidarity and pride.

Why be concerned? One reason is that disaster compensation tends to be regressive. Although the precipitating decisions about payment are made under a welter of provincial programs which seem continually under renovation, disaster-assistance programs typically compensate people and businesses for some portion of uninsured losses. Despite whatever ceilings a program may impose, the logic of compensating losses means that, in total, businesses are likely to receive more compensation than individuals, and wealthy people are likely to receive more compensation than individuals of lesser means.

For example, consider the regime for home and furniture replacement introduced by the social-democratic Parti Québécois in 1996 (see Thompson 1996a, A1; 1996b, A3). Under the Quebec program, the single owner of a $500,000 house is potentially eligible for $415,000 in compensation, the single owner of a $200,000 house can receive up to $190,000, and a single tenant can apply for a maximum of $10,000. Although information about business, as opposed to homeowner, compensation is harder to come by, the case of the 1987 Edmonton tornado is suggestive. Of the roughly $59 million transferred by the Alberta government to businesses and individuals, $40 million went to businesses, $10 million to farmers, and $9 million to individuals (Kondro 1987, F1).

Conclusion

This is not to say that disaster compensation is itself wrong or is poised to dwarf the disappearing redistributive elements of a dying welfare state. But disaster compensation may be filling an ideological void left by the neoliberalization of the Canadian welfare state. In egalitarian redistribution, the connections between suffering and desert seem less publicly accepted, as a renewed emphasis on the individual's responsibility for her economic fate returns poverty to its Victorian status as a stigmatic emblem of moral failure (cf. Beck 1992, 91-101). In such a context, disaster compensation assumes ideological power; it offers an island of respite from market individualism by allowing the polity to display sensitivity toward "genuine" victims, while summoning performances of community spirit that recall the days before we went "bowling alone" (Putnam 2000). Here, then, is the spectre of the permanent-emergency compensation state. To be clear, this is a dramatized scenario of future political warning and not a cool exercise in social-scientific prediction. Although potent taboos around "special interests" constrain reparative sensibilities where questions of racism and colonialism are concerned, disaster compensation seems almost incapable of attracting critics. The targets of its compassion are as uncontroversial as its performances of solidarity are memorable. Meanwhile, the frequency and costs of natural disasters are increasing. If this trend continues unabated, the financial costs and ideological effects of our move toward the permanent-emergency compensation state would constitute an immense barrier to the project of building a fairer and less class-ridden society.

ACKNOWLEDGMENTS
The author wishes to thank Paul Dyck, Shauna McRanor, and Diane Vermilyea for superb research assistance, Michael Orsini and Jeremy Wilson for inspiring conversations, Lianne Bellisario, Dianne Borg, Frank Cosentino, and Margaret Purdy for insights and information about disasters and disaster compensation, Alan Cairns, Michael Orsini, Miriam Smith, and an anonymous reviewer for extremely helpful feedback on earlier drafts of the chapter, and the Social Sciences and Humanities Research Council of Canada for financial support (grant no. 410-2004-0301).

NOTES
1 Thanks to Alan Cairns for helping me to conceptualize disaster compensation as a change within the broader architecture of the welfare state.
2 Mentioning the case of Japanese Canadians, Trudeau first introduced the "just in our time" theme while defending the White Paper on Indian Policy in 1969. See Sally Weaver (1981, 179).
3 Iacovetta and Ventresca (2000) stress the appeasement dynamic in reference to the Italian Canadian case. On the ethnic-minority opposition to Meech more generally, see Matt James (2006b).
4 For a similar assessment, see Gerald L. Gall, May M. Cheng, and Keiko Miki (2001).

5   For analysis of the decision, see the contributions in David Dyzenhaus and Mayo Moran (2005).

6   Wayn Hamilton, interim executive director, Office of African Nova Scotian Affairs, personal communication, 30 April 2004.

7   Calculated in current (2003) dollars using GDP data from the CANSIM database at the University of Toronto CHASS facility (see http://datacenter2.chass.utoronto.ca/cansim2/index.jsp) and Canada (2003c).

8   Figures in current (2003) dollars from Canada (2005). "Income-security programs" comprise the following: federal and provincial tax expenditures targeting families with children, Family Allowances, Old-Age Security, Guaranteed Income Supplement, Spouse's Allowance, federal training and employment programs, provincial social assistance programs, federal social assistance for registered Indians, veterans' pensions and allowances, GST credit, Canada/Quebec Pension Plan, Unemployment Insurance, and workers' compensation.

9   Frank Cosentino, Treasury Board Secretariat, personal communication, 2 December 2003.

REFERENCES

Abu-Laban, Yasmeen. 2001. "The Future and the Legacy: Globalization and the Canadian Settler-State." *Journal of Canadian Studies* 35: 262-76.

Adam, Barbara, Ulrich Beck, and Joost Van Loon, eds. 2000. *The Risk Society and Beyond: Critical Issues for Social Theory.* London: Sage Publications.

Assembly of First Nations. 2004. "AFN Residential Schools Unit Update." http://www.afn.ca/Assembly_of_First_Nations.htm.

—. 2006. "Assembly of First Nations National Chief Applauds Historic Reconciliation and Compensation Agreement as a Major Victory for Residential School Survivors." http://www.afn.ca/residentialschools/index.html.

Authier, Philip. 1998. "Martin Avoids Scoring Points: Ice Storm Not a Political Football, Minister Says." *Ottawa Citizen*, 31 January, A4.

Barkan, Elazar. 2000. *The Guilt of Nations: Restitution and Negotiating Historical Injustices.* New York: Norton.

Barry, Brian. 2001. *Culture and Equality: An Egalitarian Critique of Multiculturalism.* Cambridge, MA: Harvard University Press.

Beck, Ulrich. 1992. *Risk Society: Towards a New Modernity*, trans. Mark Ritter. London: Sage Publications.

Beinart, Peter. 1997. "Courting Disaster." *New Republic* 217(1): 11-12.

Boswell, Randy. 2003. "Acadians to Finally Receive Apology for Deportations." *Vancouver Sun*, 4 December, A5.

Brooks, Roy L., ed. 1999. *When Sorry Isn't Enough: The Controversy over Apologies and Reparations for Human Injustice.* New York: New York University Press.

Bryden, Joan. 1998. "PM Promises Compensation." *Windsor Star*, 13 January, A1.

Butler, Judith. 1997. "Merely Cultural." *Social Text* 15: 265-77.

Cairns, Alan C. 1995. *Reconfigurations: Canadian Citizenship and Constitutional Change: Selected Essays,* ed. Douglas E. Williams. Toronto: McClelland and Stewart.

"Calgary MP to Deliver Aid to Quebec Flood Victims." 1996. *Vancouver Sun,* 1 August, A3.

Canada. 1994a. Ministry of Canadian Heritage. "Ministry of Canadian Heritage News Release: Sheila Finestone Tables and Sends Letter on Redress to Ethnocultural Organizations." 14 December.

—. 1994b. Royal Commission on Aboriginal Peoples. *The High Arctic Relocation: A Report on the 1953-55 Relocation.* Ottawa: Minister of Supply and Services.

—. 1997. Department of Canadian Heritage. *Final Report on the Implementation of the Japanese Canadian Redress Agreement, 1988.* Ottawa: Department of Canadian Heritage.

—. 2003a. Office of Indian Residential Schools Resolution Canada. "Negotiations Update." http://www.irsr-rqpa.gc.ca/English/information_sheets.html.

—. 2003b. Privy Council Office. "Acadia Forever!" Notes for an Address by the Honourable Stéphane Dion, President of the Privy Council and Minister of Intergovernmental Affairs, Delivered on the Occasion of the Royal Proclamation Recognizing the Acadian Deportation, 10 December 2003. http://www.pco-bcp.gc.ca/AIA/default.asp?Language=E&Page=pressroom&Sub=Speeches&Doc=20031210_e.htm.

—. 2003c. Public Safety and Emergency Preparedness Canada. "DFAA Payments Made by Government of Canada, Per Year." Prepared for the author by Dianne Borg, Office of Critical Infrastructure Protection and Emergency Preparedness, 8 December.

—. 2004a. Department of Canadian Heritage. "Department of Canadian Heritage News Release: Minister Copps Announces a Day of Commemoration of the Great Upheaval." http://www.pch.gc.ca/newsroom/index_e.cfm?fuseaction=displayDocument&DocIDCd.

—. 2004b. Public Safety and Emergency Preparedness Canada. Canadian Disaster Database. http://www.ocipep.gc.ca/disaster/search.asp?lang=eng.

—. 2004c. Public Safety and Emergency Preparedness Canada. Canadian Disaster Database Version 4.2. Custom edition prepared for the author by Lianne Bellisario, Division of Research and Development, Public Safety and Emergency Preparedness Canada, 16 February.

—. 2004d. Public Safety and Emergency Preparedness Canada. "Public Safety and Emergency Preparedness Canada Fact Sheet: Disaster Financial Assistance Arrangements." http://www.ocipep-bpiepc.gc.ca/info_pro/fact_sheets/general/FA_df_assist_e.asp.

—. 2004e. Public Safety and Emergency Preparedness Canada. "Securing Canada's Health and Safety." http://www.sgc.gc.ca/publications/news/20031212_e.asp.

—. 2004f. Royal Commission on Aboriginal Peoples. "Residential Schools." Chap. 10 in *Looking Forward, Looking Back*. Vol. 1 of *Report of the Royal Commission on Aboriginal Peoples*. http://www.ainc-inac.gc.ca/ch/rcap/sg/.

—. 2005. Social Development Canada. Social Security Statistics, Canada and Provinces, 1978-79 to 2002-03. http://www.sdc.gc.ca/en/cs/sp/sdc/socpol/tables/page02. shtml.

Chen, Xiaobei. 2003. "The Birth of the Child-Victim Citizen." In *Reinventing Canada: Politics of the 21st Century*, ed. Janine Brodie and Linda Trimble, 189-202. Toronto: Prentice-Hall.

Chinese Canadian National Council. 1988. *It Is Only Fair! Redress for the Head Tax and Chinese Exclusion Act*. Toronto: Chinese Canadian National Council.

—. 2004. "Chinese Head Tax and Exclusion Act Redress Backgrounder." http://www.ccnc. ca/currentIssues/Redress-Backgrounder.doc.

Clarkson, Stephen. 2002. *Uncle Sam and Us: Globalization, Neoconservatism, and the Canadian State*. Toronto: University of Toronto Press.

Dafoe, Christopher. 1994. "Lining Up for Compensation." In *Righting an Injustice: The Debate over Redress for Canada's First National Internment Operations*, ed. Lubomyr Luciuk, 40. Toronto: Justinian Press.

Doern, Bruce, Allan Maslove, and Michael Prince. 1988. *Public Budgeting in Canada*. Ottawa: Carleton University Press.

Dore, Mohammed, and David Etkin. 2000. "The Importance of Measuring the Social Costs of Natural Disasters at a Time of Climate Change." *Australian Journal of Emergency Management* 15: 46-51.

Douglas, Mary. 1966. *Purity and Danger: An Analysis of Concepts of Pollution and Taboo*. London: Routledge and Kegan Paul.

—. 1992. *Risk and Blame: Essays in Cultural Theory*. London: Routledge.

Dyzenhaus, David, and Mayo Moran, eds. 2005. *Calling Power to Account: Law, Reparations, and the Chinese Canadian Head Tax Case*. Toronto: University of Toronto Press.

Egan, Kelly. 1998. "Premier Praises Storm-Hit Towns." *Ottawa Citizen*, 21 March, C1.

Fisher, Matthew. 1987. "Mulroney Visits Edmonton's Devastated Trailer Park." *Globe and Mail*, 4 August, A9.

Fraser, Nancy. 1997. *Justice Interruptus: Critical Reflections on the "Postsocialist" Condition*. New York: Routledge.

—. 2000. "Rethinking Recognition." *New Left Review* 3: 107-20.

—. 2001. "Recognition without Ethics?" *Theory, Culture and Society* 18: 21-42.

Fraser, Nancy, and Axel Honneth. 2003. *Redistribution or Recognition: A Political-Philosophical Exchange*. London: Verso.

Gall, Gerald L., May M. Cheng, and Keiko Miki. 2001. "Redress for Past Government Wrongs." Issue position paper, Working Group on Issues Development, Advisory

Committee to the Secretary of State (Multiculturalism) (Status of Women) on Canada's Preparations for the UN World Conference against Racism. http://www.pch.gc.ca/progs/multi/wcar/advisory/redress_e.shtml.

Giddens, Anthony. 1998. *The Third Way: The Renewal of Social Democracy.* Cambridge: Polity Press.

Hacker, Jacob S. 2004. "Privatizing Risk without Privatizing the Welfare State: The Hidden Politics of Social Policy Retrenchment in the United States." *American Political Science Review* 98: 243-60.

Hamber, Brandon. 2004. "Reparations as Symbol: Narratives of Resistance, Reticence and Possibility in South Africa." Paper presented at Reparations: An Interdisciplinary Examination of Some Philosophical Issues, Queen's University, Kingston, 8 February.

"Hefty Price Tag Delays Settlements." 1993. *Calgary Herald,* 1 June, A12.

Henstra, Dan. 2003. "Federal Emergency Management in Canada and the United States after 11 September 2001." *Canadian Public Administration* 46: 103-16.

Hewitt, Kenneth. 2000. "Safe Place or 'Catastrophic Society'? Perspectives on Hazards and Disasters in Canada." *Canadian Geographer* 44: 325-41.

Hobson, Barbara, ed. 2003. *Recognition Struggles and Social Movements: Contested Identities, Agency, and Power.* Cambridge: Cambridge University Press.

Honneth, Axel. 1995. *The Struggle for Recognition: The Moral Grammar of Social Conflicts,* trans. Joel Anderson. Cambridge: Polity Press.

Howard-Hassmann, Rhoda E. 2004. "Getting to Reparations: Japanese Americans and African Americans." *Social Forces* 83: 823-40.

Hurtig, Mel. 1999. *Pay the Rent or Feed the Kids: The Tragedy and Disgrace of Poverty in Canada.* Toronto: McClelland and Stewart.

Iacovetta, Franca, and Robert Ventresca. 2000. "Redress, Collective Memory, and the Politics of History." In *Enemies Within: Italian and Other Internees in Canada and Abroad,* ed. Franca Iacovetta, Roberto Perin, and Angelo Principe, 379-412. Toronto: University of Toronto Press.

James, Matt. 1999. "Redress Politics and Canadian Citizenship." In *The State of the Federation 1998: How Canadians Connect,* ed. Harvey Lazar and Tom McIntosh, 247-81. Kingston: Queen's University Institute of Intergovernmental Relations.

—. 2001. "Being Stigmatized and Being Sorry: Past Injustices and Contemporary Citizenship." In *A Passion for Identity: Canadian Studies in the 21st Century,* ed. David Taras and Beverly Rasporich, 55-75. Scarborough: Nelson.

—. 2006a. "Do Campaigns for Historical Redress Erode the Canadian Welfare State?" In *Multiculturalism and the Welfare State: Recognition and Redistribution in Contemporary Democracies,* ed. Keith Banting and Will Kymlicka. Oxford: Oxford University Press.

—. 2006b. *Misrecognized Materialists: Social Movements in Canadian Constitutional Politics, 1938-1992.* Vancouver: UBC Press.

Jenson, Jane, and Denis Saint-Martin. 2003. "New Routes to Social Cohesion? Citizenship and the Social Investment State." *Canadian Journal of Sociology* 28: 77-99.

Johnston, Richard, André Blais, Elisabeth Gidengil, and Neil Nevitte. 1996. *The Challenge of Direct Democracy: The 1992 Canadian Referendum*. Montreal and Kingston:
McGill-Queen's University Press.

Kobayashi, Audrey. 1992. "The Japanese-Canadian Redress Settlement and Its Implications for 'Race Relations.'" *Canadian Ethnic Studies* 24: 1-19.

Kondro, Wayne. 1987. "Farmers Given $10 Million in Tornado Aid." *Calgary Herald*, 21
August, F1.

Lazar, Harvey. 1998. "Non-constitutional Renewal: Toward a New Equilibrium in the
Federation." In *Canada: The State of the Federation 1997 – Non-Constitutional Renewal*, ed. Harvey Lazar, 3-35. Kingston: Queen's University Institute of Intergovernmental Relations.

Leys, Colin. 2003. *Market-Driven Politics: Neoliberal Democracy and the Public Interest*.
London: Verso.

MacKinlay, Shaune. 2004. "City Won't Attend Africville Meeting." *Halifax Daily News*, 1
May, 8.

Macpherson, Don. 1996. "Why Be Shy over Aid to Quebec Flood Victims?" *Toronto Star*,
8 August, A21.

Maioni, Antonia. 2002. "Health Care in the New Millennium." In *Canadian Federalism:
Performance, Effectiveness, and Legitimacy*, ed. Herman Bakvis and Grace Skogstad,
87-104. Don Mills, ON: Oxford University Press.

Marshall, Thomas H. 1964. *Class, Citizenship and Social Development*, ed. Seymour Martin Lipset. Garden City, NY: Doubleday.

McBride, Stephen, and John Shields. 1997. *Dismantling a Nation: The Transition to Corporate Rule in Canada*. Halifax: Fernwood.

Miki, Arthur K. 2003. *The Japanese Canadian Redress Legacy: A Community Revitalized*.
Winnipeg: National Association of Japanese Canadians.

"MPs Vote to Protect Gays under Hate Law." 2003. CBC.CA News, 18 September. http://
www.cbc.ca/stories/print/2003/09/17/hate030917.

Mullaly, Robert. 1994. "Social Welfare and the New Right: A Class Mobilization Perspective." In *Continuities and Discontinuities: The Political Economy of Social Welfare
and Labour Market Policy in Canada*, ed. Andrew F. Johnson, Stephen McBride, and
Patrick J. Smith, 76-95. Toronto: University of Toronto Press.

Norris, Alexander, and Susan Semenak. 1987. "1,400 Storm Victims File Claims with
City." *Montreal Gazette*, 20 July, A1.

Nuutilainen, Janet. 2002. "OCIPEP: Leading the Way." *Emergency Preparedness Digest*
(January-March). http://www.ocipep.gc.ca/ep/ep_digest/jm_2002_fea1_e.asp.

Orsini, Michael. 2002. "The Politics of Naming, Blaming, and Claiming: HIV, Hepatitis
C, and the Emergence of Blood Activism in Canada." *Canadian Journal of Political
Science* 35: 475-98.

Pal, Leslie A. 2001. *Beyond Policy Analysis: Public Issue Management in Turbulent Times.* Scarborough: Nelson.

Putnam, Robert D. 2000. *Bowling Alone: The Collapse and Revival of American Community.* New York: Simon and Schuster.

Rorty, Richard. 2000. "Is 'Cultural Recognition' a Useful Concept for Leftist Politics?" *Critical Horizons* 1: 7-20.

Scott, Alan. 2000. "Risk Society or Angst Society? Two Views of Risk, Consciousness, and Community." In *The Risk Society and Beyond: Critical Issues for Social Theory,* ed. Barbara Adam, Ulrich Beck, and Joost Van Loon, 33-46. London: Sage Publications.

Scott, Sarah, and Lewis Harris. 1987. "Storm Victims to Get $40 Million for Losses." *Montreal Gazette,* 6 August, A1.

Simpson, Jeffrey. 1994. "Compensation Queue." In *Righting an Injustice: The Debate over Redress for Canada's First National Internment Operations,* ed. Lubomyr Luciuk, 78-79. Toronto: Justinian Press.

Thompson, Elizabeth. 1996a. "Flood Payouts Doubled." *Montreal Gazette,* 25 July, A1.

—. 1996b. "Quebec Offers Generous Deal to Victims of Raging Flood." *Vancouver Sun,* 6 July, A3.

"Tornado Claims Could End in Fraud Charges." 1987. *Vancouver Sun,* 16 October, F9.

Torpey, John. 2001. "'Making Whole What Has Been Smashed': Reflections on Reparations." *Journal of Modern History* 73: 338-58.

—, ed. 2003a. *Politics and the Past: On Repairing Historical Injustices.* Lanham, MD: Rowman and Littlefield.

—. 2003b. "Reparations Politics in Southern Africa." Paper presented at the annual meeting of the Social Science History Association, Baltimore, 15 November.

Tully, James. 2000. "Recognition Redux: Struggles over Recognition and Redistribution." *Constellations* 7(4): 469-82.

United Nations Commission on Human Rights. 2000. *The Right to Restitution, Compensation and Rehabilitation for Victims of Grave Violations of Human Rights and Fundamental Freedoms.* 56th Session, E/CN.4/2000/62, 18 January.

—. 2004. *Report by Mr. Doudou Diène, Special Rapporteur on Contemporary Forms of Racism, Racial Discrimination, Xenophobia, and Related Intolerance: Mission to Canada.* 60th Session, E/CN.4/2004/18/Add.2, 1 March.

Van Parijs, Phillipe, ed. 2004. *Cultural Diversity versus Economic Solidarity.* Brussels: De Boeck Université.

Weaver, Sally. 1981. *Making Canadian Indian Policy.* Toronto: University of Toronto Press.

Young, Iris Marion. 1997. "Unruly Categories: A Critique of Nancy Fraser's Dual Systems Theory." *New Left Review* 222: 147-60.

16

Discourses in Distress: From "Health Promotion" to "Population Health" to "You Are Responsible for Your Own Health"

Michael Orsini

Keeping up with competing health discourses is bewildering at the best of times. On the one hand, the media are dominated by discussions of the so-called bread and butter health "care" reform issues – how to trim waiting lists for surgeries, how to resolve provincial-federal bickering over the publicly funded medicare system, how to ensure that doctors who train in Canada stay in Canada, how to deal with the nursing shortage, and so on. Embedded in these discussions is a firm belief that we can fix the system – and improve the health of Canadians as a result – by making the appropriate changes. On the other hand, there is a growing recognition that health "care" is only one aspect of health. Providing access to MRI machines or the latest health technology may do little to improve the health of Canadians unless, it is argued, these are accompanied by broader structural changes related to the economy and society. Added to this is the realization that unless we have a strong public health infrastructure and fundamentals such as safe water and a safe blood supply, we will be unable to cope with the unforeseen health emergencies that may loom on the horizon. And, finally, if the health landscape weren't complicated enough, the genetics revolution is forcing us to rethink how much of our health may be beyond our individual control, with some thinkers asking profound questions regarding how genetics is altering our relationship to our bodies and our individual and collective identities (see, among others, Petersen and Bunton 2002; Rose and Novas 2005).

Although, with the autumn 2004 announcement of the creation of the Public Health Agency of Canada, public health is back on the government agenda, how we understand terms such as "public health," "health policy," and "health care policy" goes largely underexplored, and this despite the voluminous government documents and reports on the subject, including *Building On Values*, the report of the Commission on the Future of Health

Care in Canada (by Roy Romanow). Although the concept may seem some-what dated, the creation of a federal public health agency, with "pillars" in Ottawa and Winnipeg, has revived interest in the notion that there is such a thing as a public health, one that is worth defending. Public health normally includes two distinct branches: health promotion and health protection. Former national health and welfare minister Marc Lalonde's 1974 report, *A New Perspective on the Health of Canadians*, was the blueprint for the federal government's foray into health promotion. In the report, Lalonde (Govern-ment of Canada 1974, 36) argued that behaviours would have to change and self-imposed risks reduced in order to cut the death rate: "The ultimate philo-sophical issue ... is whether and to what extent government can get into the business of modifying human behaviour, even if it does so to improve health." As is clear, public health encompasses a far broader meaning than is usually allowed. Public health is bound up with moralistic notions of acceptable and unacceptable behaviours. The defence of public health itself is predi-cated on a vision of a "good society."

The impetus for the new public health agency, which is being modelled after the US Centers for Disease Control and Prevention in Atlanta, is related to the much-publicized outbreak in 2003 of Sudden Acute Respiratory Syn-drome (SARS), which killed fifty-six Canadians, as well as a number of scan-dals that shook the public health system to its foundations. In 2000, after their water system was contaminated with *E. coli*, seven residents of the On-tario community of Walkerton died and many others became sick. In the 1980s, the country's blood system became contaminated with HIV and hepa-titis C, resulting in thousands of infections, not to mention a protracted battle between governments and victims demanding compensation (Orsini 2002). Similarly, the 2003 SARS outbreak wreaked havoc on the Toronto economy and cut deeply into its tourism industry. Each of these events ex-posed, in different ways, the fragility of the public health infrastructure.

This chapter explores changing conceptions of the public health and how these have been translated – sometimes without much reflection – into public policy. Although discourses on health may appear to fade in and out of significance, it would be incorrect to assume that this is an arbitrary pro-cess (Robertson 1998, 155). Such discourses "emerge and gain widespread significance primarily because they are more or less congruent with the pre-vailing social, political and economic context within which they are pro-duced, maintained and reproduced" (ibid., 155). It is critical, then, to explore in greater detail these discourses because they help us to uncover how we conceptualize health and how we understand the moral economy of "good" and "bad" health, as well as the respective roles of individuals, societies, governments, and wider structures in explaining health and health outcomes. I begin by exploring the "health promotion" paradigm, which took off in the 1970s following the 1974 release of *A New Perspective on the Health of Canadians* (often called the Lalonde Report). Among health promotion advocates, the early focus on lifestyle eventually gave way to a concern with the role of communities, in particular that of community development, in improving health. This new version became known as the "new public health." Health promotion has since been eclipsed, but not completely obliterated, by the "population health" approach, which was influenced by the work of health economists such as Robert Evans, co-author of the often-cited book *Why Are Some People Healthy and Others Not?* (1994). Although health promotion programs and policies have not been entirely successful in preventing disease and promoting healthy lifestyles – except for some noticeable achievements in the area of tobacco use – I argue that the population health approach suffers from some critical weaknesses of its own, namely, its sloppy insertion of the "social" into its discussion of the determinants of health. Although population health advocates claim to be concerned with the "social determinants of health," they conveniently drop the "social" in discussion with like-minded persons to focus on the "determinants of health." Not surprisingly, it is a short step from speaking about "determinants" of health to positing oversimplified cause-and-effect relationships which purport to explain "health" or the lack of it.

Not unrelated to this shift toward a population health approach is the emergence of a "shadow" paradigm which might be termed a "responsibilization paradigm." Drawing on the governmentality literature (Foucault 1979), researchers are calling our attention to an increasing shift toward the individualization of health and illness (Lupton 1999; Petersen and Bunton 2002). Critics of neo-liberalism are correct to point out that these developments are not confined to the health field (see Smith 2005), noting that the welfare state is being reshaped less around collective redistribution and more around individualized citizens seemingly empowered to take charge of their own affairs. I contend that in order to rescue the social, health research needs to take seriously the insights offered by narrative analysis. Listening to the voices of people living with illness and disease will help us to shape responses to the public health crises and challenges of tomorrow. Already, a number of medical schools in the United States are using an approach called "narrative medicine," which was pioneered by Rita Charon (2004), a medical doctor and professor at Columbia University in New York. The approach helps medical students learn the art of listening to their patients' stories.

That '70s Show: Health Promotion Enters the Lexicon

In 1974, the release of the Lalonde Report marked a watershed in the federal government's approach to health. Interestingly, however, when the report was released as a "green paper" – a "think piece" rather than a government policy – it was dismissed by opposition parties "as solidly in the motherhood realm" (McKay 2000, 1). Many government documents spark initial interest only to fade into the black hole of well-intentioned irrelevance, but interest in the Lalonde Report increased steadily, confounding even its most ardent supporters. Just ten years after its release, it was being hailed as a groundbreaking document, "one of the great achievements of the modern public health movement" (ibid., 2).

Although the "health field" concept had been discussed as early as 1973 in the Canadian Medical Association's journal, the report is credited with introducing the concept into popular discourse. Improving the nation's health, the report argued, required that the concept of health be expanded beyond traditional public health and medical care to consider broader social determinants of health, initially linked mainly to income (Glouberman and Millar 2003; Poland et al. 1998). According to one account (McKay 2000), federal bureaucrats who worked on the report were influenced by the research of Thomas McKeown, a professor of social medicine at the University of Birmingham in England, who shocked his colleagues in the medical community when he argued that the decline in English mortality rates was directly related to changes in living standards, not to advancements in medicine. This argument, later called the "McKeown thesis," is cited in much of the literature on the historical roots of the population health approach. As Simon Szreter explains (2003, 427), however, McKeown's influence should be placed in its proper intellectual context. Although he was primarily interested in knocking scientific medicine off its pedestal, his findings had the effect of reinforcing a form of "simplistic economic determinism," which all too conveniently aided the neo-liberal assault within the field of economics in the 1970s and 1980s.

In particular, the Lalonde Report outlines four components of what became known as the health field concept: human biology, health care systems, environment, and lifestyle. This last component is often viewed as the cornerstone of health promotion as it was defined in its original incarnation, and, indeed, it became the main target of critics in the population health camp. After all, who can forget those television commercials for the *ParticipACTION* program, featuring groups of men and women jogging through the streets in their fashionable seventies athletic apparel? The program long goaded Canadians with ads suggesting that a sixty-year-old Swede was as fit or fitter than a thirty-year-old Canadian.

In the lean, cost-cutting 1990s, however, health promotion began to fall out of favour with policy makers for a number of reasons. As Sholom Glouberman and John Millar (2003, 389) note, health promotion policies did not generate the type of cost savings that had been envisaged. In addition, health promotion programs were showing greatest success in changing the behaviours of the more advantaged members of society, with the situation actually worsening for the less advantaged in areas such as tobacco use, for example. The final nail came with an external evaluation of the federal government's health promotion programs, which concluded that "the paradigm which envisages health as the product of anything and everything does not readily lend itself to being actioned" (ibid.). The stage was therefore set for health researchers to narrow the focus to those determinants of health which, if improved, would provide the most "bang for the health buck."

"Show Me the Evidence": The Ascendancy of Population Health

The intellectual inspiration for the population health approach came from the Canadian Institute for Advanced Research (CIAR) and its founder, neuroscientist Fraser Mustard. Although the research published by key members associated with the CIAR's Population Health program, including Mustard and health economist Robert Evans, identified ten health determinants,[1] socioeconomic status (SES) clearly received the lion's share of attention. The main point, which seems unsurprising, is "that, on average, people with higher levels of income, education, and social position live longer and are healthier than those at lower levels" (CIAR, quoted in Raphael and Bryant 2002, 191). Although the CIAR terminated the program in 2003 after sixteen years, its influence has been significant. The CIAR website boasts of some of the program's accomplishments, including the generation of a new conceptual framework for population health research, its impact on public policy in Canada and internationally, and its influence on the creation of new research institutes and on health research granting agencies (CIAR 2004). Internationally, CIAR notes, *Why Are Some People Healthy and Others Not?*, the definitive book outlining the approach, is the most widely used text in American university courses on social determinants of health.

When the term was adopted by the federal government, however, it was enlarged to include some aspects of health promotion, including an emphasis on community responses, as well as a "framework for taking action" (Raphael and Bryant 2002, 191). Population health, according to Health Canada (2001, 2), "refers to the health of a population as measured by health status indicators and as influenced by social, economic, and physical environments, personal health practices, individual capacity and coping skills, human biology, early childhood development, and health services." As an approach, population health is interested in the impact of these factors and conditions on the health of populations as a whole. Using quantitative (and qualitative) data, researchers look for disparities or variations among population groups and try to identify policies or interventions that might mitigate these effects. Indeed, proponents of population health have emphasized how this approach is novel because it reverses the traditional epidemiologic approach by "starting with subgroups of the population that displayed systematic differences in health status, and then working backwards to understand their sources" (CIAR 2004). Although its meaning is not always clear, the term "population health" has nonetheless gained widespread recognition and acceptance, as its many appearances in the Health Canada website demonstrate. In the late 1990s, the federal government renamed one of its branches the Population and Public Health Branch to reflect this new orientation. Its website features many links to documents outlining the importance of this concept as a unifying framework for all that is done in the name of health. (To confuse matters further, the Population and Public Health Branch has now moved to a new organization home with the Public Health Agency of Canada.)

Although advocates of population health – and there are many – focus their analytical lens on the social determinants of health, exactly what makes this approach social is not always explicit. This may be due partly to the fact that quantitative research has traditionally been the dominant mode of inquiry in the health field, and not surprisingly in the population health field, as well. Rooted in the methodological tradition of the natural sciences, this approach has historically been conceptualized as the best form of empirical data acquisition. Population health advocates are influenced heavily by evidence-based medicine (EBM). Developed originally in the 1980s, EBM offered a new approach to clinical problem solving for medical practitioners. It utilizes quantitative methods, such as meta-analysis, decision analysis, and cost-effectiveness analysis, to synthesize evidence needed to make clinical decisions and formulate public policy in health care. EBM calls upon clinicians to adopt the rigours of science when deliberating on decisions about patient care. According to the Evidence-Based Medicine Working Group (1992, 2420), evidence-based medicine constitutes a new paradigm for medical practice, which "de-emphasises intuition, unsystematic clinical experience, and pathophysiologic rationale as sufficient grounds for clinical decision-making, and stresses the examination of evidence from clinical research. Evidence Based Medicine requires new skills of the physician, including efficient literature-searching, and the application of formal rules of evidence in evaluating the clinical literature." The adoption of evidence-based medicine as the guiding principle in health policy inevitably privileges disciplines that can produce "hard" facts through sound methodology. EBM claims to provide health care managers and policy makers with the best available evidence to make decisions on the effects of therapies, the benefits of diagnostic tests, and the prognosis of disease.[2]

As Ann Robertson (1998) makes clear, the population health approach clings to a set of positivist epistemological assumptions about the nature of knowledge, many of which are rarely questioned. In defending the approach, Robert Evans, one of its leading proponents, has said, "theory divides, data unite" (quoted in ibid., 158). This leaves little room for the recognition that data are socially constructed in the sense that what "counts as data depends on what we judge to be important to notice in the first place, and then to measure" (Robertson 1998, 158). Although some who self-identify as population health researchers are not openly hostile to qualitative research, especially if it helps to triangulate the quantitative data that do exist, the balance is normally tilted in favour of "reliable" scientific evidence of a quantitative nature. It may seem ironic, given their opposition to "theories that divide," that advocates of the population health approach are partly responsible for the upsurge in qualitative health research. Indeed, qualitative health research has been embraced by research-granting bodies such as the Canadian Institutes of Health Research, which changed its name from the Medical Research Council of Canada to reflect this opening toward health research that is rooted in the social sciences.

Critics have rightly pointed out that traditional population health research can be excessively reductionist and insensitive to the context in which health (and illness) is experienced by the individual as mediated through community and societal structures, what Dennis Raphael and Toba Bryant

(2002) term "context stripping." Such research privileges expert knowledge at the expense of experiential lay knowledge, which is viewed as messier and more difficult to quantify than the former. Civil society does matter, but only insofar as its members can participate in carefully designed research studies. Although health promotion advocates were criticized in the past for their inability to value community/citizen involvement, the later focus of health promotion on building community capacity demonstrates that they heeded the message. Population health, according to Raphael and Bryant (2000, 9), is less interested in collaborating with communities to understand the influence of health determinants on the ground. Nor is it interested in allowing community members to participate in discussions of research priorities, in the way that advocates of "popular epidemiology," a progressive branch of epidemiology, have been. Moreover, given their focus on socio-economic status, it is surprising that population health researchers neglect the political and socio-economic forces which underpin societies. In particular, the concern with increasing overall wealth in society as a precursor to producing good health overlooks the social forces that produce and reproduce poverty and inequality. In addition, the population health mantra that "health care does not produce population health" can be used to justify the continued assault on the welfare state (Poland et al. 1998, 786).

Certainly, it would not be constructive to dismiss the claim of population health advocates that health has important social – and economic – determinants. On this issue, one can find almost universal agreement among those interested in improving the health of citizens. But, as several commentators have noted (Coburn et al. 2003; Poland et al. 1998; Raphael and Bryant 2000, 2002; Robertson 1998), we should pay closer attention to the assumptions embedded in what may seem, at first blush, a progressive position vis-à-vis the determinants of health. The next section argues that one of the dangers of a traditional population health approach is that it can provide moral and intellectual support for a renewed form of victim blaming.

From Population Health to the Politics of Blame: The Responsibilization Paradigm

It might seem surprising, and somewhat counter-intuitive, that the health discourse could shift in the direction of blaming individuals for the circumstances in which they find themselves. A smoker has lung cancer because she "chose" to continue smoking even though her cigarette package carried frightening warnings of the dangers of doing so. A gay man is infected with HIV because he chose to engage in condomless sex despite being aware of the dangers associated with unsafe sex with multiple partners. A middle-aged woman is condemned to monitor her blood sugar on a regular basis because she ignored her doctor's warnings that being overweight increases the risk of developing diabetes. Given that a growing body of research suggests that individual behavioural factors interact with the social, environmental, biological, and physical in myriad ways, one might assume that individuals are getting "off the hook," so to speak, absolved of any responsibility for the situation in which they find themselves. Despite the recognition that health and the absence of it is complex and multifaceted, facile explanations are somewhat easier to accept in a world in which citizens and consumers are presumably armed with the information to make meaningful changes in their lives. The shift toward responsibilization is connected to broader political and social forces. In particular, neo-liberalism is concerned with the individualization of responsibility, and with reinforcing the supremacy of an unfettered market. Even movements that organize in response to neo-liberalism may find themselves reinforcing the very categories they intended to resist (Smith 2005). It is therefore not surprising that health discourses would be affected by the language of participation, empowerment, and capacity building. Communities are urged to get busy building the necessary "social capital" that will enable them to take charge of issues that affect them, and empower themselves in the process. Yet, as Barbara Cruikshank (1994) has explained in an important study of the American War on Poverty, "empowerment" can wear diverse ideological masks. For neo-conservatives, empowerment is a polite euphemism for "pick yourself up by the bootstraps." It conveniently recasts the debate away from victim blaming, which is the typical modus operandi of right-wing forces. The poor are seen to have choices, to have a say in their own salvation. For those on the left, empowerment carries the promise of emancipation. For Cruikshank (ibid., 30), it is crucial to see beyond the good intentions of those who seek to empower others, and recognize that "relations of empowerment are in fact relations of power in and of themselves." First, the logic of empowerment treats power and powerlessness as unique phenomena. To be the subject (to be powerless) is explicitly anti-democratic. Conversely, to exercise one's subjectivity "is upheld as the method of democratic self-government" (ibid.). Second, the politics of empowerment focuses solely on empowerment maximization. It presumes that empowerment can be measured in outcomes. Cruikshank notes that this process is circular. How does one in fact satisfy the conditions of empowerment? What criteria can judge whether a citizen is sufficiently empowered? Advocates of empowerment mistakenly treat power in quantitative terms. Relations of empowerment, however, are similar to relations of government in that "they both constitute and fundamentally transform the subject's capacity to act; rather than merely increase that capacity, empowerment alters it as well" (ibid., 32). Relationships of empowerment include four features:

- they are established by "expertise," by practitioners in the field
- they involve some democratic exercise of power, with one party attempting to empower another
- they rely upon a "knowledge" concerning those to be empowered (academic disciplines such as sociology are seen as helpful in this regard)
- they are both voluntary and coercive. (Cruikshank 1999, 72)

Cruikshank attempts to demonstrate that the American War on Poverty was essentially a war against the poor; she is not suggesting that it *degenerated* into a war against the poor, but rather that it began as one. It was "the power-lessness of the poor, not the actions of the powerful," that was seen as "the root cause of poverty" (1994, 36).

Within a health discourse centred on responsibilization, the language of empowerment meets the language of risk. Individual citizens become re-duced to a collection of abstract risk factors. Robert Castel (1991, 281), in a discussion borrowing heavily from Foucault, argues that a risk discourse rests on the presumption of the disappearance of the subject: "The essential com-ponent of intervention no longer takes the form of the direct face-to-face relationship between the carer and the cared, the helper and the helped, the professional and the client. It comes instead to reside in the establishing of flows of population based on the collation of a range of abstract factors deemed liable to produce risk in general."

More importantly, a focus on risk factors conveniently shifts the respon-sibility from the state to the individual citizen. The proliferation of health "information," spread across the pages of daily newspapers and other media including the Internet, is evidence of this creeping responsibilization. Health consumers are urged to avoid or limit particular products and activities, all in the hope of diminishing their chances of being afflicted with a particular ailment or condition. Although lowering one's risk factor does not necessar-ily eliminate the possibility of avoiding disease *x*, the assumption is that a responsible citizen would want to at least limit the probability. As David

Armstrong explains (1995, 401) in an interesting discussion of the rise of surveillance medicine, "The problem is less the illness *per se* but the semi-pathological pre-illness at-risk state." Indeed, this has been influenced by the genetics revolution, which heralds a new era in what is termed "predictive medicine." As some scholars have noted, the "new genetics" encourages citizens to learn more about their own genetic makeup, not to mention that of their potential offspring (Petersen and Bunton 2002). Although a genetic predisposition does not have absolute predictive power, to "know thy genetic self" nonetheless becomes a critical component of citizenship in the age of risk.

Putting Patients in Their Place: A Narrative-Centred Approach to Population Health

As a form of qualitative health research, narrative analysis takes into consideration the patient's lived experience; thus, it has the potential to discover previously undocumented dimensions of disease and illness. This allows researchers and respondents to make important contributions to health promotion research and to the broader field of population health. As Mary Gergen (2001, 21) explains, qualitative research methods "avoid the pitfalls of traditional standardized measures that squelch or deform the localized and personal knowledge of research participants and support the hierarchy of the researcher over the researched." In situating health issues within the larger socio-political context, qualitative researchers not only contribute to the advancement of knowledge in their field but also express an interest in "generating useful or practical knowledge, interrupting patterns of power, participating in socially transformative processes towards such ideals as justice, equity and freedom" (Sparkes 2001, 543).

Only recently has public policy – much less health policy – begun to take seriously the perspective that narrative brings. As Dvora Yanow (2000) explains, the so-called interpretive turn in the social sciences has begun to influence political science generally and public policy studies specifically. In public policy terms, however, narrative analysis has centred on examining "the issue-oriented stories told by policy actors, using such analysis to clarify policy positions and perhaps mediate among them" (ibid., 58). The preoccupation with "framing processes," currently popular among social movement scholars, is another direction in which narrative analysis has moved. The key here, however, is that the analysis of storytelling is viewed from the perspective of a strategic policy actor, be it a pressure group or government agency, seeking to influence or shape the policy agenda with its "version" of events. It is not concerned with democratizing public policy: rather, it clings to a pluralist vision that the act of including more voices in the policy process is somehow sufficient. Whether those voices are heard or actually contribute to policy making is of lesser importance.

Conversely, there is a strong tradition in a number of social science disciplines (such as anthropology, sociology, and social medicine, for example) of using narrative analysis to make cognitive sense of how patients come to experience their illness. In fact, the focus on *illness*, as distinguished from disease, is significant. The former, according to Arthur Kleinman (1988, 3), "refers to how the sick person and the members of the family or wider social network perceive, live with, and respond to symptoms and disability." *Disease*, on the other hand, "is what the practitioner creates in the recasting of illness in terms of theories of disorder ... In the narrow biological terms of the biomedical model, this means that disease is reconfigured only as an alteration in biological structure or functioning" (ibid., 5-6). Moreover, it is recognized that the process of telling these stories of illness and disability can be critical – and sometimes transformative – for patients who may be overwhelmed by feelings of isolation or stigmatization. Mark Swain (1999) makes this point in his discussion of the limitations of "traditional markers of disease" (for example, life expectancy, symptoms) in measuring the health-related quality of life of patients. The traditional markers of disease "often do not parallel a patient's feelings or perceptions concerning the disease" (ibid., 1). Lately, interest has focused on identifying how patients perceive their illness and quantifying its impact on their lives.

Illness stories have been used extensively to uncover patients' experiences of their relationships with doctors, or, more recently, to try to understand the experience of "suffering." Most recently, they have been recognized by Arthur W. Frank (1995) as the voice of "the illness experience" – not previously heard in its totality by the medical profession. These stories, often told by "wounded storytellers," are now seen as standing alone, without need for analysis or interpretation but as truths in their own right.

Building on the work of Kleinman (1988), Frank, a sociologist, identifies three main types of illness narratives: restitution, chaos, and quest. In the West, we are mainly preoccupied with the restitution narrative, which maintains a belief in restorable health. In contemporary culture, this is the narrative that most people want to hear: "I was sick and now I am good as new." For Frank (1995, 90), these narratives fulfill two important functions: "For the individual teller, the ending is a return to just before the beginning: 'good as new' or status quo ante. For the culture that prefers restitution stories, this narrative affirms that breakdowns can be fixed. The remedy, now secure in the family medicine cabinet, becomes a kind of talisman against future sickness." People with chronic illness and disability, however, "do not always fit this model and can find it difficult to tell a story which does not appear to have a happy ending" (Kilty 2000, 17-18).

The chaos narrative or story "remains the most frequently unheard. When people are overwhelmed by the intensity of their illness, to speak coherently becomes impossible. Only when there is a tentative ability to stand outside the chaos can the story begin to emerge" (ibid. 2000, 18). Frank (1995, 98) calls this "the anti-narrative of time without sequence, telling without mediation and speaking about oneself without being fully able to reflect on oneself." The third form of illness story is the quest narrative, in which a person journeys through and faces suffering head-on in the belief that he or she was destined to learn something from the illness experience. Quest stories search for alternative ways of being ill. These may include becoming politically active, forming a patients' rights group, attending support group meetings, or helping others who may be in a similar situation. As Frank (ibid., 76) makes abundantly clear, he is not suggesting that an individual will create only one narrative. Indeed, in many illnesses, all three types are told, depending upon where the patient is on his or her journey. The three narratives should be viewed as "patterns in a kaleidoscope: for a moment, the colours are given one specific form, then the tube shifts and another one emerges."

Narrative analysis is offered here as a way to bring the patient back into the study of health and illness. As Charles Rosenberg and Janet Golden explain (1992, 309), researchers in general have failed to "focus on the connection between biological event, its perception by patient and practitioner and the collective effort to make cognitive and policy sense out of those perceptions." But, perhaps more importantly, narrative analysis need not focus solely on eliciting patients' illness narratives, but can be illuminating for population health researchers interested in understanding the social context in which health-related behaviours take place. For instance, ethnographers who have studied the lives of injection drug users were able to discover why some users might place themselves at risk of acquiring HIV or other blood-borne diseases. In their risk calculus, the danger of overdose was more immediate than the risk of acquiring a disease (Rhodes 1997).

Conclusion

In charting the contesting discourses in health policy, this chapter has tried to provide a context through which to examine key debates in the health field. Public policy specialists and political scientists more generally with an interest in health have restricted their focus to examining health policy, in particular the intricacies of and conflicts associated with intergovernmental relations in the health arena. This chapter has attempted to step back from these key issues to emphasize the importance of discursive shifts in the health field, which have major effects on the ground. I argued that the shift from health promotion to population health has opened the door for a new counter-discourse, one which redraws the boundaries of deserving and un-deserving citizens. In this new discourse, the proliferation of information and knowledge about the health risks present in society purports to em-power citizens to make the proper choices. Paradoxically, at a time when we are increasingly aware of the complexity inherent in understanding what af-fects the health of citizens – at the very least the product of the interaction of the physical, social, and biological environments – we seem to be returning to a position in which individuals qua rational, self-interested actors are re-sponsible for their actions. These actors, seemingly aware of the possible outcomes of engaging in a particular behaviour that might negatively affect their health, are expected to choose the wise course. Their decisions are pre-sumably made in isolation, in the absence of any countervailing social and political forces.

Finally, I offered narrative analysis specifically as a possible tool to en-rich the study of health, recognizing of course that it should complement, not replace, other social theories. In general, narrative analysis can encour-age the "reflexive engagement" of researchers interested in the health of popu-lations. As Frohlich et al. (2004, 394) argue, researchers interested in population health need to move beyond "simplistic cognitive models" that attempt to explain health behaviour, and examine how social theory can help us explore the complex relationship between individuals and the so-cial structure.

NOTES

1   As defined in "What Determines Health?" (Public Health Agency of Canada n.d.), the ten determinants are income and social status; social support networks;

education, employment, and working conditions; physical environments; social environments; personal health practices and skills; biology and genetic endowment; healthy child development and health services; gender; and culture.

2   It would be misleading, however, to suggest that EBM and evidence-based policy making have been uncritically embraced. Indeed, as Kumanan Wilson et al. (2004) have argued, some "evidence" suggests that evidence-based decision making has been trumped by the precautionary principle, a term borrowed from the environmental field which maintains that it is just to exercise caution – and even unjust not to do so – especially when scientific evidence of potential harm is limited. Or, at the very least, governments should be careful when communicating to the public about risk-related issues. For instance, the British government was roundly criticized for its handling of the BSE crisis. As Martin J. Smith (2004) notes, officials made a crucial mistake in proclaiming that there was "no evidence" of a link between BSE and vCJD (the human form of mad cow disease), rather than saying, more accurately, that they "did not have evidence" of such a link.

REFERENCES

Armstrong, David. 1995. "The Rise of Surveillance Medicine." *Sociology of Health and Illness* 17(3): 393-404.

Canadian Institute for Advanced Research (CIAR). 2004. "Accomplishments of CIAR's Population Health Program." http://www.ciar.ca.

Castel, Robert. 1991. "From Dangerousness to Risk." In *The Foucault Effect: Studies in Governmentality*, ed. Graham Burchell, Colin Gordon, and Peter Miller, 281-98. Chicago: University of Chicago Press.

Charon, Rita. 2004. "Narrative and Medicine." *New England Journal of Medicine* 350(9): 862-64.

Coburn, David, Keith Denny, Eric Mykhalovskiy, Peggy McDonough, Ann Robertson, and Rhonda Love. 2003. "Population Health in Canada: A Brief Critique." *American Journal of Public Health* 93(3): 392-96.

Cruikshank, Barbara. 1994. "The Will to Empower: Technologies of Citizenship and the War on Poverty." *Socialist Review* 23(4): 29-55.

—. 1999. *The Will to Empower: Democratic Citizens and Other Subjects.* Ithaca and London: Cornell University Press.

Evans, Robert G., M.L. Barer, and Theodore R. Marmor. 1994. *Why Are Some People Healthy and Others Not? The Determinants of Health of Populations.* New York: Aldine de Gruyter.

Evidence-Based Medicine Working Group. 1992. "Evidence-Based Medicine: A New Approach to Teaching the Practice of Medicine." *Journal of the American Medical Association* 268(17): 2420-25.

Foucault, Michel. 1979. "On Governmentality." *Ideology and Consciousness* 6: 5-22.

Frank, Arthur W. 1995. *The Wounded Storyteller: Body, Illness, and Ethics*. Chicago and London: University of Chicago Press.

Frohlich, Katherine L., Eric Mykhalovskiy, Fiona Miller, and Mark Daniel. 2004. "Advancing the Population Health Agenda." *Canadian Journal of Public Health* 95(5): 392-95.

Gergen, Mary. 2001. *Feminist Reconstructions in Psychology: Narrative, Gender, and Performance*. Thousand Oaks: Sage Publications.

Glouberman, Sholom, and John Millar. 2003. "Evolution of the Determinants of Health, Health Policy, and Health Information Systems in Canada." *American Journal of Public Health* 93(3): 388-91.

Government of Canada. 1974. *A New Perspective on the Health of Canadians*. Ottawa: Minister of Supply and Services Canada.

Health Canada. 1998. "Taking Action on Population Health." Position paper for Health Promotion and Programs Branch Staff.

—. 2001. *The Population Health Template: Key Elements and Actions That Define a Population Health Approach*. Ottawa: Health Canada, Population and Public Health Branch, Strategic Policy Directorate.

Kilty, Sharon. 2000. "Telling the Illness Story: The Healing Power of Words." *Patient's Network Magazine* 5(3): 17-18.

Kleinman, Arthur. 1988. *The Illness Narratives*. New York: Basic Books.

Lupton, Deborah. 1999. *Risk*. London: Routledge.

McKay, Lindsey. 2000. *Making the Lalonde Report*. Ottawa: Canadian Policy Research Networks.

Orsini, Michael. 2002. "The Politics of Naming, Blaming and Claiming: HIV, Hepatitis C and the Emergence of Blood Activism in Canada." *Canadian Journal of Political Science* 35(3): 475-98.

Petersen, Alan, and Robin Bunton. 2002. *The New Genetics and the Public's Health*. London and New York: Routledge.

Poland, Blake, David Coburn, Ann Robertson, and Joan Eakin. 1998. "Wealth, Equity, and Health Care: A Critique of the Population Health Perspective on the Determinants of Health." *Social Science and Medicine* 46(7): 785-98.

Public Health Agency of Canada. N.d. "What Determines Health?" http://www.phac-aspc.gc.ca/ph-sp/phdd/determinants/index.html#determinants.

Raphael, Dennis, and Toba Bryant. 2000. "Putting the Population into Population Health." *Canadian Journal of Public Health* 91(1): 9-10.

—. 2002. "The Limitations of Population Health as a Model for a New Public Health." *Health Promotion International* 17(2): 189-99.

Rhodes, Tim. 1997. "Risk Theory in Epidemic Times: Sex, Drugs and the Social Organization of Risk Behaviour." *Sociology of Health and Illness* 19(2): 208-27.

Robertson, Ann. 1998. "Shifting Discourses on Health in Canada: From Health Promotion to Population Health." *Health Promotion International* 13(2): 155-66.

Romanow, Roy. 2002. *Building On Values.* Final report, Commission on the Future of Health Care in Canada. Ottawa: Library and Archives Canada.

Rose, Nikolas, and Carlos Novas. 2005. "Biological Citizenship." In *Global Assemblages: Technology, Politics, and Ethics as Anthropological Problems,* ed. A. Ong and S. Collier, 439-63. London: Blackwell.

Rosenberg, Charles, and Janet Golden, eds. 1992. *Framing Disease: Studies in Cultural History.* New Brunswick, NJ: Rutgers University Press.

Smith, Martin J. 2004. "Mad Cows and Mad Money: Problems of Risk in the Making and Understanding of Policy." *British Journal of Politics and International Relations* 6: 312-32.

Smith, Miriam. 2005. "Resisting and Reinforcing Neoliberalism: Lesbian and Gay Organizing at the Federal and Local Levels in Canada." *Policy and Politics* 33(1): 75-93.

Sparkes, Andrew C. 2001. "Myth 94: Qualitative Health Researchers Will Agree about Validity." *Qualitative Health Research* 11(4): 538-52.

Swain, Mark. 1999. "Health-Related Quality of Life (HRQOL) in Viral Hepatitis." *Hepatitis Update* (18). http://www.hepnet.com/update18.html.

Szreter, Simon. 2003. "The Population Health Approach in Historical Perspective." *American Journal of Public Health* 93(3): 421-31.

Wilson, Kumanan, Catherine Code, Christopher Dornan, Nadya Ahmad, Paul Hébert, and Ian Graham. 2004. "The Reporting of Theoretical Health Risks by the Media: Canadian Newspaper Reporting of Potential Blood Transmission of Creutzfeldt-Jakob Disease." *BMC Public Health* 4(1). http://www.biomedcentral.com/1471-2458/4/1.

Yanow, Dvora. 2000. *Conducting Interpretive Policy Analysis.* Thousand Oaks, London, and New Delhi: Sage Publications.

Contributors

FRANCES ABELE is Professor in the School of Public Policy and Administration at Carleton University. She is interested in Aboriginal political development and public administration, as well as in federal northern policy. She has published widely on Aboriginal policy and governance in Canada.

YASMEEN ABU-LABAN is Associate Professor in the Department of Political Science at the University of Alberta. She specializes in gender and ethnic politics, nationalism and globalization, and immigration policies and citizenship theory. Among her other publications is *Selling Diversity: Immigration, Multiculturalism, Employment Equity, and Globalization* (Broadview Press, 2002), co-authored with Christina Gabriel.

CAROLINE ANDREW is Professor in the School of Political Studies at the University of Ottawa. She specializes in urban development and municipal politics, women and politics, intergovernmental relations in Canada, and social policies. Her publications include *Urban Affairs: Back on the Policy Agenda* (McGill-Queen's University Press, 2002), co-edited with Katherine A. Graham and Susan D. Phillips.

PETER GRAEFE is Assistant Professor in the Department of Political Science at McMaster University. His work focuses on Quebec political economy and public policy. He also does research on social assistance and social economy policies, as well as intergovernmental relations in social policy. His recent work has appeared in *Theory and Society* and *Global Social Policy*.

OLENA HANKIVSKY is Associate Professor, Public Policy Program, Co-Director of the Institute for Critical Studies in Gender and Health, and Faculty Associate, Department of Political Science, Simon Fraser University. She specializes in public policy and political theory, and has a particular interest in gender and social and health policy. She is the author of *Social Policy and the Ethic of Care* (UBC Press,

2004) and co-author, with Sandra Kirby and Lorraine Greaves, of *The Dome of Silence: Sexual Harassment and Abuse in Sport* (Fernwood, 2000).

MATT JAMES is Assistant Professor in the Department of Political Science at the University of Victoria. His areas of interest include reparations for historical injustices, social movements, and constitutional politics. His publications include *Misrecognized Materialists: Social Movements in Canadian Constitutional Politics* (UBC Press, 2006).

ROBERT JOHNSON is Lecturer in the School of Political Studies at the University of Ottawa. His interests include the political economy of the welfare state, social and labour-market policy, and regulation and social citizenship. He is co-editor with G. Bruce Doern of *Rules, Rules, Rules, Rules: Multi-level Regulatory Governance* (University of Toronto Press, 2006).

LUC JUILLET is Associate Professor in the School of Political Studies at the University of Ottawa. He is interested in ecology, environment, and politics, theories of public policy analysis, and new forms of governance and democracy. He is the author of numerous works on public policy, the environment, and democratic governance.

RACHEL LAFOREST is Assistant Professor and head of the Public Policy and Third Sector Initiative in the School of Policy Studies at Queen's University. Her research areas include the voluntary sector and public interest groups, with a special emphasis on representation, advocacy, and new forms of political activism. Her work has been published in *Politique et Sociétés, International Journal of Canadian Studies,* and *Social Policy and Administration.*

RIANNE MAHON is Chancellor's Professor in the School of Public Policy and Administration, and Director of the Institute of Political Economy at Carleton University. She specializes in political economy and social policy, especially child care policy. Her many publications include *Child Care Policy at the Crossroads: Gender and Welfare State Restructuring* (Routledge, 2002), co-edited with Sonja Michel.

KAREN BRIDGET MURRAY is Associate Professor of Political Science at York University. Her research draws upon neo-Foucauldian themes to examine governmental realignment in urban settings, with a primary focus on policies pertaining to poverty and social marginalization. Her recent work has been published in *Canadian Historical Review, Canadian Journal of Urban Research, Canadian Public Administration,* and *Social Theory and Health.*

MICHAEL ORSINI is Associate Professor in the School of Political Studies at the University of Ottawa. He specializes in public policy, with a focus on health policy, interest groups, and social movements. His recent work has appeared in *Canadian Journal of Political Science* and *Social Policy and Administration*.

SUSAN PHILLIPS is Professor and Director of the School of Public Policy and Administration at Carleton University. Her areas of interest focus on Canadian public administration, the relationship of the state and the third sector in comparative perspective, citizen engagement, and urban governance. Her many publications include *Urban Affairs: Back on the Policy Agenda* (McGill-Queen's University Press, 2002), co-edited with Katherine A. Graham and Caroline Andrew.

DENIS SAINT-MARTIN is Associate Professor in the Department of Political Science at Université de Montréal. His interests include comparative and Canadian public policy and public administration. He is the author of *Building the New Managerialist State: Consultants and the Politics of Public Sector Reform in Comparative Perspective* (Oxford University Press, 2004).

MARK B. SALTER is Assistant Professor in the School of Political Studies at the University of Ottawa. He is interested in international mobility regimes, the history of the passport, international relations theory, and globalization. His publications include *Rights of Passage: The Passport in International Relations* (Lynne Rienner, 2003) and *Barbarians and Civilization in International Relations* (Pluto Press, 2002).

FRANCESCA SCALA is Associate Professor in the Department of Political Science at Concordia University. She specializes in biotechnology policy, social policy, and citizen engagement and public policy. Her work has appeared in *Politique et Sociétés, Canadian Journal of Political Science,* and *Policy Sciences.*

MIRIAM SMITH is Professor in the Department of Politics at Trent University. Her areas of interest are Canadian and American politics, and, in particular, social movements, and lesbian, gay, bisexual, and transgender movements. Her publications include *A Civil Society? Collective Actors in Canadian Political Life* (Broadview, 2005).

STUART N. SOROKA is Associate Professor in the Department of Political Science at McGill University. He is interested in public opinion and policy, agenda-setting and issue definition, mass media and political communications, and immigration and diversity. His works include *Agenda-Setting Dynamics in Canada* (UBC Press, 2002).

Index

NOTE: Page numbers in **bold** refer to figures or tables; "LGBT" stands for lesbian, gay, bisexual, and transgender; "SWC" for Status of Women Canada

Printed and bound in Canada by Friesens

Set in Giovanni and Scala Sans by Artegraphica Design Co. Ltd.

Copyeditor: Deborah Kerr

Proofreader: Megan Brand

Indexer: David Luljak